Foundations of English (12)

SUE HARPER

DOUGLAS HILKER

Harcourt
Canada

Harcourt Canada

Toronto Orlando San Diego London Sydney

National Library of Canada Cataloguing in Publication Data

Harper, Sue, 1952-
        Foundations of English 12

Includes index.
ISBN 0-7747-1515-4

1. Readers (Secondary) I. Hilker, Douglas II. Title.

PE1121.H388 2002   428.6   C2001-903533-0

Authors

Sue Harper
Cross-curricular Literacy Head, John Fraser Secondary School, Mississauga, ON, and Developer for the Ontario Secondary School Grade 10 Literacy Test

Douglas Hilker
Writing Team Leader for the Ontario Curriculum Policy Document for English and Lead Developer for the Ontario Secondary School Grade 10 Literacy Test

Consulting Editor

Peter J. Smith
Writer for the Ontario Curriculum Policy Document for English, Grades 11 and 12, General Editor of *The Harcourt Writer's Handbook*, and author of *Elements of English* 11 and 12.

Reviewers

The authors and publisher gratefully acknowledge these reviewers for their contribution to the development of this project:

Tish Buckley, English Teacher, Notre Dame Secondary School, Halton Catholic District School Board, Burlington, ON
Rick Carter, English Department Head, St. Benedict Catholic Secondary School, Sudbury Catholic District School Board, Sudbury, ON
Brenda Crawford, English Teacher, Monsignor Paul Dwyer Catholic High School, Durham Catholic District School Board, Oshawa, ON
Linda Henshaw, English Teacher, John Fraser Secondary School, Peel District School Board, Mississauga, ON
Roy Lalonde, English Department Head, Holy Trinity Catholic High School, Ottawa-Carleton Catholic School Board, Kanata, ON
Anne Lamie, Georges Vanier Secondary School, Toronto District School Board, North York, ON
John Liandzi, Curriculum Leader, Ernest Manning Senior High School, Calgary School District 19, Calgary, AB
Mary Lou Smitheram, Curriculum Consultant and Special Assignment Teacher, Upper Canada District School Board, Prescott, ON
Gina Tousignant, English Department Head, St. Francis Xavier Secondary School, Dufferin-Peel Catholic District School Board, Mississauga, ON

Editorial Project Manager: Ian Nussbaum
Developmental Editor: Su Mei Ku
Editor: Brett Savory
Production Editor: Sheila Barry
Production Coordinator: Cheri Westra
Permissions Coordinator: Karen Becker
Cover Design, Interior Design, and Art Direction: Sonya V. Thursby, Opus House Incorporated
Page Composition: Carolyn Sebestyen
Cover Illustration: Kevin Ghiglione/i2i art inc.
Printing and Binding: Friesens

 Printed in Canada on acid-free paper

1 2 3 4 5   06 05 04 03 02

> Contents

> Unit 3: Media

> Unit 4: The Reference Shelf

> Alternative Groupings of the Selections

> Genres

> Authors According to Country

> Themes

> To the Students

The purpose of this book is to help you further develop your literacy skills to increase your chances of success in your personal lives, in school, and in the world of work. You will have an opportunity to read short stories, poems, dramas, essays, comic strips, articles, and informational texts. The voices you will hear when you read represent a wide variety of experiences from Canada and from around the world.

The selections and activities invite you to

Think
- about new ideas
- critically and creatively
- about your own and others' values

Apply
- previous knowledge
- learned skills

Understand
- a variety of types of texts
- explicit and implicit meanings in what you read
- new ways of thinking about ideas and issues

Write
- using the writing process
- in a variety of forms for a variety of purposes and audiences
- in your own and others' voices

Research
- independently and with a group
- using electronic, print, and human resources

Speak and Listen
- in pairs, in small groups, and as a class
- in formal and informal situations

Create and Evaluate
- media works
- presentations

Reflect
- on your own work
- on the work of your classmates

This book is divided into four units.

Unit 1, Language and Forms, reviews some skills you acquired in Grade 11 and introduces you to important skills you will be working on throughout this year.

Unit 2, Literature, contains seven parts, each having a theme: "Practical Matters," "The World of Work," "The World of Play," "The Way We Communicate," "Parents and Parenting," "Race and Culture," and "Law and Order." In each of these parts, you will read a variety of types of writing, from short stories to informational texts. Each of the themes explores ideas and issues relevant to contemporary young Canadians.

Unit 3, Media, focuses on furthering your understanding of the impact of the media on you and on the world around you.

Unit 4, The Reference Shelf, gives you information, rules, and tips for using language in oral, written, and visual forms. You will also find information about life skills that are important to your success at work, school, and home.

The Glossary provides definitions of key words and phrases that are used in the activities and that you will encounter throughout your study of English. Glossary terms appear in boldface in the activities.

In Units 1 through 3, the activities are divided into the following sections:

Before Reading: You will think, talk, or write about something that will help you read and understand the selection that follows.

Responding: You will talk or write about the way in which the selection has affected you and how the writer has made you feel the way you do.

Understanding: You will practise reading skills such as understanding implicit and explicit meanings, recognizing elements of both fiction and non-fiction, and interpreting ideas and information in texts.

Thinking About Language: You will work with specific aspects of language: grammar, vocabulary, voice, intent, and structure.

Extending: You will be asked to extend your knowledge and understanding of your reading through writing, oral presentations, and media creations.

A Note About the Icons: You will notice two different icons in a number of activities. This icon indicates language and grammar activities.

 This one indicates media-related activities. The media icon does not appear in the Media Studies unit because, by nature, most activities in this unit are media related.

Where to Go from Here

It is important for you to be aware of your progress throughout this English course. Although your teacher will continually assess your skills and knowledge, it is important that you also monitor your progress. Here are some things you can do to evaluate your successes and your weaknesses:

- Keep track of your marks on tests, assignments, and group projects.
- Make a list of the comments that you have received from your teacher and your peers and update your action plan as necessary.
- Keep a portfolio of your own work that includes written reflections on how you think you are doing.
- Keep a log of the reading you have done throughout the course.
- Keep a response journal.
- Keep a list of new words and their definitions.
- Keep a list of the spelling and grammatical errors that you have made on assignments and the corrections for those errors.
- Keep track of your homework, making sure that you have specific directions for each assignment.

Enjoy this book, and good luck in your learning this year.

Sue Harper
Doug Hilker

Foundations of English

UNIT 1

> Language and Forms

At Seventeen

JANIS IAN

BEFORE READING

As a class, discuss how dating has changed since your parents' generation. In your notebooks, write a reflective paragraph in which you talk about whether dating was better in the "old days."

I learned the truth at seventeen
That love was meant for beauty queens
— And high school girls with clear skinned smiles
Who married young and then retired.
The valentines I never knew,   5
The Friday night charades of youth
Were spent on one more beautiful —
At seventeen I learned the truth.

    And those of us with ravaged faces
    Lacking in the social graces,   10
    Desperately remained at home
    Inventing lovers on the phone
    Who called to say, "Come dance with me,"
    And murmured vague obscenities.
    It isn't all it seems,   15
    At seventeen.

A brown-eyed girl in hand-me downs
Whose name I never could pronounce
Said, "Pity, please, the ones who serve,
They only get what they deserve.   20
The rich relationed home-town queen
Marries into what she needs
A guarantee of company
And haven for the elderly."

Remember those who win the game   25
Lose the love they sought to gain
In debentures of quality
And dubious integrity.
Their small town eyes will gape at you
In dull surprise when payment due   30
Exceeds accounts received,
At seventeen.

    To those of us who know the pain
    Of valentines that never came,
    And those whose names were never called   35
    When choosing sides for basketball.
    It was long ago and far away,
    The world was younger than today,
    And dreams were all they gave for free
    To ugly duckling girls like me.   40

We all play the game and when we dare
To cheat ourselves at solitaire
Inventing lovers on the phone
Repenting other lives unknown,
That call and say, "Come dance with me,"   45
And murmur vague obscenities
At ugly girls like me
At seventeen.

AFTER READING

Responding

1. a) In your notebook, describe what you know about the **narrator** by the end of the song.

   b) Explain why you do or do not feel sympathy for the narrator in this song.

Understanding

2. Identify the main idea in each **stanza** of this song.

3. Identify the mood of the narrator. In a paragraph, explain what specific evidence from the song supports your judgement about the narrator's mood.

4. With a partner, read the lyrics to this song aloud, stressing the natural rhythm of the words. Determine why the rhythm pattern breaks for certain lines. Be prepared to explain your conclusions to the class.

5. Explain why the point about valentines that the narrator never received and the line "Inventing lovers on the phone" are repeated in the song.

Thinking About Language

6. With a partner, write **definitions** of charades, debentures, dubious, and integrity as they are used in this song. Add any new or unfamiliar words you have defined to your personal word list.

7. a) Identify the **rhyme scheme** of these song lyrics.

   b) Explain whether the rhyme scheme creates any awkwardly phrased sentences.

   c) Explain any other positive or negative effects of the rhyme scheme.

Extending

8. With a partner, locate a recording of these song lyrics. Prepare a **report** on how the music and singing influence your response to the words.

9. Rewrite this song from the perspective of a 17-year-old male. In a small group, read your lyrics aloud and discuss any differences in perspectives.

The Fun They Had

"This is the old kind of school..."   ISAAC ASIMOV

BEFORE READING

Imagine what it would be like if you stayed at home and were taught by a computerized teacher. Write about a typical day at that "school."

Margie even wrote about it that night in her diary. On the page headed May 17, 2155, she wrote, "Today Tommy found a real book!"

It was a very old book. Margie's grandfather once said that when he was a little boy *his* grandfather told him that there was a time when all stories were printed on paper.

They turned the pages, which were yellow and crinkly, and it was awfully funny to read those words that stood still instead of moving the way they were supposed to —on a screen, you know. And then, when they turned back to the page before, it had the same words on it that it had had when they read it the first time.

"Gee," said Tommy, "what a waste. When you're through with the book, you just throw it away, I guess. Our television screen must have had a million books on it and it's good for plenty more. I wouldn't throw *it* away."

"Same with mine," said Margie. She was eleven and hadn't seen as many telebooks as Tommy had. He was thirteen.

She said, "Where did you find it?"

"In my house." He pointed without looking, because he was busy reading. "In the attic."

"What's it about?"

"School."

Margie was scornful. "School? What's there to write about school? I hate school." Margie always hated school, but now she hated it more than ever. The mechanical teacher had been giving her test after test in geography and she had been doing worse and worse until her mother had shaken her head sorrowfully and sent for the County Inspector.

He was a round little man with a red face and a whole box of tools with dials and wires. He smiled at her and gave her an apple, then took the teacher apart. Margie had hoped he wouldn't know how to put it together again, but he knew how all right and, after an hour or so, there it was again, large and black and ugly with a big screen on which all the lessons were shown and the questions were asked. That wasn't so bad. The part she hated most was the slot where she had to put homework and test papers. She always had to write them out in a punch code they made her learn when she was six years old, and the mechanical teacher calculated the mark in no time.

The inspector had smiled after he was finished and patted her head. He said to her mother, "It's not the little girl's fault, Mrs. Jones. I think the geography sector was geared a little too quick. Those things happen sometimes. I've slowed it up to an average ten-year level. Actually, the over-all pattern of her progress is quite satisfactory." And he patted Margie's head again.

Margie was disappointed. She had been hoping they would take the teacher away altogether. They had once taken Tommy's teacher away for nearly a month because the history sector had blanked out completely.

So she said to Tommy, "Why would anyone write about school?"

Tommy looked at her with very superior eyes. "Because it's not our kind of school, stupid. This is the old kind of school that they had hundreds and hundreds of years ago." He added loftily, pronouncing the words carefully, "*Centuries* ago."

Margie was hurt. "Well, I don't know what kind of school they had all that time ago." She read the book over his shoulder for a while, then said, "Anyway, they had a teacher."

"Sure they had a teacher, but it wasn't a *regular* teacher. It was a man."

"A man? How could a man be a teacher?"

"Well, he just told the boys and girls things and gave them homework and asked them questions."

"A man isn't smart enough."

"Sure he is. My father knows as much as my teacher."

"He can't. A man can't know as much as a teacher."

"He knows almost as much I betcha."

Margie wasn't prepared to dispute that. She said, "I wouldn't want a strange man in my house to teach me."

Tommy screamed with laughter, "You don't know much, Margie. The teachers didn't live in the house. They had a special building and all the kids went there."

"And all the kids learned the same thing?"

"Sure, if they were the same age."

"But my mother says a teacher has to be adjusted to fit the mind of each boy and girl it teaches and that each kid has to be taught differently."

"Just the same, they didn't do it that way then. If you don't like it, you don't have to read the book."

"I didn't say I didn't like it," Margie said quickly. She wanted to read about those funny schools.

They weren't even half finished when Margie's mother called, "Margie! School!"

Margie looked up. "Not yet, mamma."

"Now," said Mrs. Jones. "And it's probably time for Tommy, too."

Margie said to Tommy, "Can I read the book some more with you after school?"

"Maybe," he said, nonchalantly. He walked away whistling, the dusty old book tucked beneath his arm.

Margie went into the schoolroom. It was right next to her bedroom, and the mechanical teacher was on and waiting for her. It was always on at the same time every day except Saturday and Sunday, because her mother said little girls learned better if they learned at regular hours.

The screen was lit up, and it said: "Today's arithmetic lesson is on the addition of proper fractions. Please insert yesterday's homework in the proper slot."

Margie did so with a sigh. She was thinking about the old schools they had when her grandfather's grandfather was a little boy. All the kids from the whole neighborhood came, laughing and shouting in the schoolyard, sitting together in the schoolroom, going home together at the end of the day. They learned the same things so they could help one another on the homework and talk about it.

And the teachers were people...

The mechanical teacher was flashing on the screen: "When we add the fractions _ and _ ..."

Margie was thinking about how the kids must have loved it in the old days. She was thinking about the fun they had.

AFTER READING

Responding

1. "She was thinking about the fun they had." Write a letter to Margie in which you either talk about what is fun about going to school, or tell her the "real" story of schools.

Understanding

2. a) Describe the **setting** (time and place) of the **story**.
   b) Explain how the writer tells the reader when the story takes place without saying "The story takes place in...."
3. According to Margie, what were the advantages of schools in the "old days"?
4. When the County Inspector comes to fix the mechanical teacher, he gives Margie an apple. Explain how this is **ironic**.

Thinking About Language

5. Examine the technical language used to describe how Margie handed in her homework (paragraph 11, page 8). Explain how you can tell that this story was written before modern technology.

6. Using technical language, write a description of how you could send homework by e-mail to your teacher.

Extending

7. In a small group, write a short **play** in which young people, 100 years from now, find a "relic" from today. Rehearse and perform your play.

8. "[M]y mother says...that each kid has to be taught differently." Create a **graphic organizer** (see The Reference Shelf, pages 381–82) that shows the pros and cons of being taught individually and being taught with other students. Take one side and or the other and organize a class discussion on the subject.

9. With a partner, research e-books, making notes from your reading and keeping a record of the sources you have used. Prepare a proposal for the school board in which you recommend that schools provide students with e-books instead of printed textbooks.

Imagistic Poems

BEFORE READING

With a partner, discuss whether, in your experience, very short **poems** or longer poems are easier to read and understand. Be prepared to present your conclusions and your reasons for them to the class.

haiku
Kikaku

Translated from the Japanese by Lucien Stryk and Takashi Ikemoto

Above the boat,
bellies
of wild geese.

The Sun
Judah Al-Harizi

Translated from the Hebrew by T. Carmi

Look: the sun has spread its wings
over the earth to dispel the darkness.

Like a great tree, with its roots in heaven,
and its branches reaching down to the earth.

The Red Wheelbarrow
William Carlos Williams

So much depends
upon

a red wheel
barrow

glazed with rain   5
water

beside the white
chickens.

Midsummer, Tobago
Derek Walcott

Broad sun-stoned beaches.

White heat.
A green river.

A bridge,
scorched yellow palms   5

from the summer-sleeping house
drowsing through August.

Days I have held,
days I have lost,

days that outgrow, like daughters,   10
my harbouring arms.

AFTER READING

Responding
1. After reading all four poems in this section, explain which one appealed to you most. Give reasons for your choice.

Understanding
2. Read the explanation of "imagistic poetry" in The Reference Shelf, page 367. How does knowing the **definition** of an imagistic poem help you understand the four poems?
3. List several characteristics of a haiku. (See The Reference Shelf, page 366.) Explain whether the haiku in this section is or is not an effective example of a haiku.
4. In your own words, explain what is being emphasized about midsummer in Tobago in the poem "Midsummer, Tobago."
5. In your notebook, explain whether the comparison (**simile**) in the second part of "The Sun" is an effective choice to describe the **image** in the first half. In a small group, discuss your ideas.
6. With a partner, list specifics that the poet might have been referring to in the words "So much" in the poem "The Red Wheelbarrow."

Thinking About Language
7. a) Identify which of the four poems in this section uses the most grammatically correct sentence structure. Give reasons for your choice.
   b) Explain how the manipulation of grammar in the other poems enhances or detracts from the meaning.

Extending
8. Write your own short poem. As a class, prepare a bulletin board display or an **anthology** of the poems written by members of the class for this activity.

9. a) With a partner or individually, create a print advertisement for a product using words or phrases from one of the four poems.
   b) As a class, create an assessment form for the advertisements.
   c) Present your work to the class, explaining your production choices and problems that you might have encountered during the production, and how you resolved them.
   d) Use the assessment form to assess each advertisement presentation.

All About Food

COMPILED BY ERIC VOLMERS,
THE CAMBRIDGE REPORTER

BEFORE READING

As a class, discuss current issues about the safety and quality of our food and water supplies. Consider such issues as cases of food poisoning, food-handling in restaurants, and genetically modified food.

FOOD ISSUES THROUGH THE AGES

PREHISTORY

- Cooking meat with fire, which kills germs as well as making it taste better, improves the health of cavemen.
- A catastrophic flood in the Black Sea may have caused stone-age settlers to take their farming skills to dry lands in Europe and Asia. This flood, which may have also spurred the Biblical story of Noah's Ark, may have led to the revolution of farming. Sheep, swine, and cattle domestication happens between 9000 B.C. and 6500 B.C.

1484

Witches are blamed for the outbreak of the so-called Saint Anthony's fire, which is widespread in medieval Europe. The mysterious affliction, which causes burning in the extremities, convulsions, and hallucinations, killed thousands. It's now believed the illness was caused by ergotic toxins, a fungus that infects grains of all kinds, especially rye.

1493

London's Grocer's Company, created in 1420, receives permission to appoint a garbeller, whose function is to garbel (inspect) groceries, especially spices, and destroy adulterated products. A number of garbellers will be employed to fit seals of purity on spice cargoes before they can be weighed.

1569

London bans the sale of fresh fruit in the streets for fear it will spread disease.

1634

Dijon, France, imposes regulations on mustard makers requiring, among other things, that mustard be made only by workers wearing clean and modest clothes. Later rules will require that mustard be made only from brown or black mustard seeds and seasoned with wine or vinegar plus spices and herbs.

1675

 Antonie Van Leeuwekhoek, inventor of the microscope, reports seeing animalcules — minute organisms — through his newly designed device. Nearly two centuries would pass before these micro-organisms were recognized as the causes of food poisoning.

1762

 The sandwich gets its name when John Montagu, the 4th Earl of Sandwich, spends 24 hours at a gaming table without other food.

1795

Nicholas Appert, a French chef determined to win the prize of 12 000 francs offered by Napoleon for a way to prevent military food supplies from spoiling, creates the canning process in jars.

1805

 Upper Canada passes legislation to regulate the inspection and packing of beef and pork for foreign markets.

1835

 Allan McIntosh learns the art of grafting and begins to produce apples on a major scale in Upper Canada.

1855

England is scandalized by reports that all but the most costly beer, bread, butter, coffee, pepper, and tea contains trace amounts of arsenic, copper, or mercury, but Crosse & Blackwell announces that it has stopped coppering pickles and fruits.

1864

In France, Louis Pasteur investigates the diseases that are afflicting wine and shows the cause is micro-organisms that could be killed by heating the wine to 55 degrees Celsius. This process, which becomes known as pasteurization, would soon be applied to beer, juice, and milk and used throughout the world.

1884

French monk and physics teacher Abbe Marcel Audriffren develops a prototype for the first airtight refrigeration system.

1886

A pharmacist in Atlanta, Dr. John Pemberton, creates Coca Cola as a headache remedy.

1891

U.S. Congress enacts a law requiring the country of origin to appear prominently on product labels following revelations that Maine herring is being labeled and sold in fancy boxes as imported French sardines.

1892

The first cross between an early-ripening Indian wheat and Red Fife took place at an experimental farm in Manitoba. By 1911, so-called Marquis Wheat was commercially established. Because of its early maturing quality, Marquis greatly extended the area where wheat may be safely grown.

1894

An act is passed in Canada establishing penalties for selling adulterated or deteriorated milk.

1897

Adelaide Hoodless, of St. George, Ont., motivated by the 1889 death of her infant son from infected milk, creates what is now the Federated Women's Institutes of Ontario. The primary aim of the organization for rural women is to educate and improve health, nutrition, and safety in the home. Within 10 years there are more than 500 institutes organized across Canada.

1906

The *Pure Food and Drug Act* is created in the U.S. after the publication of *The Jungle* and its exposure of conditions in Chicago slaughterhouses.

1909

Chicago imposes the first milk-pasteurization law in the U.S.

1914

Lettuce, asparagus, watermelons, cantaloupes and tomatoes grown in irrigated fields in California are transported up to 3000 miles to customers in refrigerated rail cars.

1916

Peterborough becomes the first Canadian municipality to add chlorine to water. Chlorine, discovered in 1774, destroys bacteria, virtually eliminating typhoid fever, cholera and other waterborne diseases.

1920

Botulism from commercially canned food strikes 36 Americans, killing 23. Falling sales motivates the U.S. canning industry to impose new production safety standards.

1927

General Electric introduces the revolutionary monitor-top refrigerator. But, until after the Second World War, many people still use iceboxes, which have to be constantly reloaded with ice and the trays of melted water underneath discarded.

1929

Clarence Birdseye masters the quick-freezing of vegetables, allowing all sorts of foods to be frozen to maintain freshness and nutrition.

1931

Doctor Frederick Tisdall of Toronto's Hospital for Sick Children gives babies their first taste of Pablum — the pre-cooked and dried infant cereal that revolutionizes the diets of toddlers around the globe. The hospital credits Pablum with saving thousands of children from death and malnutrition-related disease.

1940

- The first Dietary Standard for Canadians is developed by the Canadian Council on Nutrition. Recommendations are made for total calories, protein, fat, calcium, iron, iodine, ascorbic acid and vitamin D intake.
- Food for Health in Peace and War is prepared by the Canadian Medical Association with assistance from the Canadian Dietetic Association. It lists milk products, potatoes and other vegetables, whole-grain breads, raw fruits and canned tomatoes, eggs, meat, and fish as foods that supply nearly all the substances necessary for good health.
  - A&P supermarkets sell the first pre-cut cellophane-wrapped meat. People no longer have to eat as much

  preserved meat, such as corned beef, hams, and sausages.

1941

South Carolina becomes the first state to require enrichment of white bread with vitamins and iron.

1942

The frozen food industry balloons as producers look for alternatives to metal cans during the war years, so the metal can be used for the war effort.

1944

Newfoundland establishes a program for the fortification of flour with riboflavin, thiamin, niacin, calcium, and iron and of margarine with vitamin A to help reduce the incidence of nutrient deficiency diseases such as night blindness, beriberi, rickets, and scurvy, which are seen in some isolated villages.

1945

Earl W. Tupper invents resealable plastic food containers.

1949

The addition of potassium iodine to table salt becomes mandatory and eliminates iodine deficiency goitre, which is common in some areas of Canada. Ascorbic acid is added to evaporated milk and is responsible for eliminating infantile scurvy in some eastern parts of the country.

1955

Raymond Kroc, sales distributor of a milk shake maker called the Multimixer, hears about brothers Mac and Dick McDonald, running eight of the mixers at a time at their hamburger stand in California. Kroc suggests more restaurants so he can sell more mixers. He becomes their franchise agent and opens the first in Des Plaines, Illinois.

1957

Nitrite poisoning creates a scandal in Germany, where butchers are found to be using sodium nitrite to make meat look fresh and red, exposing consumers to the hazards of methemoglobinemia, which can produce dizziness, fatigue, nausea, and even death.

1960s

For NASA, Pillsbury develops Hazard Analysis Critical Control Point (HACCP), which is still today the standard approach to managing food-borne risks.

1964

The first Tim Hortons doughnut store is opened in Hamilton.

1976

The U.S. Food and Drug Administration bans Red No. 2 dye, citing new concern that it may be carcinogenic, but does not order a recall of foods containing Red No. 2, which is the nation's most commonly used food colouring.

1977

Health Canada researchers identify a sub-species of E. coli that produces a poison called verotoxin.

1982

The world first hears about E. coli 0157:H7 in 1982, when dozens of McDonald's customers in Oregon and Michigan fall ill with food poisoning. McDonald's sets higher minimum cooking standards and introduces time-controlled grills to prevent undercooking.

1983

Mohamed Karmali, chief microbiologist at Toronto's Hospital for Sick Children, establishes the link between E. coli 0157:H7 and hemolytic uremic syndrome. HUS is characterized by severe anemia, a decrease in the number of platelets in the blood, and the failure of the renal system. It becomes known as the "hamburger disease."

1993

An outbreak of E. coli poisoning is traced to contaminated and undercooked burgers from Jack-in-the-Box fast-food restaurants in the U.S. It resulted in four deaths and hundreds of illnesses, mostly in Washington State.

1996

Mad cow disease is identified in Britain. The related brain-wasting disease known as new-variant Creutzfeldt-Jakob disease (nvCJD) eventually kills 90 people in Britain.

1997

The Canadian Food Inspection Agency is formed and takes over Health Canada's responsibilities for investigating the cause of food-borne illness outbreaks.

1998

Salmonella poisons 800 Canadians, mostly school children. The outbreak is traced to cheese packaged in Lunchmates, a popular snack made by J.M. Schneider Inc.

2000

An outbreak of E. coli in the drinking water of Walkerton claims the lives of seven people and sickens thousands.

2001

- The Canadian Cattle Identification Program requires that all cattle in Canada have an approved ear tag by the time they leave their herd of origin. The program is on the heels of the mad cow scare that continues to plague Europe.
- More than 1600 cases of foot and mouth disease are detected in Europe and, to prevent the spread, more than 3 million animals are killed.

PROPER FOOD STORAGE

Keeping food stored properly can prevent food-related illnesses. Some tips:

CHILLING: Refrigerate or freeze perishables, prepared foods, and leftovers within two hours or less. Marinate foods in the refrigerator.
THAW: Never defrost food at room temperature. Thaw food in the refrigerator, in cold water, or in the microwave if you will be cooking it immediately.
DIVIDE: Separate large amounts of leftovers into small, shallow containers for quicker cooling in the refrigerator.
DISCARD: Don't overstuff the refrigerator. Cold air needs to circulate above and beneath food to keep it safe.
BEST BEFORE: Placed on packaged foods that have a durable life of 90 days or less, such as dairy products, eggs, vacuum-packed foods, and salad dressings. This date does not apply once a food package has been opened.
DAIRY PRODUCTS: Should be used within three days after opening, even if the best before date indicates that they are good for a few weeks more. That's because foods begin to spoil once they have been opened and exposed to air, bacteria, and warm temperatures.
PACKAGED FOOD: Including vacuum-packed meats and prepared foods such as salads, salad dressings, dips, and jarred sauces. Need to be refrigerated and used within a reasonable amount of time to keep them safe to eat.
PERISHABLES: Cottage cheese, salads made with mayonnaise, meat, fish, or poultry, and combination foods like pasta dishes and casseroles can only be kept for a few days in the refrigerator and should be discarded if they have sat out at room temperature for more than two hours.

(continued)

PROPER FOOD STORAGE (CONTINUED)

FRESH FOOD: Deli meats, meat, fish, poultry, and cheeses are labeled with a packaging date. Should only be kept a few days after opening.

CANNED FOOD: Generally has a long storage time, about one to two years. Some canned foods, such as soups, have a best before date stamped on their lid. Avoid swollen or leaking cans, or damaged packages. That may indicate that the contents have been exposed to bacteria.

FROZEN FOOD: Also has a long storage time. Frozen fruits and vegetables, for example, keep for about one year. Foods stored in the freezer should be covered tightly with freezer wrap, or in airtight containers or freezer bags to prevent spoilage and freezer burn. Foods that have thawed and been refrozen before being cooked are unsafe to eat and should be discarded.

MISC: Jams, jellies (once opened, store covered in refrigerator), and syrup can be kept for about a year. Honey can be kept in the cupboard for about 18 months.

IF IN DOUBT throw it out.

PROPER FOOD HANDLING

Improper handling of raw meat, poultry, and seafood can create an inviting environment for cross-contamination. As a result, bacteria can spread to food and throughout the kitchen. Some tips on preparing food safely:

LATHER UP: Always wash hands, cutting boards, dishes, and utensils with hot, soapy water after they come in contact with raw meat, poultry, and seafood. Sanitize them for the safest results.

SANITIZE: Clean and then sanitize counter tops, cutting boards, and utensils with a mild bleach solution (5mL/1 tsp. bleach per 750mL/3 cups water) before and after food preparation.

WASH: Always wash fruit and vegetables carefully to remove any trace of pesticides as well as micro-organisms that could cause food poisoning. Discard the outer leaves of greens such as lettuce and cabbage before washing.

CUTTING BOARDS: If possible, use one cutting board for fresh produce and use a separate one for raw meat, poultry, and seafood.

SEPARATION: Separate raw meat, poultry, and seafood from other foods in your grocery shopping cart and in your refrigerator.

SEAL IT: To prevent juices from raw meat, poultry, or seafood dripping on to other foods in the refrigerator, place these raw foods in sealed containers or plastic bags on the bottom shelves.

CLEAN PLATE: Never place cooked food back on the same plate or cutting board that previously held raw food.

(continued)

PROPER FOOD HANDLING (CONTINUED)

MARINADE: Sauce that is used to marinate raw meat, poultry, or seafood should not be used on cooked foods. Boil leftover marinade or prepare extra for basting cooked food. Wash and sanitize your brush or use separate brushes when marinating raw and cooked foods.

COOKING: Cook to proper temperatures. Cooking times vary for meats, poultry, and fish. Following cooking, keep foods out of the "danger zone" (4°C to 60°C or 40°F to 140°F) by preparing them quickly and serving them immediately.

KEEP IT HOT: When serving hot food buffet-style, keep it hot (at 60°C or 140°F) with chafing dishes, crock pots, and warming trays.

CHECK: Use a clean thermometer that measures the internal temperature of cooked foods, to make sure meat, poultry, egg dishes, casseroles, and other foods are cooked all the way through. Insert the thermometer in different spots to ensure even cooking. Wash your food thermometer with hot soapy water before using it again. Sanitize it for the safest results.

MICROWAVE: Do not use plastic children's tableware, plastic containers, polystyrene foam meat trays and cups, margarine tubs, or yogurt containers to defrost, cook, or reheat foods in the microwave. Containers that are not labeled "microwave safe" may release chemicals into food when heated.

PLASTIC WRAP: Fine as a cover for reheating or cooking foods in the microwave, but shouldn't touch food. The concern is that food may absorb some of the plasticizer, a material that helps make the wrap flexible.

WIPE UP: Consider using paper towels to wipe kitchen surfaces or change dishcloths daily to avoid the possibility of cross-contamination and the spread of bacteria. Avoid using sponges because they are harder to keep bacteria-free.

AFTER READING

Responding

1. Identify
   - the most important or interesting fact on each of the charts
   - a piece of information you would like to have about food that is not on these charts

Understanding

2. With a partner
   - assess the organization and ease of finding specific information on each chart
   - analyze the vocabulary used in these charts to determine their intended audience (age, socio-economic position, education, and their experience with computers and the Internet)
   - identify publications where charts like these are published

   Be prepared to discuss your observations with the class.

3. In your notebook, explain any graphic changes you would make to these selections to enhance their effectiveness.

4. a) Write a serious or humorous **personal essay** explaining why one piece of information on these charts is of greatest benefit to you. Use an appropriate method of development to organize your essay. (See The Reference Shelf, pages 386–391.)

   b) With a partner, revise and edit your essay, focusing on content, organization, and use of transitions. (See The Reference Shelf, page 393.)

   c) Using feedback from your partner, update your Writing Skills Action Plan for improvement. (See The Reference Shelf, page 395.)

Thinking About Language

5. The time line "Food Issues Through the Ages" is written in sentences; the time line "How Writing Evolved" (page 164) uses point form. With a partner, assess the advantages and disadvantages of the two approaches. Be prepared to report to the class on your discussion.

Extending

6. Add another entry to the time line (with a date, an illustration, and a sentence or two) describing another historically important food issue. You may need to do research to prepare your entry.

7. **Debate** the following resolution: Be It Resolved That Consumers Can Be More Confident in the Quality of Their Food Supply Today Than Ever Before in History. (See The Reference Shelf, page 401.) You may need to do research to prepare your arguments.

8. Using a "plain language style" (see The Reference Shelf, page 352) and the charts "Proper Food Storage" and "Proper Food Handling" as models, create instructions to help your audience perform a practical task. Be sure to format your work, either by hand or with computer software, with a **layout** that is easy to read, uses headings to organize information, and incorporates other design elements.

9. Find another graphic selection in a newspaper or magazine that presents information that is important or interesting to you. Prepare a presentation to the class explaining aspects of the graphic and the information it contains that appealed to you.

10. Create an advertisement for a print or electronic medium to reassure consumers about a product after a widely publicized health scare related to that product.

What Goes Around

"...nothing truly disappeared..."   SARAH SHEARD

BEFORE READING

Complete the expression referred to in the title of the **story**. As a class, discuss the meaning of the expression and predict the content of the story.

A six-quart basket of peaches, of zucchini and new potatoes. I set them down, side by side on the kitchen counter. They had been picked at the moment of perfect ripeness and looking at them gave me a thrill of pleasure. I reached for my cookbook and began thumbing through for a recipe that might combine all three. Crossing the room, I disturbed the cloud of fruit flies hovering over the compost bucket I had meant to empty before going out shopping. Food scraps rotted fast in this heat. Insects helped. I draped a clean tea towel over the peaches to hide them from the valkyrie. When I kicked open the back door and carried the bucket out, the cloud followed like a genie chasing its bottle.

The *County Echo* had begun reporting a garbage crisis. Residents were being urged to recycle, so we all began bundling up newspapers and tin cans and dropping them off at the depot downtown, waiting to be unobserved before pitching in our liquor bottles. The *Echo*'s how-to article on composting made it sound easy and inexpensive, so I bought a plastic garbage pail, cut the bottom out as recommended, punched holes for ventilation below the lid and around the sides and planted it beside the flower bed.

What I'd begun out of civic obligation became intensely satisfying. To redirect the river of squandered material flowing through my life freed me of guilt.

It was heavy work. Like the human body, organic kitchen waste was eighty per cent water. My kitchen accumulation of banana peels, bread crusts, egg shells, tea bags, pea hulls, cantaloupe rinds, dillweed stems and coffee grounds had to be aerated every few days with a pitchfork but tending my compost now displaced most of the pleasures of my day. I became fanatical about not letting the smallest chip of vegetable matter escape into the regular garbage. These six-quart baskets sitting on my counter: zucchinis — discrete tubes of green light, peaches glowing like blood-quickened skin, potatoes, small and freckled-like eggs laid by the ground itself — were bright links in a chain of coexistence — teaching me something of where they and I were positioned on that chain. These vegetables were on their way to two mouths — mine and the other, hidden under the lid of the bin. Between us, every atom — and I was becoming more sensible of the molecular universe — would be put to good use, a Jack Sprat and his wife symbiosis. My soul, fed on reassurances like that, was nourished spiritually by such insights. Around other people eating, I found myself scrutinizing their plates, almost compulsively assessing the scraps, longing to carry them off, marvelling at my self-restraint.

Occasionally, I lapsed back into old habits. My hand mindlessly pitched a newspaper I'd been reading into the fireplace, rinsed out the teapot under the tap, coming to with horror just as the swirl of leaves escaped through the holes in the drain basket. Waste, waste. I paid penance for these lapses by meticulously collecting the nest of garlic papers and peppercorns strewn about my condiment shelf and transporting them between prayerful palms to the bucket.

But today I just lay down on the grass beside my bin with my cookbook under my head and stared into the sun, waiting for the willpower to pull myself up again and sort out the chaos around me. Like continents that had once been attached, the armoured plates of my psyche were drifting apart while I lay passive as an ocean beneath them, powerless to nudge them back together.

The ground was cold.

I stood up and brushed the blades of grass off my legs. I walked down Belevedere Hill to the mall, drawing nigh to the place as though it were a hearth to warm me with its freneticism of shoppers pursuing their lists, herding their kids, loading up the family wagon, darting back out onto the highway like needleflies. I'd seen films of such places speeded up, the headlights fusing into streamers — and slow–mo photography too, that elevated the simplest of human gestures to the eloquence of poetry.

I found myself out behind Family Restaurant staring at the battered dumpster bins socked full of leftover dinners jumbled in with paper garbage and industrial-sized tins that had once held shortening, mayonnaise, gravy: the fats, salts, sugars, alcohols and blood that a restaurant combusted into meals. All that squandered possibility. In the dying light, the dumpsters looked like giant six-quart baskets of organic, recyclable material — if only the owners and staff could be persuaded to — why, each of the dumpsters could be labeled so that the different categories of offal could be sorted before disposal, saving people at the other end a horrible job. If I could persuade Family Restaurant to act as a model — and it was a franchise — then perhaps Burger King might follow suit and McDonald's. A chain reaction across North America. Triggered by me. I paced the lot, rehearsing how to pitch the idea to the manager. I'd probably have to approach the Chamber of Commerce first, confront the polyester opportunists responsible for

everywhere were braiding into oily rivers, roaring down mountains into the seas, taken up as rain, seeping through our skins, staining the unborn.

I sat down.

I couldn't undertake the global consciousness-raising of restauranteurs and their patrons. I couldn't reclaim the ocean of refuse and turn it into good earth, build my own Zeider Zee, single-handedly. Why did I want to? I hated the process of decay and change. Every year, when the lake turned cool, the daylight shrank and leaves began blowing across the sidewalks, I was seized with a melancholia so sharp its pangs felt almost physical while the fragrant air of spring, the receding crust of winter only reminded me of lilies and death. Another year gone.

My thoughts and impulses lately were like paint thrown onto a spinning turntable, blurring into a pattern that was always different and yet, somehow, always the same. Cycles of remembering intentions and forgetting and remembering again.

No escape.

No relief.

No insight.

I had started my compost bin the previous winter, so decomposition really didn't strut its stuff until the spring. I first checked the contents in April, but nothing had happened. The corn cobs and broccoli trunks were still quite recognizable (even the beansprouts).

By June, I noticed that the contents had dropped substantially and by the end of the month no matter how many buckets I emptied into it the level always fell a little by the next day.

putting this mall here in the first place. Sure, or end-run them all, shame the merchants' association into taking responsibility by writing an impeccably worded "We the People" torpedo to the *Echo*. On the other hand, the same letter coming from a politician...who was my Member of Parliament?

A pair of kitchen workers came staggering out with garbage bags which they swung overhand into a dumpster. The smell, punched loose by the impact, hit me in the throat and I had to retreat quite a distance. The asphalt beneath the bins was greasy and stained with spoilage. Tributaries of spoilage from dumpsters

The transformative process of decay no longer dismayed me as it once had. In a way, I was getting over my fear of death. It comforted me to think that nothing was wasted, nothing truly disappeared — or therefore appeared. Whenever friends dropped by I showed them my bin, rolling it aside to reveal the muck percolating through. I wanted to convert them to my new pleasure, seduce them with my enthusiasm for this philosophy of decay. Some listened. Others did not.

The telltale stink of anaerobia could be cured by vigorous pitch-forking and basting with hay and I was doing just that after a particularly wet week in July when I noticed masses of thin red worms, a decompositional milestone. By now, my fork was turning something over that resembled dirt but was somewhat slushier.

August 24th.

Today, I lifted the lid and pitched the contents out into the flower bed. The characteristic forms of all the fruits and vegetables I had thrown in for a year had been assimilated into a material indistinguishable from store-bought gardening soil. I picked up a handful, felt it, studied it, squeezed it. When I opened my hand the earth held its shape like a cake. I spread the grains apart with my thumb, red-black crumbs, purple-black, some flecks of orange but basically uniform in colour, and free of insects.

There it was, the whole story, spread out on the palm of my hand, the elegant proof of ashes to ashes, dust to dust.

We come out. We go back in. We are dissolved into one another.

AFTER READING

Responding

1. In a small group, make a list of things you and your families do to help the environment. Discuss your list with the rest of the class and decide what more you could be doing.

Understanding

2. Look up the meanings of the following words: valkyrie, symbiosis, offal. Find these words in the story and explain why it is important to understand their meanings when trying to understand the story.

3. Explain why the **narrator** got involved in recycling and composting.
4. Record two examples from the story that show the narrator is obsessed with composting. How does her obsession make you feel about her?
5. a) The story ends with "ashes to ashes, dust to dust," words that are often heard at funerals. With a partner, talk about what this expression means.

    b) In this story, the narrator's successful composting teaches her something about herself and about life. With your partner, brainstorm the lessons she has learned from the experience. Together, using your brainstorming, write a series of paragraphs explaining what she has learned and how the composting helped her learn it.

Thinking About Language

6. Look up the meaning of "**allusion**." What is the writer alluding to when she refers to "Jack Sprat and his wife" (page 25)? Why is the allusion appropriate for the story?

Extending

7. a) With a partner, look back at your response to activity 1. Using a **graphic organizer** (see The Reference Shelf, pages 381–382), gather ideas for a story that would encourage children to help keep the environment healthy. Decide on the age of your audience. Choose your best idea and write your story. In your story, use **inclusive language** to reflect the many people who live in Canada. Illustrate your story so that it appeals to your audience.

    b) Have another pair read and comment on the content and organization of your story.

    c) Present your story to the class.

Remembrances of Calcutta

"...her leathery touch clings to my fingertips."   SHIKHA BHATTACHARJEE

BEFORE READING

Locate the city of Calcutta on a map. Why is it important to know where Calcutta is before reading this essay?

The smell grows dank, as the streets become narrower. Walls are replaced by trickling streams running along the side of the road. Children dart around the rick-shaws, bicycles, and the occasional car as garbage piles rise high in the streets. The piles steadily grow higher, mocking their patrons in doing the impossible: rising from the streets where they began their lives. In a day to day struggle, children grow up quickly, too quickly, though the rapid ascent is not swift enough.

In a world where meals are uncertain, there is little room for childhood. Responsibility is required, the burden forc-ing backs to grow strong. Girls are married immediately upon crossing the threshold of physical womanhood. Once married, she is no longer a mouth to be fed, making the transition from dependent to provider. Looking out the doorway upon children of her own, she wishes for them a childhood better than the one laid upon her, but

without money to send them to school, the cycle will continue.

The laughing eyes are quieted, as all focus now belongs to me. I am conscious of my clothes, showing no signs of wear, in a dark contrast to threadbare coverings, draped loosely over bony shoulders. My bracelets jingle. As earrings bob from my ears, the polished silver reflects the dusty streets and empty stares. I am ashamed of the sparkle, as new sandals protect my lily petal feet from the heat of the sun beaten ground. My feet are kept cool, as the breeze gently tickles. This same playful breeze does nothing for my burning face, as it is warmed by the army of stares.

The home of my Father's Aunt, shown to be spotlessly clean by the light creeping in through the solitary window. The living area: the size of my present bedroom. I am ashamed of what I have, and even more so, of what I wanted.

Savory aromas fill the air; I am hungry. Summoning my voice, though it is weak from the burden of a new perspective, I think to voice my hunger. Hunger: the young mother huddled at the street corner, reaching out with a hand hardened by work, begging alms while gesturing towards her child. Dropping the coins into her hand, her leathery touch clings to my fingertips. Their eycs plead to me as I allow myself to remember: I am not really hungry, I do not know what hunger is. At night, when the darkness is full, and the sound empty, I return to the place of remembrance. I tiptoe through the streets, a silent visitor, watching the struggle for all that I have….

Memories weight my head, reminding me to look straight. The sight is beautiful, for I have nothing to make me unhappy. I live in a beautiful home. Nine pairs of shoes lined neatly in a stacked closet: because of this, I am not completely at ease. My days harbor constant reminders of the injustices in this world. I want the pain of knowing; I keep it as a reminder of the good that cares enough to hurt.

I do not wish to portray my India this way. I can set this scene over and over again, from the villages of Central America to the City of New York where the people struggle daily to rise.

AFTER READING

Responding
1. Reread the third paragraph and write about a time you felt embarrassed when you thought your clothing, hair, jewellery, or other personal items made you stand out in a group.

Understanding
2. Describe three **images** that have stayed with the writer from her visit to Calcutta. How has the writer been changed by her visit?
3. Explain the meaning of the last paragraph. Why is it an important paragraph in this **essay**?
4. In a small group, provide feedback to the Grade 10 student who wrote this essay. Include comments on the following: content (reorder, add, delete, substitute), organization, clarity (transitions, word use), and **style** (sentence structure, language level, audience). (See the Writing section in The Reference Shelf, pages 380–395.) As a class, compare your comments.

Thinking About Language
5. Find the meanings of the following words from the first paragraph of this essay, and add them to your personal word list: dank, ascent. How does your knowledge of these words increase your understanding of the essay?
6. The writer's guilt comes across in the emotional language she uses. With a partner, find examples of this type of language and explain how it emphasizes the main idea of her essay.
7. Explain the effects of the two sentence fragments in the fourth paragraph in this essay. Rewrite the fragments as full sentences.
8. Locate the word in the sixth paragraph that uses American spelling. How is it different from the Canadian spelling? Make a list of other words, in both Canadian and American spelling, that are similar in pattern to this one (e.g., colour).

Extending
9. a) With a partner, choose one of the first five paragraphs to create a shooting **script** for part of a documentary on Calcutta. Re-create the **mood** of this essay using sound and video elements. (See The Reference Shelf, pages 418–422.)
   b) Present your shooting script to another group for evaluation.
10. Research and record at least 10 facts about Calcutta. Using these facts, write one coherent paragraph (or more, if needed) about this city. With a partner, compare the information you found.
11. Using "Remembrances of Calcutta" as a model, write a similar essay about your remembrances of a town or city close to you.

Because I could not stop for Death

EMILY DICKINSON

BEFORE READING

1. As a class, discuss why humans are so interested in death.
2. Using classroom and library resources, make a chalkboard outline of some beliefs about death from various time periods, countries, and cultures.

Because I could not stop for Death —
He kindly stopped for me —
The Carriage held but just Ourselves —
And Immortality.

We slowly drove — He knew no haste   5
And I had put away
My labor and my leisure too,
For His Civility —

We passed the School, where Children strove
At Recess — in the Ring —   10
We passed the Fields of Gazing Grain —
We passed the Setting Sun —

Or rather — He passed Us —
The Dews drew quivering and chill —
For only Gossamer, my Gown —   15
My Tippet — only Tulle —

We paused before a House that seemed
A Swelling of the Ground —
The Roof was scarcely visible —
The Cornice — in the Ground —   20

Since then — 'tis Centuries — and yet
Feels shorter than the Day
I first surmised the Horses' Heads
Were toward Eternity —

AFTER READING

Responding

1. Reread the **poem** and decide whether or not you like the way Dickinson has used rhyme and
   rhythm in a poem that has such a serious subject. (See The Reference Shelf, pages 366–367.)
   Explain your decisions in your notebook.

Understanding

2. a) In a group, reread the poem aloud at least twice. Discuss the poem and come to a com-
      mon understanding of its meaning. Write a statement of **theme** for the poem starting
      with the words, "In 'Because I could not stop for Death,' Dickinson was saying that...."
   b) Be prepared to discuss your group's theme, using support from the poem, with the class.
3. In your notebook, describe the **tone** of the poem. Choose words and **images** from the poem
   that create that tone. Compare your list with a partner's.
4. In **stanza** 3, the **narrator** passes the school, the fields, and the setting sun, but in stanza 4,
   pauses in front of a house. From the group discussion in activity 3, explain why the carriage
   pauses at that point. As a class, discuss this change of words.

Thinking About Language

5. a) Look up and include in your personal word list the meanings of the following words:
      civility, cornice, surmised.

b) Look up other words that you found difficult. Explain how knowing their meanings helped your understanding of the poem.

6. Use The Reference Shelf to review the purpose of the semicolon (page 356). Explain why Dickinson would use a semicolon instead of a period in verses 1, 3, 5, and 6.

Extending

7. Locate and read the poem "In Flanders Fields." How does John McCrae feel about death? Why do you think McCrae and Dickinson have such different views of death?

8. a) With a partner, research the influence popular music has on the beliefs and behaviours of young people who listen to it. Create inquiry questions, assess information needs, and design a plan for a **report** on the **topic**. Find lyrics to a popular song that romanticizes death (makes it seem better than it is).

b) In addition to subtopics of your own, include the following in your report:
   • the possible effects the song could have on those who hear it
   • the pros and cons of radio stations censoring music that has been labelled "harmful" to listeners
   • the pros and cons of giving music a rating for parents to see

9. Write your own poem about death. Use words and phrases that create mental pictures for your reader. (Note: Your poem does not have to rhyme.)

Dracula

"A vampire...is a man or a woman who is dead and yet not dead."

HAMILTON DEANE AND
JOHN L. BALDERSTON

ADAPTED FROM
BRAM STOKER'S NOVEL *DRACULA*

BEFORE READING

As a class, brainstorm a list of places, things, and behaviours associated with the word "Dracula."

The original novel *Dracula*, written by Bram Stoker, was published in 1897 and has become a classic in the genre of horror. Since its first publication, *Dracula* has been adapted numerous times into **plays**, films, and television shows.

CHARACTERS

Miss Wells, maid
John Harker, betrothed to Lucy Seward
Dr. Seward, Director of a sanitarium
Abraham Van Helsing, doctor; friend of Dr. Seward
R.M. Renfield, patient at the sanitarium
Butterworth, attendant at sanitarium
Lucy Seward, Dr. Seward's daughter
Count Dracula

SETTING

Act One
The library in Dr. Seward's Sanitarium, Purley, England

Act Two
Lucy's bedroom; following day

Act Three
Scene 1
The library 32 hours later
Scene 2
A vault, just after sunrise

Act One

(*The library on the ground floor of Dr. Seward's Sanitarium at Purley. Room is medieval, the walls are stone with vaulted ceiling supported by two stone pillars, but is comfortably furnished in modern style. Wooden paneling around walls. Tapestries hang on the wall. Medieval fireplace in wall Right. Fire burning. There is a couch Right Center, a large armchair Right. At Left, a desk with armchair back of it, a small chair to Right of desk. Double doors in the rear wall. Large double window across angle of room, Left rear, leading out into garden. The curtains are drawn. Door Downstage Left. Invisible sliding panel in bookcase rear wall Right.*)

(*Maid, an attractive young girl, enters, showing in John Harker. Harker is a young man of about twenty-five, handsome in appearance; a typical Englishman, but in manner direct, explosive, incisive and excitable.*)

Harker: (*Agitated.*) You're sure Miss Lucy is no worse?

Maid: (*Soothingly.*) Just the same, sir.

(*Dr. Seward comes in, Downstage Left. He is a psychiatrist of about fifty-five, intelligent, but a typical specialist who lives in a world of textbooks and patients, not a man of action or force of character. The Maid exits, closing doors.*)

Seward: Oh! John.

Harker: (*As Seward extends hand.*) Doctor Seward. What is it? Why have you sent for me?

Seward: My dear John. I told you in my wire there was nothing new.

Harker: You said "no change, don't worry," but to "come at once."

Seward: (*Approvingly.*) And you lost no time.

Harker: I jumped in the car and burned up the road from London. Oh, Doctor, surely there must be something *more* we can do for Lucy. I'd give my life gladly if it would save her.

Seward: I'm sure you would, my boy. You love her with the warm blood of youth, but don't forget I love my daughter, too. She's all I have. You must see that nothing medical science can suggest has been left undone.

Harker: (*Bitterly.*) Medical science couldn't do much for Mina. Poor Mina.

Seward: Yes, poor Mina. She died after these same incredible symptoms that my Lucy has developed.

Harker: *My* Lucy too.

Seward: *Our* Lucy, then.

(*Wild, maniacal laugh is heard offstage left.*)

Harker: Good God, what was that?

Seward: (*Sits at desk.*) Only Renfield. A patient of mine.

Harker: But you never keep violent patients here in your sanitarium. Lucy mustn't be compelled to listen to raving madmen.

Seward: I quite agree, and I'm going to have him sent away. Until just lately he was always quiet. I'll be sorry to lose him.

Harker: What!

Seward: An unusual case. Zoophagous.

Harker: What's that?

Seward: A life-eating maniac.

Harker: What?

Seward: Yes, he thinks that by absorbing lives he can prolong his own life.

Harker: Good Lord!

Seward: Catches flies and eats them. And by way of change, he feeds flies to spiders. Fattens them up. Then he eats the spiders.

Harker: Good God, how disgusting. (*Sits.*) But tell me about Lucy. Why did you send for me?

Seward: Yesterday I wired to Holland for my old friend Van Helsing. He'll be here soon. The car has gone down to the station for him now. I'm going to turn Lucy's case over to him.

Harker: Another specialist on anemia?

Seward: No, my boy, whatever this may be, it's not anemia, and this man, who speaks a dozen languages as well as his own, knows more about mysterious diseases than anyone alive.

Harker: Heaven knows it's mysterious enough, but surely the symptoms are clear.

Seward: So were poor Mina's. Perfectly clear. (*A dog howls at a distance. Other dogs take up the chorus far and near.*) There they are, at it again, every dog for a mile around.

Harker: (*Crosses to the window.*) They seem howls of terror.

Seward: We've heard that chorus every night since Mina fell ill.

Harker: When I was traveling in Russia, and the dogs in the village barked like that, the natives always said wolves were prowling about.

Seward: I hardly think you'll find wolves prowling around Purley, twenty miles from London.

Harker: Yet your old house might be in a wilderness. (*Looks out of window.*) Nothing in sight except that place Carfax that Count Dracula has taken.

Seward: Your friend, the Count, came in again last evening.

Harker: He's no friend of mine.

Seward: Don't say that. He knows that you and I gave our blood for Lucy as well as for Mina, and he's offered to undergo transfusion himself if we need another volunteer. (*Sits on couch.*)

Harker: By Jove, that's sporting of him. I see I've misjudged him.

Seward: He seems genuinely interested in Lucy. If he were a young man I'd think…

Harker: What!

Seward: But his whole attitude shows that it isn't that. We need sympathy in this house, John, and I'm grateful for it.

Harker: So am I. Anyone who offers to help Lucy can have anything I've got.

Seward: Well, I think he does help Lucy. She always seems cheered up when he comes.

Harker: That's fine. May I go to Lucy now?

Seward: (*Rises.*) We'll go together. (*Bell rings off.*) That must be Van Helsing. You go ahead and I'll come presently.

(*Harker exits. Maid shows in Abraham Van Helsing, who enters briskly. Man of medium height, in his early fifties, with clean-shaven, astute face, shaggy gray eyebrows and a mass of gray hair which is brushed backward showing a high forehead. Dark, piercing eyes set far apart; nervous, alert manner; an air of resolution, clearly a man of resourceful action. Incisive speech, always to the point; raps his words out sharply and quickly. Van Helsing carries small black bag.*)

Maid: Professor Van Helsing.

Seward: (*He and Van Helsing shake hands warmly as Maid goes out.*) My dear Van Helsing, I can never repay you for this.

Van Helsing: Were it only a patient of yours instead of your daughter, I would have come. You once rendered me a service.

Seward: Don't speak of that. You'd have done it for me. (*Starts to ring.*) Let me give you something to eat. (*Stopped by Van Helsing's gesture.*)

Van Helsing: (*Places bag on table back of couch.*) I dined on the boat train. I do not waste time when there is work to do.

Seward: Ah, Van Helsing, you cast the old spell on me. I lean on you before you have been two minutes in my house.

Van Helsing: You wrote of your daughter's symptoms. Tell me more of the other young lady, the one who died.

Seward: (*Shows Van Helsing to chair. Seward sits at desk.*) Poor Mina Weston. She was a girl just Lucy's age. They were inseparable. She was on a visit here when she fell ill. As I wrote you, she just grew weaker; day by day she wasted away. But there were no anemic symptoms; her blood was normal when analyzed.

Van Helsing: You said you performed transfusion.

Seward: Yes, Sir William Briggs ordered that. (*Baring forearm.*) You see this mark? Well, Lucy herself, and her fiancee, John Harker, gave their blood as well.

Van Helsing: So…Three transfusions…And the effect?

Seward: She rallied after each. The color returned to her cheeks, but the next morning she would be pale and weak again. She complained of *bad dreams*. Ten days ago we found her in a stupor from which nothing could rouse her. She…died.

Van Helsing: And…the other symptoms?

Seward: None, except those two little marks on the throat that I wrote you about.

Van Helsing: And which perhaps brought me here so quickly. What were they like?

Seward: Just two little white dots with red centers. (*Van Helsing nods grimly.*) We decided she must have run a safety pin through the skin of her throat, trying in her delirium to fasten a scarf or shawl.

Van Helsing: Perhaps. And your daughter's symptoms are the same?

Seward: Precisely. She too speaks of *bad dreams*. Van Helsing, you've lived in the tropics. May this not be something alien to our medical experience in England?

Van Helsing: (*Grimly.*) It may indeed, my friend.

(*Laugh is heard from behind curtain at window. Van Helsing rises, followed by Seward, who crosses to window and draws curtain. Renfield is standing there. Repulsive youth, face distorted, shifty eyes, tousled hair.*)

Seward: (*Astounded, drawing Renfield into room.*) Renfield. How did you…?

Van Helsing: Who is this man?

Seward: (*Crosses to bell; rings.*) One of my patients. This is gross carelessness.

Van Helsing: Did you hear us talking?

Renfield: Words…words…words…

Seward: Come, come, Renfield, you know you mustn't wander about this way. How did you get out of your room?

Renfield: (*Laughs.*) Wouldn't you like to know?

Seward: How are the flies? (*To Van Helsing.*) Mr. Renfield makes a hobby of eating flies. I'm afraid you eat spiders, too, sometimes. Don't you Renfield?

Renfield: Will you walk into my parlor, said the spider to the fly. Excuse me, Doctor, you have not introduced me to your friend.

Seward: (*Reprovingly.*) Come, come, Renfield.

Van Helsing: Humor him.

(*Enter Maid.*)

Seward: Tell the Attendant to come here at once.

Maid: Yes, sir. (*Exits.*)

Seward: Oh, very well. Professor Van Helsing, Mr. Renfield, a patient of mine. (*Van Helsing steps toward him. They shake hands. Van Helsing rubs Renfield's fingers with his thumb and Renfield jerks hand away.*)

Renfield: Ah, who does not know of Van Helsing! Your work, sir, in investigating certain obscure diseases, not altogether unconnected with forces and powers that the ignorant herd do not believe exist, has won you a position that posterity will recognize. (*Enter Attendant dressed in uniform. He starts at seeing Renfield, then looks at Seward sheepishly.*)

Seward: (*As severely as his mild nature permits.*) Butterworth, you have let your patient leave his room again.

Attendant: No, really, sir, I locked the door on him, and I've got the key in my pocket now.

Seward: But this is the second time. Only last night you let him escape and he tried to break into Count Dracula's house across the grounds.

Attendant: He didn't get out the door this time, sir, and it's a drop of thirty feet out of the windows. (*Crosses to Renfield.*) He's just an eel. Now you come with me. (*As they start toward door; holds Renfield by coat collar and right arm.*)

Seward: Renfield, if this happens again you will get no more sugar to spread out for your flies.

Renfield: (*Drawing himself up.*) What do I care for flies…now? (*Attendant gives Van Helsing a look.*) Flies. Flies are but poor things. (*As he speaks he follows with his eyes a fly. Attendant sees fly too; releases Renfield indulgently. With a sweep of his hand he catches fly, holds closed hand to ear as if listening to buzz of fly as he crosses a few steps, then carries it to his mouth. Then seeing them watching him, releases it quickly.*) A low form of life. Beneath my notice, I don't care a pin about flies.

Attendant: Oh, don't you? Any more of your tricks and I'll take your new spider away.

Renfield: (*Babbles; on knees.*) Oh, no, no! Please, dear Mr. Butterworth, please leave me my spider. He's getting so nice and fat. When he's had another dozen flies he'll be just right, just right. (*Gives little laugh. Rubs hands together, then catches fly and makes gesture of eating.*)

Van Helsing: Come, Mr. Renfield, what makes you want to eat flies?

Renfield: (*Rises.*) The wings of a fly, my dear sir, typify the aerial powers of the psychic faculties.

Seward: (*To attendant, wearily.*) Butterworth, take him away.

Van Helsing: One moment, my friend. (*To Renfield.*) And the spiders?

Renfield: (*Impressively.*) Professor Van Helsing, can you tell me why that one great spider lived for centuries in the tower of the old Spanish church—and grew and grew? He never ate, but he drank, and he *drank.* He would come down and drink the oil of all the church lamps.

Seward: (*To attendant.*) Butterworth.

Renfield: One moment, Doctor Seward…(*Van Helsing gets wolfsbane from bag on table.*) I want you to send me away, now, *tonight*, in a straitjacket. Chain me so I can't escape. This is a sanitarium, not a lunatic asylum. This is no place for me. My cries will disturb Miss Lucy, who is ill. They will give your daughter *bad dreams*, Doctor Seward, *bad dreams.*

Seward: (*Soothingly.*) We'll see about all this in the morning. (*Nods to Attendant, who moves toward Renfield.*)

Van Helsing: Why are you so anxious to go?

Renfield: (*Crosses to Van Helsing; hesitates, then with gesture of decision.*) I'll tell you. Not that fool Seward. He wouldn't understand. But you…(*A large bat dashes against window. Renfield turns to the window, holds out his hand and gibbers.*) No, no, no, I wasn't going to say anything…

(*Attendant crosses up; watches Renfield.*)

Seward: What was that?

Renfield: (*Looks out window, then turns.*) It was a bat, gentlemen. Only a bat! Do you know that in some islands of the Eastern seas there are bats which hang on trees all night? And when the heat is stifling and sailors sleep on the deck in those harbors, in the morning *they* are found dead men… white, even as Miss Mina was.

Seward: What do you know of Miss Mina? (*Pause.*) Take him to his room!

Van Helsing: (*To Seward.*) Please! (*To Renfield.*) Why are you so anxious to be moved from here?

Renfield: To save my soul.

Van Helsing: Yes?

Renfield: Oh, you'll get nothing more out of me than that. And I'm not sure I hadn't rather stay. After all, what is my soul good for? Is not…(*Turns to window.*)…*what I am to receive worth* the loss of my soul?

Seward: (*Lightly.*) What's got him thinking about souls? Have you the souls of those flies and spiders on your conscience?

Renfield: (*Puts fingers in his ears, shuts eyes, distorts face.*) I forbid you to plague me about souls! I don't want their *souls*. All I want is their life. The blood is the life.

Van Helsing: So?

Renfield: That's in the Bible. What use are souls to me? (*To Van Helsing.*) I couldn't eat them or dr…(*Breaks off suddenly.*)

Van Helsing: Or drink…(*Holding wolfsbane under his nose, Renfield's face becomes convulsed with rage and loathing. He leaps back.*)

Renfield: You know too much to live, Van Helsing! (*He suddenly lunges at Van Helsing. Seward and Attendant shout at the attack and as they drag Renfield to door he stops struggling and says clearly:*)

Renfield: I'll go quietly. (*Seward lets go of him.*) I warned you to send me away, Doctor Seward. If you don't, you must answer for my soul before the judgment seat of God!

(*Renfield and Attendant exit. Wild laughter can be heard off. Van Helsing puts wolfsbane in bag as Seward closes door.*)

Seward: My friend, you're not hurt?

Van Helsing: No.

Seward: My deepest apologies. You'll think my place shockingly managed.

(*Van Helsing waves apology aside with impatient gesture.*)

What was your herb that excited him so?

Van Helsing: Wolfsbane. (*A little look out of window as he crosses.*)

Seward: Wolfsbane? What's that? I thought I knew all the drugs.

Van Helsing: It grows only in the wilds of Central Russia.

Seward: But why did you bring it with you?

Van Helsing: It is a form of preventive medicine.

Seward: Well, we live and learn. I never heard of it.

Van Helsing: Seward, I want you to have that lunatic securely watched.

Seward: Anything you say, Professor Van Helsing, but it's my Lucy I want you to look after first.

Van Helsing: I want to keep this man under observation.

Seward: (*Annoyed and hurt.*) An interesting maniac, no doubt, but surely you'll see my daughter.

Van Helsing: I must see the records of his case.

Seward: But Doctor…

Van Helsing: Do you think I have forgotten why I am here?

Seward: (*As they start to go out left.*) Forgive me. Of course I'll show you the records, but I don't understand why you're so curious about Renfield, because in your vast experience…

(*They exit. The room is empty for a few seconds; then Lucy enters, supported by Harker. She is a beautiful girl of twenty, clad in filmy white dressing gown, her face unnaturally pale. She walks with difficulty. Round her throat is wound a scarf. She crosses to desk and leans on it as Harker closes door.*)

Harker: Why, I thought they were here, Lucy.

Lucy: John, do you think this new man will be any better than the others?

Harker: (*Moving her to the couch.*) I'm sure he will. Anyway, Lucy, now that I'm back I'm going to stay with you till you get over this thing.

Lucy: (*Delighted.*) Oh, John. But can you? Your work in town?

Harker: (*Seating her, then sitting next to her.*) You come first.

Lucy: (*A change comes over her.*) I…don't think you'd better stay, John. (*A look about room.*) Sometimes…I feel that I want to be alone.

Harker: My dear. How can you say that you don't want me with you when you're so ill? You love me, don't you? (*Taking her hand.*)

Lucy: (*Affectionately.*) Yes, John, with all my soul.

Harker: Just as soon as you're well enough I'm going to take you away. We'll be married next month. We won't wait till June. We'll stretch that honeymoon month to three months and the house will be ready in July.

Lucy: (*Overjoyed.*) John, you think we could?

Harker: Of course, why not? My mother wanted us to wait, but she'll understand, and I want to get you *away*. (*Starts to kiss her. She shudders as he does so.*) Why do you shrink when I kiss you? You're so cold, Lucy, always so cold…now…

Lucy: (*With tenderness but no hint of passion.*) Forgive me, dear. I am yours, all yours. (*Clings to him. He embraces her. She sinks back.*) Oh, John, I'm so tired…so tired. (*Seward and Van Helsing return.*)

Seward: Lucy dear, this is my old friend, Professor Van Helsing.

(*She sits up; extends her hand to him.*)

Van Helsing: My dear Miss Seward, (*He kisses Lucy's hand.*) you don't remember poor old Van Helsing. I knew you when you were a little girl. So high, and now what charm, what beauty. A little pale, yes, but we will bring the roses back to the cheeks.

Lucy: You were so kind to come, Professor.

Van Helsing: And this, no doubt, is the fortunate young man you are to marry?

Seward: Yes, John Harker, Professor.

Harker: Look here, Professor. I'm not going to get in your way, but if Doctor Seward will have me I'm going to make him give me a bed here until Lucy gets over this thing. (*Turns to Seward.*) It's absolute hell, being away in London, and of course I can't do any work.

Seward: You're most welcome to stay, my boy.

Van Helsing: Indeed, yes. I should have asked you to stay. I may need you. (*Takes chair from desk to left of couch; turns to Lucy.*) Now lie back, so. (*Examines her eyelids carefully and feels her pulse.*) And now tell me when did this, this weakness first come upon you? (*Sits, after examining eyelids; looks at her gums, examines tips of fingernails, then takes out watch as he feels her pulse.*)

Lucy: Two nights after poor Mina was buried I had…a bad dream.

Van Helsing: (*Releases pulse, after looking at watch.*) A bad dream? Tell me about it.

Lucy: I remember hearing dogs barking before I went to sleep. The air seemed oppressive. I left the reading lamp lit by my bed, but when the dream came there seemed to come a mist in the room.

Van Helsing: Was the window open?

Lucy: Yes, I always sleep with my window open.

Van Helsing: Oh, of course, you're English. (*Laughs.*) We Continentals are not so particular about fresh air. And then…

Lucy: The mist seemed so thick I could just see the lamp by my bed, a tiny spark in the fog, and then…(*Hysterically.*) I saw two red eyes staring at me and livid white face looking down on me out of the mist. It was horrible, horrible!

(*Harker makes move toward her. Van Helsing stops him by a gesture.*)

Van Helsing: There, there. (*Soothingly, taking her hands from her face.*) Go on, please.

Lucy: (*Gives little start when Van Helsing touches her hands. Looks at Harker and starts; and at Seward and starts, then at Van Helsing and relaxes.*) The next morning my maid could scarcely wake me. I felt weak and languid. Some part of my life seemed to have gone from me.

Van Helsing: There have been other such dreams?

Lucy: Nearly every night since then has come the mist…the red eyes and that awful face.

(*She puts hands to her face again. Van Helsing soothes her, "There, there, now."*)

Seward: We've tried transfusion twice. Each time she recovered her strength.

Lucy: But then would come another dream. And now I dread the night. I know it seems absurd, Professor, but please don't laugh at me.

Van Helsing: I'm not likely to laugh.

(*Gently, without answering, he unwinds scarf from her throat. She puts hand up to stop him and cries, "No, no." A look at Harker when her neck is bare. As Van Helsing does so he starts, then quickly opens small black bag on* table and returns with magnifying glass; examines two small marks on throat. Lucy with eyes closed. Controlling himself with difficulty, Van Helsing puts magnifying glass back in bag, closes it, puts back chair by desk.)

And how long have you had these little marks on your throat?

(Seward and Harker start violently and come to couch. They look at each other in horror.)

Lucy: Since…that first morning.

Harker: Lucy, why didn't you tell us?

Seward: Lucy, you've worn that scarf around your throat to hide them!

(Lucy makes convulsive clutch at throat.)

Van Helsing: Do not press her. Do not excite her. (To Lucy.) Well?

Lucy: (Constrained; to Seward and Harker.) I was afraid they'd worry you, for I knew that…Mina had them.

Van Helsing: (With assumed cheerfulness.) Quite right, Miss Lucy, quite right. They're nothing, and old Van Helsing will see that these dreams trouble you no more.

Maid: (Appears at door.) Count Dracula.

(Dracula enters. He is a tall, mysterious man of about fifty. Polished and distinguished. Continental in appearance and manner. Lucy registers attraction to Dracula.)

Seward: Ah, good evening, Count.

Dracula: Gentlemen. (He bows to men; then goes to the couch and bows in courtly fashion.) Miss Seward, how are you? You are looking more yourself this evening.

(Lucy registers thrill. Alternate moods of attraction and repulsion, unaccountable to herself, affect Lucy in Dracula's presence. But this should be suggested subtly.)

Lucy: (Quite natural.) I feel better already, Count, now that father's old friend has come to help me.

(Dracula turns to Van Helsing. Lucy looks up at Dracula, recoils, and turns to Harker.)

Seward: Count Dracula, Professor Van Helsing.

(The two men bow.)

Dracula: A most distinguished scientist, whose name we know even in the wilds of Transylvania. (To Seward.) But I interrupt a consultation.

Seward: Not at all, Count. It's good of you to come, and we appreciate your motives.

Harker: Doctor Seward had just told me of your offer, and I can't thank you enough.

Dracula: It is nothing. I should be grateful to be permitted to help Miss Lucy in any way.

Lucy: But you do, Count. I look forward to your visits. They seem to make me better.

Van Helsing: And so I arrive to find a rival in the field.

Dracula: (Crosses to Lucy.) You encourage me, Miss Seward, to make them more frequent, as I should like to.

Lucy: (Looking at him fixedly.) I am always glad to see you.

Dracula: Ah, but you have been lonely here. And my efforts to amuse you with our old tales will no longer have the same success, now that you have Professor Van Helsing with you, and especially now that Mr. Harker is to remain here.

Harker: How did you know I was going to stay, Count?

Dracula: (Little start.) Can the gallant lover ask such a question? I inferred it, my friend.

Harker: You're right. Nothing is going to shift me now until Lucy's as fit as a fiddle again.

Dracula: Nothing?

Lucy: Please come as before, Count, won't you?

(*Dracula bows to her; kisses her hand. Van Helsing meanwhile has been talking to Maid.*)

Van Helsing: You understand, you will not answer bells. She must not be alone for a single moment under any circumstances, you understand.

(*As Dracula crosses to below desk, Lucy leans toward him, extends her hand, then recovers herself. Van Helsing registers that he sees her look at Dracula.*)

Maid: Yes, sir.

Van Helsing: (*To Lucy.*) Good. Your maid will take you to your room. Try to rest for a little, while I talk to your father.

(*Maid comes to couch to get Lucy. Pause, as Lucy looks at Dracula.*)

Seward: Wells, remember, don't leave her alone for a moment.

Maid: Oh, no, sir.

(*Lucy exchanges a long look with Dracula as Maid takes her out.*)

Dracula: Professor Van Helsing, so you have come from the land of the tulip, to cure the nervous prostration of this charming girl. I wish you all the success.

Van Helsing: Thank you, Count.

Dracula: Do I appear officious, Doctor Seward? I am a lonely man. You are my only neighbors when I am here at Carfax, and your trouble has touched me greatly.

Seward: Count, I am more grateful for your sympathy than I can say.

Van Helsing: You, like myself, are a stranger in England, Count?

Dracula: Yes, but I love England and the great London, so different from my own Transylvania, where there are so few people and so little opportunity.

Van Helsing: Opportunity, Count?

Dracula: For my investigations, Professor.

Seward: I hope you haven't regretted buying that old ruin across there?

Dracula: Oh, Carfax is not a ruin. The dust was somewhat deep, but we are used to dust in Transylvania.

Harker: You plan to remain in England, Count?

Dracula: I think so, my friend. The walls of my castle are broken, and the shadows are many, and I am the last of my race.

Harker: It's a lonely spot you've chosen, Carfax.

Dracula: It is, and when I hear the dogs howling far and near I think myself back in my Castle Dracula with its broken battlements.

Harker: Ah, the dogs howl there when there are wolves around, don't they?

Dracula: They do, my friend. And they howl here as well, although there are no wolves. But you wish to consult the anxious father and the great specialist. May I read a book in the study? I am so anxious to hear what the Professor says and to learn if I can be of any help.

Seward: By all means, Count. (*Dracula bows; exits. Seward watches him leave. Dogs howl offstage.*) Very kind of Dracula, with his untimely friendliness, but now what about my daughter?

Harker: Yes, Professor, what do you think is the matter with Lucy?

Van Helsing: (*Crosses to window, looks out. Long pause before he speaks.*)

Your patient, that interesting Renfield, does not like the smell of wolfsbane.

Seward: Good Heavens. What has that got to do with Lucy?

Van Helsing: Perhaps nothing.

Harker: In God's name, Professor, is there anything unnatural or occult about this business?

Seward: Occult? Van Helsing! Oh…

Van Helsing: Ah, Seward, let me remind you that the superstitions of today are the scientific facts of tomorrow. Science can now transmute the electron, the basis of all matter, into energy, and what is that but the dematerialization of matter? Yet dematerialization has been known and practiced in India for centuries. In Java I myself have seen things.

Seward: My dear old friend, you can't have filled up your fine old brain with Eastern moonshine.

Van Helsing: Moonshine?

Seward: But anyway, come now, what about my daughter?

Van Helsing: Ah! Seward, if you won't listen to what will be harder to believe than any Eastern moonshine, if you won't forget your textbooks…keep an open mind, then, Seward, your daughter's life may pay for your pig-headedness.

Harker: Go on, go on, Professor!

Seward: I am listening.

Van Helsing: Then I must ask you to listen calmly to what I am going to say. Sit down. (*Van Helsing crosses to window; closes curtains. Seward and Harker exchange glances, then both look at Van Helsing as they sit.*) You have both heard the legends of Central Europe, about the Werewolf, the Vampires?

Seward: You mean ghosts, who suck the blood of the living?

Van Helsing: If you wish to call them ghosts. I call them the undead.

Harker: (*Quickly.*) For God's sake, man, are you suggesting that Mina, and now Lucy…

Seward: (*Interrupting.*) Of course, I have read these horrible folk tales of the Middle Ages, Van Helsing, but I know you better than to suppose…

Van Helsing: (*Interrupting.*) That I believe them? I *do* believe them.

Seward: (*Incredulously.*) You mean to tell us that vampires actually exist and…and that Mina and Lucy have been attacked by one?

Van Helsing: Your English doctors would all laugh at such a theory. Your police, your public would laugh. (*Impressively.*) *The strength of the vampire is that people will not believe in him.*

Seward: (*Shaking head.*) Is this the help you bring us?

Van Helsing: (*Much moved.*) Do not despise it.

Harker: (*To Seward.*) Doctor, this case has stumped all your specialists. (*To Van Helsing.*) Go on, Professor.

Van Helsing: Vampires are rare. Nature abhors them, the forces of good combine to destroy them, but a few of these creatures have lived on for centuries.

Harker: (*Excited.*) What *is* a vampire?

Van Helsing: A vampire, my friend, is a man or a woman who is dead and yet not dead. A thing that lives after its death by drinking the blood of the living. It must have blood or it dies. Its power lasts only from sunset to sunrise. During the hours of the day it must rest in the earth in which it was buried. But, during the night, it has the power to prey upon the living. (*Incredulous move from Seward.*) My friend, you are thinking you will have to put me amongst your patients?

Seward: Van Helsing, I don't know what to think but I confess I simply can't follow you.

Harker: What makes you think that Lucy has been attacked by such a creature?

Van Helsing: (*From now on dominating them.*) Doctor Seward's written account of these ladies' symptoms at once aroused my suspicion. Anemia? The blood of three people was forced into the veins of Miss Mina. Yet she dies from loss of blood. Where did it go? Had your specialist any answer? The vampire attacks the throat. He leaves two little wounds, white with red centers. (*Harker rises slowly.*) Seward, you wrote me of those two marks on Miss Mina's throat. An accident with a safety pin, you said. So I thought, I suspected, I did not know, but I came on the instance, and what do I find? These same wounds on Miss Lucy's throat. Another safety pin, Doctor Seward?

Seward: Do you mean to say that you've built up all this nightmare out of a safety pin? It's true I can't make out why she hid those marks from us.

Van Helsing: I could tell you that.

Seward: (*Pause.*) What! I don't believe it. Of course Lucy's trouble can't be *that*.

Harker: I do believe it. This theory accounts for all the facts that nobody has been able to explain. We'll take her away where this thing can't get at her.

Van Helsing: She will not want to go.

Seward: What!

Van Helsing: If you force her, the shock may be fatal.

Harker: But why won't she go if we tell her that her life depends on it?

Van Helsing: Because the victim of the vampire becomes his creature, linked to him in life and after death.

Seward: (*Incredulous, shocked; rises.*) Professor, this is too much!

Harker: Will Lucy become an unclean thing, a demon?

Van Helsing: Yes, Harker. *Now* will you help me?

Harker: Yes, anything. Tell me what to do.

Van Helsing: It is dangerous work. Our lives are at stake, but so is Miss Lucy's life, so is her soul. We must stamp out this monster.

Harker: How can we stamp it out now?

Van Helsing: This undead thing lies helpless by day in the earth or tomb in which it was buried.

Seward: A corpse, in a coffin?

Van Helsing: A corpse, if you like, but a living corpse, sustained by the blood of the living. If we can find its earth home, a stake driven through the heart destroys the vampire. But this is our task. In such a case the police, all the powers of society, are as helpless as the doctors. What bars or chains can hold a creature who can turn into a wolf or a bat?

Harker: A wolf! Doctor Seward, those dogs howling! I told you they howl that way in Russia when wolves were about. And a bat, Renfield said there was a bat.

Seward: Well. What of it?

Van Helsing: (*Reflectively.*) Your friend Renfield does not like the smell of wolfsbane.

Seward: But what in the world has your wolfsbane to do with all this?

Van Helsing: A vampire cannot stand the smell of wolfsbane.

Harker: You suspect that lunatic?

Van Helsing: I suspect no one and everyone. Tell me, who is this Count Dracula?

Seward: Dracula? We really know very little about him.

Harker: When I was in Transylvania I heard of Castle Dracula. A famous Voivode Dracula who fought the Turks lived there centuries ago.

Van Helsing: I will make inquiries by telegraph. No, but after all this Thing must be English. Or at least have died here. His lair must be near enough to this house for him to get back there before sunrise. (*To Seward.*) Oh, my friend, I have only the old beliefs with which to fight this monster that has the strength of twenty men, perhaps the accumulated wisdom and cunning of centuries.

Harker: This all seems a nightmare. But I'm with you, Professor.

Van Helsing: And you, Doctor Seward?

Seward: It all seems preposterous to me. But everyone else has failed. The case is in your hands at present.

Van Helsing: (*Sternly.*) I need allies, not neutrals.

Seward: Very well, then, do what you will.

Van Helsing: Good. Then bring your daughter here.

Seward: What are you going to do?

Van Helsing: To set a trap. Miss Lucy is the bait.

Harker: We can't let you do that!

Van Helsing: There's no other way. I believe this Thing knows that I plan to protect Miss Lucy. This will put it on its guard and the first moment she is alone it will no doubt try to get at her, for a vampire must have blood or its life in death ceases.

Harker: No, I forbid this.

Seward: She's my daughter, and I consent. We'll show the Professor he's mistaken.

Harker: You allow it only because you don't believe, and I do believe. Doctor, I've heard that lunatic laugh; life-eating, you said he was, and you subject Lucy to that risk.

Van Helsing: (*Interrupting harshly.*) I must be master here or I can do nothing! I must know in what form this Thing comes before I can plan how to stamp it out. Bring your daughter here.

(*Seward turns and sees Harker looking at him; stares at Harker. There is a short pause, then Harker reluctantly exits. Seward follows him. Van Helsing thinks a moment, then looks about, noting the positions of doors, furniture, etc. He then turns out lights. The room is dark except for the firelight. Van Helsing moves into firelight, looks at couch, then walks back to door and turns, looking at couch, satisfying himself that the light from the fire is sufficient to see anything that happens. Opens curtains. Suddenly, the double doors open sharply and Van Helsing starts violently; the Attendant enters.*)

Attendant: Beg pardon, sir. Is Doctor Seward here?

Van Helsing: What do you want with him?

Attendant: Old Flycatcher's escaped again, sir.

Van Helsing: Escaped, how?

Attendant: Out of the window. The door's still locked and I was in the corridor all the while. It's a drop of thirty feet to the stone flagging. That loonie's a flyin' squirrel he is.

Van Helsing: (*Commandingly.*) Say nothing to Doctor Seward at present. Nothing, do you hear? Now go.

(*Attendant exits. Van Helsing switches on lights again. Enter Lucy, supported by Harker and Seward.*)

Lucy: Oh! Oh!

Seward: Lucy, you have nothing to fear.
(*They take her to the couch.*)

Van Helsing: I want you to lie down here, my dear.

Lucy: But, Doctor…

Van Helsing: You trust me, do you not?
(*She smiles weakly at him; nods. They place her on the couch.*) I want you to lie here for just a little.

Lucy: But I am so frightened.

Van Helsing: Make your mind passive. Try not to think. Sleep if you can.

Lucy: I dare not sleep. It is when I sleep…
(*Harker takes her hand.*)

Van Helsing: (*Arranging her on the couch, head on pillows, soothingly.*) I know, my dear. I know. I am going to cure you, with God's help.

Lucy: Oh, but Father…

Seward: You must do as the Professor says. Come, Harker.

Van Helsing: Come, Harker.
(*Van Helsing leads Seward to the door. Seward exits. Harker lingers and Van Helsing calls him. Van Helsing switches off lights as he and Harker go out. No movement. Lucy closes her eyes. Low howl is heard outside, howl of a wolf. It is followed by a distant barking of dogs. Firelight grows dimmer. Dracula's hand appears from back of couch, then his face. Lucy screams; swoons. Harker and Seward are heard offstage.*)

Harker: Lucy! Lucy!

Seward: Professor, what is it?
(*Van Helsing enters, followed by Seward and Harker. Van Helsing switches on lights. They are just in front of door as a bat flies in the room from window to center, then out of the window.*)

Van Helsing: You saw?

Seward: What was that?

Harker: Lucy, Lucy, speak to me!

Van Helsing: Take her to her room, Harker, quickly.
(*Harker carries Lucy to door as Dracula enters. He looks about, his glance taking in everyone.*)

Dracula: (*Mildly, sympathetically.*) The patient is better, I hope?
(*Renfield gives a wild laugh offstage right. Van Helsing, Seward and Harker turn. Renfield gives a second wild laugh.*)

CURTAIN

Act Two

(*Lucy's bedroom. Window Right rear closed but curtains open. Chairs, small table with toilet articles on it by window. Couch against wall up Left Center. Mirror on wall. Small stand, with flowers in vase, near couch. Doors, Right, leading into bedroom, Left, leading into hall. Arch Left Center. The next evening.*)

Dogs howling. As curtain rises, Maid enters from bedroom, glances up at window over her left shoulder, takes a few steps, looks back over right shoulder, then to couch and takes newspaper. Sits on couch; reads newspaper. As she turns a page, Attendant knocks on hall door.)

Maid: (*Starts.*) Who is that?

Attendant: (*Enters; smiles at her.*) Excuse me, Miss. Did you happen to have seen anything of the Guv'ner's pet looney? He's out again, he is.

Maid: (*Holding paper.*) And what would he be doing here? You'll not hold your job, you won't, if you can't keep that man safe and sound. Why, he gets out every night.
(*She crosses toward bedroom door.*)

Attendant: Don't go, miss.

Maid: Miss Lucy's asked for the evening paper.
(*Maid smiles as she goes off; indicates speedy return. Attendant looks out of window and then*

looks under couch. Maid returns. Her line comes just as Attendant bends over, causing him to jump back, frightened.)

Maid: Well, have you found him?

Attendant: No, I haven't. (*Confidentially.*) And I'll tell you, Miss, this job is gettin' on my nerves.

Maid: Your nerves? And what about *my* nerves? Isn't it enough to have dogs howling every night and foreign counts bobbing up out of the floor, and Miss Lucy taking on the way she does, with everybody having their veins drained of blood for her, and this Dutch Sherlock Holmes with the X-ray eyes about, without you letting that Renfield loose?

Attendant: (*Grieved.*) I haven't let him loose. Just now I hears a noise like a wolf howling. I opens his door with me key, and what do I see but his legs goin' through the window as though he was goin' to climb down that smooth wall. He ain't human, he ain't.

Maid: Climb down the wall?

Attendant: (*Gloomily.*) I don't expect no one to believe it, but I seen it, and what's more, I grabbed hold of his feet, I did.

Maid: (*Laughs unbelievingly.*) Climbing down, head first, like a bat?

Attendant: Queer your mention of bats, for just as I got hold of him, a big bat flies in the window and hits me in the face.

Maid: (*Mysteriously.*) I know where that bat came from.

Attendant: (*Startled.*) You do? Where?

Maid: Out of your belfry. (*Crosses to head of couch and arranges pillows, then to dresser.*)

Attendant: No, miss, it's the truth I'm tellin' you. (*Look from her.*) Out that bat flies, and the looney is gone, but I heard 'im laugh. And what a laugh! I'll catch it from the Guv'ner for this.

Maid: (*At dressing table.*) If you tell the Governor any such tales he'll shut you up with the looney.

Attendant: Gosh, miss, but you're a smart one. That's just what I've been thinkin', and I daren't tell him what I see or what I heard. But he's harmless, this guy.

Maid: (*Ironically.*) Wouldn't hurt a fly, would he?

Attendant: Hurt a fly? Oh, no, not him. He only *eats* 'em. Why, he'd rather eat a few blue-bottles than a pound of the best steak, and what he does to spiders is a crime.

Maid: It seems to me somebody will be coming after *you* in a minute, you and your spiders.

Attendant: I say, miss. This is a queer neighborhood. (*Looking out of window.*) What a drop that is to the ground. (*Turns to her.*) You don't have to be afraid of burglars, do you? No way of getting up here unless they fly. Don't you never feel a bit lonesome like, out there (*Points to window.*) on your nights off?

Maid: Just lately I have a bit. (*Looks toward window.*) I never noticed trees had such shadows before.

Attendant: Well, if you feel you'd like an escort, miss.

Maid: I'll not walk with you in your uniform. People might be taking me for one of your loonies.

Attendant: (*Puts arm around her.*) In mufti, then, tomorrow night.

Maid: I say, you haven't wasted much time, have you?

Attendant: I've had my eye on you.

Maid: Better keep that eye on your looney, or you'll be looking for a new job.

(*Attendant tries to kiss her. She pushes him off and slaps him.*) Here, you. Be off. Your Governor will be in any minute. (*Gestures to door.*) Go find your looney.

Attendant: Oh, all right, but I've got somethin' here that'll tempt him back to his room.

Maid: Why, what's that?

(*He fumbles in pocket. She comes up to him.*)

Attendant: (*Takes white mouse by tail out of pocket; holds it in her face.*) This here.

Maid: (*Screams; climbs on chair, holds skirt.*) Take it away! Take it away!

Attendant: (*Mouse climbs up his arm to shoulder. To mouse.*) Come on, Cuthbert. We ain't too popular. (*Offended, walks off left with dignity, remarking from door:*) Some people have no sense of humor.

Seward: (*Enters hastily from bedroom.*) What was that?

Maid: (*Puts down her skirt.*) Pardon, sir. He frightened me with that…that animal.

Seward: (*Agitated.*) Animal, what animal?

Maid: A white mouse, sir.

Seward: (*Relieved.*) You mustn't scream, not in this house, *now*.

Maid: I'm sorry, sir, but that nasty little beast...

Seward: You alarmed Miss Lucy so. She's dreadfully upset as it is by something in the paper.

Maid: Oh, do you mean about that Hampstead Horror, sir? The lady in white who gives chocolates to little children.

Seward: (*Interrupts impatiently.*) Never mind that, but I will not have Miss Lucy disturbed.

(*Seward returns to bedroom. Dogs howl. Lights go out. Maid screams. Green spot comes up on Dracula who stands in center of room. Maid screams again as she sees him.*)

Dracula: (*Soothingly.*) Forgive me. My footfall is not heavy, and your rugs are soft.

Maid: It's all right, sir, but how did you come in?

Dracula: (*Smiling.*) The door of this room was ajar, so I did not knock. How is Miss Lucy and her nervous prostration?

Maid: I think she's better, sir.

Dracula: Ah, good. But the strain of Miss Lucy's illness has made you also ill.

Maid: How did you know, sir? But it's only a pain in my head that runs down into the neck.

Dracula: (*Winningly.*) I can remove this pain.

Maid: I don't understand, sir.

Dracula: Such pains yield readily to suggestion.

Maid: (*Raises arm slightly to shield herself.*) Excuse me, sir, but if it's hypnotism you mean, I'd rather have the pain.

Dracula: Ah, you think of hypnotism as an ugly waving of arms and many passes. That is not my method. (*As he speaks he gestures quietly with his left hand and she stares at him, fascinated. Placing his left thumb against her forehead, he stares straight into her eyes. She makes a feeble effort to remove his hand, then remains still. He now speaks coldly; turns her face front before speaking.*) What is given can be taken away. From now on you have no pain. And you have no will of your own. Do you hear me?

Maid: (*Murmurs.*) I hear you.

Dracula: When you awake you will not remember what I say. Doctor Seward ordered you today to sleep with your mistress every night in the same bed because of her bad dreams. Is it not so?

Maid: (*Murmurs.*) Yes, Master.

Dracula: Your mistress is threatened by horror and by death, but I will save her. A man whose will is at cross purposes with mine has come to this house. I will crush him. Receive your orders. You hear me?

Maid: Yes, Master.

Dracula: Hear and obey. From now on you will carry out any suggestion that reaches you from my brain instantly without question. When I will you to do a thing it shall be done. My call will reach you soon.

(*Green spot dims out slowly. Dracula exits through window. Lights come on. Dogs howl outside. Maid looks up at window as Van Helsing enters left. She starts when door shuts.*)

Van Helsing: (*His face is paler. He looks drawn and weak. He carries box tied with string.*) You've not left your mistress alone?

Maid: Doctor Seward is with her, sir. (*Sways a little.*)

Van Helsing: (*Looking at her keenly.*) What's wrong with you, my girl?

Maid: Nothing, sir.

Van Helsing: You've just had a severe shock.

Maid: It's nothing, sir. I...I suddenly felt queer. (*Looks toward window.*) That's all. I can't remember anything.

Van Helsing: Mr. Harker has just arrived. Ask Doctor Seward to come here. Remain with Miss Lucy yourself.

Maid: Yes, sir. She's dreadfully upset, sir.

Van Helsing: Upset over what?

Maid: It's in the evening paper, sir. About the Hampstead Horror. (*Van Helsing motions Maid to silence.*) Yes, sir.

Van Helsing: (*Shaken.*) Oh, God, she has seen it!

(*Maid goes into bedroom. Harker enters left.*)

Harker: (*Worried.*) Everything just the same? (*Van Helsing nods. Harker closes door.*) When I leave this house even for a few hours I dread what I...I dread what I may find when I come back.

Van Helsing: And well you may, my friend. (*He places box on table under mirror.*)

Harker: God must have sent you here to help us. Without you there'd be no hope. And this morning, Professor, when you opened your veins to revive Lucy again...

Van Helsing: It was the least I could do, for my lack of foresight was responsible for this attack.

Harker: Don't say that.

Van Helsing: Her maid slept with her and yet we found the wolfsbane thrown off the bed to the floor.

Harker: She was so weak, so pale, the two little wounds opened fresh again.

Van Helsing: (*With gesture to box.*) I have prepared a stronger defense. But our main task is not defense, but attack. What have you found in London?

Harker: A lot, but heaven knows what it means or whether it's any use.

Van Helsing: I, too, have had news of which I can make nothing.

Seward: (*Enters.*) Ah, John, back from town.

Harker: Yes. (*Sits.*)

Van Helsing: We must try to piece together what we have learned today. (*Producing telegram of several sheets.*) My colleague in Bucharest wires that the Dracula family has been extinct for five hundred years.

Seward: Can the Count be an impostor?

Van Helsing: (*Referring to telegram.*) The castle he calls his own is a desolate ruin near the border. It was built, as you said, Harker, by the terrible Voivode Dracula, who was said to have had dealings with evil spirits. He was the last of his race. But for many generations the peasants have believed the Castle Dracula inhabited by a vampire.

Harker: Then it must be he.

Van Helsing: (*Shakes head; puts telegram back in pocket.*) My friends, I am bewildered.

Seward: But surely this confirms your suspicions. I was incredulous till I saw that creature hovering over Lucy.

Van Helsing: A vampire from Transylvania cannot be in England.

Seward: But why?

Van Helsing: Because, as I have told you, the vampire must rest by day in the earth in which the corpse it inhabits was buried.

Harker: (*Rises.*) In the earth.

Van Helsing: The vampire must return to its burial place by sunrise.

Harker: (*Excited.*) I found today that Dracula arrived at the Croydon airdrome in a three-engined German plane, on March sixth.

Seward: March the sixth? Three days before Mina first was taken ill.

Harker: This plane had made a nonstop flight from Sekely in Transylvania. It left just after sunset. It arrived two hours before dawn. It carried only the Count and six packing cases.

Van Helsing: Did you learn what was in those cases?

Harker: He told the customs people he wanted to see whether Transylvania plants would grow in a foreign climate in their native soil.

Van Helsing: Soil? What was in those boxes?

Harker: Just plain dirt. He left in a truck, with the six coffinlike boxes, before sunrise.

Van Helsing: Before sunrise! The King of Vampires, my friends. (*Crosses between Seward and Harker.*) This creature is the terrible Voivode Dracula himself! In his satanic pride and contempt, he even uses his own name. For who could suspect? For five hundred years he has been fettered to his castle because he must sleep by day in his graveyard. Five centuries pass. The airplane is invented. His chance has come, for now he can cross Europe in a single night. He prepared six coffins filled with the earth in which he must rest by day. He leaves his castle after sunset. By dawn he is in London and safe in one of his cases — a great risk, but he has triumphed. He has reached London with its teeming millions, with its "opportunity," as he said.

Seward: God protect my Lucy!

Harker: (*To Van Helsing, new tone.*) I saw the estate agent from whom he bought Carfax here and got the address of four old houses he has leased in different parts of London.

Van Helsing: One of his coffin retreats is in each of those houses.

Seward: Two heavy boxes were delivered at Carfax the day after he took possession.

Van Helsing: He has scattered them, for safety. If we can find all six, we can destroy him.

Seward: But how?

Van Helsing: His native earth will no longer receive his unclean form if each box is sanctified with holy water.

Harker: Then we must get at those boxes, tear them open one by one. If we find him, Professor, I demand that my hand shall drive the stake into this devil's heart and send his soul to hell!

(*Seward motions no noise because of Lucy.*)

Van Helsing: Your plan is too dangerous.

Seward: But why? These attacks on Lucy continue. Are we to delay while my child is dying?

Harker: No, not for a moment.

Van Helsing: Patience, my friends. This creature is more than mortal. His cunning is the growth of the ages. What if we find five of his boxes and close them against him, and cannot find the sixth?

Seward: Well?

Van Helsing: Then he will bury himself in his last refuge, where we can never find him and sleep until we are all dead.

Harker: Then Lucy will be safe.

Van Helsing: For her life, yes, but his unclean kiss has claimed her for his own. When she dies she will become as he is, a foul thing of the night. The vampire can wait. No, my friends, there is only one way to save her from him, to destroy him.

Seward: You're right, as always.

Van Helsing: We have one great advantage. By day he is a coffined corpse. Of our search by day he can know nothing, if we leave no traces.

Harker: God, this delay!

Van Helsing: We must make the round of his houses and find all six boxes, without his knowledge, and *then* we act.

Seward: But what about the caretakers or servants?

Van Helsing: All the houses will be empty. The vampire plays a lone hand. (*Maniacal laugh heard behind curtains of window. Seward crosses quickly to window.*)

Seward: Renfield!

(*He grabs Renfield by arm and throws him into room. Renfield laughs cunningly.*)

Van Helsing: He's been here all the time we've been talking.

Seward: Did you hear what we were saying, man?

Renfield: Yes, I heard…something… enough…(*With gestures to Seward and Harker.*) Be guided by what he says. (*Points to Van Helsing.*) It is your only hope. It is her only hope. (*Crosses to Van Helsing.*) It is *my* only hope. (*Falls on knees before Van Helsing.*) Save my soul! Save my soul! I am weak. You are strong. I am crazy. You are sane. You are good and he is evil.

Van Helsing: (*Impressively.*) I will save you, Renfield, but you must tell me what you know. Everything.

Renfield: (*Rises.*) Know? What should I know? I don't know anything. (*Taps head.*) You say I'm mad and Doctor Seward will tell you about that. You musn't pay any attention to anything I say.

Seward: We can't waste time with this fellow. I'll have him taken away. (*Crosses to bell.*)

Renfield: (*To Seward.*) Fool, fool, and I thought you were wise! The whole world is mad just now, and if you want help you must come to a madman to get it. (*Little laugh, cunningly.*) But I'll not give it to you, I'm afraid. (*Turns to window.*) A wise madman will obey him who is strong and not the weak.

Van Helsing: (*Moves to him fiercely.*) Him? Whom do you mean?

Renfield: Need we mention names among friends? Come, Professor, be reasonable. What have I got to gain by being on your side? The Doctor keeps me shut up all day, and if I'm good he gives me a little sugar to spread out for my flies, but on the other hand, if I serve *him*…(*Points to window.*)

Van Helsing: (*Sharply, taking him by coat.*) The blood is the life, eh, Renfield?

(*Dragging him again.*) What have you to do with Count Dracula?

Renfield: (*Convulsed with terror.*) Dracula! (*Drawing himself up defiantly.*) I never even heard the name before!

Van Helsing: You are lying!

Renfield: Madmen, Professor, lack the power to discriminate between truth and falsehood, (*Breaks away.*) so I take no offense at what most men would consider an affront. (*Crosses to Seward.*) Send me away! I asked you to before and you wouldn't. If you only knew what has happened since then. I dare not tell you more. I dare not! I should die in torment if I betrayed…

Van Helsing: Doctor Seward will send you away if you speak.

Seward: Yes, Renfield. (*Renfield moans.*) I offer you your soul in exchange for what you know.

Renfield: God will not damn a poor lunatic's soul. God knows the devil is too strong for us who have weak minds. But send me away. I want you to promise, Doctor Seward!

Seward: If you will speak.

Van Helsing: Come, Renfield.

Renfield: (*Pause. Looks at Seward, Van Helsing, Harker, and Seward again, then speaks as a sane man.*) Then I will tell you. Count Dracula is…(*Bat comes in window; flies out again. Renfield rushes to window with arms outstretched, screaming.*) Master! Master, I didn't say anything! I told them nothing. I'm loyal to you. I am your slave.

(*Seward and Harker rush to window.*)

Seward: (*Looking out window.*) There's a big bat flying in a circle. It's gone.

Harker: What's that, just passing that small shrub? It looks like a big gray dog.

Van Helsing: Are you sure it was a dog?

Harker: Well, it might easily be a wolf. Oh, but that's nonsense. Our nerves are making us see things.

Van Helsing: Come, Renfield. What were you about to say?

Renfield: Nothing, nothing.

(*Lucy comes in from bedroom with newspaper.*)

Lucy: Professor, have you seen what's in this…

Van Helsing: Miss Lucy, give it to…

Renfield: (*Crosses to her.*) Are you Miss Seward?

Lucy: I am.

(*Seward moves closer to her; indicates Harker to ring bell.*)

Renfield: Then, I beg you, leave this place at once!

(*She turns to him. Van Helsing motions silence to others.*)

Lucy: But this is my home. Nothing would induce me to leave.

Renfield: (*Sane.*) Oh, that's true. You wouldn't go if they tried to drag you away, would you? It's too late. What a fool I am. I shall be punished for this and it can't do any good. It's too late. (*In tone of pity.*) You are so young, so beautiful, so pure. Even I have decent feelings sometimes, and I must tell you, and if you don't go your soul will pay for it. You're in the power of…(*Bat flies in window and out. Renfield rushes to window and screams. Seward moves toward couch. Harker crosses to Lucy to protect her.*) The Master is at hand!

(*Renfield crosses back on knees. Attendant appears at door.*)

Seward: Butterworth!

(*Seward helps Renfield up, then Attendant grasps him and takes him to door.*)

Renfield: (*At door.*) Goodbye, Miss Seward. Since you will not heed my warning, I pray that I may never see your face again.

(*He exits with Attendant.*)

Lucy: What did he mean, Professor? What did he mean? Why did he say that?

(*She goes off into bedroom, in hysterics. Harker follows her.*)

Seward: That crazy thing in league with the devil; horrible, and Lucy already upset by something in the paper.

Van Helsing: Go in and get that paper from her.

Seward: Whatever it is, she keeps on reading that article again and again.

Van Helsing: Take it away from her, man, and come back to me. (*Places hand on forehead as if faint.*)

Seward: Don't overdo it, Van Helsing. God knows where we should be if you went under. After a transfusion operation, at your age you really ought to be in bed…the loss of so much blood is serious.

Van Helsing: I never felt more fit in my life.

Seward: I only ask you not to overestimate your strength now, when we lean on you. (*As he exits.*) Feeling fit, are you? Just look at yourself in the glass.

(*Van Helsing, alone, registers as tired and exhausted, and walks slowly across room, looking at his drawn face in mirror. Dracula, with stealthy tread, in evening dress and cloak as before, enters from window and walks slowly to directly behind Van Helsing.*)

Van Helsing: (*Looking at himself, touching face, shakes head.*) The devil.

Dracula: Come. (*Van Helsing turns suddenly to him and looks back into the mirror.*) Not as bad as that. (*Suave, cold, ironical.*)

Van Helsing: (*Long look in mirror, then turns to Dracula. Controlling himself with difficulty.*) I did not hear you, Count.

Dracula: I am often told that I have a light footstep.

Van Helsing: I was looking in the mirror. Its reflection covers the whole room, but I cannot see…

(*Pause. He turns to mirror. Dracula, face convulsed by fury, picks up small vase with flowers from stand, smashes mirror, pieces of mirror and vase tumbling to floor. Van Helsing steps back; looks at Dracula with loathing and terror.*)

Dracula: (*Recovering composure.*) Forgive me, I dislike mirrors. They are the playthings of man's vanity. And how's the fair patient?

Van Helsing: (*Meaningly.*) The diagnosis presents difficulties.

Dracula: I feared it might, my friend.

Van Helsing: Would you care to see what I have prescribed for my patient?

Dracula: Anything that you prescribe for Miss Lucy has the greatest interest for me.

(*Van Helsing crosses to table to get box. Dracula crosses, meets Van Helsing coming back with box. Van Helsing deliberately turns away from him, goes to small table right of arch, turns front as he opens pocketknife and, in cutting string of parcel, cuts his finger. Dracula starts for Van Helsing with right hand raised, then keeping control with difficulty, turns away so as not to see blood. Van Helsing stares at him a moment, then walks up and sticks bleeding finger in front of him.*)

Van Helsing: The prescription is a most unusual one.

(*Dracula, baring teeth, makes sudden snap at finger. Van Helsing turns away quickly; ties handkerchief around it. Dracula again regains poise with an effort.*)

Dracula: The cut is not deep. I…looked.

Van Helsing: (*Opening parcel.*) No, but it will serve. Here is my medicine for Miss Lucy. (*Dracula comes up to Van Helsing, who quickly holds handful of wolfsbane up to his face. Dracula leaps back, face distorted with rage and distress, shielding himself with cloak. Putting wolfsbane back in box.*) You do not care for the smell?

Dracula: You are a wise man, Professor, for one who has not lived even a single lifetime.

Van Helsing: You flatter me, Count.

Dracula: But not wise enough to return to Holland at once, now that you have learned what you have learned.

Van Helsing: (*Shortly.*) I preferred to remain. (*Meaningly.*) Even though a certain lunatic here attempted to kill me.

Dracula: (*Smiling.*) Lunatics are difficult. They do not do what they are told. They even try to betray their benefactors. But when servants fail to obey orders, the Master must carry them out for himself.

Van Helsing: (*Grimly.*) I anticipated as much.

Dracula: (*Gazing at him intently.*) In the past five hundred years, Professor, those who have crossed my path have all died, and some not pleasantly. (*Continues to gaze at Van Helsing; lifts his arm slowly; says with terrible emphasis and force.*) Come…here. (*Van Helsing pales, staggers, then slowly takes three steps toward Dracula. Very slight pause as Van Helsing attempts to regain control of himself, then takes another step toward Dracula; pauses, places hand to brow, then completely regains control of himself and looks away.*) Ah, your will is strong. Then I must come to you. (*Advances to Van Helsing, who takes out of breast pocket small velvet bag. Dracula stops.*) More medicine, Professor?

Van Helsing: More effective than wolfsbane, Count.

Dracula: Indeed? (*Starts for Van Helsing's throat. Van Helsing holds bag out toward him. Dracula's face becomes convulsed with terror and he retreats left before Van Helsing, who follows him.*) Sacrilege.

Van Helsing: (*Continuing to advance.*) I have a dispensation. (*Van Helsing has cut him off from the door and unpityingly presses him toward window. Dracula, enraged and snarling, backs out of the window. As Dracula is just outside the window he spreads his cape like a bat and gives a long satirical laugh as he makes exit. Van Helsing almost collapses; puts bag back in pocket; crosses himself; mops perspiration from brow with handkerchief. A shot is heard. Van Helsing leaps up; rushes to window. Bat circles almost into his face. He staggers back. Seward hurries in, carrying newspaper.*)

Seward: Van Helsing, what was that? (*Dropping newspaper on table.*)

Van Helsing: A revolver shot. It came as a relief. That at least is something human.

Seward: Who broke the mirror?

Van Helsing: I.

(*Harker enters.*)

Harker: Sorry if I startled you. I saw that infernal bat around this side of the house. I couldn't resist a shot.

Seward: Did you hit it?

Harker: Why, I…

Van Helsing: The bullet was never made, my friend, that could harm *that* bat. *My* weapons are stronger.

Harker: What do you mean?

Van Helsing: Dracula has been here.

Seward: Good God!

Harker: How did he get in?

Van Helsing: You ask how the Vampire King, during the hours of night, the hours that are his, comes and goes? As the wind, my friend, as he pleases. He came to kill me. But I carry a power stronger than his.

Harker: What power?

Van Helsing: I expected an attack. I secured a dispensation from the Cardinal. I have with me…(*Crosses himself.*)…the Host. (*Harker crosses himself.*) He came. I proved my case if it needed proof. The mirror does not reflect this *man that was*, who casts no shadow. See, I cut my finger, *it* leapt at the blood, but before the sacred wafer *it* fled.

Seward: Lucy must not know.

Van Helsing: (*Gently, worried.*) Miss Lucy knows more than you think.

Harker: How can she? If she knew, she'd tell me.

Van Helsing: As these attacks continue she comes more and more under his power. There is a mystic link between them. (*Seward sighs.*) Oh, it is hard to bear, but you must face it. It may be that he can already learn what passes in her mind. And so Miss Lucy must not be told that we know about earth boxes, for he may learn whatever she knows.

(*Lucy enters.*)

Seward: But Professor, that would mean that Lucy is in with this creature. That's impossible.

(*Lucy crosses to table; takes newspaper.*)

Van Helsing: No, no, Miss Lucy, you must not.

Harker: Lucy, what's in this paper that's upset you?

Lucy: (*Hands newspaper to Harker.*) Read it, John.

(*Harker takes newspaper; reads. Van Helsing moves as if to stop him, then checks himself.*)

Van Helsing: No, Harker, no.

Lucy: Read it!

(*Lucy sits on couch. They all listen.*)

Harker: (*Reading.*) "The Hampstead Horror. Further attacks on small children, committed after dark by a mysterious and beautiful woman in Hampstead, are reported today. Narratives of three small girls, all under ten years of age, are alike in essential details. Each child speaks of a beautiful lady in white who gave her chocolates, enticed her to some secluded corner and there bit her slightly in the throat." (*He looks at Seward and Lucy.*)

Lucy: Go on.

Harker: (*Reading.*) "The wounds are trivial. The children suffered no other harm and do not seem to have been frightened. Indeed, one small girl told her mother she hoped she might see the beautiful lady again."

(*He turns to Lucy. Seward takes paper from Harker.*)

Van Helsing: So soon…so soon.

(*Harker and Seward look at each other.*)

Seward: You know what has been happening, Lucy? (*Lucy nods.*)

Harker: Professor Van Helsing knows, too, Lucy, and he knows how to protect you.

Lucy: It is not too late?

Van Helsing: No, Miss Lucy, it is not too late.

Seward: These poor innocent children…

Van Helsing: (*To Seward.*) You think Count Dracula…

Lucy: (*Shudders.*) Not that name.

Van Helsing: You think the Werewolf has done this too?

Seward: Of course, in the form of a woman. Who else could it be?

Van Helsing: It is worse. Far worse.

Harker: Worse? What do you mean?

(*Lucy is motionless, her face frozen in horror.*)

Van Helsing: Miss Lucy knows.

Lucy: The woman in white…is Mina.

Harker: Mina. But she's dead, Lucy.

Lucy: She has joined…the Master.

Seward: Oh, God, have pity on us all. (*Drops newspaper on chair.*)

Van Helsing: My dear Miss Lucy, I will not ask you how you know. After tonight no more little children will meet the woman in white. She will remain at rest in the tomb where you laid her. And her soul, released from this horror, will be with God.

Lucy: How can you do this?

Van Helsing: Do not ask me.

Lucy: (*Takes hold of Van Helsing's arm.*) Professor, if you can save Mina's soul after death, can you save mine?

Harker: Oh, Lucy! (*Sitting on couch, arm around her.*)

Van Helsing: (*Takes her hand.*) I will save you. I swear it. In this room tonight.

Lucy: Then promise me one thing. Whatever you plan to do, whatever you know, do not tell me. (*Turns to Harker.*) Not even if I beg *you* to tell me, swear that you will not, now, while I am still yours, while I am myself, promise it.

Harker: I promise it. (*Takes her in his arms; tries to kiss her.*)

Lucy: (*Breaks away from him, horrified.*) No, no, John! You mustn't kiss me. Promise that you never will, not even if I beg you to.

Harker: I promise.

Van Helsing: My dear Miss Lucy, from tonight on one of us will be awake all night, here in this room, next to your bedroom, with your door open.

Lucy: (*Murmurs.*) You are so good.

Van Helsing: Yes, and I will make the room safe for you. Your maid will be with you. (*Harker talks to Lucy on couch while Van Helsing takes handful of wolfsbane.*) Doctor, rub these over the window in the little room there. See, like this. (*He starts rubbing around edge of window.*) Rub it around the sashes and especially above the lock. (*Seward watches Van Helsing rubbing, then takes wolfsbane from Van Helsing quickly, and goes out through arch. Van Helsing turns, goes to table and takes out wreath of wolfsbane.*) See, I have made this wreath that you must wear around your neck tonight. While you wear this those…dreams…cannot come to you. (*Hangs wolfsbane around her neck. Takes out of pocket crucifix on cord, which he also hangs around her neck.*) Swear to me that you will not take these off.

Lucy: I promise.

Van Helsing: Swear it on the cross.

Lucy: (*Kisses cross.*) I swear it!

(*Van Helsing crosses toward door.*)

Harker: Professor, surely the Host is more powerful than this wolfsbane.

Van Helsing: Of course.

Harker: Then leave the Host with her, nothing can harm her then.

Van Helsing: No, the Host cannot be used where there has been pollution. (*Screams off left.*) What is it?

(*Attendant enters left. Maid comes in from bedroom; Seward enters from arch.*)

Attendant: It's Renfield, sir.

Seward: Why haven't you got him locked up?

Attendant: Because he's barred himself in, sir. He got hold of one of the patients. He had her by the throat.

(*He exits. Lucy rises.*)

Van Helsing: Ah, human blood now! (*Starting.*) Come, Seward! Come, Harker!

Seward: I should have had him sent away!

(*Maid crosses to Lucy. Van Helsing and Seward exit. Harker hesitates then follows them off. Harker ad libs during exit. "It's all right, Lucy. I'll be right back," etc.*)

Lucy: John…(*To maid.*) Don't you leave me, too.

Maid: Of course I won't, Miss Lucy. It's nothing but a quarrel among the patients. Mr. Harker will be back soon. (*Maid places her on couch. Lucy swoons. Maid gets smelling salts.*) Here, Miss Lucy. (*Dracula's face appears back of tapestry on rear wall; disappears. Maid steps down right, gets message, then returns. Puts salts back on dresser; crosses to Lucy.*) These evil-smelling flowers have made you faint. (*Takes crucifix and wreath from around Lucy's neck, throws them on floor; crosses two steps down right. Another message comes to her. Puts hand to head, turns slowly, looks at window, steps toward couch.*) It is so close, Madam. A little air. (*Turns to window. Lucy moans again. Maid pulls back latch; opens window. As window opens, clouds of mist roll in. Steps down. Gets message. Switches out lights, then exits into bedroom. The stage is now dark. Dogs without, far and near, howl in terror. A gauze curtain comes down and a green light dims up covering the couch and center of the stage, revealing Dracula standing center with back to audience, hands outstretched to resemble a large bat. As he moves up a few steps, Lucy slowly rises from couch and falls into his arms. A long kiss and then, as she falls back on his right arm, he bares her throat and starts to bite her as:*)

CURTAIN

Act Three

SCENE I:
The library. Thirty-two hours later, shortly before sunrise.

A stake and hammer are on desk. Dogs howl. Curtains move as if someone is entering window. Then chair back of desk, which is turned Upstage, moves around, facing front. After a moment, Van Helsing enters with Seward. Van Helsing paces up and down; Seward sits at desk. The Center doors are flung open and the Attendant comes in.

Van Helsing: What is it?

Attendant: (*To Van Helsing.*) Anybody who wants my job, sir, can have it. (*Seward rouses himself.*)

Seward: What's the matter?

Attendant: I know what I knows, and what I seen I saw, and I hops it by the first train, and don't ask for no wages instead of notice.

Van Helsing: Where's Renfield?

Attendant: If you asks me, I says he's probably payin' a little visit to hell.

Seward: You've let him escape again?

Attendant: Look here, sir. Having, so to speak, resigned, I don't have to put up with any more from any of you. (*Look at Van Helsing and Seward.*) What a man can't help, he can't help, and that's that. (*Seward shrinks back on desk, head in hands.*)

Van Helsing: Can't you see, man, that Doctor Seward is not well? Will you desert him when he needs all the help he can get?

Attendant: Puttin' it that way, sir, I ain't the man to run under fire. But I'm sick and tired of being told off for what ain't my fault.

Van Helsing: We don't blame you. No bolts or bars could hold Renfield.

Attendant: (*Seward looks up at him.*) Now, sir, you're talkin' sense. I had him in a straitjacket this time. Nearly all yesterday I worked at clampin' bars across the window. Now I finds them bars pulled apart like they was made o' cheese and him gone.

Van Helsing: Then try to find him.

Attendant: Find him, sir? Find him? I can't chase him up and down the wall. I ain't no bloody mountain goat! (*Exits.*)

Van Helsing: The Thing mocks us. A few hours after he finds out what we know, and what we have done, he comes here, and drags that poor creature of his to himself.

Seward: (*In dull, hopeless tone.*) What can the vampire want with Renfield?

Van Helsing: Renfield is serving an apprenticeship to join the Vampire King after his death. We must prevent that.

Seward: What does Renfield matter? If we are beaten, then there is no hope.

Van Helsing: (*Crosses to him.*) We dare not despair, Seward.

Seward: To figure out in advance what anyone would do who got on his track!

Van Helsing: I thought we had him when we broke into Carfax and found two earth boxes there and then found one box in each of his four other houses, and when I pried up the lid of the sixth box I was sure we would find him there, helpless.

Seward: (*Bitterly.*) Empty.

Van Helsing: An empty packing case, left as a blind.

Seward: He only brought six in his plane, so there can be only the one left.

Van Helsing: Only one, but hidden where we can never find it. And now we've put him on his guard.

Seward: Yes. (*Chair turns back. Curtains flap out. Seward looks at wrist watch.*) It's not half an hour till sunrise. (*Rises and crossing to fireplace.*) Poor John has been sitting up with Lucy for nine hours. She'll be safe at dawn and he can get some sleep, if anyone can sleep in this house.

Van Helsing: Whoever else sleeps or does not sleep, Miss Lucy will sleep at dawn.

Seward: Another horror?

Van Helsing: Oh, you've noticed how she keeps awake all night now and sleeps by day.

Seward: Is that part of…the change?

Van Helsing: Of course. And sometimes the look that comes into her face.

Seward: (*Turns face away in horror.*) Don't, man. I can't bear it!

Van Helsing: We must face the facts, for her sake.

Seward: How could it have got at her with the wolfsbane and the cross around her neck? (*Pause.*) Suggestion, conveyed from the Monster?

Van Helsing: Yes. He must have impelled the maid to take away the wolfsbane and cross and open the window. I should have foreseen that.

Seward: Don't blame yourself. The devil is more cunning than we are. (*Sits on couch.*) Yet Lucy seems better. Until this last attack she's always been exhausted, but at sunset last night, when she woke up after sleeping all day…

Van Helsing: There was blood in her cheeks again.

Seward: Yes, thank goodness.

Van Helsing: (*With terrible emphasis.*) My poor friend, *where does that blood come from?*

Seward: What do you suggest now? What fresh horror…

(*Door left opens a crack. Long skinny hand protrudes into room. Seward sees it first and starts in alarm. Rises. Van Helsing turns quickly. Door opens slowly and Renfield slinks in.*)

In această casă a locuit
intre anii 1431–1435,
domnitorul Tãrii Romãnesti
VLAD DRACUL,
fiul lui
Mircea cel Bãtrin

Renfield: Is not half past five in the morning a strange hour for men who aren't crazy to be up and about? (*Crosses to window.*)

Van Hesling: (*Aside to Seward.*) We may get help from this thing that's still half-human. (*To Renfield.*) Renfield.

Renfield: (*Crosses, with growing hysteria.*) He's after me! He's going to kill me!

Van Helsing: Help us, Renfield, and we'll save you.

Renfield: You, you poor puny man, you measure your brains against his? You don't know what you're dealing with! You, a thick-headed Dutchman and a fool of a psychiatrist, and a young cub of a boy. Why, not all the soldiers and police in London could stop the Master from doing as he likes.

Van Helsing: But God can stop him!

Renfield: God permits evil. Why does he permit evil if He is good? Tell me that?

Seward: How did you escape through those iron bars?

Renfield: (*Cunningly.*) Madmen have a great strength, Doctor.

Van Helsing: Come, Renfield, we know you didn't wrench those bars apart yourself.

Renfield: (*Sane.*) No, I didn't. I wanted them there. I hoped they'd keep him out. He did it, then he called to me and I had to come. (*Back to insanity.*) The Master is angry. He promised me eternal life and live things, live things, big ones, not flies and spiders; and blood to drink, always blood. I must obey him but I don't want to be like him. I am mad, I know, and bad, too, for I've taken lives, but they were only little lives. I'm not like him. I wouldn't like a human life. (*Lucy laughs offstage and says, "Oh, John!" as she enters with Harker. Lucy has changed; there is blood in her cheeks, she is stronger and seems full of vitality. She and Harker stop in surprise at seeing Renfield. To Lucy.*) And why did I seek to betray him? For you. (*She smiles.*) I said I'd serve the devil, but I didn't serve him honestly. I don't like women with no blood in them. (*Lucy laughs.*) And yet I warned you and made him angry, and now…(*Working into frenzy.*)…perhaps he will kill me. (*Lucy laughs.*) And I won't get any more live things to eat. There'll be no more blood. (*Renfield starts for Lucy's throat. Harker grasps him by right arm, Van Helsing by left arm, then Seward steps in and takes Harker's place as Renfield struggles violently. Seward and Van Helsing bear him away, struggling and screaming.*)

Harker: Lucy, darling, you mustn't mind that poor, crazed creature.

Lucy: (*With low laugh as before.*) I don't. He amuses me.

(*She crosses to the couch and sits.*)

Harker: Oh, Lucy, how can you? The poor devil! Thank goodness, it will soon be dawn now.

Lucy: Dawn. The ebb tide of life. I hate the dawn. How can people like daylight? At night I am really alive. The night was made to enjoy life, and love. (*Harker turns to her; hesitates.*) Come to me, John, my own John.

(*He comes and sits next to her.*)

Harker: Lucy, I'm so happy that you are better and strong again.

Lucy: I've never been so well, so full of vitality. I was only a poor, washed-out, pale creature. I don't know what made you love me, John. There was no reason why you should. But there is *now*.

Harker: I worship you.

Lucy: Then tell me something, John. (*Harker turns slightly away.*) If you love me, you'll tell me. Now don't turn away from me again.

Harker: (*Wearily and sadly.*) You made me promise that I wouldn't tell you…anything.

Lucy: Oh, but I release you from your promise. There, now. What were you and Father and the funny Professor doing all day?

Harker: I can't tell you, I promised.

Lucy: (*Angrily.*) You say you love me, but you don't trust me.

Harker: I would trust you with my life, my soul.

Lucy: Then prove it. What were you doing over there in Carfax? With the hammer and the horrible iron stake. (*He shakes his head. She registers anger. He puts his head in his hands, as though crying.*) You don't think I'm asking you because…I'm just trying to find out whether you really love me. (*Harker recoils from her, facing up.*) So you try to hide your schemes and your plots. Afraid I'd give them away, are you? You fools. Whatever *he* wants to know, he finds out for himself. He knows what you do. He knows what you think. He knows everything.

Harker: Lucy!

(*He puts his head in her lap and sobs. Lucy makes claw-like movement with both her hands, then as he sobs she changes attitude and gently strokes his head.*)

Lucy: My dear, I'm sorry. Let me kiss away the tears.

(*She starts to kiss him. He quickly rises; backs away a few steps.*)

Harker: No, you mustn't kiss me! You made me promise not to let you kiss me.

Lucy: You don't know why I said that, John darling. It was because I love you so much. I was afraid of what might happen. You've always thought me cold, but I've blood in my veins, hot blood, my John. And I knew if I were to kiss you…but I'm not afraid now. Come, will you make me say it?

Harker: Lucy, I don't understand you.

Lucy: (*Moves toward him.*) I love you. I want you. (*Stretches out her arms to him.*) Come to me, my darling. I want you.

Harker: (*Goes to her, his resistance overcome, carried away by her passion.*) Lucy, Lucy!

(*He seizes her in his arms. Slowly she takes his head and bends it back. Slowly, triumphantly she bends her head down; her mouth hovers over his. Dogs howl outside. She bends his head further back quickly. Her mouth seeks his throat. Doors center open. Van Helsing rushes in, holding crucifix.*)

Van Helsing: Harker! Harker, save yourself! (*Harker rises, draws away. With outstretched arm, Van Helsing holds crucifix between them. Lucy's face becomes convulsed with loathing and rage. She snarls like an animal, retreats, fainting onto the couch. Van Helsing follows, holds crucifix to her; strokes her forehead with left hand.*) I warned you, my poor friend. (*He kneels beside Lucy; begins to chafe her temples. She revives slowly, looks about her, sees cross and seizes it and kisses it passionately. Van Helsing, fervently:*) Oh, thank goodness!
(*Pause. Harker crosses to couch.*)

Lucy: (*Broken-hearted.*) Don't come to me, John. I am unclean.

Harker: (*Sits beside her.*) My darling, in my eyes you are purity itself.

Van Helsing: You love her, and in love there is truth. She is pure, and the evil thing that has entered her shall be rooted out.

Lucy: (*In a weak voice as in previous acts; to Van Helsing.*) You said you could save Mina's soul.

Van Helsing: Mina's soul is in heaven.

Lucy: (*Murmurs.*) Tell me how.
(*Seward enters, comes up to group in alarm, but Van Helsing motions silence.*)

Van Helsing: It is your right to know now. I entered her tomb. I pried open the coffin. I found her there, sleeping, but not dead, not truly dead. There was blood in her cheeks, a drop of blood like a red ruby on the corner of her mouth. With a stake and hammer I struck to the heart. One scream, a convulsion, and then...the look of peace that came to her face when, with God's help, I had made her truly dead.

Lucy: If I die, swear to me that you will do this to my body.

Van Helsing: It shall be done.

Harker: I swear it.

Seward: And I.

Lucy: My lover, my father, my dear friend, you have sworn to save my soul. And now I am done with life. I cannot live on to become...what you know.

Van Helsing: No, no, Miss Lucy, by all you hold sacred, you must not even think of suicide. That would put you in his power forever.

Lucy: I cannot face this horror that I am becoming.

Harker: (*Rises.*) We will find this *Thing* that has fouled your life, destroy him and send his soul to burning hell, and it shall be by *my* hand.

Lucy: You must destroy him if you can, but with pity in your hearts, not rage and vengeance. That poor soul who has done so much evil needs our prayers more than any other.

Harker: No, you cannot ask me to forgive.

Lucy: Perhaps I, too, will need your prayers and your pity.

Van Helsing: My dear Miss Lucy, now, while you are yourself, help me. (*Takes her hand.*)

Lucy: How can I help you? Don't tell me, no, you mustn't tell me anything.

Van Helsing: Each time the white face, the red eyes came you were pale, exhausted afterwards. But that last time...

Lucy: (*Shudders.*) Last time he came he said I was his bride, he would seal me to him for the centuries to come.

Van Helsing: And then?

Lucy: And then...(*Rises; crosses toward door.*) No, no, I can't tell you. I can't.

Van Helsing: But you must.

Seward: You must, Lucy!

Lucy: He scratched open one of his veins. He pressed my mouth down to it. He called it a mystic sacrament. He made me…he made me drink…I can't, I can't…go on…(*Lucy rushes off hysterically. Seward follows her.*)

Van Helsing: I warned you, my poor friend. I broke in when I heard the dogs howling.

Harker: The dogs. Then the Werewolf is about.

Van Helsing: He is pursuing Renfield.

Harker: We must do something!

Van Helsing: And at once. I shall leave Renfield here, as I did Miss Lucy. If the *Thing* appears, we three will bar the two doors and the window.

Harker: (*Crosses Up toward window. Laughs bitterly.*) Bar? Against *that*?

Van Helsing: Even against *that*, for we shall each carry the sacred element.

Harker: And then?

Van Helsing: Then I do not know. It will be terrible, for we do not know his full powers. But this I know…(*Looks at watch.*) It is eight minutes to sunrise. The power of all evil things ceases with the coming of day. His one last earth box is his only refuge. If we can keep him here till daybreak he must collapse. And the stake and the hammer are ready. (*Dogs howl. Harker crosses to window, goes out.*) He is here. Quickly! (*Van Helsing runs to window. Seizes Renfield.*)

Renfield: (*As he is dragged in by Van Helsing.*) No, no!

Van Helsing: But you must, man, and this may save your soul and your life as well.

Renfield: No, no, no, not alone! Don't leave me alone! (*Van Helsing shoves him forward. Renfield falls. Van Helsing hurries out, closing door and putting lights out. Renfield slowly rises; looks about him. Renfield howls in terror; crouches in firelight as far away as possible from doors and window. Dracula appears, door center, in pale blue light, in evening clothes, dress and cloak as before. Red light from fireplace covers Dracula. As Dracula moves, Renfield's back is to audience.*) Master! I didn't do it! I said nothing. I am your slave, your dog! (*Dracula steps toward him.*) Master, don't kill me! Punish me…torture me…I deserve it…but let me live! I can't face God with all those lives on my conscience, all that blood on my hands.

Dracula: (*With deadly calm.*) Did I not promise you that you should come to me at your death, and enjoy centuries of life and power over the bodies and souls of others?

Renfield: Yes, Master, I want lives, I want blood, but I didn't want human life.

Dracula: You betrayed me. You sought to warn my destined bride against me.

Renfield: Mercy, mercy, mercy, don't kill me!

(*Dracula raises right arm very slowly toward Renfield, who screams, this time in physical pain. Renfield, like a bird before a snake, drags himself to Dracula, who stands motionless. As Renfield reaches Dracula's feet, Dracula, with swift motion, stoops, seizes him by the throat, lifts him up, his grip stifling Renfield's screams. Doors Center are thrown open. Van Helsing switches on lights. Dracula drops Renfield, who falls into corner below couch and remains there during following scene. Dracula starts toward Van Helsing, who takes case containing Host out of inside breast pocket and holds it out toward Dracula in his clenched right fist. Dracula recoils; turns quickly to window. Harker appears through window and holds crucifix toward Dracula in clenched fist. Dracula recoils. Seward enters window, holding crucifix. The three men stand during the following scene with right arms pointing toward Dracula. He turns, walks to fireplace, turns and faces them.*)

Dracula: (*Ironically.*) My friends, I regret I was not present to receive your calls at my house.

Van Helsing: (*Looks at wrist watch.*) Four minutes until sunrise.

Dracula: (*Looking at wrist watch.*) Your watch is correct, Professor.

Van Helsing: Your life in death has reached its end.

Seward: By God's mercy.

Dracula: (*Harker steps toward Dracula. Dracula, turning to them, suavely.*) Its end? Not yet, Professor. I have still more than three minutes to add to my five hundred years.

Harker: And three minutes from now you'll be in hell, where a thousand years of agony will not bring you one second nearer the end of your punishment.

Van Helsing: Silence, Harker. Miss Lucy forbade this. She asked for prayer, and for pity. (*To Dracula.*) Make your peace with God, Man-That-Was. We are not your judges, we know not how this curse may have come upon you.   •

Dracula: (*Furiously.*) You fools! You think with your wafers, your wolfsbane, you can destroy me, me, the king of my kind? You shall see. Five of my earth boxes you have polluted. Have you found the sixth?

Van Helsing: You cannot reach your six refuge now. Take your true form as Werewolf if you will. Your fangs may rend us, but we have each sworn to keep you here (*looks at watch*) for two minutes and a

half, when you must collapse and we can make an end.

Dracula: *You* keep *me*. Fools, listen and let my words ring in your ears all your lives, and torture you on your deathbeds! I go, I go to sleep in my box for a hundred years. You have accomplished that much against me, Van Helsing. But in a century I shall wake, and call my bride to my side from her tomb, my Lucy, my Queen. (*Harker and Seward move closer.*) I have other brides of old times who await me in their vaults in Transylvania. But I shall set *her* above them all.

Harker: Should you escape, we know how to save Lucy's soul, if not her life.

Dracula: (*Moving left.*) Ah, the stake. Yes, but only if she dies by day. I shall see that she dies by night. She shall come to an earth box of mine at her death and await her Master. To do to her what you did to my Mina, Van Helsing, you must find her body, and that you will not.

Harker: Then she shall die by day.

Dracula: You will kill her? You lack the courage, you poor rat of flesh and blood!

Seward: Silence, John, he is doomed. This is his revenge. He hopes to trouble us…afterwards.

Van Helsing: (*Looks at watch.*) Thirty seconds. (*They move in.*)

Dracula: (*Calmly, suavely again.*) I thank you for reminding me of the time.

Van Helsing: Harker, open the curtains. (*Harker opens curtains. Red light of approaching dawn outside.*) That is the East. The sun will rise beyond the meadow there. (*Dracula pulls cape over his head.*)

Seward: (*Glancing behind, leaves wolfsbane on desk as he looks up at window.*) The clouds are coloring.

Harker: Daybreak.

(*Harker leaves crucifix on desk. Van Helsing checks watch. Seward and Harker step in.*)

Dracula: (*Coolly. Turns Upstage, with back to them.*) A pleasant task you have set yourself, Mr. Harker.

Van Helsing: Ten seconds. Be ready when he collapses.

(*Seward crosses to hold Dracula's cape on Left of Dracula. Harker holds cape on Right of Dracula.*)

Harker: *The sun*! The stake, Professor, the stake! Hold him, Doctor.

Seward: I've got him.

(*Dracula, with loud burst of mocking laughter, vanishes on the word "sun," leaving the two men holding the empty cape. A flash goes off in front of fireplace. Harker backs Down Left, drops empty cape in front of desk. The three men look around them.*)

Harker: Up the chimney, as a bat. You heard what he said?

Seward: God will not permit it. What's to be done now, Van Helsing?

Van Helsing: (*Crosses, after looking at the prostrate Renfield; motions Harker and Seward to him. Whispers to them.*) We'll trick Renfield into showing us! (*Then, loudly:*) Dare we leave Renfield on earth to become the slave when he dies?

Seward: But he's human. We can't do murder?

Harker: I'll do it if you won't, Doctor!

Van Helsing: (*To Seward.*) Go to your office and get some painless drug.

Renfield: (*Sensing their drift without hearing their words, has been edging toward panel. Looks around room, then at panel.*) They're going to kill me, Master! Save me! I am coming to you.

(*Panel in bookcase opens, Renfield exits and panel closes.*)

Van Helsing: He has shown us the way! Where does that passage go?

Seward: I never knew there was a passage.

(*Harker hastens to desk; gets stake and hammer. They rush to panel.*)

Van Helsing: Only that devil has the combination. We'll break through somehow. Harker, quick, the hammer.

BLACKOUT

CURTAIN

SCENE II:

A vault.

Absolute darkness. Coffin Right Center and back of gauze drop. Flash of electric torch seen coming slowly downstairs Center. Coffin contains body of Dracula.

Van Helsing's voice: Be careful, Seward.

Seward's voice: These stairs go down forever.

Van Helsing's voice: May God protect us.

Seward's voice: Is Harker there?

Van Helsing's voice: He's gone for a lantern.

Seward's voice: I've got to the bottom.

Van Helsing's voice: Be careful. I'm right behind you.

(*Torch flashes around vault and they walk about slowly.*)

Seward's voice: What can this place be?

Van Helsing's voice: It seems an old vault. (*Stifled scream from Seward. Torch out. The torch is seen to jerk back.*) What is it? Oh, where are you, man?

Seward's voice: Sorry. I'm all right. A big rat ran across my foot.

(*Light seen coming downstairs. Harker appears carrying lighted lantern which reaches floor; partially illuminates bare vault. He has stake and hammer in left hand.*)

Harker: Where are you? What is this place?

Van Helsing: We can't see.

(*Harker moves with lantern.*)

Harker: The place smells horribly of bats.

Van Helsing: It has an animal smell, like the lair of a wolf.

Harker: That's what it is.

Seward: (*Still flashing torch about.*) There's absolutely nothing here.

Harker: (*At extreme Left with lantern.*) Here's another passage.

Van Helsing: (*Moving Left.*) I thought so. That must lead to Carfax. The sixth earth box is hidden somewhere here.

Harker: And the monster is in it.

Seward: You can't be sure. (*As he speaks, light from his torch falls on Renfield, stretched on floor. Renfield screams as light falls on him; scurries off right into darkness.*) Renfield! (*Harker and Van Helsing hurry across.*)

Van Helsing: Where is he?

Seward: Over there somewhere. Even if Renfield knew about this place, that doesn't prove the vampire's here.

Van Helsing: (*As Seward is speaking Van Helsing moves Right; seizes Renfield.*) It is the vampire's life or yours! (*Drags Renfield into light of lantern.*) Look at him, man, look at him. He knows.

Renfield: I know nothing. Let me go! Let me go, I say! (*Breaks away; goes Right.*)

Van Helsing: He was stretched out here, but he wouldn't let me drag him back. Ah! Here it is. Quick, that stake.

(*Harker and Van Helsing, with stake, pry up stone slab and open coffin. The three men gaze in horror and triumph at coffin.*)

Seward: What a horrible undead thing he is lying there!

Harker: Let me drive it in deep!

(*Van Helsing takes stake from Harker, lowers it into the coffin. Renfield stands at right end of coffin.*)

Van Helsing: (*Almost in a whisper.*) That's over the heart, Doctor?

Seward: (*Back of coffin.*) Yes. (*Van Helsing hands hammer to Harker. Harker raises hammer high over head; pounds stake with full force. Low groan. Silence. Stake remains fixed in Dracula's body.*)

Van Helsing: See his face now...the look of peace.

Seward: He is crumbling away.

Renfield: We're free!

Lucy: (*Comes down stairway and halts at bottom.*) Father, Father, John!

Harker: Lucy!

Van Helsing: (*Takes handful of dust; scatters it over the body.*) Dust to dust...ashes to ashes.

CURTAIN

(*The curtain rises again and the entire cast comes Downstage before a black drop for curtain speech.*)

Van Helsing: (*To Audience.*) Just a moment, ladies and gentlemen! Just a word before you go. We hope the memories of Dracula and Renfield won't give you bad dreams, so just a word of reassurance. When you get home tonight and the lights have been turned out and you are afraid to look behind the curtains and you dread to see a face appear at the window...why, just pull yourself together and remember that after all *there are such things.*

THE CURTAIN FALLS

AFTER READING

Responding

1. In your notebook, compare the perceptions the class had of Dracula with the narrative as it is told in this **drama**. Try to explain why there are differences between the class' perceptions and the reality of this play.

Understanding

2. a) In a small group, write a **definition** for each of the following words from the **play**, using only the **context** and the root words to predict their meanings.

   maniacal, page 36   preventive, page 41
   sanitarium, page 36   battlements, page 44
   rendered, page 38   dematerialization, page 45
   rallied, page 38

   b) As a class, compare your definitions. After your discussion, use a dictionary to check the accuracy of your definitions, making changes as necessary.

3. Explain how **foreshadowing** is used in this play to help the audience figure out who the vampire is before Dr. Van Helsing does. As a class, explain why a writer would want the audience to be able to have this information first.

4. List the purpose of each act in the play. Be prepared to explain your ideas to a small group.

5. When reading fantasy, science fiction, or supernatural stories, readers have to suspend their disbelief. Make a list of points in the drama when you had to suspend your disbelief. With a partner, compare your lists and add new ideas to your own. Discuss any differences between the lists, and suggest reasons why readers may respond in different ways.

Thinking About Language

6. Ellipses are used in two different ways in this play. Describe the ways they are used, who uses them, and whether a **character** uses them in the same way each time. Explain any patterns you find.

Extending

7. With a partner, from the descriptions of the set at the beginning and throughout the play, draw and label a picture of the stage and its furnishings, as it would be seen from above. Post your drawing on the bulletin board and compare it with those of your classmates.

8. a) With a partner, write a **scene** between Dracula and another character that you believe should be included in the play. Imitate the language **styles** of the existing characters. Be prepared to read your scene to the class.

b) As a class, create an evaluation form to assess the quality of the content and the style of the **dialogue**.

9. Choose one part of a scene from the play. Using both the dialogue and stage directions as guides, create a shooting **script** with a series of camera shots that increase or maintain the suspense of the scene. Present your shooting script ideas to a small group, who will give you feedback on the success of your ideas.

10. Find the story of Dracula presented through a different medium than drama (comic book, cartoon, film, or television show). Write a short **report**, using logical headings, on the differences and similarities between the two forms.

UNIT 2

> Literature

Ladies and Gentlemen, Start Your (Search) Engines

"...a library...[with an] estimated one billion pages in its holdings..."

LISA SLONIOWSKI

BEFORE READING

As a class, discuss experiences you have had doing research on the Internet. Identify both problematic and successful experiences. Share strategies that address any problems or frustrations identified.

The Internet, it has been said, is a library in which all the books are scattered on the floor. That's a modest description for the estimated one billion pages in its holdings, since they are, in fact, scattered around the world in a variety of individual computers. Each time you log on to the Internet to track down information, you're sifting through those far-flung mountains of data, tethered by only a tangle of telecommunications cables.

There are a variety of tools available to help you search the Internet. Search tools are basically indexes that organize the contents of the web, and each one searches, sorts, and retrieves data according to its own principles. Altavista, HotBot, and Northern Light, for example, are known as search engines. They work best when you search for a specific phrase or name. These tools let you search through all those web pages piled on the floor of the virtual library according to specific "keywords." Such engines are far-reaching tools that rely on "spiders," or

"crawlers," to index web pages one at a time, recording the occurrences of the specified keywords within.

Yahoo or the Google Web Directory, on the other hand, are known as search directories and are generally smaller than the more expansive search engine. They work much like the Yellow Pages in the telephone book. A directory organizes web sites into hierarchical subject categories moving from broad to specific, as in Canada > Science > Geography > Cartography > Maps. By providing lists of subcategories related to your general request, this kind of tool helps focus your search, allowing you to fine-tune your search as the subtopics arise. If this kind of tool seems more satisfying, it may be because humans have created the index.

Search tools that can explore several engines or directories themselves, rather than individual sites, are known as meta-engines. The most popular are Metacrawler, Profusion, and Ask Jeeves.

They automatically submit your chosen keywords to several different kinds of tools at once and produce a summary of your hits within each one. Meta-engines are great for information on current events or very broad topics. But it's kind of an apples-and-oranges approach since the meta-engine is simultaneously searching tools that have different characteristics and restrictions. Your results will vary in relevancy, and it may make your search less systematic. In the end, you might have greater success searching each tool separately.

The last type of Internet search tool is called a "subject guide." Guides are web-based bibliographies of sites, or lists of links, on a particular topic. The upside is that the sites in a subject guide are often hand-picked and evaluated and sometimes provide a few lines of description that save you from entering irrelevant sites. The downside, however, is that their scope is limited. About.com, for example, is a subject guide that provides bibliographies for many topics including physical and cultural geography, rivers, maps, disasters, and climatology.

In general, searching for information on a broad topic calls for using more than one tool. Studies indicate that there are not significant overlaps among different search tools; each one indexes a different part of the web. Your best bet is to choose a couple of search sources, read the help instructions to get familiar with their idiosyncrasies, and then get in the habit of working with a couple each time you search a subject.

FIVE TIPS FOR MAXIMUM EFFICIENCY

1. **Read the online help.** A quality search engine or directory will have instructions

---

WEBLIOGRAPHY

Search Tutorials
The following tutorials offer information on how to search effectively:
Search Engine Watch (www.searchenginewatch.com)
Finding Information on the Internet: A Tutorial (www.lib.berkeley.edu/TeachingLib/Guides/Internet/Findinfo.html)

Search Engines
Altavista Canada (www.altavista.ca/cgi-bin/query)
Excite Canada (www.excite.ca/)
Southam's Canada.com (www.canada.com)
Maplesquare (www.maplesquare.com)
Sympatico (www.sympatico.ca)

Search Directories
Google's Canada Directory (www.directory.google.com/Top/Regional/North_America/Canada/)
National Library of Canada's Canadian Information by Subject (www.nlc-bnc.ca/caninfo/ecaninfo.htm)
Yahoo Canada (www.yahoo.ca)
Canadian Eh? (www.canadianeh.com)

Subject Guides
About.com (www.about.com)
Geo Guide (www.sub.uni-goettingen.de/ssqfi/geo/)
Canadian Communities Atlas (www.cgdi.qc.ca/ccatlas)
Earth Sciences Virtual Library (www-vl-es.geo.ucalgary.ca/VL/hrml/es-resources.html)
UNB (St. John Campus) Geography Resources (www.unbsj.ca/library/subject/geogl.htm)

---

to guide you through its quirks. You can increase the relevancy of your results and save a lot of time by reading help screens and checking back once in a while to see whether anything has changed.

2. **Devise a strategy before you search.** First, define your topic and think about what kind of tools will work best for your search. Decide on your keywords, and develop a few alternatives to help you

revise a search. If, for instance, you're looking for information on Canada's East Coast, plan to search under the Maritimes, the Atlantic Provinces, and Atlantic Canada.

3. **Use search operators.** "And," "or," and "+" are common operators that allow you to combine concepts or add additional keywords to help make your search results more accurate. Entering "pollution and illness and Canada" in a search box, for example, will produce records containing all three concepts, rather than just all the web sites from around the world that refer to "pollution" alone.

   "Or" and "match any," on the other hand, help to broaden your search if you aren't certain about the correct word to use. For example, "Pollution" and (illness or disease or sickness or health) and (Canada or Canadians) searches for any of the words in each set of parentheses but returns only those records that contain at least one of the specified words in each of the sets.

   Most major search engines allow you to type in operators as part of your search phrase. You can choose not to use operators, but be aware that many search engines default to the "or" operator if you don't instruct them to do otherwise. For instance, if you enter "pollution illness Canada," you will retrieve articles that contain any one of those terms, but not necessarily all three. If all three concepts are important, using operators will enhance the accuracy of your results.

4. **Be specific.** If you're looking for information on birds, decide whether you want general information on birds or a particular kind of bird. If it's a particular species you're after, use the name of the bird as your keyword.

5. **Refine your search.** If the first search doesn't yield the results you're looking for, don't give up. Think of your first attempt as simply a way of gathering information, ideas, and keywords for narrowing your focus. A first search on "earthquakes and Canada," for example, may call up the term "tectonics," which should then be added to your next search round.

EVALUATING YOUR RESULTS

Feeling some doubt and anxiety because you don't know whether the information you have found is credible? Apply the following four criteria to test its quality:

Accuracy. Double-check the facts against another source. Watch for other documentation. Does the author cite data from other sources? Are these sources valid? Are there links to other sources on the web?

Authorship. Look for the affiliations and credentials of the author. Use the web to search an author's credibility independently, and see whether others cite the research.

Goals. Identify the goals of the site. Is this a commercial site with a URL ending with ".com"? Is the site trying to sell you something? Is it a vanity page created by someone with a fancy desktop and lots of free time? Is the site affiliated with a reputable not-for-profit organization or an academic or research group?

Currency. Check the date to determine when the site was created and last updated.

WEBCABULARY

Keywords, which you enter in the search box, are the most important concepts in your search.

Location bar is a space at the top of a browser where you can type a URL to go directly to that site.

Search bar is a box in a search engine or directory where you enter keywords and operators.

URL (Uniform Resource Locator) is the unique address of a web page.

HTML (Hypertext Markup Language) is a programming code that allows information to be displayed on the World Wide Web.

Hyperlink (sometimes known as a link) is a piece of highlighted text or an icon that joins two pages on the web. When you click on a link, the browser jumps directly to that page.

Browser is a computer program that lets you view web pages on the Internet. The most common browsers are Netscape and Internet Explorer.

Search engine is a tool that helps you find information by indexing words on the web. You may use an engine to search for pages that contain particular words.

Search directory is a tool that organizes web pages into hierarchical subject categories. This tool allows you to browse through the subject headings or conduct keyword searches in a directory.

Meta-engine is a tool that allows you to search several engines or directories at once.

Subject guide is an electronic bibliography of web sites on a particular topic.

Operators are symbols or words that relate keywords in a search. Commonly used operators are: "and"; "+"; "or"; "not"; "-"; "near."

AFTER READING

Responding
1. As you read this **article**, make notes on advice that you think will help you with your Internet searches. Compare your notes with those of a partner.

Understanding
2. In your notebook, explain the differences among search engines, search directories, meta-engines, and subject guides.

3. With a partner, discuss how the methods of searching the Internet outlined in this article address problems described during the "Before Reading" activity.

4. Create a graphic presentation of information in this selection for the use of younger students who are being introduced to the Internet as a research tool.

Thinking About Language

5. Define the word "currency" as it is used in the **context** of this article. Explain how this **definition** differs from the more common definition of the word.

6. Explain the derivation of the "coined" words "Webliography" and "Webcabulary." For each, explain whether the new word is helpful or confusing for readers of this article.

7. With a partner, examine and analyze the technical vocabulary and level of language used in this article. (See The Reference Shelf, page 351.) Identify the intended audience of the article (age, socio-economic position, education, and experience with computers and the Internet).

Extending

8. With a partner, visit one of the Web sites mentioned in this selection. Prepare a **report** to the class on helpful information found on the Web site. In your report, provide additional "Webcabulary" terms you encounter, and define them.

9. In a group of three, select an author or **topic** from the "Contents" pages of this textbook. Have each member of the group use either one of the Internet search engines, one of the search directories, or one of the meta-engines mentioned in this article to research information on the author or topic. (Note: Each member of the group should use a different search method.) Compare the results obtained from each search method. Be prepared to share the results of your study with the class.

Credit: What Do You Really Know?

"...the wise and responsible use of credit cards should be as commonplace as brushing our teeth twice a day."

JOANNE THOMAS YACCATO

BEFORE READING

1. Take a poll of the class to find out how many people have a credit card (including gas, store, and bank credit cards).

2. As a class, discuss the pros and cons of having a credit card.

PUTTING YOU IN CHARGE WITH CREDIT

Buying a computer? Taking a trip to some glorious destination? What about university textbooks? Little Katie's orthodontist's bill? Thinking about replacing that cool white suit you bought while disco was the rage?

Life sometimes seems like an endless stream of purchases. Thankfully we have convenience in a 3×2 piece of plastic that makes buying fast and easy — the credit card. A recent nationwide survey on credit shows that convenience is the number one reason Canadians use their cards. In fact, we carry an average of 3.4 credit cards in our wallets. But we must treat that plastic as respectfully as we would a thousand-dollar bill. Credit cards are a financial tool that puts tremendous buying power into our hands, so they must be handled with care.

The kind of power we'd like from credit cards comes from knowing how to use them properly. Of course, the wise and responsible use of credit cards should be as commonplace as brushing our teeth twice a day. When we neglect either, the consequences aren't pleasant. Despite this, and even though credit affects every aspect of our lives, we don't know nearly enough about it. The credit study shows a wide discrepancy between what consumers think they know and what they actually know. The intent of this brochure is to provide you with the right knowledge to improve your credit literacy. This knowledge will put you in charge.

Credit lenders decide on your credit worthiness based on three principles known as the three C's of credit:

Your Character

Are you dependable? Do you pay your bills on time? Does your past show you to be a financially responsible person?

Your Capacity

Do you have a steady means to pay back what you are borrowing? Do you own a home or rent? Have you lived at your current address for long? Credit lenders like to see your name on one mailbox for at least a year.

Your Collateral

When everything is added up, is what you are worth more than what you owe? Do you own something that is worth at least as much as your credit limit or the amount you want to borrow? This might include the equity in your house, household goods, a car, savings, investments, and life insurance.

If Yes figures prominently in your answers, then you are a good candidate for credit.

WHAT'S A CREDIT RATING?

Your credit rating is a scorecard of your credit behaviour. Everything you do with credit is tracked and rated according to how responsible you have been in paying it back. Most of your credit transactions are kept on file at an independent credit bureau. These transactions include things like loans and credit cards but not rent or utility bills.

Financial institutions, retailers, and other lenders who have an interest in your financial status check your rating before deciding whether you get credit. To be sure your record is accurate, contact the bureau for a free copy of your history.

HOW CAN YOU ESTABLISH CREDIT?

The best way to create a credit rating that will allow you to borrow money is...to borrow money. Confusing? Yes, but it's easier than you think. Credit lenders often like to see a good repayment history before lending money or offering credit. You can begin to develop this history by trying any of the following:

- Make regular deposits to a savings account.
- Pay all your bills on time.
- Get a credit card at a department store with a $500 limit and repay quickly.
- Obtain a small loan and have a friend or relative co-sign for you.
- Take out a car loan and pay it back promptly.

This is how you establish a good credit rating.

KEEPING A GOOD CREDIT RATING

As soon as you've been approved for any type of credit, you are rated from 1 to 9 — depending on your performance as a debtor. If you miss payments or are late paying, your rating will deteriorate from an enviable 1 all the way down to 8 or 9 which could mean repossession, scissors, and a destroyed credit rating. Count on seven years before your record is clean again.

The way to keep a good rating is to make all your payments on time and to take on only as much debt as you can handle. Don't put anything on a credit card unless you know you can pay for it by the time the bill comes in, or within a couple of months. It's to your advantage to keep your credit performance clean because a bad record can affect your ability to borrow money for a car or your home. It can damage your ability to get insurance and maybe even a job.

LOOK AFTER YOUR OWN AFFAIRS

The merits of having your own driver's license and social insurance number are obvious. It is equally important to have your own credit rating. If you have lived under the umbrella of your partner's credit, for example, by using a supplementary card instead of one in your own name, the credit bureau may not have a record on you. This can become dangerous should you wake up one morning to find yourself handling money matters on your own. Something you always took for granted — credit — is gone; so be sure you are establishing a credit history of your own.

WILL THAT BE CHARGE OR CREDIT?

It's a little known fact that there is actually a difference between credit cards and charge cards. Knowing this difference is the first step to an informed choice.

CHARGE CARDS

Some gas companies and certain financial and travel service companies tend to be the issuers of these types of cards. They offer no pre-set spending limits and must be paid in full every month. They don't charge interest per se but they do levy delinquency fees on unpaid balances. Charge cards are really designed for short-term credit needs, usually 30 days or less. Annual fees cover the full range from $15 to $350.

CREDIT CARDS

Credit cards allow you to carry a balance from month to month as long as a minimum portion of the bill is paid each month. You are charged interest for this benefit. Unless, of course, you pay off your balances in full each month.

You can choose from two categories of credit cards. The first is offered by banks, trust companies, credit unions, and other financial institutions. The second is offered by retailers and certain gas companies. The major difference is store and gas cards charge higher interest rates.

WHAT ARE MY CHOICES?

It used to be that a credit card was a credit card was a credit card. Choosing the right credit card has become almost as mind-boggling as choosing running shoes these days. In response to demand for options and added-value, financial institutions are introducing a large variety of products to address different consumer needs.

Standard Cards

Interest rates on these cards range from 16–18% and some offer various incentives like points toward travel, entertainment, and merchandise. Annual fees range from no-fee cards up to $35.

Low Rate Cards

These cards are generally stripped down versions of standard cards without the added benefit of a points programs and can offer interest rates up to 6 points below conventional cards. Some come with an annual fee, so be sure to ask.

Premium Cards

Otherwise known as gold cards, these are enhanced products with generally a higher annual fee and a range of benefits. Features may include higher credit limits, cash back, travel insurance, purchase protection plans, guaranteed hotel reservations, collision insurance on rental cars, credit card registry services, and itemized annual spending records. The same points programs attached to standard cards apply to premium cards as well. Premium cards usually charge $50–$130 in annual fees.

THE REAL COSTS OF CREDIT CARDS

Let's look at the anatomy of a credit card. To determine the real costs of a card, be sure to consider the interest rate, the grace period, and the annual fee.

HOW IS INTEREST CALCULATED?

It's pretty simple. Cards from financial institutions charge interest on daily outstanding balances. No interest is charged on new purchases if you pay the entire balance by the due date. In most cases, if you carry a balance, interest is charged from the date you make purchases until the balance is paid in full.

Retailers, on the other hand, tend to charge interest on monthly as opposed to daily balances. In most cases you'll pay less interest if you pay at least half the balance each month.

GRACE PERIODS

The number of days you have on a card before a company starts charging you interest is called a grace period. Usually that period is the number of days between the statement date and the payment due date.

Grace periods on credit cards are usually 21 days for financial service cards and 25 to 30 days for retail cards. Charge card balances are typically due on receipt of statement. Be aware, though, that there are some low-interest credit cards that have no grace period at all.

When you carry balances from month to month, there is likely no grace for balances carried forward from previous months.

FEES

Watch for annual and administrative fees. Depending on your balance, the fee may end up costing you more than a card with a higher interest rate but no fee. For instance, on an average yearly outstanding balance of $1500, a card with an interest rate of 13.5% with a $60 annual fee ends up costing you the same as a no-fee card at 17.5%.

Today your card may chip in money toward a new car or long distance calls. It can send you on a trip to Istanbul, no charge. It can give you a free night out on the town with dinner and theatre.

To choose the right rewards program, consider the following:
- Evaluate your lifestyle and figure out what you're after. A trip, a dinner out, or merchandise?
- Compare program fees and value. To be sure the rewards program works for you, do the math. Consider the annual fee against the reward you might qualify for.
- Evaluate what type of spender you are. Rewards or points programs only work if you spend money. If you spend more than $250 a month, they are a good bet.

Whatever program you choose, stick with it so you can rack up the points faster.

For a free copy of your credit report, contact:

Equifax Canada

P.O. Box Jean-Talon Station
Montreal, Quebec
H1S 2Z2
1-800-465-7166

Trans Union of Canada

1-800-663-9980

For help managing your finances, call: Credit Counselling Services/Orderly Payment of Debt, a not-for-profit organization 1-800-267-2272 for the location nearest you or check out their Web site: http://www.creditcanada.com

**For information about credit card costs, check out:
Industry Canada Consumer Connection Web Site**
http://strategis.ic.gc.ca./OCA

AFTER READING

Responding

1. Write about one new thing you learned from this guide. How has the information in this guide changed the ideas you had about credit?

Understanding

2. List two of the most important points included in each subsection in this guide.
3. The writer uses plain language in this guide to inform her audience. Look closely at the language she uses and answer the following questions:
   - How does she make her writing sound friendly?
   - How does she make her writing sound knowledgeable?
   - Is her writing **style** effective for a high-school audience?
4. Under "Credit Ratings & the Credit Bureau," the writer asks a series of questions before she makes a statement. Explain whether or not this approach is effective for the reader.

5. This guide was originally a **brochure**. In a small group, analyze the effectiveness of the graphic design (use of fonts and font sizes, subtitles, and other graphic elements) in enhancing readability and increasing audience appeal. Be prepared to report your conclusions to the class.

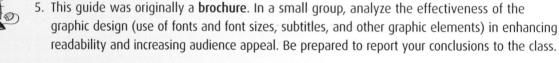

Thinking About Language

6. a) Under "How Can You Establish Credit?" (page 78), explain why the writer has used ellipses between "money is" and "to borrow."
   b) Make a list of other times when a writer may use ellipses. (See The Reference Shelf, page 357.)
   c) Use ellipses correctly and effectively in one piece of writing you complete for this selection.
7. Choose three words or phrases from this selection that would be considered "technical" words. Add these words, correctly spelled, to your personal word list.

Extending

8. a) Find another source of information on credit. Compare the advice from the new source to this selection. Cite your source in the correct form. (See The Reference Shelf, page 379.)
   b) With a partner, discuss the sources you found. Decide which source is more credible and explain the reasons for your choice.

9. a) Choose a product or service that you might be interested in purchasing in the near future that would require you to use credit. Prepare a research plan for getting information about the product, the model you could most afford to buy, and the way you could finance the purchase.

b) Conduct your research and prepare a computer-assisted oral **report**, using presentation software, on the proposed purchase.

c) With a partner, rehearse your presentation. Comment on the organization and clarity of information and expression.

d) As a class, create an evaluation form for the presentation, focusing on the quality of the research, the level of language used in the presentation, and the quality of the technological portion of the presentation.

e) Identify your strengths and weaknesses in the Oral Communication Skills Action Plan. (See The Reference Shelf, page 395.)

10. Create an advertisement for a credit card, using information from the selection.

How to Buy or Sell a Car

"You can learn a great deal just by using
your eyes, ears, and nose."

CONSUMER REPORTS

BEFORE READING

As a class, list on the board all the items that you would need to check if you were going to buy a used car.

ASK THE RIGHT QUESTIONS

The answers you get to basic questions about a used car—even over the telephone—can help you avoid a heap of trouble later. That's especially true when you're buying from a private party. The following queries will help you separate the cream puffs from the clunkers in your used-vehicle search. Any strange, far-fetched, or odd-sounding answers to routine questions should put you on guard.

"What color is the car?" Color is important, but this question is meant mostly to break the ice. Whatever the answer, follow up with, "Are the body and upholstery in good shape?" You want to get a general idea of the car's condition.

"How is it equipped?" If the ad doesn't specify, ask about key features: number of doors; automatic or manual transmission; air conditioning; antilock brakes; air bags; sound system; power windows, locks, seats, or mirrors; cruise control; sunroof; upholstery material; and so forth.

"Have you owned it since it was new?" You want to be able to piece together as much of the car's service history as you can. Be concerned about a car that's changed hands quite a bit—three or four times in two years, say.

"Are you the person who drove it the most?" Ideally, you want to meet the car's principal driver or drivers to see if they strike you as responsible people. Be wary of a car that has spent years in the hands of a teenager.

"How many miles does it have?" If the mileage is higher than, say, 20 000 [km] per year or lower than 5000, ask why. If a car has high mileage because its owner had a long commute to work, that's better than if a car was used on a delivery route. Stop-and-go use is a lot rougher on a car than freeway miles. Low mileage is a good thing, but you'll have to make a careful inspection to determine if the mileage claimed is too good to be true.

"Has it ever been in an accident?" If so, ask about the extent of the damage, cost of repairs, and the sort of shop that did the work. Don't worry too much about minor scrapes, but think twice about buying a car that has been in a serious accident—crucial components such as the frame may be irreparably damaged.

"Do you have service records?" You want a car that has been well maintained. That means that it should have gone back to the dealer or service station at specified service intervals. You also want to see the receipts for any new muffler, brakes, tires, or other "wear" parts that have been replaced. Repair-shop receipts normally note the car's odometer reading, verifying the car's history.

"Why are you selling the car?" Look for a plausible explanation rather than an interesting story. If the answer sounds evasive, be wary. If you're buying from a dealer, you probably won't be able to glean all that much information about the car's history because the dealer simply may not know it. Take with a grain of salt any tale about how the previous owner pampered the car. But you should still ask to see service records and other evidence that the car was maintained properly.

INSPECTING THE CAR

Whether you buy from a dealer or private party, always inspect the vehicle thoroughly before bringing it to a mechanic for a final inspection. You don't have to be an expert to give a car a good, revealing going–over. You can learn a great deal just by using your eyes, ears, and nose. Dress in old clothes and take along a friend to help you out. Do your inspection in broad daylight on a dry day or in a well-lit garage. The car must be parked on a level surface and shouldn't have been driven for at least an hour before you take a look.

Check out the exterior

First, walk around the car and see if it's standing level. If it sags to one side, it may have broken springs or another suspension problem. Bounce each corner of the car up and down. If the shock absorbers are in good shape, the car should rebound just once or twice and not keep bouncing up and down. Then grab the top of each front tire and tug it back and forth. If you feel play in it or hear a clunking sound, the wheel bearings or suspension joints may be shot.

Body Condition. Check each body panel and the roof, looking for scratches, dents, and rust. The gaps between the panels and surrounding surfaces should be uniform. Examine the lines of the fenders and doors. Misaligned panels or large gaps can indicate either sloppy assembly at the factory or repair.

The easiest way to find out if the car has been in an accident is to ask the owner. But you should still take a look for yourself. Paint color and finish should be the same everywhere. A repainted body panel might not quite match the original in color or gloss. It's very hard for a body shop to duplicate the texture and finish of a factory's baked-on paint. Look for differences in color on the outside edges of panels. A repainted panel may even look more mirrorlike than the original, but the paint may not weather the same or last as long.

Sometimes a repair is obvious. Other times, you'll have to peer closely, moving your head slowly to catch the light. If you think a dent may have been patched up, use a magnet to see if it sticks to the suspect area. If a dent was filled with plastic body filler, the magnet won't stick. (This test won't work if the car has plastic or fiberglass body parts, such as a Saturn or Chevrolet Corvette.)

Look for signs of body repair on the sills around door openings, the hood, and trunk lid. If parts of the car have been repainted, there may be signs of "overspray," or paint adhering to the rubber seals around the body openings. Look carefully at the underside of the hood and trunk lid for signs of damage or repair.

Minor cosmetic flaws are no cause for concern, but rust is. Look particularly for blistered paint or rust spots around the wheel wells and rocker panels (the sheet metal beneath the doors) and the bottoms of the doors themselves. Use a flashlight to look inside the wheel wells for rust and corrosion caused by salt.

Open and close each door, the hood, and the trunk. Do they ride freely on their hinges and close properly? Gently lift and let go of each door, particularly the driver's door. If the door is loose on its hinges, the car has seen hard or long use. Also inspect the rubber seals around all openings to be sure they're intact. Loose, deteriorated, or missing rubber can create water leaks, drafts, and wind noise.

Lights and Lenses. Have your friend stand outside the car and confirm that all lights are working. Try out both low-beam and high-beam headlights, the parking lights, the turn signals, and any ancillary

SHOPSMART
Used-car inspection kit
Paper and pencil
Flashlight
Magnet
Rag or paper towels
Work gloves
Old blanket
Audio tape or CD (to check the sound system)

lights, such as fog lights. Make sure all the light lenses are intact and not cracked, fogged with moisture, or missing.

Tires. You can tell a lot from the tires. If the car has less than, say, 30 000 miles [48 300 km] on the odometer, it should probably still have its original rubber. If a car with low miles on the odometer has new tires, be suspicious. Turn the front wheels all the way to the right or left, so you can get a good look at them. All four should be the same brand and size (except on a few performance cars, which use different sizes on the front and rear). If there is a mix of brands or sizes on the car, ask why.

Tread wear should be even across the width of the tread. It should also be the same on the left and the right sides of the car. Ask if the tires have been rotated front-to-rear regularly. If not, the wear is usually more severe on the drive wheels.

An aggressive driver tends to put heavy wear on the outside shoulder of the tire, at the edge of the sidewall. If the shoulder is badly worn, assume that the car has been driven hard.

Check the tread depth, either with a tread-depth tool (available at auto-parts stores) or with a penny. To be legal, tires must have at least 1/16 inch [1.6 mm] of tread. If you don't have a tread gauge, insert a penny into the tread groove, with Lincoln's head down. If you can see the top of the head, the tire should be replaced.

On each tire, lightly stroke the tread with the flat of your hand. If you feel raised areas, the tire was not aligned properly. That symptom could point to a simple maladjustment or a costly suspension repair; have your mechanic check it out. Tires with that sort of wear will tend to make the steering wheel vibrate at highway speeds.

Examine the sidewalls for scuffing, cracks, or bulges, and look on the edge of each rim for dents or cracks. A hard impact with a pothole or curb could have knocked a tire out of alignment or damaged a tire, rim, or suspension part.

Brake Discs. Check the rotors on disc brakes. Most cars have disc brakes in front and drum brakes in the rear; some have disc brakes all around. With a flashlight, peer through the front wheel rims. The rotor discs should be smooth, with no deep grooves. Don't worry about traces of surface rust on the discs. After your test drive, when you've used the brakes, the discs should look clean and smooth.

Glass. Look carefully at the windshield and other windows to make sure there are no cracks. A small bull's-eye from a stone hit on the windshield may not be cause for alarm, though you should point it out as a bargaining chip. Cracks in the windshield often grow worse over time and can lead to a costly repair.

Check out the interior

Odor. When you first open the car door, sniff the interior. A musty, moldy, or mildewy smell could indicate water leaks. Be diligent here because water leaks can be very hard to find and fix. Remove the floor mats, and feel and sniff for wet spots on the carpet beneath. If there's doubt, find another car.

Pedal Rubber. The rubber on the brake, clutch, and gas pedals gives an indication of use. A car with low miles shouldn't show much wear. If the pedal rubber is worn through in spots, it indicates high kilometres. If the clutch-pedal rubber is badly worn, it may mean the driver is in the habit of riding the clutch, which puts a strain on it and the gearbox.

Instruments and Controls. Start the car and let it idle. Note if it's hard to start when cold. Note too whether the engine idles smoothly. Then methodically try out every switch, button, and lever. Check all the doors and their locks, and operate the windows. If there's a sunroof, open and close it. Try the interior lights, overhead dome light, any reading lights, and the lighted vanity mirrors on the sun visors. Honk the horn.

Turn on the heater full blast and see how hot it gets, how quickly. Switch on the air conditioning and make sure it blows cold (for more on issues raised by old air conditioners, see the next section). If there are seat heaters, turn them on and see how warm they get.

Try the sound system. Check radio reception on AM and FM, and try loading, playing, and ejecting a tape or compact disc if there is a tape or CD player.

Seats. Try out all the seats even though you may not plan on sitting in the rear. The driver's seat typically has more wear than the passenger's, but it shouldn't sag. The upholstery shouldn't be ripped or badly worn, particularly in a car that's supposed to have low kilometres on it. Try all the driver's-seat adjustments, along with the steering wheel height-and-reach adjustment, to make sure you can have a good driving position.

AIR-CONDITIONING ISSUES

Particularly if you're considering a 1994 or older car or truck, check the air conditioner: Fixing one that's broken or leaking could prove expensive. The reason is the R-12 refrigerant that chilled all cars and light trucks through the early 1990s. Because R-12 is a chlorofluorocarbon (CFC), which depletes the earth's ozone layer, production was banned in the U.S. and most other countries in 1995 as automakers switched to non-CFC R-134a. Shrinking supplies have since driven prices for R-12 to around $128 per kilogram compared with just $19 to $30 per kilogram for R-134a—and made the time-honored act of simply adding R-12 to a leaking system expensive as well as irresponsible.

Most 1994 vehicles and all subsequent models were switched over to R-134a at the factory, though some '94 models still rolled off the line with R-12. An R-12 system with minor problems can often be fixed for less than $100. But major repairs can set you back anywhere from $300 to more than $1000, depending on the model. You may also face service problems and even a fire hazard if the vehicle you're

considering has been contaminated with other refrigerants that were added as a cheap fix.

Take Its Temperature. A healthy air-conditioning system should produce cold air within a few minutes. Turn it on with the temperature set to full cold and the blower at medium speed. Then keep it running when you road-test the vehicle. Be wary if the air coming through the dash vents turns warm and stays that way. While the problem could be minor—a faulty switch or excess moisture in the system, for example—a shift from cold air to warm could mean an expensive repair bill down the road.

Know What's in There. A decal on the underside of the hood should reveal which refrigerant the factory installed or whether the vehicle was retrofitted with something else. Unfortunately, decals can't tell you whether the original system was properly maintained or how well any retrofits were performed. That's why the surest way to know which air-conditioning system a vehicle has and what shape it's in is to have it checked by an air-conditioning specialist. An air-conditioning shop can use an electronic leak detector and trace dyes, if needed, to find any leaks. The shop can also inspect the system to see if it contains more than one refrigerant. Refrigerant mixes pose added problems and expense because purging them requires special equipment. And while both R-12 and R-134a can be recycled, blends must be collected and shipped off-site for reclamation—another expensive procedure to go through. Few shops are equipped to service systems with contaminated refrigerant, which alone makes the vehicle worth less. Mixes are also a tell-tale sign that the system was leaking and probably wasn't fixed before the other refrigerant was added. Worse, if the system has been filled with propane or some other flammable gas and it leaks into the passenger compartment, the gas may cause a fire or an explosion.

Does It Pay to Switch? Industry observers estimate that, thanks largely to recycling, there will be enough R-12 to service older systems well into the new century. If an R-12 system is sound, it usually makes sense to keep it R-12, since a converted system may not cool as effectively. Most air-conditioning shops recommend switching to R-134a only for later models with R-12 systems, and only when the compressor—the engine-driven pump that circulates refrigerant through the system—fails. At anywhere from U.S. $300 to U.S. $1000 [Cdn $480–$1600], the compressor is the costliest part of any air-conditioning system and the one most crucial to retrofit.

If the compressor needs replacing, the new one that goes in will probably be R-134a-compatible anyway, so it makes sense to switch to the new refrigerant. A specialist can tell you for sure and give you an estimate that you can use as a bargaining chip to lower a used vehicle's price. Then again, if the cost to repair or convert represents a significant portion of that price—and the owner won't discount it accordingly—you may want to pass on the vehicle and continue your search.

Look in the trunk

The trunk is another place to use your nose as well as your eyes. Again, sniff and look for signs of water entry. See if the carpeting feels wet or smells musty. Take up the trunk floor and check the spare-tire well for water or rust.

Check the condition of the spare tire. (If the car has alloy wheels, the spare-tire rim is often plain steel.) With many minivans, pickups, and sport-utility vehicles, the spare tire may be suspended beneath the rear of the vehicle. You'll have to get down on your knees to examine it. Also be sure the jack and all the jack tools are present and accounted for.

Under the hood

If the engine has been off for a few minutes, you can do most under-the-hood checks. Look first at the general condition of the engine bay. Dirt and dust are normal, but watch out if you see lots of oil spattered about, a battery covered with corrosion, or wires and hoses hanging loose.

Wiring. Feel the crinkly, plastic-armored covering on electrical wires. If the covering is brittle and cracked, the wires have overheated at some point. Look for neat plastic connectors where wires run into other wires, not connections made with black electrical tape.

Hoses and belts. Try to squeeze the various rubber hoses running to the radiator, air conditioner, and other parts. The rubber should be supple, not rock-hard, cracked, or mushy. Feel the fan belt and other V-belts to determine if they are frayed.

Fluids. Check all the fluid levels. Dipsticks usually have a mark indicating the proper level.

The engine oil should be dark brown or black, but not too dirty or gritty. If the oil is honey-colored, it was just changed. White spots in the oil cap indicate water is present. Transmission fluid should be pinkish, not brown, and smell like oil, with no "burnt" odor. It shouldn't leave visible metal particles on your rag—a sign of serious problems. With most cars, you're supposed to check the automatic-transmission fluid with the engine warmed up. On some, the transmission-fluid dipstick has two sets of marks for checking when the engine is either cold or warm. Also check the power-steering and brake-fluid levels. They should be within the safe zone.

Radiator. Don't remove the radiator cap unless the engine has cooled off completely. Check the coolant by looking into the plastic reservoir near the radiator. The coolant should be greenish, not a deep rust or milky color. Greenish stains on the radiator are a sign of pinhole leaks.

Battery. If the battery has filler caps, wipe off the top of the battery with a rag, then carefully pry off or unscrew the caps to look at the liquid electrolyte level. If the level is low, it may not mean much, or it may mean that the battery has been working too hard. Have a mechanic check it out.

Under the car

Spread an old blanket on the ground, so you can look under the engine at the pavement. Use a flashlight. If you see oil drips, other oily leaks, or green coolant, it's not a good sign. If you can find the spot where the car was habitually parked, see if that part of the garage floor or driveway is marred with puddles of oil, coolant, or transmission fluid. Check the ground beneath the fuel tank for fuel drips from the fuel-filler tube and gas tank.

Don't be alarmed if some clear water drips from the car on a hot day. It's probably just water condensed from the air conditioner.

Examine the constant-velocity-joint boots behind the front wheels. They are round, black rubber bellows at the ends of the axle shafts. If the rubber boots are split and leaking grease, assume that the car has or shortly will have bad C-V joints— another item that's costly to repair.

Feel for any tailpipe residue. If it's black and greasy, it means the car is burning oil. The tail-pipe smudge should be dry and dark gray. Look at the pipes. Some rust is normal. Heavy rust is sometimes normal but could mean that a new exhaust system might be needed soon.

Take a test drive

If you're still interested in the car, ask to take it for a test drive. Plan to spend at least 20 minutes behind the wheel, to allow enough time to check the engine's cooling system and the car's heater and air conditioner.

Comfort. Make sure the car fits you. Set the seat in a comfortable driving position and attach the safety belt. Make sure that you're at least 10 inches [25 cm] away from the steering wheel and that you can still fully depress all the pedals. Typically, seats fit some bodies better than others, so make sure the seat feels right for you. Make sure that you can reach all the controls without straining, that the controls are easy to use, and that the displays are easy to see.

Steering. With the engine idling before you start your test drive, turn the steering wheel right and left. You should feel almost no play in the wheel before the tires start to turn.

Once under way, the car should respond to the helm quickly and neatly, without lots of steering–wheel motion. At normal speeds, the car should maintain course without constant steering corrections.

If the wheel shakes at highway speed, suspect a problem with wheel balance or the front-end alignment, which is easily fixed, or with the suspension, which may not be. Likewise, if the car constantly drifts to one side, suspect that a tire is under-inflated or that there is some suspension problem—something to have a mechanic check.

Engine and Transmission. The engine should idle smoothly without surging or sputtering, and accelerate from a stand-still without bucking or hesitating. When you accelerate up a hill, you shouldn't hear any pinging or clunking. The car should be able to keep up with highway traffic without endless down-shifting.

With an automatic transmission, don't confuse smoothness with slippage. When you accelerate, there should be no appreciable hesitation between the engine's acceleration and the car's. If there is, it's an almost sure sign of transmission wear—and a costly fix down the road.

With a manual transmission, the clutch should fully engage well before you take your foot all the way off the pedal. If there isn't at least an inch [2.5 cm] of play at the top of the pedal's travel, the car may soon need a new clutch.

Brakes. Test the brakes on an empty stretch of road. From a speed of 45 mph [70 km/h], apply the brakes hard. The car should stop straight and quickly, without pulling to one side and without any vibration. The pedal feel should be smooth and linear, and stopping the car shouldn't take a huge effort. If the car has antilock brakes, you should feel them activate with a rapid pulsing underfoot when you push hard on the brake. (It's easier to make the antilock braking system activate on a stretch of wet road.)

Try two or three stops; the car should stop straight and easily each time. Then pull into a safe area, stop, and step firmly on the brake pedal for 30 seconds. If the pedal feels spongy or sinks to the floor, there may be a leak in the brake system.

Look, Listen, Feel. At a steady speed on a smooth road, note any vibrations. You shouldn't feel shuddering through the steering wheel, nor should the dashboard shake or the image in your mirrors quiver noticeably.

Drive at 30 mph [50 km/h] or so on a bumpy road. You want a compliant, well-controlled, quiet ride. If the car bounces and hops a lot on routine bumps and ruts, it may mean the car has suspension problems or the car's chassis wasn't designed well in the first place. Listen, too, for rattles and squeaks—they're annoying to live with and often difficult to track down and fix.

Where there's smoke...

A little smoke from the tailpipe in the first seconds after startup is nothing to worry about. Smoke that persists is cause for concern.

After driving awhile at highway speeds, take your foot off the accelerator for a few seconds and check the rearview mirror for exhaust smoke. Step firmly on the accelerator and look back again.

- *Black smoke* comes from partially burned fuel. This means the fuel system needs service.
- *Blue smoke* indicates burning oil—a bad sign. Clouds of blue smoke on startup may indicate worn valve guides, seals, or piston rings, which can mean a cylinder-head or engine rebuild is needed.

TECH TIP

Battery check
On maintenance-free batteries, there are no filler caps. Instead, check the color of the "eye" on the top of the battery. It should be green or blue. If the battery is weak, the eye will be black or not visible. A clear or light-yellow eye means the battery should be replaced.

- *Billowy white smoke* may indicate that coolant is getting into the combustion chambers, possibly through a cracked cylinder block or head or a blown head gasket.

It's normal when starting an engine in cold weather for condensation in the exhaust pipe to blow out as vapor.

AFTER READING

Responding
1. Do you feel more or less able to judge a used car now that you have read this selection? Explain your feelings, referring specifically to the text.

Understanding

2. a) List the eight questions you should ask when talking to a person who is selling a used car.

   b) Why shouldn't you buy a car based only on the answers to these eight questions?

3. This guide says that when buying a used car, you should (a) wear old clothes, (b) take a friend, (c) see the car in good light and dry conditions, (d) see the car on a level surface, and (e) see it when it has not been driven for at least an hour. Explain the reason for each of these rules. Compare your answers with those of a partner.

4. The writer of this guide suggests that you need sharp eyes, good hearing, and a good nose. With a partner, make a list of how you would use each of these senses when buying a used car.

5. Describe the **tone** and level of language used in this selection. (See The Reference Shelf, pages 349–351.) How do the tone and language make the reading easier or harder? Be prepared to defend your opinion in front of the class.

6. a) Describe the design elements in this selection. Explain why an editor would choose to use these design elements in an informational text such as this one.

Thinking About Language

7. Create a list of the information contained in the "Tires" section (page 86). Be sure that each point in your list is written using parallel grammatical structure.

Extending

8. Using technology where possible, design a **brochure** based on the most important information in this guide. Use a level of language and tone appropriate to a student who might be buying his or her first car. Display your brochure, highlighting the design elements you have used to increase readability and enhance understanding.

9. With a partner, study a television or print advertisement for used cars. Write an explanation of the advertisement, highlighting the techniques used to capture the interest and attention of the audience and to convince them to buy the product. (See The Reference Shelf, pages 428–429.) Present your advertisement and your explanation to the class.

10. With a partner, write a **dialogue** between a knowledgeable used car buyer and a used car dealer who is trying to sell a "less-than-perfect" car. Perform your dialogue for the class.

11. With a small group, research Lemon-Aid, a company that provides information for used-car buyers. Compare the information that the company provides with this selection.

Helping Out

"...make an impact...and gain valuable skills..."   SCOTT EDMONDS

BEFORE READING

1. As a class, make a list of volunteer jobs you or friends have held.

2. As a class, brainstorm a list of reasons why anyone would want to volunteer and work without pay.

Although looking for sea turtles and putting together chicken coops might sound like child's play, Sherene Nabatian says the activities she did while on a 10-week volunteering excursion to Guyana really made her grow up.

"I was looking for something meaningful and worthwhile to do between graduating from high school and starting university," says Nabatian, 18, who will attend the University of British Columbia in September. "Volunteering in Guyana was the perfect answer."

While Nabatian's desire to help others took her far from her home in Ottawa, it isn't the only way to make a difference. There are tons of rewarding ways to contribute your time and effort in your own community.

In 1999, it became mandatory for high school students in Ontario to complete at least 40 hours of volunteer work to graduate. In other provinces, students can get credit for volunteering their time. Some young people just want to be given the satisfaction of lending a hand to those in need.

Whatever your reasons for volunteering, you'll be able to make an impact on others and gain valuable skills at the same time.

Seventeen-year-old Nafisa Jadavji started volunteering when she was 12 and, despite having a part-time job and a heavy course load at school, she doesn't plan on stopping any time soon.

"I can't stand to stay at home and laze around," Jadavji says. "It's just kind of built in me to volunteer."

Jadavji, who lives in Calgary, has been assigned to various projects. They range from painting murals to brighten up construction sites to helping out at a day camp for physically challenged youths. Recently, while taking care of children at a women's shelter as their mothers were getting counselling, Jadavji was told by a worker that her presence was invaluable.

"Before she said that to me, I thought it was just babysitting, having fun with the kids. But when she made me realize that I was actually helping these women get a second chance at life, I thought, 'wow, I feel so amazing right now,'" she says.

Making the decision to volunteer your time is a selfless one. After all, why would you want to spend your free time doing something you're not even getting paid for?

Besides the fact that being selfless is a good thing, in the long run it will pay other dividends too, Jadavji and Nabatian both agree.

The skills you will get from applying yourself to different volunteering situations will count for a lot when you apply for a "real" job or for college or university.

It can be tough to get a job without experience, but how do you get experience without a job? That's where volunteering comes in.

When Jadavji applied for her part-time job at a Calgary public library, she brought with her a portfolio of the volunteering projects she'd been involved with.

"They were really impressed that I had already done so much," she says.

Listing all of the skills she's gained would take a long time, Jadavji says, but some of the more valuable ones include time management, organization and leadership. She has also learned about people with disabilities and addictions.

While in Guyana, Nabatian says she gained "a ton of confidence" to keep travelling and volunteering.

During her 10-week stay in the South American country—arranged through the Toronto office of Youth Challenge International—Nabatian was called on to do everything from painting schools to teaching English, and from monitoring sea turtles to building chicken coops at a women's shelter.

"To be honest, I think (the people I helped) impacted me more than I impacted them," she says. That's an important thing for youth volunteers to realize.

"I think I'm a much richer person (since volunteering in Guyana), and I think everyone I come into contact with will in some way benefit from my experience there."

WHAT'S ONLINE?

Want to learn more?
Check out these Internet sites:

Volunteer Canada
www.volunteer.ca

Charity Village
www.charityvillage.com

United Way
www.unitedway.org

Youth Volunteer Corps of Canada
www.yvcc.ca

Youth Challenge International
www.yci.org

Students Partnership Worldwide
www.spw.org

Christian Children's Fund of Canada
www.ccfcanada.ca

VOLUNTEERING ABROAD OFFERS ADVENTURE BUT IT'S NO FIVE-STAR VACATION

So you'd like to volunteer your time but you also want a little adventure? Perhaps volunteering in another country might be the perfect fit for you.

Before you decide to hop on a plane for destinations unknown, there are some things you should know.

"It definitely isn't a five-star vacation," says Susan Tabar of Youth Challenge International. "You'll definitely be roughing it and shouldn't be surprised if your accommodations might be the floor of a school house one night or a tent another night."

Potential volunteers should also be aware that the communities in greatest need are also those that are the most isolated. The closest telephone might be an hour's hike away, says Tabar. And the chances of finding an Internet cafe are about as likely as seeing Jennifer Lopez wearing a baggy track suit.

Volunteers should also be prepared to get required vaccinations and should be in tip-top shape before leaving.

Also note that some volunteering agencies get absolutely no funding. This means you might be asked to pay for part or all of your expenses.

Despite all of that, volunteering in another country is a fantastic way to learn about different cultures and to travel.

Opportunities for foreign volunteering include: community-building projects and health-care education in countries like Costa Rica, Guyana and Nicaragua; teaching English, French or computer skills at Palestinian refugee camps in Lebanon; helping people rebuild and return to normal life in post-conflict regions in eastern Europe, the Middle East and South America.

JUST THE FACTS

Value of volunteering: There are roughly 7.5 million Canadians who volunteer each year. The services they inject into the community are worth more than $16 billion a year.

Young volunteers: Youth aged 15-24 are more likely to be volunteers than Canadians in any other age group, says Statistics Canada. A national survey found the volunteer participation rate of young Canadians nearly doubled from 1987 to 1997.

Year of Volunteers: The United Nations General Assembly declared 2001 the International Year of Volunteers.

National Volunteer Week: This event was started in Canada in 1943 to honour the contributions of women during the Second World War and has since changed to include volunteers in every sector. National Volunteer Week is the third week in April.

JUST THE FACTS (CONTINUED)

I'm still not convinced about giving up my time. What's in it for me?
By volunteering you will:
- Meet new people.
- Learn valuable social skills and job skills.
- Get a chance to discover hidden talents.
- Get great experience to add to your résumé.
- Help solve community problems.
- Promote a cause you passionately believe in.
- Get the satisfaction of helping those less fortunate than you.
- Have fun.

QUESTIONS? WE GOT ANSWERS

What does it mean to volunteer?
Volunteers are regular people who donate their time and effort to help individuals, organizations and causes without getting paid. There are many opportunities for volunteers, including cleaning up the environment, working with children, visiting elderly people in nursing homes, helping out at homeless shelters and food banks, and coaching sports.

Can anyone volunteer?
Absolutely, but certain opportunities might not be for everyone. For instance, some volunteering positions might require specific skills like medical training or a teaching background. Others might have a minimum age requirement (usually for safety/liability reasons). Organizations will match you with a position that best suits your background and ability.

If I do decide to volunteer, how do I get involved?
Make a list of your interests and the kind of job you think you might like to have down the road. Then pull together a list of organizations, companies or people that might be able to use your skills and contact each of them. If you're not sure who to call, contact a volunteering organization and let them place you.

How much of my time is required?
That's mostly up to you. While some placements might require the same time commitment from you every week (like a scheduled shift), others have more of an open policy where you can just "drop in." Regardless of the time requirement, it's considered bad volunteering etiquette to commit yourself and then not show up without a phone call or a good explanation.

AFTER READING

Responding

1. In your notebook, record one argument from this **article** that most convinced you that volunteering is worthwhile.

Understanding

2. Explain how Jadavji's volunteer experiences helped her get her part-time job at the library.

3. Describe what might be contained in a job portfolio. What would be the advantage of having a job portfolio as well as a **résumé** when you go for an **interview**?

4. a) If volunteering abroad, describe the kinds of accommodations you could expect to find.

   b) In a well-written **personal essay**, write a **summary** of the pros and cons of accepting a volunteer position outside of your own country. Be sure to use an appropriate method of development to organize your essay. (See The Reference Shelf, pages 386–391.)

5. In your own words, write the author's conclusion regarding volunteerism. Explain how each of the sections of the article reinforces that conclusion.

6. Assess the effectiveness of the graphic design used to present information in this article to its audience.

Thinking About Language

7. a) With a partner, describe the **voice** of this article. Analyze how the language and sentence structures are used to create that voice. (See The Reference Shelf, pages 349–353.)

   b) In point-form notes, decide whether you like the voice and explain why or why not.

Extending

8. According to "Just the Facts," volunteerism nearly doubled between 1987 and 1997. In a small group, list the factors that would increase volunteerism. Predict whether there will be an increase or decrease in the first decade of the 21st century. (You may need to do some research to help you make your predictions.) Be prepared to present your findings and predictions to the class.

How Do You Procrastinate?

LINDA SAPADIN WITH
JACK MAGUIRE

BEFORE READING

Write or talk about a time you procrastinated (put off something you had to do) until it was too late. What were the consequences? How did you feel about not completing the task?

HOW MANY STYLES DO YOU RELATE TO?

Find yourself in this chart of the six styles of procrastination.

PROCRASTINATION TYPE	PERSONALITY TYPE	THINKING STYLE	SPEAKING STYLE	ACTING STYLE	PSYCHOLOGICAL NEED FOR
Perfectionist	Critical	All-or-nothing	I should I have to	Flawless	Control
Dreamer	Fanciful	Vague	I wish	Passive	Being Special
Worrier	Fearful	Indecisive	What if?	Cautious	Security
Defier	Resistant	Oppositional	Why should I?	Rebellious	Non-Conformity
Crisis-Maker	Over-Emotional	Agitated	Extremes... "Unbelievable"	Dramatic	Attention
Overdoer	Busy	Compelled	Can't say "no"	Do-it-all	Self-Reliance

"It drives me crazy!" Andy cried. For six years, he had been an assistant manager for an insurance firm, and most of that time he had yearned for a better job. When he first consulted me for psychotherapy, he agonized over his career misfortunes: "I never seem to get a break, and I can't understand why. It makes me furious sometimes, just thinking about it!"

Soon afterward, Andy's company offered to send him to executive development seminars, and he was very pleased. "This could be my way out of a dead-end job!" he confided. I waited for weeks to hear more about the seminars, but he didn't mention them. Finally, I brought up the subject myself. He shrugged and said, "Oh, them! I went for a while, but I didn't have the time to keep up with all the reading. Then, with one thing and another, I started missing some classes. Before long, I'd fallen too far behind to go back."

Maureen, an emergency room nurse, had only recently begun to tire of her job when she became my client. "I'm burned out," she declared. "I want to do something different, something more stimulating for my mind and less hectic for my body."

Following through with her idea, Maureen started researching job opportunities in medical publications. She pressed for any interview she could get and eventually spoke to every hospital administrator in the city. Time after time, her applications were rejected. "It gets to me every now and then," she admitted to me, "but I'm going to keep on keeping on. All that counts is that first 'yes,' and I've got to believe it will happen." It took several months of steady effort, but it did happen.

Today, she's a pediatric nurse in a first-class teaching hospital, and she loves the work.

Both Andy and Maureen had the same basic goal—to get a better job—but one failed, while the other succeeded. What made the critical difference? Andy suffers from a lifelong habit of procrastination. Maureen does not.

Despite Andy's sincere intention to improve his career, he was unable to perform accordingly. He even acted against his own best interests: giving up too soon rather than sticking with the seminars that seemed almost certain to open up new opportunities for him. It was not sheer laziness that sabotaged his dream, nor was it simply a weak will or negative thinking. Instead, it was a firmly entrenched predisposition to procrastinate, featuring its own complicated mixture of self-defeating habits and attitudes. Fortunately, Maureen doesn't have such a chronic predisposition. In pursuing her dream of a better job, she was able to maintain a strong connection between what she wanted to do and what she actually did.

Of course, everybody procrastinates occasionally. An unusually messy closet gets cursed for months without ever being cleaned, or the task of writing an especially difficult letter is put off until the last possible minute. For many people, however, procrastination is chronic, pervasive, and deeply rooted. Because of how, as children, they were conditioned to think, speak, and behave, these individuals have a built-in tendency not only to procrastinate whenever they face a challenging situation but also to do so consistently, in the same way. They don't understand why they do this, and as a result, they're terribly frustrated.

So are their family members, friends, and coworkers!

How serious is *your* procrastination problem? To get an idea, ask yourself each of the following questions, circling "yes" if you *often* do what's described, and "no" if you *rarely or never* do it:

Do I put off taking care of important things that jeopardize my relationships, career, finances, or health?	YES NO
Do I put off doing what I need to do until a crisis develops?	YES NO
Do I put off doing tasks unless I can do them perfectly, or until I can find the perfect time to do them?	YES NO
Do I hesitate taking action that needs to be taken because I fear change?	YES NO
Do I think too much about things I'd like to do but rarely get around to doing?	YES NO
Do I think I am special and don't need to do all the things that other people need to do?	YES NO
Do I commit myself to so many things that I can't find time for many of them?	YES NO
Do I tend to do only what I *want* to do instead of what I *should* do?	YES NO
Do I tend to do only what I think I should do instead of what I want to do?	YES NO

If you answered "yes" to *any* of these questions, you have a procrastination problem. The more questions you answered affirmatively the more you will relate to several of the procrastination styles described in this book.

Fortunately, you *can* solve your problem, no matter how long you've suffered from it or how hopelessly trapped you may feel.

THE SIX STYLES OF PROCRASTINATION

The first step toward positive change is to develop a better understanding of procrastination as a complex *pattern* of living, rather than just a collection of bad habits. Essentially, procrastination is caused by an internal conflict: You feel a want or a need to do something, but you also feel resistant toward doing it. Usually, the two feelings are so evenly matched that you experience a halt in your natural flow of energy until, eventually, the conflict is somehow resolved — often in a way that's not at all satisfying.

In effect, this blockage of energy functions as an approach–avoidance conflict: Like a Hamlet in the world of action, you're torn between two impulses — "to do" or "not to do." Temporarily, at least, you're torn by ambivalence, incapable of making a clear choice or commitment one way or the other. Maybe you actually start doing what you want or need to do, even though your lingering resistance makes you waste a lot of time and energy as you go along. Or maybe you stay stuck in your conflict until the last possible moment, when you finally plunge into doing what you want or need to do (probably with a strong push from someone — or something — else). If so, the task may not get done on time, and if it is, most likely it won't be done nearly as well as it could have been with an earlier start. Or maybe you won't do it at all. You'll stay halted at your sticking point: your flow of energy dammed and, ultimately, damning you to yet another failure.

Far from being lazy, as the stereotype would have it, chronic procrastinators generally have sufficient energy—it just doesn't flow smoothly from mental preparation to physical execution. Instead, it remains mostly mental. Some procrastinators simply can't get beyond the planning stage of a project. They keep elaborating or revising their plans, or generating alternative plans, far beyond the real need to do so. Others preoccupy themselves with wishful thinking: "If only [fill in the blank] happens, I won't have to worry about [fill in the blank]." All get caught up to some degree in the rationalize-regret-and-obsess syndrome we've already observed.

What each chronic procrastinator needs to cultivate is a more natural, more fluid transition from mental activity to physical activity, so that an appropriate amount of time and energy gets allotted to each phase. To do this, the procrastinator first needs to understand the inner conflicts that produced the procrastination pattern. Without that knowledge, the predisposition to procrastinate will sabotage any efforts the individual makes to change, no matter how earnest those efforts may be. It's a situation familiar to that faced by many people who try to diet and lose weight without really understanding the inner conflicts that lead them to overeat: Until they learn more about the origins of their eating pattern, their problem will not go away.

I call the sticking point in this kind of internal conflict the *BUT* factor, because the chronic procrastinators I've counseled frequently use the word "but" in describing their action:

"I'd like to finish what I'm doing, *BUT* I want it to be perfect!"

"I'd like to start doing it, *BUT* I hate all those bothersome details!"

"I could do it, *BUT* I'm afraid to change!"

"I could do it, *BUT* why should I have to do it?"

"I'd do it now, *BUT* I only get motivated at the last minute!"

"I'd do it now, *BUT* I have so much to do!"

In my thirty years as a psychologist in schools and in private practice, I have helped hundreds of people from all walks of life overcome their chronic procrastination. Based upon my experiences as a clinician, I have identified six fundamental procrastination styles, which relate to the six major *BUT* factors:

1. **The Perfectionist: "...BUT I want it to be perfect!"** Perfectionists can be reluctant to start—or finish—a task because they don't want to do anything less than a perfect job. Although their primary concern is not to fall short of their own lofty standards, they also worry about failing the high expectations that they believe (rightly or wrongly) other people have of them. Unfortunately, once they've begun a task, they often can't resist spending far more time and energy on it than is required—a commonly unacknowledged or misunderstood form of procrastination that involves delaying the completion of a task by *over*-working.

2. **The Dreamer: "...BUT I hate all those bothersome details!"** The dreamer wants life to be easy and pleasant. Difficult challenges that

confront the dreamer can automatically provoke resistance: "That might be hard to do" gets translated into "I can't do it." Dreamers are very skillful in developing—and, usually, promoting—grandiose ideas, but they seem incapable of turning their sketchy ideas into full-blown realities: a pattern that frustrates themselves as well as the people around them. Uncomfortable with the practical world, they tend to retreat into fantasies: "Maybe I'll get a lucky break," or "I'm a special person—I don't have to do things the typical [i.e., hardworking] way."

3. **The Worrier: "...BUT I'm afraid to change!"** Worrier procrastinators have an excessive need for security, which causes them to fear risk. They proceed too timidly through life, worrying incessantly about the "what ifs." Faced with a new situation or demand, they become especially anxious, because anything new involves change and, therefore, unknown and potentially undesirable consequences. Thus, they tend to put off making decisions, or following through on decisions, as long as they can. Once they start working on a project, they're likely to drag it out in an effort to help "soften the blow." Many times, consciously or unconsciously, they avoid finishing projects altogether, so that they never have to leave the "comfort zone" of the familiar and move on to new territory. Much to their own dismay and frustration, they resist change even when they know, intellectually, that the change

is almost certain to improve their life situation.

4. **The Defier: "...BUT why should I have to do it?"** The defier is a rebel, seeking to buck the rules. Some defiers are openly proud of their tendency to procrastinate, precisely because it goes against the "normal" or "logical" way to do things. By procrastinating, they are setting their own schedule—one that nobody else can predict or control. In other words, they are establishing their individuality, against the expectations of others. Other defiers are more subtle, perhaps because they are less consciously aware of what they are doing. They don't flaunt their opposition toward doing something. They simply don't take on the responsibility to do it in a timely manner. This more subtle type of defiance is called "passive–aggressive" behaviour. Both kinds of defier procrastinators are inclined to see relatively simple tasks—like doing the laundry, paying the bills, or maintaining the car—as big impositions on their time and energy, rather than as things they should take in stride as mature adults.

5. **The Crisis-Maker: "...BUT I only get motivated at the last minute!"** The crisis-maker needs to live on the edge. Addicted to the adrenaline rush of intense emotion, constant challenge, and emergency action, crisis-makers delight in pulling things off at the last minute. To them, procrastination is a form of adventure. Adventures, however, are by nature risky, and the

crisis-maker procrastinator is often a loser. Despite the heroic, last-minute run, the train is missed. Despite working day and night all weekend, the status report doesn't get completed by Monday. Despite a year-long intention to spend July in Europe, the flight isn't booked on time and the deadline for a reduced fare passes quietly by, too quietly for the crisis-maker to notice.

6. **The Overdoer: "...BUT I have so much to do!"** Overdoer procrastinators say "yes" to too much because they are unable—or unwilling—to make choices and establish priorities. In other words, they haven't really mastered the art of decision-making. Because of this liability, they tend to be inefficient in managing time, organizing resources, and resolving conflicts. The result is that they try to do too much and, inevitably, fail. Overdoers are often hard workers, and many of them do accomplish some things very well; however, other things never get done at all, or else get done poorly or late. With so much to do and so little time to do it in, overdoers are prime candidates for early burnout.

Each of these six procrastination styles—the perfectionist, the dreamer, the worrier, the defier, the crisis-maker, and the overdoer—involves a distinctly differ-

ent pattern of impeding the productive flow of energy. But rarely does a flesh-and-blood procrastinator display only *one* of these styles. Instead, each person employs a distinctive *mix* of styles: perhaps two or three styles that are most operative—the major styles—along with two or three that are displayed less often but are still reasonably active—the minor styles.

For example, a person initially identified as a perfectionist procrastinator may also have a dreamer inside, who, among other activities, delights in imagining "perfect" life situations. As a result, sometimes the person's procrastination style is recognizably that of a perfectionist; other times, that of a dreamer. Within this same person, there may also be a bit of the crisis-maker, who performs best under pressure.

In fact, chronic procrastinators tend to harbor several—or even all—of the six procrastination styles to some degree, with different kinds of life situations triggering different kinds of styles. For example, a woman may identify herself as primarily a crisis-maker procrastinator—especially at work, where she has plenty of opportunities to find, or engineer, emergency situations. Nevertheless, with a little more self-analysis, she may realize that she procrastinates somewhat differently in other areas of her life. When it comes to fulfilling her innermost desires, she may function more like a dreamer procrastinator. And with her husband, the strongest relationship in her life, she may adopt a defier style.

AFTER READING

Responding

1. In your **journal**, write about what you learned about your procrastinating styles from reading this excerpt.

Understanding

2. Based on information in the selection, make a chart, listing the six procrastination patterns in the first column and one key characteristic of each in the second column. Compare your chart with that of a classmate.

3. Examine the chart of procrastinating styles on page 99. Write a note on how the graphic artist has effectively designed the page so it
   • is interesting to look at
   • makes it easy to find specific information

4. The name of the book that includes this excerpt is called *It's About Time*. Explain why this is a good title for a book about procrastination.

Thinking About Language

5. Look up the meanings of the following words and add them to your personal word list: ambivalence, sabotage, incessantly, impeding, insidious. Write a sentence for each word that shows you understand its meaning.

6. Create a chart like the one below for the four sentences in the first paragraph of the section called "The Six Styles of Procrastination."

SENTENCE #	# OF WORDS	SENTENCE TYPE	SENTENCE ORDER

Extending

7. Read at least two other kinds of publications (e.g., **articles** or **reports**) on procrastination. Take notes on the information in each publication, being sure to document the sources for each. Evaluate which publication of the three you have read has the best information on procrastination and explain the reasons for your choice.
   • How has the designer made the book look interesting and inviting?
   • Would you keep reading this book on your own time? Why or why not?

Everyone Can't Be a Superstar

MINDY BINGHAM,
JUDY EDMONDSON, AND
SANDY STRYKER

"For every superstar, there are dozens of
people on the sidelines."

BEFORE READING

Write a paragraph explaining how information about a famous person or someone who is an expert
at what they do has caused you to consider a job or career that you might otherwise never have
considered.

Considering all the things you know about
yourself, what are two careers you think
you might like? Be sure to consider all the
alternatives. For example, it's easy to think
of well-known glamour jobs, and jobs that
have great appeal. You might think it
would be fun to be a star like Shania
Twain. Unfortunately, those jobs are rare.
However, if you look beyond the obvious,

there are thousands and thousands of different jobs. For every superstar, there are
dozens of people on the sidelines. The others may not get their pictures in the paper
all the time, but they do take part in all the
excitement, meet important people, travel
and make a living at it. Perhaps you've
never thought about all the "behind the
scenes" jobs. Here are just a few of them,

to get you started. Put on your thinking cap and see if you can come up with others and put them on the blank lines. Maybe one of them is *the* job for you.

Behind every television star there's a:

Make-up artist	Hairdresser
Personal secretary	Stunt person
Photographer	Answering service
Wardrobe consultant	Manager
Accountant	Agent
Writer	Caterer

Every brain surgeon needs a:

General physician	Dietician
Physical therapist	Anesthetist
Pharmacist	Speech pathologist
Hospital administrator	Secretary
Occupational therapist	Head nurse
X-ray technician	Counselor

A movie director can't operate without a:

Camera operator	Stage hand
Props director	Light technician
Producer	Publicity agent
Set director	Music director
Electrician	Film editor
Cinematographer	Special effects designer

Professional athletes work with a:

Coach	Agent
Statistician	Equipment manager
Sportscaster	Photographer
Doctor	Referee/umpire
Sportswriter	Physical therapist
Scoreboard operator	Time keeper

If you can't be a rock musician, maybe you can be a:

Disc jockey	Sound editor
Concert co-ordinator	Recording technician
Record producer	Lighting director
Piano tuner	Song writer
Costume designer	Album cover designer
Cutting designer	Dancer

The Prime Minister of Canada has at least one:

Advisor	Chauffeur
RCMP officer	Personal assistant
Pilot	Parliament Hill tour guide
Speech writer	Chef
Campaign manager	Security guard
Administrative assistant	Fund raiser

The Chief Executive Officer of a major oil corporation is backed by a:

Corporate planner	Lobbyist
Computer programmer	Accountant
Geologist	Data entry operator
Lawyer	Petroleum engineer
Financial analyst	Marketing manager
Publicity director	Researcher

What would you like to do? List two choices. They might be in fields you've been thinking about for a long time, or they could be jobs that have occurred to you since you started doing these exercises. You don't have to know a lot about them. That's the purpose of this exercise. *Let your imagination soar here.*

Choose *one more* job from the following list. These are non-traditional careers that men often overlook even though they can be very rewarding.

Nursery school teacher	Nurse
Fashion designer	Interior decorator
Secretary	Caterer
Telephone operator	Cruise director
Social worker	Flight attendant
Tailor	Dental hygienist
Hair stylist	Elementary school teacher
Piano teacher	Dancer
Marriage counselor	Travel agent
Sales clerk	

These are non-traditional careers that women often overlook:

Firefighter	Personal trainer
Mechanic	Carpenter
Sports reporter	News anchor
Police officer	Welder
Construction worker	Plumber
Bank manager	Hockey coach
Basketball coach	Detective
Pilot	Army personnel
Electrician	Music conductor
Movie director	Photographer

AFTER READING

Responding

1. Identify three or four jobs listed in this selection about which you would like more information.

Understanding

2. a) For the jobs you identified in activity 1, research the nature of the work done, the knowledge, skills, and education required, the pay scales, and the current and long-term projections for job opportunities.

   b) As a class, create a template for recording the information about each job.

   c) Place the information you have gathered on specific jobs into the template.

   d) As a class, create a bulletin board display about the jobs researched by members of the class.

Thinking About Language

3. Explain why "the" is in italics in the last sentence of the introductory paragraph of this selection (page 107).

Extending

4. a) With a partner of the opposite sex, brainstorm a list of occupations that traditionally have been dominated by members of one gender in particular. Using print and/or electronic sources, prepare a research **report** on why one of the occupations became gender-related, whether more members of the other sex are choosing the occupation now, and whether more members of the other sex should be considering the occupation.

  b) Try to present your report using interesting **layout**, headings for organizing the information, and other visual elements (e.g., charts and graphs) that will appeal to your audience.

  c) Include a correctly formatted bibliography of all the sources that you use. (See The Reference Shelf, pages 378–379.)

5. a) Conduct an **interview** with someone who has a job that interests you. Ask for the interview in a polite manner and thank the interviewee in writing for granting the interview. Prepare your questions in advance. Plan the order you will ask your questions. At the interview, don't press for answers that the interviewee is reluctant or doesn't want to answer. If you are going to tape the interview, ask for permission first. Be polite.

  b) With the information that you collected from the interview, prepare it in either an interview or a written report format.

6. a) Prepare a business plan for creating your own business, related to a career that interests you.

  b) Present your plan to a group of your classmates who will provide you with feedback on the soundness and viability of your plan.

Rookie Errors Close Hiring Doors

"Some made rookie mistakes, dressing too casually or showing up empty-headed and empty-handed."

KENNEDY PIRES

BEFORE **READING**

As a class, discuss the following questions: What is a job fair? What is its purpose? Who holds job fairs? How can you find out about a job fair?

Each spring brings high anxiety for a new wave of graduating students at Ontario's 25 community colleges. It's crunch time, as they try to find their place in the job market and take the first step towards a long and hopefully satisfying career.

Typically the colleges play matchmaker, organizing job fairs that bring together companies with targeted needs and students looking for a foothold.

Earlier this year [2001], about 1000 students turned out when Centennial College held a career fair for its business and technology majors at the Progress campus in Scarborough, Ontario.

There to greet them were recruiters at 59 booths, including such blue-chip entities as IBM, Amex Canada and Celestica. The turnout on both sides was such that, at the last minute, the event was switched to the campus gym.

On the big day, students milled about on the blue plastic tarp protecting the gym floor. Some toured in boisterous groups of three or four, eagerly approaching recruiters arrayed under cardboard posters bearing their company logos. Others quietly surveyed booths from a distance while glancing down at the floor plan provided at the door.

There was a flea-market buzz in the air as recruiters talked shop with applicants, rustled papers and tendered business cards. People assembled on the gym's balcony to take in the action.

By the end of the day, when the last handshakes had been made, recruiters interviewed had three words of advice for the crush of young job seekers—be better prepared.

For every student with a confident smile and a polished résumé at the ready, there were others who seemed confused about what to say to employers, or even which booths to approach. Some made rookie mistakes, dressing too casually or showing up empty-headed and empty-handed.

Tayo Alliu, a store manager for Reitman's, said many students she met seemed unaware that "selling themselves" was part of landing a job.

Her clothing chain was looking for business majors with some retail sales experience. Alliu said there was no set number of positions to fill. Her team took in about 50 résumés and intended to interview probably half that many applicants.

Many of the others, Alliu said, had inflated hopes and were unwilling to consider entry-level positions.

"You have to be flexible, ask what we have available," she said. "Don't come in with a preset mind, and don't ask for a salary range."

Alliu said people succeed at Reitman's by starting low and "easing" up the management ladder. She was impressed by students who had a grasp of that fact, and who had the sense to open up a dialogue with her, ask questions about the company and pay attention to the replies.

How do you stand out in a crowd of job seekers?

"Don't be a floater," she said. "We want people who care, not people who don't know what they want."

"It's good to start low, because we tend to hire internally for the high-level positions," agreed another recruiter, Walter Craib of Scotiabank. The bank was there to hire as many as 20 graduates to work phones at its electronic banking call centres.

Craib listed excellent interpersonal skills, adaptability and Internet know-how as qualities he was looking for.

In recent months, about 80 per cent of applicants hired for Scotiabank's Toronto call centre submitted their résumés online, he said. "We encourage this. A lot of companies are. Using e-mail is our first indication that (an applicant) is Web-savvy."

Even so, Craib believes in the importance of job fairs, because recruiters get a chance to meet applicants in person and gauge their ability to communicate with others.

He suggested a common-sense rule for preparing a résumé. Make sure it's error-free and neat. Sloppy résumés with key-boarding mistakes are typically passed over, he said, pointing to the two stacks of applications accumulated on his table.

Actually, it seems there's an even more basic rule: Make sure you *have* a résumé. Nichole Harrison, a human resources officer at State Farm Insurance, estimated 25 per cent of students she met at the fair didn't bother to bring one.

It also bugged her that many students approaching her table hadn't done any research on her company. "You would be surprised how many ask me what we do," she said. "Look at the sign — we sell insurance."

Like the other recruiters, Harrison said she was encountering unreasonably high job expectations. "Some just want to get their foot in the door," she said. "But somebody here actually asked if we had an executive position available."

In the scrum of a busy job fair, recruiters say, an applicant should consider his or her first encounter with an employer to be an important event — a pre-interview of sorts. As such, the standard rules of conduct should be considered and taken seriously. Dress professionally, be confident and introduce yourself with a firm handshake.

"Some students seem to think they're just dropping off their résumé and they'll worry about an interview later," Harrison said.

Wrong. "This is the first impression you're making," she said. "I decide now which people I want to talk to later."

Making good eye contact and clearly stating your objectives are two ways to impress recruiters, said Scott Timpson of SynreVoice Technologies, a Markham software firm that sells administrative packages to schools.

Timpson, a sales and marketing director, said he had his eye out for students who had questions of their own to ask, to demonstrate they hadn't come to his booth by chance.

"Don't blindly hand in your résumé or dump it on the table," said Timpson. "Interview the interviewer."

Bill Eisan, a technical sales representative for Cowper Inc., echoed that sentiment. He said many in the gym were not prepared for meaningful conversation about a job. "They don't want to know who you are or what you're about," he said. "They're giving out their résumé as they're flying by."

His team was after a couple of students to fill junior sales jobs at Cowper, which is a distributor of fluid power products. But

Eisan was disappointed by the way applicants were dressed. While he didn't necessarily expect suits and ties, the sight of baggy jeans, bomber jackets and sports wear clearly didn't impress him.

"If we were here hiring maintenance people, that's one thing," he said.

It's not like the staff and faculty at Centennial College didn't see these problems coming.

Well in advance of its two job fairs, the college staged open-invitation seminars for its student body, designed to get job seekers primed and ready to knock the socks off employers. Topics included dress guidelines, which questions to ask (and not ask) a recruiter, how to research a company before the first contact and how to follow up afterwards.

Just about all the aspects, in other words, that the job-fair recruiters later found lacking.

So what happened? No one showed up for the seminars, said Linda Lugli, a student employment advisor at Centennial.

"We only got about 20 people each time," she said.

Many students find it difficult to squeeze in such an event while juggling courseloads and part-time jobs, she said. "We definitely need to do more to prepare students for (meeting) an employer," she said.

AFTER READING

Responding

1. a) With a partner, brainstorm a list of reasons why many young job seekers have "unreasonably high job expectations."
   b) Make another list of reasons why prospective employers expect young new employees to consider "entry-level positions."
   c) Prepare a **report** to the class explaining which group's expectations are the most valid.

Understanding

2. List four common errors the college students made at the job fair, according to the recruiters. Compare your list with that of a partner and add any points you missed.

3. Using information in this **article** and your own ideas, make a list of advice or instructions for a young person planning to attend a job or career fair.

Thinking About Language

4. In this article, some numbers are written in Arabic numerals (20, 80) and others as words (two, three). With a partner, look for the pattern. Check any pattern you find against other reading selections in this textbook. Consult a style sheet to find if there are rules covering the proper way to present numbers as part of a written text.

Extending

5. Bring your current **résumé** to class. Using the suggestions in The Reference Shelf (pages 410–412), revise your résumé, giving it a content and presentation that would make recruiters take a second look at it.

6. a) In a small group, create a plan for a job fair. Be sure to include the types of jobs you would like to see represented.
   b) Select a spokesperson to present your group's plan. At the end of the presentations, vote for the best plan to be presented to the principal or the Guidance Department as a suggestion for future action.

7. a) Choose and research one company, as you would in preparation for a job **interview**. Prepare an oral report on the company for the class. With a partner, rehearse your report to get feedback on content, organization, and visual presentation. Remember to use correct language (both Standard Canadian English and technical language). Plan to have your presentation videotaped for later review.
   b) As a class, create a feedback form to assess the presentations. Include feedback on the content, presentation manner, organization, and use of visual aids or technology. (See The Reference Shelf, page 404.)
   c) Review the feedback sheets and the videotape of your presentation and update your Oral Communication Skills Action Plan. (See The Reference Shelf, page 395.)

Opening Doors

"The list of hidden barriers for anyone with a disability is long..."

JOHANNA WEIDNER

BEFORE READING

In a small group, discuss the following questions:

- What difficulties do disabled persons with good job skills face when applying for a job?
- Is your community doing enough to help persons with disabilities become employed participants in society?

Be prepared to present the ideas discussed in your group to the class.

[Waterloo, Ontario's] Peter Hulme is hunting for a job, but he's not going to circle just any ad in the classified section.

Hulme, who is a quadriplegic because of a spinal tumour that developed when he was a child, has to be picky because he can't do many of the basic tasks listed in job descriptions.

"(With) my level of disability, even pushing paper is a concern. I can't file," said Hulme, who recently finished a year-long position with the Independent Living Centre, his first job since graduating with a B.A. four years ago.

And even if he has the required skills, Hulme, 31, also has to read between the lines to determine if he's able to do a job.

The list of hidden barriers for anyone with a disability is long: transportation to the office, work place accessibility, whether an employer will accommodate his special needs and whether he would require an attendant or help in the office.

After he's narrowed the choices, then comes the hard part: convincing an employer he can do the job.

"You have to be aggressive and go out there and break down the barriers," said [Kitchener, Ontario's] Wayne Tuttle.

Tuttle, who is legally blind with minimal vision in his left eye, said people with disabilities have to combat a lot of negative attitudes during a job search.

He's looking for work after being laid off from his job as a sales marketing manager for an area security system dealer. Before that job, Tuttle worked in a Rogers Cable call centre for a decade.

"Employers today, they still have the ignorance factor of what people are capable of doing," said Tuttle, 46.

During an interview for a managerial position in a call centre, he said the interviewer told him, "You know, Wayne, quite frankly I have no idea how you'd do this job."

This is when a disabled person needs to flex his powers of persuasion, Tuttle said, and explain how he plans to do the job.

Yves Bergeron, an employment counsellor for the Canadian National Institute for the Blind, agrees that the key to success is demonstrating a person's abilities, which are independent of any disabilities.

"Employers have certain jobs that need to be done," Bergeron said. "I think that any barriers and fears are overcome when the person comes to them with a skill set."

Bergeron, who helped more than 20 visually impaired people find work last year, said it's often easy to break down the barriers simply by meeting with the employers and tackling any worries head on.

For a blind person, this means something as simple as explaining to a potential employer that all he needs is a tour of the building and then he'll be able to move around the office on his own.

Technology is by far the most important tool to open the world of work for people with disabilities.

"Technology now makes things much more even as far as the playing field goes," said Hulme, who deftly operates his computer by punching on a tiny key pad with his tongue and scrolling a track ball with his chin.

BACKGROUND

- One in eight Canadians aged 15 to 64 reported a disability in 1991, the latest figures available from Statistics Canada.

- Disability is defined as difficulties performing routine tasks of daily living due to a long-term physical, mental or health condition.

- Of 2.3 million disabled Canadians, nearly half were employed, compared to almost 75 per cent of people without a disability.

- About 44 per cent of people with disabilities are not working or looking for work, more than double the number of able-bodied Canadians not in the labour force.

STARTING A BUSINESS

For people with disabilities, a new course shows how to be their own boss. The program, launched in March and free for anyone with a physical disability, teaches people how to research a market, create a business plan and prepare a presentation to possible financial backers. After getting a business up and running, participants also get free business coaching for almost a year.

Program manager Ron Grant of K-W Access-Ability, one of the groups running the program, said being self-employed offers new working opportunities for people who may be unable to work in an office. "The limit is what they want to make it," Grant said.

Tuttle can go into any office and start working in minutes with the help of high-tech gadgets such as a type and speak (basically a laptop computer without a screen that reads commands and typing aloud) and special programs that let him hear what's on the screen.

With all these accessibility devices available, most of which are at least partially paid for by the ministries of health or community and social services, Tuttle said there's virtually no limit to job possibilities.

It's a matter of finding the right job for an individual—and the right person for the job.

"It has to be a fit on both sides," Tuttle said simply.

His advice to employers and people with disabilities, "Don't be afraid to take a chance."

AFTER READING

Responding

1. Explain whether the information in this **article** and the way it is presented would encourage an employer to "take a chance" and hire a person with a disability.

Understanding

2. a) With a partner, compare the list of barriers to employment for the disabled people presented in this article with the points that came up in the group and class discussion in the "Before Reading" activity.

   b) Assess the level of awareness the class had about the issue before reading this selection.

   c) Brainstorm reasons for the level of awareness that you identify.

3. With a partner, plan an alternative **layout** of the information in this article for publication. Explain how your layout and use of graphic elements would improve the presentation of the information.

Thinking About Language

4. This article contains many short paragraphs. With a partner, select two places where paragraphs could be combined and still act as unified, well-constructed paragraphs. Consider why the writer originally chose to have so many paragraphs. Be prepared to present your ideas to the class.

Extending

5. The **bias** against people with disabilities has been called "ableism" by some. As a class, discuss possible reasons for this bias and how it compares to other forms of bias or prejudice such as sexism, racism, and ageism.

6. a) Use information from this article to create a radio or television commercial encouraging employers to hire people with disabilities. Consider using a slogan like "When you hire a person with disabilities to work for your company, we all win."

   b) Rehearse and present your commercial (either taped or live) to the class, who will provide you with feedback. Using their feedback, update your Oral Communication Skills Action Plan as necessary. (See The Reference Shelf, page 395.)

7. With a partner, discuss how technology assists people with disabilities to participate more fully in society and the workplace. Using print and/or electronic sources, research a particular disability to find out how recent advances in technology are providing even more assistance. Be prepared to share your findings with the class.

Beware of Illegal Questions in Employment Interviews

"...illegal questions can result in discrimination against anyone."

BARBARA SIMMONS

1. As a class, create a list of questions that would make you uncomfortable in an **interview**. When you have finished reading this **article**, note how many of these questions are illegal.

2. Using the Internet, look up the Web site for the Ontario Human Rights Commission. What kinds of information can you find there?

Sher Singh was optimistic the morning of his very first job interview in Canada. But his hopefulness plummeted when his interviewer asked him, "Where exactly is that accent from?" and "What religion do you people practice?"

Singh had serious misgivings about answering these illegal questions, but he had no idea how to handle the situation appropriately.

All newcomers are vulnerable targets and illegal questions can result in discrimination against anyone. Imagine being asked: Do you have any disabilities or health problems? With whom do you live? Are you married? Do you plan to have children? How old are you?

Did you know that all these questions fall into the prohibited areas of inquiry (disabilities, sexual orientation, marital/family status and age), based on the Ontario Human Rights Code?

Francois Larsen, manager of communication and public education for the Ontario Human Rights Commission (OHRC), says the code applies to full, part-time and contract work, work done by temporary staff from agencies and may include volunteer work.

Human rights guidelines for employment interview questions are clear: Applicants for employment may be asked to divulge only information which has relevance to the position applied for. Employers, by law, must focus on gathering relevant information in order to decide if the applicant is able to perform the functions of the position.

Some employers erroneously believe that they have a right to ask any question they choose since they are paying the salary. Others are simply awkward in their technique and a question comes out as unlawful. However, human rights law does not distinguish between the interviewer who is asking questions with the intent to discriminate and the one who is just curious or inept at interviewing.

Anne Charette, president of the Human Resources Professional Association of Ontario, reminds interviewers: "No employer today can plead ignorance of the law when it comes to knowing what are legal or illegal interview questions. The government has done a very good job in providing the proper information for us all."

Career counsellor Roni Chaleff helps work searchers at Times Change Women's Employment Service in Toronto prepare

approaches to address the question and the questioner. Chaleff's suggestions include:
- "You can answer the question. It is your choice to do so. But be aware that you might be offering information that could be used against you."

- "You are justified in telling the interviewer, 'The question is illegal (or not appropriate) and I prefer not to answer it. Could we move on to the next question, please?' But your refusal to answer might create a negative impression and lead to your not being hired."

- "If you know the question is unlawful, or if you have difficulty in understanding the intent of the question, you could ask for clarification. Put the onus on the interviewer to reword the question properly to relate to the position, by saying diplomatically, 'Could you tell me please how this is relevant to the work I'd be doing? I'm trying to get a handle on what you mean.'" To say this effectively, a nonconfrontational tone is important.

Another approach is to try to determine the hidden worry or information the interviewer is trying to illicit, then respond with an answer that addresses it. For example, the illegal question many women get, "Do you have children?" falls under the human rights category of marital/family status.

A confident answer, if true, might be, "I understand my work will require some travel and I'm excited that this position offers such a variety of opportunity."

Pre-interview preparation is key to handling illegal questions. Start by anticipating any objections to hiring you. Develop your strategies to handle the objections. Anticipate possible areas of illegal questioning and the direct or indirect questions you might be asked. Practice your answers.

Pay close attention to the tone of the interview. Are you feeling uncomfortable? Did your interviewer lob several illegal or inappropriate questions or only one that you might choose to ignore? Aim for overcoming your discomfort or anger by focusing on your skills and abilities.

Are code phrases or questions used such as, "How do you handle criticism from someone younger than yourself?" Does your response help you to market yourself well and still address the interviewer's worry?

Keep in mind that the vast majority of employers strive to hire the most qualified staff and do so fairly. For employers who don't play by the rules, remember that assistance is as close as your nearest Ontario Human Rights Commission office. Contact them. To access the complaint procedure, visit the OHRC Web site at *http://www.ohrc.on.ca*.

AFTER READING

Responding

1. Explain the illustration accompanying this article. Write a short opinion paragraph about whether the illustration is effective for the article.

Understanding

2. **Paraphrase** and explain the Ontario Human Rights guidelines for interview questions.
3. Write out the contact information for two places where you could get more information about illegal interview questions.
4. According to Francois Larsen, who may be covered by the Ontario Human Rights Code? Why is this an important piece of information to know, especially for high school students?
5. a) As a class, discuss the suggested ways to handle illegal interview questions and how you can use them confidently. Add some suggestions of your own.
   b) **Roleplay** some of these situations with a partner so that you will become comfortable dealing with the questions.

Thinking About Language

6. With a partner, look at the paragraph starting "Are code phrases..." (page 120). From the **context** of the article and this paragraph, as well as your personal knowledge and experience, define "code phrases or questions." Compare your **definition** with another pair and then with the class.

Extending

7. In a small group, choose a job that you might be interested in. Make up some questions, both direct and "coded," that might be asked at the interview. Take turns roleplaying the interview, using some of the suggestions provided in the article to handle illegal or coded questions, and practising the correct body language and tone of voice.
8. Study the graphic elements (excluding the illustration) that the designer has used, and show how these elements make the article interesting and easy to read.

9. Write a research **report** on how to lodge a complaint through the Ontario Human Rights Commission. Create this report on a computer, using various graphic elements to increase the readability of your report. Have a partner edit your work for content, organization, and **layout**.
   Or
   With a partner, create a short video on how to lodge a complaint through the Ontario Human Rights Commission. The intended audience of your video should be other students your age.

25 Things Your Boss Wants You to Know

"...be aware of these guidelines."

SHIRLEY SLOAN FADER

BEFORE READING

As a class, list the fears that you might have about starting a new job.

When you report to work those first days and weeks of your new job, your boss doubtless will mention the visible, mechanical portions of your responsibilities. She or he probably will say almost nothing about the crucial, invisible parts. You'll be told about hours, meetings, reports, general performance goals. Beyond vague clichés like "We all work together as a team," who will tell you what attitudes and behaviour separate the also-rans from those who win promotions?

Usually no one. You are supposed to be aware of these guidelines. It is essential because, although no one will educate you in the Dos and Don'ts, people will notice when you violate unspoken performance expectations. Then your superiors' private reaction will be, "She ought to know better" and "She doesn't have what it takes."

Beyond our basic 25 expectations, your boss may have additional, personal behaviour expectations for you. Listen and watch. Soon you'll recognize your boss's

pet behaviour criteria. Some bosses, for example, value an employee only if she comes early and stays late. Other bosses interpret such long work hours as incompetence—an inability to complete your work in the allotted time. These are variations you have to search out about your individual supervisor. Add your boss's expectations to the 25 below and you'll be well along to standing out as a valued performer. If you're the boss, you can help your staff members do the best job possible by informing them of these business axioms.

1. **Forget about excuses.** With rare exceptions, such as a true life-and-death crisis, no boss hears or cares why an assignment wasn't done. It's your job to get it done on time.

2. **Don't aim for perfection.** Getting it done well and on time is much more important than doing it "perfectly." To your boss, absolutely perfect performance counts against you if it interferes with your carrying your share.

3. **Simply carrying your share is not enough.** Doing only what is expected of you and no more sets you among the expendable mass of performers. Bosses value people who do their job and look around for or create or ask for more real work, not busy work.

4. **Follow through on your own.** Pick up the pieces; tie the loose ends of your assignments. Don't wait to be reminded, particularly by a supervisor.

5. **Anticipate problems.** Ask yourself what could go wrong? When your responsibilities depend on input from others, check their plans and understanding of what you're requesting. There is no substitute for having your projects come out right.

6. **Be resilient about foul-ups.** Part of carrying your responsibilities is understanding that commotions, mistakes, "unforeseeable" failures by others (supplies or contributions) are a normal, routine part of work life. When foul-ups occur, no one is picking on you and you can't excuse it as "bad luck." You are supposed to know that Murphy's Law — "if something can go wrong, it will and at the worst possible time" — operates everywhere. Realize this, and it won't be so hard to adapt to unfavourable conditions and make your projects successful. Pass on to your staff the same expectations.

7. **Take care of problems, don't take them to your boss.** (Bosses have enough of their own.) If you lack the authority, come prepared with solutions when you broach the problem. Even though your boss may not use your solutions, you've made your point as a problem solver — not as a problem collector.

8. **Punctuality counts.** No amount of staying late makes up for your not being available when other people need you in order to do their work. And, as a boss, set an example: let your staff know when you'll be late or have to leave early.

9. **Attendance counts.** People quickly become aware of who makes an effort to be there and who uses any excuse to miss a day.

10. **Don't be a squeaking wheel.** As a daily work style, this approach is self-defeating. Don't be seen as "Here comes a problem."

11. **Don't carry grudges over routine losses.** You cannot win them all. No one can. Even Babe Ruth, Roger Maris, Hank Aaron, and the other home-run champions were out at bat about 65 per cent of the time. Expect to lose some. So don't squander your energy, the goodwill of your allies, and the patience of your boss by turning every issue into a crusade. Concentrate on winning some of the big ones, and you'll be ahead of most people.

12. **Choose your battles carefully.** To decide if something is worth fighting for, ask yourself: How much difference does this problem really make in my job? Is it permanent or transitory? Is it worth making an enemy (enemies)? Most important, do I have a realistic chance of winning? Don't be among the astonishing number of people who fling themselves into no-win job situations.

13. **Deal directly with the person who can make the decision.** This is the

way to get action (and thus be an effective employee). Dealing with people with less authority may be easier on your nerves, but you'll be wasting time and effort. Your most elaborate and smashing presentation may be passed on to the real power reduced to something feeble, such as "Riva thinks we ought to change this procedure." When you're in charge, set aside time to have your staff members present their ideas directly to you.

14. **Whenever possible, keep control of solving your own problems.** This is another essential to being effective and valuable. Let's say you need a new machine or some special work done for you. Don't stop with getting approval. If the other person doesn't follow through, you're left looking inept with your explanation of how John promised to take care of it. Make it happen: "OK, thanks, I'll let them know to start on it and what's involved." Then do it.

15. **Learn to translate boss language.** "If it's not too much trouble" means, "do it…and the sooner the better."

16. **Learn what other people in the organization are doing.** What were last year's big triumphs and failures? What is being planned? What are the organization's major goals and fears? How does your job intertwine with all this? Then you'll understand when, how and where to press for your goals.

17. **Get along with your co-workers.** No boss is ever interested in who is "right" in a co-worker squabble. Internal battles mean less production. To your boss, if you're involved, you're automatically wrong.

18. **Protect the organization's reputation and privacy.** Never discuss organization business and people in detail or by name in a public place where strangers can overhear. Even in private, be reticent about organization politics, problems, business.

19. **Let others win sometimes—even when you have the power.** "Sounds like a good idea. We'll do it that way." If you don't, people will resent you and give you grief.

20. **Learn timing.** This often involves developing the patience to wait for an appropriate occasion.

21. **Don't lie.** Nothing is so serious that lying won't make it worse. If you're caught in a lie, you lose your credibility. Then you're dead.

22. **Read your business's professional and trade publications.** Indicating that you haven't the time or money to read or subscribe will shock your bosses. When they were at your career stage, they were ravenous for trade information. To them, your lack of interest indicates no real career goals on your part. Or worse yet, they may think that you are ignorant of the importance of professional/trade news. Let your staff know which publications apply to your industry.

23. **Get to know your peers in your industry.** Be active in one or more professional/trade organizations. The contacts you make and information you glean aid you on a personal level whenever you change jobs—while improving your status with your current boss.

24. **Never assume other people are operating from your premises,**

your standards, your goals or your rules. When you find yourself thinking, "I never would have expected such behaviour from her," you know you've made the mistake of projecting your outlook onto others' behaviour. That's a narrow, problem-generating attitude that irritates bosses.

25. **Use common sense in applying these and all business-behaviour rules to your own situations.** For instance, the rules of timing and controversy obviate "making waves" when you're brand new on a job. But one MBA reported to her new executive position to find the other newly hired MBAs all had work stations while her boss had forgotten to prepare for her. The absent-minded boss gave her a makeshift table and chair in a supply closet. After a week of vague promises, the MBA decided that this was a situation worth reacting to. New job or not, she made some genteel but effective waves and obtained a suitable work setting. She was right, of course.

AFTER READING

Responding

1. In a small group, discuss the fairness of unwritten rules in the workplace. How could employers make it easier for new workers to learn unwritten rules?

Understanding

2. Group the list of "25 things the boss wants you to know" into categories (e.g., dealing with problems). Compare your categories with those of other students.

3. State the **thesis** (main idea) of this **article**. Explain how the 25 points in this article support the writer's thesis. Compare your answers with those of another classmate and discuss the similarities and differences.

4. Reread one of the 25 points and put it in your own words, expanding on the description. Think of an incident at your own job or at someone else's job that is a good example of the point, and be prepared to talk about it in a small group.

5. This article was first published in the 1980s. In your notebook, make point-form notes on what has changed in the workplace since the 1980s. (If you need help, ask your managers, teachers,

parents, or guardians.) Write a series of paragraphs explaining whether or not an article written in the 1980s is still able to inform the workers of the 21st century. Use evidence from the article, from your discussions with others, and from your personal experience to support your opinions.

Thinking About Language

6. a) Examine paragraph 3 in this article for the level of language. (See The Reference Shelf, page 351.) Create a chart like the one below and fill in the information for each sentence.

SENTENCE	# OF WORDS	DIFFICULT VOCABULARY	SENTENCE TYPE	TRANSITIONS
#1				
#2				

   b) From the information in the chart, write a paragraph on the level of language in this article.
7. Look at the bolded statements in the article. Explain how the writer has used parallel structure in these statements and why the structure is effective for the main idea of the article.

Extending

8. a) In a small group, propose a program for new employees to help them learn these and other "unspoken performance expectations." Write your proposal and present it to the class, using a variety of ways to engage your audience.
   b) With the class, create an evaluation form to evaluate the presentations of all the groups.
   c) Following the feedback from the class, update your Oral Communication Skills Action Plan. (See The Reference Shelf, page 395.)
9. a) Choose a common workplace issue (e.g., sexual harassment, inequity, safety, or office politics) on which you can write a **report**. Create a research plan for the report that includes inquiry questions, information needs, resources, note-taking forms, bibliographic forms, time lines, and reflection questions. Conference with your teacher before starting on your report.
   b) After writing the first draft of your report, form a writing group. Have each person in the group read your work and comment on one of the following: report format; level of language for audience and purpose; content; organization; and integration of research.
   c) Revise your work using feedback from your group. Ensure your bibliography is in the correct format. (See The Reference Shelf, pages 378–379.)
   d) Update your Writing Skills Action Plan using your classmates' and teacher's feedback. (See The Reference Shelf, page 395.)

Stuck in the Throat

"...the most ridiculous dream that
ever was."

XIN QI SHI
TRANSLATED BY DON J. COHN

BEFORE READING

1. With your teacher, discuss what can happen to the way a **story** is told, and how the **tone** of the story can change when it is translated from one language to another.

2. As a class, look closely at the title of the story and the margin notes accompanying the story. Predict the content of the story. Discuss what led you to the predictions you have made.

There had been thunderstorms every day for a week, and like punctual guests, they visited us once in the morning and once in the afternoon. It got so that the days were somehow incomplete without the rain. But that morning the weather suddenly turned fine. Since I believe that sunlight can make people happy, I decided to stop worrying about what had taken place the day before, and because my particular problem could not be solved overnight anyway, it seemed totally useless to get angry or upset about it. And then at the stroke of noon on that glorious sunny day, just as I was reminding myself that I should pay closer attention to the way I handle my problems, particularly those involving Peter Chen, the bad news made its way into my office.

I went to bed late the night before and was only half awake when I arrived at the office. Like an amphetamine, the insistent clacking of type-writers in the next room revived me and helped me to focus my mind on my work. I filed away the letters and other papers on my desk that had piled up the day before, locked up the documents stamped CONFIDEN-TIAL in blood-red ink, made appointments by phone with a few people the manager wanted to meet, and called the airline to check the arrival time of the flight on which the "imperial envoy" from the bank's head-quarters in the United States was travelling. Then the directors of the Research and Analysis departments called and asked to see Peter Chen,

*point of view
—near past*

foreshadowing

*indicates that
the story takes
place during a
time before
computers were
used in the
workplace*

and I put them off by telling them that he had an important morning meeting. In fact, I knew perfectly well there was no such meeting. His office was empty and it was well after ten o'clock; he simply hadn't come to work yet. My office was right next to Peter Chen's and his office door opened into my room, so Peter Chen had to pass by my desk on his way to his office. Today he was already two hours late. Perhaps I was being over-sensitive, but as I looked through the glass wall of my office, all my colleagues appeared particularly bored with their work. There was a lot of whispering going on, and they cast their glances in my direction from time to time. Like other departments in the multitude of similar institutions in Hong Kong, the atmosphere of the Credit and Investment department of the American bank where I worked was rife with a rich collection of secrets and half secrets which in greatly elaborated form could spread through the entire building in a matter of hours. Power struggles in the upper echelons, transfers and promotions in middle management, or even a minor contretemps between lovers could significantly enliven the drab routine lives of my co-workers. In a place where human relationships were so complex, it seemed that no one had any privacy.

setting of story

One of the walls in my room consisted of a large glass panel through which I could observe everything going on in the main office. But most of the time this cold and impersonal piece of glass gave me the most unpleasant feeling. When I was under pressure due to some personal or work-related problem and happened to look up from my desk, I felt like a fish swimming about in an aquarium, my every movement cruelly exposed to the scrutiny of the rest of the staff. I became accustomed to my colleagues' surveillance long ago, and after <u>three years</u> of practice, I'd developed an almost supernatural ability to fend off their hostile glances. In fact, if I hadn't found some way of defending myself from them I certainly would not have survived so long in the Credit and Investment department as Peter Chen's secretary.

time clue

I must admit that when I recall my first few weeks on the job, the idea of quitting occurred to me more than once. I wasn't some kid fresh out of high school with no experience in society, and I've had a fair share of ups and downs in my so-called "emotional life," so the heavy work load, complex human relationships and nasty rumours that infect the office like germs couldn't get me down. When I found myself in a new environment, I could adjust to the changing situation easily and with real enthusiasm. In fact I had switched jobs several times since I started working. If a young woman doesn't want to get married, her only alternative is to put all her energy into her career. Thus one of the things I wanted most in life was a steady job with good future prospects. When I landed my present job, I

shift to distant past

information about the narrator and what motivates her

was really excited and hoped that I could climb step by step up the ladder to become a senior personal assistant. You know, it's a long hard journey from personal secretary to senior personal secretary to personal assistant to senior personal assistant. Some people may have very little respect for this sort of ambition, but what other choices did I have? I'm a middle school graduate with one year of secretarial training. I know my limitations and never make unrealistic demands on myself. I'm nearly thirty now. All I want is some security, a decent job, a nice little flat of my own and a man to love me. Is that too much to ask?

When I accepted my job in the bank I told myself: I'm no spring chicken, so if I'm going to strive for my ideals I'd better do it now while I'm young. Since it was no mean feat for me to get such a good job, I decided that I would never quit unless I was in the most dire circumstances. But the best laid plans often go awry. What made me want to quit was not the heavy work load or the tough schedule, but a man, aged around forty, tall, thin and balding, the manager of the Credit and Investment department of the bank. It was Peter Chen, my boss.

I remember my first day at work. Mr. Chen called me into his office, which was furnished with a two-seater couch and a coffee table (later I learned that this furniture was issued to departmental managers as an indication of their status), and told me what his work habits were and how he wanted things done. After he finished with that, he made a point of telling me that as his private secretary, he expected me to accompany him to social functions whenever necessary, and that at such times I should dress stylishly and be sociable and elegant. As he spoke, he looked me up and down, and it was at this moment that I first felt a terrible surge of anger inside me. What did he mean by that? I have nothing against attending social functions for business reasons, but the way he sized me up was downright insulting. At that moment I reminded myself that I had to exercise a certain amount of self control, especially considering that jobs weren't easy to come by. There was a world-wide economic depression, and I had won out over ten highly-qualified competitors. Though the bank would never hire an incompetent slob, I knew that one of the reasons I was given the job, besides the fact that I'm well qualified, was because of my looks. Although what Peter Chen said left a bitter taste in my mouth, I walked out of his office with a smile on my face, while he, as a way of demonstrating to me that he hoped our association would be a happy one, patted me lightly on the shoulder.

Frankly speaking, working as an executive's private secretary isn't much different from being a nursemaid. First, you've got to be able to read your boss's mind and anticipate his wishes, including everything from

job description from main character's point of view

arranging the agenda at an important meeting to getting him a soda crack-
er and half an aspirin when he needs it; no detail can be overlooked. You
have to tell clients exactly what they want to hear for your boss's benefit,
never forgetting that his interests are your interests as well—actually, as
a secretary your own interests don't matter very much in the first place.
This may make you a complete failure as a person, but it will certainly
make you a top-notch secretary in your boss's eyes. There's a contradiction
here of course, and when I got my first job, it worried me a great deal. For
example, sometimes you know your boss is playing nasty tricks behind a
competitor's back, and will go on doing so until the poor victim is forced
into bankruptcy. But it is your job to act against your conscience, covering
up the truth with clever excuses and rationalizations. You may be earning
a secretary's wages, but your job is more like an accomplice in crime.

I had often thought of changing careers, but what else could I do? All
my qualifications and experience involved secretarial work. If I started
again from the beginning, my future prospects would certainly have been
a lot worse than they were at the bank, not to mention the fact that I
would probably never realize any of my dreams. Switching bosses one
after another and pursuing my career like a dog year after year was terribly exhausting, but gradually I learned to resign myself to it. I could see
through my situation and realized that my stubbornness and inner struggles would never make me happy. While my friends, classmates and colleagues seemed to be able to live their lives and do their jobs successfully
with very little conflict between the two, at the same time gaining both
fame and fortune (despite the irresolvable contradictions involved), my
old-fashioned way of standing by my principles and insisting on doing
what I thought was right has been self-defeating. For years I've been stuck
at the bottom of the totem pole working as an assistant personal secretary.
Let me put it another way: it's as if I were trapped in a giant whirlpool in
the middle of the ocean, clinging helplessly to a bunch of flimsy seaweed
trying to stay alive, while everyone else has safely made their way to the
shore. To go on acting like a fool in the eyes of all those on the shore is
pure stupidity. And after playing the perfect fool for many years, would
anyone in his right mind want to go on in this way? When I learned that
my application for personal secretary had been accepted at the bank, I
knew my time had come. But that's when all the trouble began.

time clue   One night about <u>three months</u> after I had begun working at the bank,
Peter Chen and I were leaving a fancy banquet we had attended with
some clients, when suddenly he turned to me and made a request that
first incident   was definitely beyond the bounds of propriety. I refused him in unequivo-
cal terms, and immediately thought of quitting my job. This was an

extraordinarily painful decision for me, and the more I thought about it the worse my head ached, so that the next day I had to stay home from work. Peter Chen called me at home to apologize. He said that he had been so excited about the deal that had been concluded the night before that he had drunk more than he should have, and said what he did as a joke without thinking very much. Realizing that I had not been compromised in any way, and how immensely difficult job-hunting had been, and that if I quit then I would still have to work with Peter Chen for another month, I decided to go on and take things as they came. But this decision landed me squarely and helplessly in Peter Chen's trap, a trap from which there was no escape.

From that day on, Peter Chen treated me with extreme courtesy and kindness. He was my boss, and in that capacity started giving me gifts one after another. Sometimes I would stay late if there was some paperwork needing urgent attention; at other times, when he would come back to the office from an appointment right before closing time, I'd take short-hand in his office for the pile of letters waiting for him to draft. If the two of us were working hard, he might stop in the middle and let me rest a while, hand me a glass of water, bring up something which had nothing to do with our work, or just start shooting the breeze. My professional training had made me an excellent listener, and I'd let him go on about his family background or his own life story. Though at times like these he never mentioned his wife, I knew they had no children. I have never understood how married men totally devoted to their work managed to keep up their relationships with their wives. Though Peter Chen spent more time with me every day than with his wife, I had no desire to play the role of an interloper, and certainly didn't want to do any harm to others. I often reminded myself that my relationship with Peter Chen was strictly professional, and that it was in my professional capacity that I knew so many details about his personal affairs. Of course we had a number of common goals, but this was simply a manifestation of our intense devotion to our work. It was this sort of dedication that made us perform so well on the job, and might lead eventually to a promotion and more power in the organization for both of us. It's true that Peter Chen treated me well—too well perhaps, but only because I took care of most of his problems in the office. I was his right-hand girl, his girl Friday. I handled all the office work without a hitch, freeing him to concentrate his energies on planning strategy and winning people over to his side, and paving the way for his future advancement. Everyone in the bank knew how Peter had his heart set on a real plum—the vice-presidency of the Hong Kong head office. This would be the crowning glory of his career, for if he were to attempt to climb one step higher and become president, he would first have to hocus-pocus himself into a blonde-haired, blue-eyed caucasian. But fate had it that Peter Chen was reincarnated in the wrong womb; a vice-presidency was the very highest honour a Chinese could aspire to. It was precisely the same sort of aspiration that motivated me to work with such enthusiasm. But events never develop along a straight course, and it's impossible to prevent something that at first glance looks quite simple from turning into a complicated mess.

foreshadowing

I don't recall precisely when, but at some point I began to notice that all my colleagues were constantly staring at me. Whenever Peter Chen stood in front of me giving instructions or chatting about something, every one of them in the next room would exchange knowing glances and turn to look in my direction. And when I passed by them on my way to the washroom, their animated gossip would suddenly cease, as if I were a porcupine they were afraid to touch. Finally I learned from a colleague in another department that rumours about Peter Chen and me had spread through the entire bank. And when I fainted one day at work, was sent to hospital and took two days off to recover, the rumours were elaborated upon to the point where I had become Peter Chen's mistress, and had gone to hospital for an abortion. I decided then that the best way to deal with such painfully compromising rumours was to pretend they didn't exist. I also wondered whether Peter Chen knew what was going on, since he hadn't batted an eyelash about any of this since it started, but it was a difficult subject for me to bring up with him, even in private. I was still confident that I could ward off my nosey colleagues' hostile glances with my "bullet-proof shield." Since Peter Chen had hinted on more than one occasion that at the end of this year he would promote me to personal assistant, this was hardly the time to consider quitting; it was too critical a moment in my career. But though my home-made shield could protect me from the after-lunch gossip in the office, it was hardly effective against Peter Chen's neurotic wife.

Mrs. Chen called the office as often as five or six times a day and was nothing but rude to me. If Peter Chen was out of the office when she called, I would tell her where he had gone, but she only half-believed me. When Peter Chen failed to return home one night, Mrs. Chen barged into my office first thing the next morning and started heaping curses on me left and right. Though my office door was shut, this event set my colleagues' tongues wagging furiously. Had I actually been Peter Chen's mistress, I certainly could have accepted being dragged over the coals in this manner. But this was obviously a case of false accusation and I was completely at a loss to defend myself. Peter Chen answered his wife's criticism by mumbling a bunch of wishy-washy nonsense, neither accepting her charges nor denying them, which left the three of us in an uncomfortable stalemate. I didn't know what Peter Chen had on his mind, but I was angry to the point of exploding. No matter how I explained things to her, Mrs. Chen simply responded with the same line: "The two of you know what dirty tricks you've been up to." When I confronted Peter Chen later and demanded that he clear up the whole misunderstanding, he just smiled at me and said, "What's wrong with being my mistress?" He told me how much he liked me, and how he wished the rumours about us were true. He then said that he was confident that by the end of the year, or at the latest by early next year, he would be promoted to vice-president, and that if I kept working for him, we'd be in the number-two slot in the Hong Kong main office, only one step away from the very top. I naturally understood all the implications of what he was saying. Though I had rejected his advances that first time, he actually had never given up his pursuit, and tried to use all sorts of tricks and promises to get me to surrender to his desires. I had always thought Peter Chen was a bit too self-confident for his own good; he couldn't imagine any woman saying "no" to him, so he played the role of the modest and self-effacing gentleman as he attempted to lure me into his trap. I now had two choices: one was to quit my job and give up all hope for a better future; the second was to give in to Peter Chen and become his mistress. I saw right through the man; in business, he made use of every means at his disposal to get ahead, often stooping to unscrupulous practices. He found failure intolerable, and so he plotted every move with the greatest care to ensure he would never suffer a single loss. For example, a move he made today might only produce the desired result in the distant future. Peter Chen only entered into battles he was sure to win. His self-confidence and relentless drive to get ahead made him one of the most insufferably arrogant people I have ever known. He was polished to the point of slickness in his dealings with others, and had a knack for stabbing people in the back while smiling at them, so his victims never knew where the knife came from. He mobilized everyone, both close friends and casual acquaintances, who might be of some use to him in futhering his career. Naturally, a clever man like Peter Chen knew all the dirty tricks in the book and could pull them off without leaving a single fingerprint anywhere, so all those he dealt with continued to praise him for his "loyalty to his friends." Since I was the one responsible for executing his plans, I perhaps knew more than I should have about his affairs. This put me in a somewhat risky situation, since Peter Chen was the last person in the world to subscribe to the professional ethic of confidentiality. In his mind, the easiest way to control a woman was

Peter Chen's character

through her heart, to become emotionally involved with her. If I became his mistress, got my promotion, started taking money from him and moved into a fancy flat, I would never be able to extricate myself from his clutches and would end up as a mere pawn in his selfish designs. I understood my own needs as well as the predicament I was in. Giving up the chance of a promotion was as difficult for me as acting against the dictates of my conscience. Our discussion had led nowhere, and so our relationship remained as ambivalent and ill-defined as before.

Mrs. Chen seemed to grow more neurotic by the day. Once when her husband failed to come home she called me in the middle of the night and asked for him. Peter Chen and I had parted after a social function earlier that evening, and I had no idea where he was. When I discovered that my colleagues' glances contained intimations to the effect that I was now a certain person's mistress in addition to being his private secretary, it was already too late for me to try to defend myself. I'd never felt so frustrated in my life, and needed desperately to get it off my chest, but who could I possibly speak to? The hot rumours on everybody's lips had metamorphosed into the truth, and any attempt I might have made to lay my heart bare before them would have only made me the laughing stock of the office. I was under a tremendous amount of pressure, and was torn by contradictions. It was as if some weird force were pushing me to the edge of a whirlpool; I was terrified that I might fall in. I detested the way Peter Chen devoted all of his energies to his own advancement, but I also had to admit that he always treated me very well. When you work with a man from morning to night every day, you get to know his good points as well as his faults. Although I kept telling myself that my relationship with Peter Chen was strictly professional, could anyone guarantee it would remain like that? And so this odd relationship of ours continued to develop in an atmosphere of darkness and gloom, much like the cloudy and rainy weather we'd been having over the last week.

shift to near past again (same point of view as the beginning of the story)

I was sitting in my little fishbowl of an office, separated by a sheet of glass from the intermittent whispering and curious glances of my colleagues. Long experience told me that the topic of their many discussions was Peter Chen's failure to show up in the office that morning. In the eighteen years Peter Chen has been a manager in this bank, he has always come to work early and left late. When we parted the night before he had not mentioned having any early outside appointments this morning. Had the negative decision by the board of directors the day before shocked him so deeply that for the first time in nearly two decades he wasn't the first one in the office? Or did his absence stem from the insulting way I had told him off in the presence of another manager, and he was too ashamed of himself to put in an appearance? That board meeting was the event Peter Chen had long been waiting for. Every time he had weighed up his adversaries, he had concluded that the vice-president's position at the Hong Kong head office belonged to him and him alone. Thus when the board's decision was announced and the job given to another man, Peter Chen's lifelong dream burst like a bubble. Something rather odd took place when I went to the toilet that day at lunch time. I was alone for a few minutes at first, but then two women came in and through their chattering and giggling I learned, for the first time, a "secret" about Peter Chen and me that everyone in the entire office seemed to be in on: the person responsible for circulating all the rumours was none other than Peter Chen himself! In order to verify the authenticity of these rumours, the professional busybodies in the office had checked their sources carefully, and each time the accusing finger pointed at Peter Chen. Since the information was issued directly from the horse's mouth, could it possibly be false?

time clue

Though I had wondered a lot about the source of the rumours, I never imagined that Peter Chen would go so far as to attempt to present our hypothetical relationship to others as a *fait accompli*, thus ruining my reputation forever. I decided to have it out with him then and there, and make him admit that the whole thing was a mistake. This was how it happened. Yesterday afternoon, Peter Chen had an appointment outside the office. When he got back, before he learned that he had failed to get this much-coveted promotion, he had a discussion about sales promotion with another manager in our branch. When their discussion was over, I walked into his office, asked the other man to stay in order to be my witness, and then had Peter Chen describe the true nature of our relationship in order to redress the injustice he had done. I asked him why he had spread so many rumours about us and, at the top of my voice, called him a shameless bastard. At this Peter Chen blushed and paled in turn, while the other man became embarrassed and started fidgeting, and then found an excuse and fled. Peter Chen then admitted to me that he had started the rumours, but swore that he had only told one person, even though they had now spread throughout the entire office. It was at that moment that I made up my mind once and for all to abandon all hope about my promotion to personal assistant. Though I was not and never had been Peter Chen's mistress, everyone in the office now regarded me as an immoral woman. Unfortunately, I could never act like a particular classmate of mine from middle school who very happily and openly lived the life of a kept woman. So once again my thoughts turned to quitting. Then, as I was mechanically arranging the papers on my desk and thinking about

time clue

whether to stay or leave, Mr. Guo, one of the bank's directors and a long-time close associate of Peter Chen, came to relate the board of directors' decision. For a few minutes no sound came from Peter Chen's office. What was going on in there? I was still stewing about my confrontation with Peter Chen and was hardly interested in the board's decision. It took me until 6:30 to finish all my work. As I was getting ready to leave, Peter Chen walked out of his office, a perfect picture of gloom. He apologized for what he had done and invited me out for a drink. I took a good look at him. I knew it was cruel to refuse him at a time like this, but I recalled my promise to myself that I would only go out with him for business reasons, especially now that the office was rife with scandal. As he walked listlessly out of the office and disappeared from view, he looked to me like an old and worn out man, though he was still in his early forties.

That night I couldn't sleep. I was trying to decide whether it was right for me to quit my job at such a difficult time in Peter Chen's life. Even if I continued working at the bank and adopted a more detached attitude, the problem remained of how to handle my complex relationship with Peter Chen in the rather absurd environment that the office had become. Could I give up my one chance for a better job and a better life and not regret it later? If I got another job elsewhere, would I have the same opportunities for advancement? Questions like these plagued me all through the night, so I slept poorly and awoke feeling woozy all over. It was a relief to discover that the weather the following morning was extremely fine. The glass walls of the office building opposite my flat glowed in the early-morning sunlight, reflecting distorted images of the objects nearby. As the noon-day sun beat down on Victoria Harbour, I tried to forget what had taken place the day before and concentrate on my work. But Peter Chen had mysteriously failed to show up at work, and since no one knew the real reason for his absence, a rumour was circulating to the effect that he was making a silent protest for not having received his promotion. Then at noon when this rumour had become the subject of the most heated debates, the personnel department announced the terrible news that Peter Chen had died the night before.

Peter Chen was not the sort of man to commit suicide on account of a single career setback. My common sense told me that he would soon recover from the shock, make an impressive comeback and eventually attain his goal. The fact that he had died at a point in his life when death was certainly the last thing on his mind proves the notion that not even the cleverest scheming can foil the workings of Fate, especially here where death came about in such a preposterous way. This was how it happened. After a night of heavy drinking, Peter Chen returned home and had a bowl of fish soup; a fish bone got stuck in his throat, and the pain was so unbearable that while groping about for some vinegar to swallow in order to dissolve the bone, he mistakenly picked up a bottle of sulphuric acid and drank it instead. The acid burned his throat and oesophagus and destroyed his insides. In less than an hour he was dead.

Peter Chen's lifetime dream was to be a vice-president in the bank. Thanks to good fortune, the position became available, but to everyone's surprise he lost out in the running. Finally, by a weird twist of fate, he lost his life as well, leaving behind a vacant post for someone else to fill. During the next few days, all of Peter Chen's associates in the office, friend and foe alike, wore looks of grief, but in most cases these were mere masks concealing ambitious plots and schemes. Of course, if the victim had been someone else in the office, Peter Chen would have displayed the same hypocritical concern. The news of Peter Chen's death had come without warning. Following a short period of general disbelief, there arose in the office the usual mixed chorus of discussion and evaluations, some of which inevitably involved me. The stares coming from my colleagues now contained a mixture of curiosity and feigned aloofness. It was as if I had suffered the sudden loss of my sole source of support and now had to struggle for my own survival in a vast and unfriendly sea. In their eyes, I had lost my good name and influence and was reduced to the pitiable status of someone's "former mistress." I couldn't tolerate this absurd situation, but there was no way for me to clarify it. As far as I was concerned, I wasn't sure whether Peter Chen's death was good or bad. On the positive side, I would never become his mistress and was thus saved from making a very unsound investment; and on the negative side, I had been an innocent victim of rumour mongering, and now the only witness who could clear my name was dead. Peter Chen's death also dashed all my hopes for a promotion, and all the hard work I had done over the years suddenly dissolved into nothingness. But what caused me the most grief was not my colleagues' sarcastic comments and glassy stares, but Mrs. Chen's hysterical behaviour in the aftermath of her husband's death.

I had asked several of my colleagues to accompany me to Peter Chen's funeral service, but each of them made up a different excuse not to go, expressing their sympathy for me in odd, offhand ways, and then silently and remorsefully turning and walking out of my office. I got so fed up with this that I shouted at the top of my voice: "I was never Peter Chen's mistress, so stop looking at me that way!" But it was too late. They showed even greater solicitude at this point and tried to get me to calm down, assuring me that with time I would recover from my loss. Since

more recent past moving to the present

they had cut themselves off from me completely, I made up my mind to be courageous for once and attend the funeral alone.

I went to the funeral parlour dressed in a simple outfit. As I stood before the coffin, bowing three times at the behest of the funeral director, I was aware that everyone was staring at me. When everyone you know starts thinking of you as Mr. So-and-so's mistress, it makes you wonder whether it's true or not. In order to get back at them, I decided to play the role of Peter Chen's mistress to the hilt, and sat down in the front row. Much to my surprise, I started crying, but whether the tears were for Peter Chen or myself it was really hard to say. Mrs. Chen was kneeling down before the coffin not far from where I was sitting. There was hardly any expression on her face, and she had grown quite thin and pale, but not for a single second did she take her eyes off me. The few times I glanced at her and our eyes met, I felt terribly sad for her. The most important thing for me was to get her to believe that I had not had any sexual relations with her husband. Peter Chen may have been an unfaithful husband, but I certainly had no responsibility in that. In the end, I had innocently been made someone else's scapegoat. Can a woman blinded by hate and jealousy take seriously anything her mortal enemy says? It was clearly too late for that. Suddenly, like a ravening beast, Mrs. Chen attacked me, slapping my cheeks with all her might. I said, "I'm afraid you've made a big mistake," but before I could say any more, a few of the kind-hearted busybodies attending the ceremony ushered me out of the funeral hall. And so by the good will of others I was denied a last opportunity to clear my name in public, though I knew full well that by confessing at that time I would have been wasting my breath.

Mrs. Chen had lost her source of financial support, so the bank arranged a job for her in the import–export department of one of the branch offices. Since we worked in different parts of town, our paths never crossed, but she continued to haunt me like a ghost, and occasionally I would see her lurking around my neighbourhood. When we met, she would always say the same thing: "Give me my husband back!" At first I put up with it, but later I had to call the police to get her off my back once and for all.

Then one night I came home late from a friend's dinner party and found her lying dead drunk on my doorstep. I carried her inside, helped her clean up a bit, tidied up her filthy clothing, and gave her some ginger tea to drink. She vomited several times and then started to come around. She tried to focus her bloodshot eyes on me, muttered something unintelligible, and in a moment of clarity confessed to me that she had murdered Peter Chen. She had always loved her husband deeply. They had fallen in love in high school, and for ten years their marriage had gone quite well.

But when Peter Chen started moving up in the bank his personality changed completely. Mrs. Chen couldn't tolerate being ignored for days on end, not to mention being brushed aside while her husband chased after other women. She told me that she hated me because everyone had told her that I was Peter Chen's mistress. The day he died, Mrs. Chen had made a pot of fish soup, a particularly good tonic, as she often did, though her husband hadn't told her whether he was coming home that night. Earlier she had put the live snakehead fish she had bought for the soup in the bathtub, but a moment later it disappeared, and she found it stuck head first in the toilet, with only the dark tip of its tail fins sticking out. It was too slippery for her to grasp, so she called in a plumber who convinced her it was better to let the fish "die in glory rather than live in dishonour"; in other words, rather than destroy the toilet to save the fish, he suggested using sulphuric acid to eliminate the fish without damaging the toilet. She concurred with him and it was the neat way the fish disintegrated in seconds with only half a bottle of sulphuric acid that gave Mrs. Chen her inspiration. She went out and bought another fish, as well as another bottle of sulphuric acid….At this point in her story, Mrs. Chen took a deep breath and said that she had bought the sulphuric acid with me in mind. If Peter Chen didn't come home that night, she was going to eliminate me. But the course of events disrupted her plans. Peter Chen actually turned up that night, and in his drunken state drank the fish soup his wife had prepared for him. When the bone got stuck in his throat, he shouted at his wife so violently that she panicked and mistakenly handed him the bottle of sulphuric acid. In this tragicomic manner Peter Chen's life came to an end.

irony of his death

Between sobs, Mrs. Chen told me that if I hadn't gotten involved with her husband, he would not have died in this manner. Then I swore to her that though her husband had made sexual overtures to me many times, I always refused him; and though our professional relationship was perhaps more intimate than most we had never crossed the line of propriety as she had imagined. Mrs. Chen listened carefully to me, and I sensed that she was ready to accept my explanation, but all of a sudden she lashed out at me again with the allegation that I was an ingrate who had bitten the hand that fed me. She accused me of having forgotten all the favours her husband had done me, and of trying to deny everything that had gone on between us. How could I be so cruel, she said, since in a sense her husband had sacrificed his life for me? This was too much for me to bear, and I felt I was losing touch with reality. The whole world seemed topsy-turvy, and I started feeling dizzy. I had tried as best I could to clear myself of the charge that I was Peter Chen's mistress; now I was fed up with the whole thing and couldn't tolerate any more. I saw no need to waste any more of my time and energy on this matter, since it now looked like I was going to be stuck with the title "Peter Chen's mistress" for the rest of my life.

Mrs. Chen finally calmed down and fell asleep, and when I woke up the next morning, she had already left. It wasn't until some six months later, on Christmas eve, that our paths crossed again at the airport, though I only caught a glimpse of her from afar. Following Peter Chen's death, some major personnel changes took place at the bank which made working there even less attractive to me. Peter Chen's replacement was, to put it mildly, a lot less of a gentleman than Peter Chen. He constantly tried to take advantage of me, with the excuse that it was part of my job. When I refused him, he would start insulting me, and at such times would always manage to bring up Peter Chen's name. I found this intolerable and six months later I handed in my letter of resignation, bringing to a close a period in my life that was nothing but one long nightmare. I planned a trip to Europe to do some sightseeing and visit a couple of friends who lived there. I wanted to distance myself from the shadows of my past and start a new life. Fame and fortune are nothing but a trap. I had two choices: either completely ignore the dictates of my conscience, or escape before it was too late.

most recent past

On Christmas eve, the departure lounge at the airport was packed with people leaving Hong Kong on their holidays. As my flight was being announced for the third time, a familiar figure came into my view. It was Mrs. Chen, arm in arm with the newly appointed vice-president of the bank's Hong Kong head office. Dressed to kill and as happy as a pair of lovebirds, the two of them disappeared through the departure gate. I could hardly believe my eyes. The new vice-president was a married man. I wanted to cry and laugh at the same time. It was as if I had stepped into the midst of the most ridiculous dream that ever was.

AFTER READING

Responding

1. In your notebook, write your assessment of the two main **characters**: the **narrator** and Peter Chen. Be sure to support your opinions with evidence from the story. Compare your responses in a small group.

Understanding

2. Having read the complete story, do you think the title is a good one? In your notebook, explain why or why not.
3. Write the **theme** of the story in a statement starting "In this story, the author is saying...." Make point-form notes supporting your theme statement.
4. In your notebook, draw a time line of the events of the story. Label the time line with events from the story. Your time line could look something like the one below.

5. With a partner, write a **character sketch** of the narrator. Divide your sketch into sections, labeling each section with appropriate titles. With another pair, compare your character sketch and add to it as necessary.
6. Compare the narrator's job from the **point of view** of the narrator and from that of her boss, Peter Chen. Be sure to include the page number where you found the information. As a class, discuss your observations.

ASPECT OF JOB	NARRATOR'S VIEW	PAGE	PETER CHEN'S VIEW	PAGE

7. With a partner, discuss the ending of the story and explain how it is **ironic**.

8. With a partner, create at least five additional margin notes that could be placed next to specific sentences or paragraphs to direct the reader to significant points in the plot of this story. For each note, identify the sentence or paragraph next to which it should be placed and the words you would use in the margin note.

Thinking About Language

9. Find five examples from the story of the use of formal language. These could include vocabulary, **tone**, or sentence structures.

Extending

10. The story takes place in Hong Kong. In a group, create a plan for research about how cultural values in Hong Kong differ from those in Canada. If time allows, carry out this research.

11. a) As a class, come up with a **definition** of "systemic **bias**." Examine the systemic biases that both the narrator and Peter Chen are fighting against. As a class, talk about other systemic biases that exist in workplaces and how they may show themselves in hiring, in daily work, in performance reviews, and in promotions.

    b) In a small group, create a poster fighting a particular type of systemic bias, to be displayed in the workplace. Write an explanation of the design elements that you used to promote understanding of systemic bias.

The Runner

WALT WHITMAN

BEFORE READING

With a partner, make two lists: activities that are best done alone and those that require participation in a group. Which list of activities do you prefer? What personality type is attracted to each list of activities? Be prepared to report to the class on your discussion.

On a flat road runs the well-train'd runner,
He is lean and sinewy with muscular legs,
He is thinly clothed, he leans forward as he runs,
With lightly closed fists and arms partially rais'd.

AFTER **READING**

Responding
1. Explain whether the runner in this **poem** is or is not a serious athlete.

Understanding
2. Explain the attitude of the poet to the runner.
3. Find or create another illustration to accompany this poem. In a small group, compare and explain your choices.
4. With a partner, predict when this poem was probably written. Explain what clues led to this prediction. Use the Internet to check the date of the poem or its poet to verify your prediction.

Thinking About Language
5. Rewrite the poem verbatim using punctuation to create grammatically correct sentences. Compare your rewrite with those of your classmates.
6. Complete a chart similar to the one below that includes adjectives and adverbs in this poem.

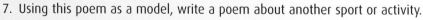

WORD	ADJECTIVE OR ADVERB	WORD THE ADJECTIVE OR ADVERB MODIFIES
flat		
well-train'd		
lean		
sinewy		
muscular		
thinly		
clothed		
lightly		
closed		
partially		
rais'd		

Extending
7. Using this poem as a model, write a poem about another sport or activity.

8. a) With a partner, track the sports coverage in a newspaper or on a television station news program for a week to determine which gets more coverage: sports played by individuals or by teams. Prepare a list of reasons for the proportion of the sports coverage that each receives.
   b) Discuss your findings with the class.

Johnny B

"My favorite thing in my mediocre world. Shinny."

PHIL "THE MALLET" VOYD

As a class, brainstorm what you know about the game of shinny. Where and when is it played? What are the rules?

I excel at mediocrity. You name it — basketball, crossword puzzles, guitar, karate, French, German, Japanese, watercolor painting, microeconomic analysis — I've done it and done it not well. Not badly, either, I guess. I can say *Ohaiyogozaimasu, genki desu ka* and talk about what a nice day it is with Hayashida *sensei*, my karate instructor. More often than not, I can accurately calculate the price elasticity of a product. Every now and again, I can paint a tree so it looks like a tree and not a head of broccoli.

Not bad and not good. Average. Ordinary. Straight Bs in everything. Except for one thing. My favorite thing in my mediocre world. Shinny.

When the outdoor rinks are finally ready, and it seems to happen later and later the last couple of years (not until January 19th this year), I put on my high tech long underwear and turtleneck, Hot Chillys socks, fleece pullover, nylon shell

pants and jacket, toque, and most importantly of all, my genuine, autographed Edmonton Oilers jersey. Number 99. The Great One.

I grab my skates, two Sher-Wood P.M.P. Feather Lam sticks and my soft-as-cream hockey gloves, jump in my Ford Escort and go searching for a Game. Sometimes I have to go to three or four rinks — Dovercourt Park, Fisher, Plouffe — before I find a real game and not just a couple of ankle skaters or a bunch of kids taking dud slapshots, trying to raise the puck off the ice for the first time.

Sometimes I don't find a Game, even if I go as far as Mechanicsville or Brewer Park, where there's a hockey rink and a speed skating oval inhabited by grim-faced, hockey stickless people. When I can't find any shinny, I stop at the park where I've been finding the best Games. I lace up my skates, get on the ice and wait, taking slapshots at the goalposts, hoping the clanging,

the rink. I sit on the snowbank surrounding the rink boards, tear off my boots and put on my Bauer Supreme Custom Flo-Fit 4000 skates. They aren't top of the line like the pros use, but I've worked them in until they're so comfortable they feel like a part of my body—peeling leather, frayed ballistic nylon, chipped plastic feet. Only the blades look new, glossy and dangerous under the rink lights, honed to thumbnail narrowness by hundreds of sharpenings.

"Hey," shouts someone from the center of the ice, "you gonna play?"

I nod, tighten the last criss-cross of the laces, tie a double knot and stand up, feeling my feet and legs flow into the skates, filling the steel, plastic, leather and nylon with warmth and speed. I put on my hockey gloves, grab a Sher-Wood and hop over the boards, ignoring the gate. I kind of like to make an entrance, I guess.

I drop my stick on the pile and an older guy—late forties, fogged-up glasses, holey green jersey—gets down on his knees and starts throwing the sticks, one to the right, one to the left, until the pile is gone.

I skate over to the side with my stick and pick it up, feeling my body lighten and tingle with unshed kinetic energy.

"You can start," says a big guy on our side. He's wearing an expensive, Flash Gordanish ski jacket. An orange lift ticket is hanging from the zipper.

A tall guy on the other team takes a puck out of their net. He's wearing a university intramural jersey, Mech Eng Scoring Machines. He's a good skater, smooth and unaware. He carries the puck over center and the Game starts. Everything else disappears. The snowbank piled around the rink, the tiny shack, the

ringing sound will bring the local players. It works every now and again.

Sometimes I get lucky and find a Game at the first rink I check out. Like tonight.

I'm not too surprised. The weather is perfect for shinny. Cold enough to make the ice hard and fast, but windless, so your face doesn't freeze solid. On a night like tonight, I can play for hours and feel like I'm on a beach in Florida.

The Game is just starting. Everybody is dropping their sticks in a pile in the center of the ice, getting ready to choose teams. I don't bother going inside the shack beside glowing houses next to the park, the noises of the city.

The teams are pretty even. Neither side has any ankle skaters or little kids. Both teams have a handful of real Players.

The group is a typical shinny mix. Teenagers with backwards baseball caps, frozen ears and jerseys from the newest NHL teams — Mighty Ducks, Coyotes, Predators. Guys in their twenties and thirties dressed warmly and wearing slightly less professional jerseys — Blosker's Pub, Tortoises, The Flying L Bows. A couple of older guys with ancient skates and gray hair sneaking out from under their toques. A girl with a long ponytail and teal tape on the blade of her stick.

I stay back, playing mostly defense and goalie, getting a feel for the ebb and flow of the Game. When my body is so light it feels like I weigh less than a snowflake, I start playing for real.

I take the puck away from the old-timer in the fogged-up glasses, slip it through the legs of the tall Mech Eng Scoring Machine, deke around two surprised teenagers and then it is only me and the goalie and the beautiful endless now of open ice.

When I'm close enough to the net, I pull the puck back to my skate, flick it behind my other skate and back up to my stick. The goalie, a stubbly guy wearing a Molson Export Ale jersey, is flummoxed by this move, legs twisting in different directions. I carom the puck off the outside of his skate and into the net, making sure I don't break two of the most important rules of shinny. No hard shots and no raising the puck. The goalie stumbles back, grabbing onto the top of the net to keep from falling.

I glide back to my side of the ice, past the reappraising glances of the other players. My favorite feeling.

"Nice goal," says the big skier with the orange lift ticket hanging from his zipper.

No one keeps score, another unwritten rule, but I've long since realized that the players do keep track of who is winning. It is the *impression* of which side is better, not the team with the most goals, although that does count. What makes more of an impression is who scores nicer goals: snappy passing plays, two-on-ones, spectacular breakaways. Cheesy goals — hard shots, raises, open net goals — don't really count. They make a bad impression.

As players leave and arrive, change teams, take breaks in the shack to warm up frozen cheeks and toes, I make sure my team is winning. I don't try to score a goal every time I touch the puck. I can't stand guys who do that. There's nothing worse than a puckhog. If there's a hog on the other side, I take the puck away from him every time he starts to show off. They get really annoyed when you do this.

I set up more goals than I score. I take my turn playing defense and goalie. I use hotdog moves — spinaramas, no-look passes, stickhandling shenanigans — only every now and again. After all these years, I have it down to a science. I excel at shinny, I guess.

"Did you every play pro?" asks the teenaged Coyote after I score an almost embarrassingly hotdoggish goal.

I smile and shake my head. I get asked this a few times every winter. It's not one of my favorite feelings. It feels pretty good for a moment but then it feels really bad. It makes me remember the rest of the world.

Out there, I'm mediocrity personified Johnny B.

I play harder after that, trying to recapture the bright kinetic forgetfulness. An impossible no-look pass and a breakaway goal later, I do. Everything disappears except the ebb and flow of the Game.

After a while, I don't know how long (two hours? three?), I decide it's time to go home. My legs are starting to feel heavy and my toes are so cold they feel like they'd shatter if something hit my skates hard enough. Besides, this Game is over. There can be no doubt about which team has made the better impression. It's written all over the rosy-cheeked faces of the players. One more goal, a hotdog move. I like to make a big exit, I guess.

I lift the stick of a guy in a baggy Dallas Cowboys shirt and Micron plastic skates, and take the puck.

"Sh—," he says and falls.

I rush down the left side of the ice, near the boards, not doing any moves, just going faster than everyone else. They chase after me but it's like they're wearing boots instead of skates.

I cut towards the net. The goalie, a chubby guy wearing a toque with a floppy blue pompom, looks like he just remembered he left his car lights on.

I do some rapid fire stickhandling. The puck is my willing collaborator, clinging devoutly to the blade of the Sher-Wood. The goalie tries to follow the pingponging of the puck. I try not to smile. His eyes are wide open, popping out of his chubby face like two matching pompoms.

I start a backwards, through-the-legs no-looker, spinning around and—

My stick is lifted into the air and flung out of my hands. The blade of one of my skates catches in a gash in the ice. I fall backwards, sliding over the ice on my rear end past the even wider-eyed goalie and into the net.

I never fall. I never let go of my stick. I never have the puck stolen from me. *Traitor*, I can't help thinking, although I'm not sure what I mean—the ice, my skate, the puck, the Sher-Wood, the player who so easily, so inconceivably took the puck away from me.

He's rocketing down the ice, slaloming effortlessly through my whole team. He is toqueless and his blond hair is flying back as he flashes towards the net. He's wearing a black and yellow Pittsburgh Penguins jersey. Number 66.

Each move is incredible. I've never seen any of them before and, obviously, neither has any of my teammates. The puck, *his* puck is in the back of our net before I can get myself out of their net.

"Wow." The chubby goalie looks down at me, pompom bouncing happily. "Did you see that?"

I look back up the ice. The other team is crowding around Number 66, congratulating him, welcoming this unbelievable Player to their side. His angular face is tanned and TV handsome.

I crawl out of the net, stand up, brush the snow off my nylon pants and then look around for the Sher-Wood. It is stuck in a snowbank piled behind the boards, perfectly perpendicular, looking almost mythical. The Stick In The Snow.

"Sh—," I say under my breath as I skate over to get it, feeling a flush of warm blood in my cold face. Dropping your stick is kind of like the shinny equivalent of leaving your fly open. Having your lumber hurled into the air and down into a snowbank, sticking up as straight as a sign post is...I don't know what it is. Leaving your zipper open and then asking a girl you've had a crush on since you were seven to dance, I guess.

I yank the Sher-Wood out of the snow-bank and skate back to my side of the ice, keeping near the boards. As I pass the crowd around Number 66, I hear the Coyote teenager ask him if he ever played pro. He laughs and then, easily, inconceivably, he says —

"Yes."

I almost fall again. I grab the boards, feeling ridiculously grateful for their blank wooden solidness.

"Cool! Awesome!" says the Coyote teenager. "For which team? The Penguins?"

Number 66 laughs again. "No, I never made the NHL. Not good enough, too small and too slow. I played in Europe."

Everybody — the teenagers, the twenty- and thirtysomethings, the oldtimers, the girl with teal tape on her stick — are blown away by him. They can't believe they get to play hockey with Number 66, although it's more like they're just sharing the ice with him. He's playing his own celestial Game, weaving through the stars, skates barely touching the ice.

Still, they love him. I can see why. He's the best Player I've ever seen. He's generous, too. Not even close to being a puckhog. He sets up more goals than he scores. He plays defense and goalie. He does every-thing I do except he does it much, much better. *He* excels.

And he's modest. He's not too small or too slow for the NHL. He's well over six

feet and his muscles are visible even under the loose Penguin jersey. If he's not good enough then my eyes are lying to me. He looks faster, more skilled than most of the millionaire sloggers who clutch and grab, dump and chase their way from Montreal to Nashville.

I hate him.

The impression of the Game changes almost instantly. The other team starts win-ning. They score more goals, a lot more, and all of them stunning, forget-me-not kind of goals.

I try harder. A bad idea, I know. I should go home. My emotions are like everything else in my life; average, straight Bs. The few occasions I've been afflicted by extreme feelings, I have humiliated myself. But I can't seem to stop playing. I try even harder.

It doesn't matter. I can't make an impression on the ebb and flow of the play. Another extreme emotion boils through me. Fury. I know I must leave. Hate and fury don't mix. They are the alloys of dis-grace. With an effort that feels like I'm tearing off a jersey made of new scabs, I skate towards the gate in the boards. No big exit for me tonight.

"Hey!" says the big skier with the orange lift ticket hanging from his zipper. "You going, man?"

I stop and nod.

"But we're getting destroyed by that guy." He looks at the whirling, slicing Number 66 with awe and disbelief. "Can't you stay for a bit more?"

"I'd like to," I say, "but my toes are frozen."

"Oh," he says, nodding sympathetically. "That's too bad."

Frozen toes are a fact of shinny. An honorable discharge.

"Thanks for the game," I say as I skate towards the gate.

"See ya," he says and rejoins the play.

I reach for the gate and a black and yellow blur cuts in front of me, knocking me off balance. I grab for the boards but this time I'm too far away. I fall flat on my butt.

I watch Number 66 deke around three players, spin and shoot while gliding backwards, a no-looker. The puck banks off a post, slides along the goal line, hits the other post and goes in. Everybody cheers at this pool-sharkist goal.

I scramble to my feet and skate over to our net.

"I thought you were going," says the big skier.

"A few more minutes can't hurt." I retrieve the puck from the net and head up the ice.

The hate and fury *have* mixed together, melding into a feeling I have no name for. It is more extreme than anything I have ever felt before, as far away from my everyday emotions as the stars are from the surface of the ice.

I rush straight at Number 66. He swoops forward to pokecheck me. I pull the Sher-Wood back, raising it high into the air. Slapshot position. Number 66 jumps out of the way, terrified I'm going to break the most sacred of shinny rules. No SLAPSHOTS.

I don't. I lower my stick and carry the puck by him. I never planned on taking a slapshot, I guess. I just needed the time a fake would give me to get past him.

I deke around a couple of their players, barely noticing them, and slip the puck between the goalie's legs, the coveted five hole.

My team loves it, slapping me on the back, laughing at my audacity, crowing, "Nice goal!" "Great move!" "Waytago!"

Number 66 is not pleased. He points his stick at me. "You almost tasted lumber," he says. "Don't do that again."

I don't. I don't need to. I've made an impression. I can play with him, I know. Match him impossible move for impossible move. I can score on him. *I can excel.*

I'm not sure why. I don't want to know why. I just want to play like this forever. I never want this night to end. After a while, I know that my team is winning. I can tell by the look on their rosy faces.

During a rest break—the teenagers smoke, the oldtimers lean against the boards, the twenty- and thirtysomethings drink Gatorade—the big skier skates up to me.

"Man," he says, "I think that pro guy's getting pissed off."

"It's just shinny," I say.

"Yeah, I know that. You know that. But does *he* know that?" He zips up his expensive jacket. "I don't know, maybe you shouldn't be smiling so much."

I almost touch my face to see if it is true. Am I smiling? I realize I am grinning from ear to frozen ear, probably have been since my fake slapshot. Something more extreme has been added to the mix of hate and fury. *Joy,* I guess.

I pull a loose piece of tape off the blade of my stick and toss it on the snowbank piled behind the boards. "He played pro. I don't think he's going to get too upset over a pick-up game."

But I close my mouth tight, making it as even and neutral as the center line of a real hockey rink. It doesn't seem very sportsmanlike to be grinning like a fool.

The big skier rips the orange lift ticket off the end of his zipper, throws it on the snowbank. "I hope so, man."

The rest break ends. Both teams head back to their own sides. The Coyote teenager still has a cigarette in his mouth. The other team, the losing side, starts off with the puck. The girl with the teal tape passes to Number 66. He turns on the jets, blasting by everybody, leaving a trail of powdery snowclouds and dumbfounded players. I go after him. I think I am smiling again.

Number 66 is closing in on our net when I catch up with him. I lift his stick and take the puck. One of my skates grazes one of his and he falls. For the first time tonight.

I stop. "Sorry about that," I say. "Are you okay?"

He looks up at me. His eyes are gone. No blood, no empty sockets, no dangling gore, his eyes haven't fallen out. There is only...nothing. Empty *absences*, deeper than the night sky.

In one smooth, swirling movement, he stands up and glides towards me.

He says, "You're starting to get on my nerves, hotshot."

I try to look away from the absences, try to remember the hardness of the ice I'm standing on, the string of the pure cold air in my nose and lungs, my frozen cheeks and toes, the intimate weight of the Sher-Wood.

"It was an accident," says our goalie. He is stocky and wearing a Jack O'Day Automotovation jersey. "He didn't mean to trip you."

"He's been going after me all night," says Number 66, looking at the goalie,

pointing his stick at me. "Playing like a maniac."

Jack O'Day smiles at Number 66, a friendly, take-it-easy smile. He looks a little worried, like maybe he thinks Number 66 is going to drop the gloves. He doesn't look like someone seeing two empty absences where eyes should be.

"It was an accident," repeats Jack O'Day. "Really. I saw the whole thing."

Number 66 glides closer to me, raises a glove. It is new and unblemished, made entirely of Kevlar. "Don't do that again." He pokes me in the chest.

There is something unfolding inside the emptiness where his eyes should be, something at the end of the absences slicing towards me. I can't see it yet but it is thumbnail narrow and made of limitless desires.

"I'm sorry," I say. My voice doesn't sound like my voice. It is hollow, as faint as an autumn leaf.

Number 66 stares at me. I can almost see the thumbnail narrow thing. The shadow of its desires is made of the pleasure of torment, the fleeting sweetness of murder.

"I...would never do something like that on purpose," my stranger's voice says.

I'm going to die, I know.

"C'mon let's play," says the big skier, sliding between us. "He didn't mean to knock you down, man."

Other players—the oldtimer in the fogged-up glasses, the guy wearing the Dallas Cowboys shirt and the plastic Micron skates—echo the big skier. None of them look like they have seen two empty absences where eyes should be.

AFTER READING

Responding

1. Explain why you think the **narrator** of this **story** is or is not a serious athlete.

Understanding

2. Explain what the narrator enjoys about playing a game of pick-up shinny.
3. a) Using a chart similar to the one below, explain the meaning and/or significance of the following words in the story.

WORD(S)	MEANING AND/OR SIGNIFICANCE
Hot Chillys socks (page 145)	
Number 99 (page 145)	
Flash Gordonish (page 146)	
Orange lift ticket (page 146)	
Cheesy goals (page 147)	
Puckhog (page 147)	
Hotdoggish goal (page 147)	
"Waytago!" (page 150)	
Hotshot (page 151)	

   b) Identify other unusual words in this story that could be included in the chart.
4. Describe one quality you admire about the narrator and another you don't.
5. The narrator of this story begins by saying "I excel at mediocrity." Explain why you agree or disagree with the statement "If something is worth doing it is worth doing badly."
6. Study the illustration that the author has created for this story. How does it reflect the **mood** of the story? Do you agree with the use of this illustration for the story?

Thinking About Language

7. Locate the following verbs in the story: deke, flick, flummoxed, and carom. Find another verb to replace each in the sentence. Explain which verb you prefer in each case.

Extending

8. Write a sequel to this story. Make sure that your new ending is consistent with the rest of the story.

The Need to Win

CHUANG TZU

TRANSLATED FROM THE CHINESE BY THOMAS MERTON

BEFORE READING

As a class, discuss which is most important: whether you win or how you play the game.

When an archer is shooting for nothing
He has all his skill.
If he shoots for a brass buckle
He is already nervous.
If he shoots for a prize of gold   5
He goes blind
Or sees two targets—
He is out of his mind!

His skill has not changed. But the prize
Divides him. He cares.   10
He thinks more of winning
Than of shooting—
And the need to win
Drains him of power

AFTER READING

Responding

1. a) In your own words, write the main idea in this **poem**.
   b) List and explain specific details in the poem that led you to the main idea.
   c) Explain why you do or do not agree with the point of the main idea.
2. In a **journal** entry, describe a personal experience that either makes the same point or contradicts the main idea in this poem.

Understanding

3. Explain the implications the main idea of this poem has for one's personal philosophy of life.
4. Use a search engine to find information on the Internet about Chuang Tzu, the writer of this poem, and Thomas Merton, the translator of this poem. Record key information about each in your notebook. Explain briefly what the two men have in common.

Thinking About Language

5. Review the main uses of the dash in Standard Canadian English. Then examine the two dashes used in this poem and explain why the dash has been used in each instance.

Extending

6. Research an Olympic athlete vying for a gold medal. How does the athlete prepare mentally in order not to have his or her performance overwhelmed by the high stakes of Olympic gold medal competition? Discuss your findings with the class.

7. a) Write an **opinion piece** agreeing or disagreeing with the following statement: Television has made sports into pure entertainment with less emphasis on athletic skill. Be sure to choose an appropriate method of development to organize your essay. (See The Reference Shelf, pages 386–391.)
   b) With a partner, revise and edit your essay before submission, focusing on content, organization, and use of evidence to support your arguments. (See The Reference Shelf, page 393.)

The Will to Win

"...determination and indomitable spirit..." LAURIE NEALIN

BEFORE READING

In a small group, discuss what you know about the other Olympic Games: the Paralympic Games. Organize your discussion around the following topics: who competes, where and when they are held, and how much media coverage they get.

When a freak accident rendered Chantal Petitclerc paraplegic at age 13, her life changed dramatically. But not in the ways you might expect.

Instead of allowing the injury she suffered to limit her life, Petitclerc channelled her drive, determination and indomitable spirit into becoming one of the greatest wheelchair athletes in the world today. This August, the 2000 Paralympic double-gold medallist hopes to reach another milestone on her incredible journey toward Olympic gold in 2004 with her first-ever victory at the International Amateur Athletics Federation (IAAF) world championships in Edmonton. At the world's premier track-and-field event, being held for the first time in North America, only eight women will compete in the 800-metre wheelchair race. Petitclerc, the world record-holder in the event, intends to be one of them.

"Petitclerc is amazing," says Faye Blackwood, Paralympic programs manager for Athletics Canada. "She works hard, trains hard and wants perfection in all her events."

Reflecting on the two months she spent in hospital and rehabilitation after a barn door fell on her while she was playing with a friend, Petitclerc, now 31, says: "I didn't get the feeling that I couldn't do things, only that I was going to do something different. The first year was a year of adaptation with ups and downs, but what's a year in a life? For one year of struggle, I've had 10 years that were really great."

Petitclerc, who hails from the small Quebec town of St-Marc-des-Carrières, started training for wheelchair racing when she was 17 and entered her first track meet a year later, competing in a racing wheelchair pieced together by a friend. The 5-foot-5, 110-pound athlete has since competed in three Paralympics, two Olympic Games and four IAAF world championships, winning 16 gold, silver and bronze medals at these global meets. Her 1999 world record of one-minute, 50.62 seconds in the 800 — some three seconds faster than any woman has ever covered that distance on foot — still stands.

Achieving that level of success involves long hours of training — at least four hours a day on average, six days a week, 11 months a year. Her regimen consists of three intensive sessions of weightlifting and seven sessions in her racing chair, covering 120 kilometres weekly. When Petitclerc is racing the 800, her average speed is 28 kilometres an hour with peaks as high as 32 km/h over the last 300 metres. "The power we give is the same as the runners. When you're finished the 800, you could not go on at that intensity for even another 200," she laughs. "We go at 95 percent of our heart-rate capacity (about 170 beats per minute) for the whole time."

When she's not training, the Montreal resident is busy lending her name to fund-raising projects, especially those that assist Quebec youth; working tirelessly as a spokesperson for Le Défi Sportif, the annual multi-disability sport event held in Montreal; and working part-time for Loto Quebec, hosting its televised lottery draws.

One of the most gratifying aspects of her career, says Petitclerc, is being seen as a role model by young, able-bodied athletes who value her advice. "It's great that a kid can see through Paralympics to see the athlete in you."

Speaking to school-children is also a priority for Petitclerc. She talks to them about how being different can be a challenge and she encourages them to see people for themselves, not for their differences.

About twice a month, Petitclerc, who was nominated for Canadian athlete of the year honours in 2000, is invited to speak at corporate events. "Achieving a goal in sport is very similar to reaching your potential in anything — in business, in school, in music..." she says. "Setting goals and achieving those goals is always important to me."

Petitclerc has long been a well-known personality in her home province. Now, she is also recognized in Australia as "the Canadian who beat Louise Sauvage" at the 2000 Paralympic Games. That victory over the Aussies' hometown favourite last fall is the one Petitclerc considers her most memorable. And she expects Sauvage will be her main competition again on August 10 at the IAAF games.

After the IAAF, Petitclerc will turn her attention to ensuring wheelchair racing becomes an "official," rather than just a demonstration event — at both the IAAF and the Olympic Games in 2004 in Athens. Wheelchair racing is the only sport with the dubious distinction of having been a demonstration event for five successive Olympiads. "I will never be satisfied being in a demo event because that is not enough," she says.

Petitclerc has already devoted a decade of her life to high-performance sport but she's not hanging up her racing gloves just yet. In 2004 in Athens, she is intent on taking one more shot at the only prize that has eluded her — an Olympic Games medal.

Petitclerc's advice to others — "Whatever happens, somehow you always find the strength to go through it" — will no doubt help her reach that goal.

AFTER READING

Responding

1. In your notebook, write a paragraph explaining what you think is the most amazing aspect of Chantal Petitclerc's story.

Understanding

2. Write a news **report** of Chantal Petitclerc winning a gold medal at the 2004 Olympics as it might appear in her hometown newspaper.

3. a) In a small group, explain
   - how Chantal Petitclerc's experiences and achievements can be an inspiration to anyone as they graduate from high school
   - what messages Chantal Petitclerc might want to present in her **speeches** at business or corporate events

   b) If time allows, work with your group to write and rehearse the speech that Chantal Petitclerc might give at a graduation or corporate event. Choose a spokesperson from your group to deliver the speech.

4. **Debate** the following resolution: Be It Resolved That Wheelchair Racing Should Be Made an Official Event of the Olympic Games. (See The Reference Shelf, page 401.) You may need to do research to prepare your arguments.

Thinking About Language

5. With a partner, discuss the function of the hyphen in the following phrases: "800-metre wheelchair race," "able-bodied athletes," "high-performance sport." Write a rule covering this use of the hyphen.

Extending

6. With a partner, research and write a short report on the history of Paralympic Games. If possible, include photos and other appropriate visuals to enhance your report.

   Or

   With a partner, research the events available to athletes who participate in the Paralympic Games. Prepare an entry form for participation in one of the events. Include requests for appropriate documentation required for any of the items on the entry form.

7. a) In a small group, create an advertisement (print, television, or radio) promoting the Paralympic Games. Ensure that all members of the group contribute during the production process.

   b) As a class, design an evaluation form to assess the impact of each advertisement.

   c) Present your work to the class, explaining the production choices that your group made.

1928 400m Relay: Bell, Cook, Rosenfeld & Smith—Women's Olympic Lib

"...their accomplishments lived on."

**FRANK COSENTINO AND
GLYNN LEYSHON**

BEFORE READING

As a class, discuss the extent to which female athletes are given the same kind of pay and media attention as male athletes. Discuss recent progress in closing the gap between the sexes in sports. Discuss possible reasons for the remaining gaps.

In 1928, women's track and field events were included in Olympic competition for the first time. Male dominance of Olympic athletics declined quickly after that, even though the inclusion of women's athletics in the ninth Olympiad was made over the protests of the Pope and Baron de Coubertin, founder of the modern Olympics.

The miniscule team of six Canadian girls made the most of their debut into the international scene by winning the team title and capturing two gold medals, one silver, one bronze, one fourth place, and one fifth place.

Four of the girls, Fanny Rosenfeld, Ethel Smith, Florence Bell, and Myrtle Cook, shared a gold medal when they won the 400m relay and set a new world record in the process.

Fanny Rosenfeld bounced and jogged on the cinder track. It was the last day of

Olympic competition in Amsterdam. A few days earlier, she had lost the gold medal in the 100m dash. A very close finish with Robinson of the USA had resulted in a judge's decision that had gone against Fanny. Her great competitive spirit was aroused. This time, her last chance, she was determined to take a gold medal.

Yet her determination was not without humour as well. Named the "life of the party," Fanny could keep her teammates loose and relaxed with an endless stream of jokes and a constantly cheerful approach to life. Fanny also happened to be one of the most talented female athletes in the world. She was later to be named Canada's female athlete of the half century.

At age 23, Fanny, a worker in a Toronto chocolate factory, held Canadian records in running long jump, standing long jump, discus and shot-put, as well as being an outstanding baseball player. Her distance in

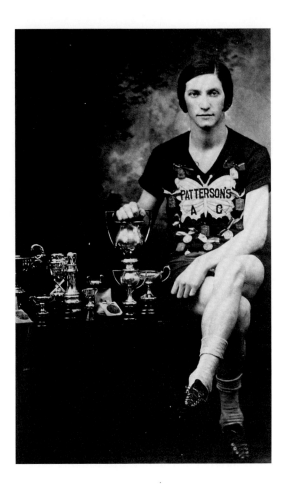

the discus during Olympic trials was 129 feet, 1 inch [39.325m] and the winning toss in Amsterdam was 130 feet [39.6m].

Fanny dropped from the discus competition in order to concentrate on track events; she entered three events and placed in three events, breaking records in two of them! She was second in the 100m, fifth in the 800m (where she surpassed the existing world record) and now was ready to win gold. The starter called the girls for the beginning of the 400m relay final.

Fanny stood in her lane looking down at the footholds dug into the cinder track. This was the track where no records were expected because it had had to be relaid just ten days prior to the start of the Olympics. How wrong the predictions had been! Twelve records were set in the twenty-two men's events and new ones set in all five of the women's events.

The experts had been right about something else, though. Back in Canada they predicted the Canadian girls would do very well. Three of the girls advanced to the finals of the 100m dash alone! All three were now in the final of the 400m relay.

Their send-off had been terrific. The mayor of Toronto was one of the many well-wishers who had come down to the train to wish them good luck. Their chaperone, Alexandrine Gibb, had pampered and ushered them around like a mother hen. On the boat crossing to the Netherlands, Gibb had seen to it that they had a daily workout in the gym, had eaten properly (no pop allowed) and had plenty of sleep (in bed by 10:30).

Awaiting the "get set" of the starter, Fanny could look down the track and see Ethel Smith, dressed in the rather controversial outfit the Canadian girls had chosen. Their shorts were daringly brief for the times and they had cut out the sleeves of their track shirts to give their arms more freedom of movement.

Ethel was another all-round athlete who played softball and basketball as well as holding the Canadian Women's title in the 200m dash. In the 100m final a few days earlier, Ethel had finished just a step behind Fanny Rosenfeld to take the bronze medal. In the Canadian finals in June, the order had been reversed with Ethel second and Fanny third. In her heat to gain the Canadian final, Ethel had had to defeat

Rosa O'Neill, the defending North American record holder, and she did it in a great upset. Thus she was familiar with tough, down-to-the-wire competition. She was eager and ready to put everything into this last attempt at gold.

The rough cinders dug into Fanny Rosenfeld's hands as she waited for the gun. Yesterday this Canadian team had established a new world mark in the 400m relay of 49.4 s and won their heat. Fanny was bursting to go. She was going to show the world how fast they really could run. A split second before the gun went off, Fanny broke. The runners were recalled and Fanny's name was taken. One more false start would disqualify the team. Only a few days before, Myrtle Cook, Canada's world record holder in the 100m dash, had been thrown out of the final for having two false starts. Fanny was determined to take no chances. As the gun went up once more, she held back deliberately. The gun sounded and the runners exploded from their starting pits. Fanny was not among the leaders. She held steady a step or two behind the front runners as they approached the first exchange.

Ethel Smith looked over her shoulder at the rapidly nearing runners. She shifted her feet restlessly. She remembered the training each morning on the *Albertic* during their passage over to the Games, and before that, the weeks of training at the Canadian Ladies' Athletic Club in Toronto — training that brought funny looks to the faces of certain people who believed it unladylike. But at 21, Ethel was more than equal to the stares. She was here in Amsterdam at the Olympics and Fanny was approaching fast with the baton. In a wink of an eye she had it and was gone.

The baton Ethel carried up the track toward Florence Bell was something special. It had been presented to the girls by one of the premier track clubs in Canada, the Hamilton Olympic Club. Not only had the HOC presented the girls with the baton, they had given the Olympic Association $2800. The baton had been passed frequently on the deck of the *Albertic* in order that the girls be fully familiar with it. It was now on the most important journey it would ever make.

At 18, Florence Bell was the youngest on the team. She, too, in keeping with the versatility of the rest of the group, was not only a runner, but a Canadian Champion hurdler, a swimmer and a baseball player.

Florence had been very impressed by the opening parade and the special significance of the flag the girls had been given by the head of the Canadian delegation, P.J. Mulqueen. The flag was the one carried by the victorious Canadian ice hockey team at the 1924 Winter Olympics in Chamonix. It had a winning tradition and Mulqueen gave it to the girls to inspire them. It seemed to be working.

Ethel pounded up the track and inched past one of her competitors. She bore down on Florence like a fury. Florence turned and began sprinting. She felt the slap of that solid baton in her palm, wrapped her fingers around it tightly and shifted into high gear. She too, had something to prove.

In the first heat of the 100m, Florence had been a victim of international stage fright. Her inexperience and youth worked against her and she got off to a bad start.

She was eliminated in the first heat—the only Canadian girl to fail her first test. Now like a reprieve, she was being given a chance to show just what she could do. She tore down the track with a vengeance toward the compact form of Myrtle Cook. The baton jumped in her right hand as though pulling her along. She held the team in steady position in the middle of the pack.

The baton. Myrtle Cook was worried about that thick cylinder of wood. Earlier in the Olympiad, the Canadian men's relay team had been disqualified for dropping their baton, and they had been one of the favoured teams. Would this happen to her? Myrtle Cook's hands were very small and Alexandrine Gibb had given her and the rest of the team daily drilling on the baton exchange to try to prevent any fumbling. But was it enough? Myrtle could not afford the emotional upset which would ensue if she dropped the baton. She was already the hard luck girl of the team. She had disqualified in the finals of the 100m. Myrtle Cook, holder of the world's record of 12 s had not even been allowed to run the race.

Myrtle Cook was very sensitive. Even though she was the only member of the team with previous international experience, she was also the only one to cry from homesickness on the trip. She also sat at the side of the track and cried for half an hour at the time of her ejection from the 100m. Her pride had been deeply hurt. However, she had strong self-discipline, and pulled herself together.

She watched as Florence Bell approached and adrenalin shot through her body. This was it. If Canada was to win a medal, Myrtle would have to run the last leg of the relay as she had never run before. Florence approached the passing zone and Myrtle started. All thoughts of fumbling the exchange had been driven from her mind. She began to accelerate when she felt the hard slap of the wood in her palm and she jumped out of the pack. Within a few strides she had taken a slight lead and with 50m to go had widened the gap. She flew down the track. All the pent-up frustration and emotion pumped her legs like pistons and she drove harder still as she approached the tape. She hit the finish line like a champion. She was out in front by several steps. Canada had won its fourth gold medal of the 1928 Olympics! The winning relay team broke its own world record by a full second with a time of 48.4 s.

The whole team jumped and ran crying and laughing and hugging one another. They were so ecstatic the photographers could not get them to stand still long enough for pictures. Photographers could wait! Right now they wanted to savour their moment. They had worked and sacrificed; they had been "unladylike"—and they had won. Their relay won them both a gold medal and the women's team title by a score of 34 points to 28 for runner-up USA.

A triumphant return home was postponed while the girls participated in meets in France and England, and shopped in Paris. When they did reach Canada, the welcome was tumultuous. In Montreal, they were given a tour of the city and presented at a civic banquet. All the women received solid silver compacts from the city. In Toronto, their hometown, the welcome was awesome. A crowd of 200 000 jammed Union Station and Front Street to greet them on their arrival. The four-mile parade route was lined by another 100 000. When the motorcade of smiling athletes passed Patterson's chocolate factory, everyone was given a box of chocolates by Fanny Rosenfeld's admiring co-workers.

When the parade reached Sunnyside, a highly charged crowd sang "See Them Smiling Just Now" as the girls mounted the platform to be presented with a silver tea set each.

Later, the team attended a special reception in Hamilton for all the Olympic team members and were given special medals to mark the occasion.

The honours and gifts did not stop. Fanny Rosenfeld, for example, was presented with a new car by an admiring group of Toronto businessmen — an unheard-of luxury for a female factory worker.

Gradually, the excitement died, but their accomplishments lived on. The women's Olympic track and field program of five events grew to more than a dozen, and other events — such as canoeing and gymnastics — were expanded to include women. The impetus for such expansion came in large measure from the success of that 1928 Olympics. And the most successful women's team of the year was Canada's.

AFTER READING

Responding

1. Explain why it is important for young Canadians to read about the events described in this selection.

Understanding

2. In a paragraph for each, describe the personality, motives, and achievements of any three of the athletes profiled in this selection.
3. In your notebook, describe how the writers build **suspense** in presenting one of the episodes in this selection.
4. As a class, explain how the events described in this selection relate to the larger story of the women's movement during the last century.

Thinking About Language

5. a) This selection, from a book that was written in 1975, refers to the female athletes as "girls." Explain why the same book written today would probably not use the word "girls" in the same way.

   b) Identify any other words or phrases in the selection that would not appear in contemporary writing for the same reason.

Extending

6. Using print and/or electronic sources, research the achievements of another prominent Canadian female athlete. Write the story of her achievements for publication in your school newspaper. If possible, include a photo, or photos, with **captions** to accompany your story.

7. a) With a partner, track the sports coverage in a newspaper or on a television news program for a week to determine which gets more coverage: sports played by women or sports played by men.

   b) Prepare a list of reasons for the proportion of the sports coverage that each receives.

   c) Discuss your findings with the class.

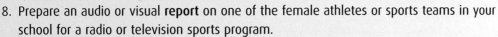

8. Prepare an audio or visual **report** on one of the female athletes or sports teams in your school for a radio or television sports program.

How Writing Evolved

BEFORE READING

Brainstorm a list of reasons to explain the advantages writing cultures had over oral cultures in history.

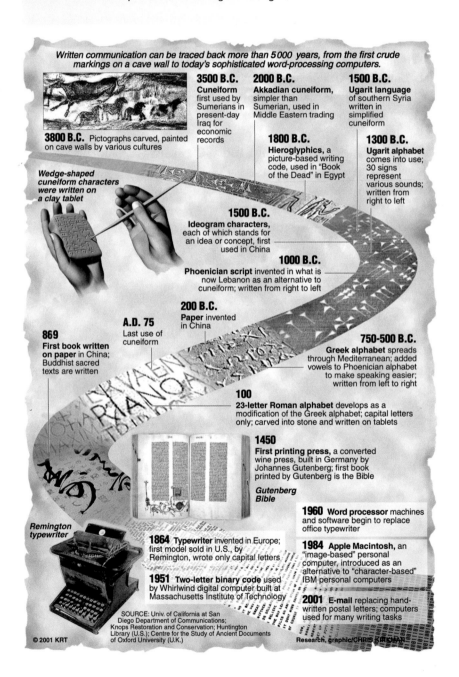

Written communication can be traced back more than 5000 years, from the first crude markings on a cave wall to today's sophisticated word-processing computers.

3800 B.C. Pictographs carved, painted on cave walls by various cultures

3500 B.C.
Cuneiform first used by Sumerians in present-day Iraq for economic records

2000 B.C.
Akkadian cuneiform, simpler than Sumerian, used in Middle Eastern trading

1500 B.C.
Ugarit language of southern Syria written in simplified cuneiform

1800 B.C.
Hieroglyphics, a picture-based writing code, used in "Book of the Dead" in Egypt

1300 B.C.
Ugarit alphabet comes into use; 30 signs represent various sounds; written from right to left

Wedge-shaped cuneiform characters were written on a clay tablet

1500 B.C.
Ideogram characters, each of which stands for an idea or concept, first used in China

1000 B.C.
Phoenician script invented in what is now Lebanon as an alternative to cuneiform; written from right to left

200 B.C.
Paper invented in China

A.D. 75
Last use of cuneiform

869
First book written on paper in China; Buddhist sacred texts are written

750-500 B.C.
Greek alphabet spreads through Mediterranean; added vowels to Phoenician alphabet to make speaking easier; written from left to right

100
23-letter Roman alphabet develops as a modification of the Greek alphabet; capital letters only; carved into stone and written on tablets

1450
First printing press, a converted wine press, built in Germany by Johannes Gutenberg; first book printed by Gutenberg is the Bible

Gutenberg Bible

1960 **Word processor** machines and software begin to replace office typewriter

1984 **Apple Macintosh,** an "image-based" personal computer, introduced as an alternative to "character-based" IBM personal computers

Remington typewriter

1864 **Typewriter** invented in Europe; first model sold in U.S., by Remington, wrote only capital letters

1951 **Two-letter binary code** used by Whirlwind digital computer built at Massachusetts Institute of Technology

2001 **E-mail** replacing hand-written postal letters; computers used for many writing tasks

SOURCE: Univ. of California at San Diego Department of Communications; Knops Restoration and Conservation; Huntington Library (U.S.); Centre for the Study of Ancient Documents of Oxford University (U.K.)

© 2001 KRT

Research, graphic/CHRIS KIRKMAN

AFTER READING

Responding

1. With a partner, identify
   - the most interesting fact on the chart
   - a piece of information you would like to have about the evolution of writing, but which is not on this chart

Understanding

2. a) With a partner, list the strengths and weaknesses of presenting historical information in a chart such as this. Be prepared to explain whether there are more strengths or weaknesses to presenting the information in this way.
   b) Explain any changes you would make to the chart to enhance its effectiveness.
3. In your notebook, prepare arguments to support one fact on the chart as being the most significant to the evolution of writing. In a small group, compare your arguments and facts. If there are differences, try to convince others in the group of the validity of your arguments.

Thinking About Language

4. Locate words in this chart that are in quotation marks and explain why this punctuation has been used.

Extending

5. The Greek philosopher, Plato, believed that writing would destroy people's ability to memorize. As a class, brainstorm what he might have meant by this. To what extent was he right?
6. Using print and/or electronic sources, research one of the points on this chart or an additional fact about the history of writing. Using your findings, prepare an oral **report** and create an illustration that could be added to the chart.

It's Etymology, Dude

"Entire conversations can be had with this one word."

RACHEL SAUER

BEFORE READING

With a partner, brainstorm a list of words that have acquired a new meaning in contemporary usage. For example, the use of the word "cool" to mean "first-rate" or "admirable" as in "I think this is a cool design." For each word on your list, write the old **definition**, the new definition, and use the word with its new meaning in a sentence.

A conversation overheard at a college:

Guy No. 1 (showing a friend something on his arm): See?

Guy No. 2: Dude.

A conversation overheard on the basketball court at a middle school:

Boy No. 1 (sinking a jump shot): Dude!

Boy No. 2: Dude, that was awesome.

This word "dude," see how it slips so effortlessly from the mouths of so many. See how it can express the entire range of human emotion: sadness (Dude.), happiness (Dude!), anger (Dude...), confusion (Dude?) and amazement (Duuuuuude).

Entire conversations can be had with this one word.

"I think when a word achieves such a basic, generic meaning, it really puts it squarely in the centre of usage so that it could just be thrown into a sentence basi-cally as filler," says Tom Pitoniak, associate editor of Merriam-Webster dictionaries.

What a victory for this underdog, to have risen in less than 100 years from obscurity to prominence.

Gerald Cohen, editor of *Comments on Etymology*, says most researchers agree the first printed occurrence of "dude" was in 1883, in Robert Sale Hill's poem "The Dude."

Prior to 1883, the word "dude" was used in some New England towns, pronounced "doo-dy" and believed to be a diminutive form of "doodle" and "dandy." It was used to describe a foppish young man.

Or, according to a poem printed in the Feb. 16, 1884, edition of *The Hatchet:* "A dude is a weak and anomalous thing with very thin legs that it gaily doth swing as it ambles along in a Newmarket coat, with a seven-inch collar caressing its throat. It stands on the corner attempting to mash the girls as it pulls at a feeble moustache."

But a May, 1883, article in *Clothier and Furnisher* said: "It is not exactly slang, but has not rooted itself in the language and has not, therefore, a precise and accepted meaning."

So, things have both changed and stayed the same. "Dude" has rooted itself in our language, but as for a precise and accepted meaning, well, it doesn't necessarily have one.

In the early 20th century, "dude" came to be used to describe city slickers who went West trying to be cowboys on dude ranches. From the 1930s through 1950s, it was used by hipsters to mean guy or man—think James Dean and Marlon Brando in leather.

"Historically, it became at one point fairly restricted to African-American populations in the 1960s," says Walt Wolfram, a sociolinguist at North Carolina State University.

"Over time, it expanded so it was used by white liberals who sort of adopted these terms because there's a sort of covert prestige to the slang of black culture."

In the mid-1960s, California surfers adopted "dude" and the use of the word spread. At first, it specifically meant a guy, as in "that dude." Soon, it came to be associated with hippies, Generation X and now Generation Y.

"I think they want to cultivate an ethos of 'nothing really fazes me,' and I think the word 'dude' is really commensurate with that," Pitoniak says. "Unflappability is sort of a hallmark of younger generations, and 'dude' just has that whole connotation of 'just catch a wave and worry about the other things later, dude.'"

According to the *Generation X Field Guide and Lexicon*, "dude" can mean a guy friend or a cool female, while the longer "duuuuude" indicates the speaker is impressed.

What remains to be seen, Pitoniak notes, is whether dude reaches "man" status. That is, a meaningless intensive word that's not really addressed at anyone, as in, "Oh, man!" At this point, "Oh, dude!" doesn't quite sound right.

"In our era of mass-media culture… there's a certain degree of snowballing that makes it harder for a word to fade out because it becomes widespread," Pitoniak says.

So far, dude has outlasted hep cats, groovy anything, rad this and gnarly that. Aging hippies and fifth-graders say dude. It has transcended just about every sociological category. But as for its future, dude, that's anyone's guess.

AFTER **READING**

Responding

1. Identify the uses and meanings of the word "dude" mentioned in this **article** that you were familiar with before you read this article.

Understanding

2. Identify the **thesis** or main idea of this article.
3. With a partner, create an illustrated time line showing the evolution of the word "dude." (For examples of time lines, see "All About Food," pages 14–21 and "How Writing Evolved," page 164.) Display your work on chart paper.

Thinking About Language

4. Write definitions of generic, obscurity, diminutive, foppish, anomalous, ethos, and ambles as they are used in this article. Add any new or unfamiliar words you have defined to your personal word list.
5. a) Look up and record the **etymology** of the word "etymology" in a dictionary.
   b) Distinguish between an etymologist and entomologist.
6. Find an example of the use of quotation marks in this article that indicate each of the following:
   • **direct speech**
   • words taken from another written source
   • the title of a short work of literature
   • a word used out of **context**

Extending

7. With a partner, discuss whether colloquial words such as "dude" are more apt to change their meaning over time than more formal and/or technical words. (See The Reference Shelf, pages 351, for a discussion of the levels of language.) Brainstorm a list of words that support your conclusion.
8. With a partner, research and write a history of the use of one of the words from the list you brainstormed in the "Before Reading" activity. Take your writing through the writing process before submitting the final draft. Be sure to include a correctly formatted bibliography of any sources that you use. (See The Reference Shelf, pages 378–379.)

Now Hear This

"Huh? What was that?"   DON OLDENBURG

BEFORE READING

Describe to a partner the listening characteristics of someone you know who is a very good listener. Have your partner describe to you the listening characteristics of someone who is a poor listener. Be prepared to report to the class on the characteristics of good and poor listeners.

Chances are you haven't given much thought to becoming a better listener.

But lend an ear to this: Effective listening is emerging as one of the important remedies for relationship angst, mental and emotional blocks, societal stress and much of what ails or derails our busy and distracted modern lives, say social scientists who study listening's impact on human activity.

Huh? What was that?

How about some attention-grabbing statistics, compiled on *www.listen.org*, the Web site of the International Listening Association:

We listen to 125 to 250 words per minute, but think at 1000 to 3000 words per minute.

We've learned 85 per cent of what we know by listening.

We are distracted, preoccupied or forgetful 75 per cent of the time.

Immediately after listening to someone talk, we recall about half of what we heard. After some time has passed, we remember about 20 per cent.

Less than 2 per cent of us have had any formal training in listening skills.

"We previously sort of assumed that if anybody can hear and has intelligence enough to listen, they could," says Larry Barker, co-author with Kittie Watson of *Listen Up: How To Improve Relationships, Reduce Stress And Be More Productive By Using The Power of Listening.*

"But we see now that's not necessarily so."

Barker is also the author of the benchmark textbook *Listening Behavior* that in 1971 began changing how scientists studied and understood the skills of effective listening.

There are four different listening styles: people-oriented, action-oriented, content-oriented and time-oriented.

"An example of people-oriented listeners are those who like to hear all the colour around the story, what time it was, what they were wearing, did it snow or rain?" Barker says.

"Another kind of listener might be bored with that. An action-oriented listener, for instance, wants to really get to the bottom line and skip the colour commentary."

So, in a conversation between a people-oriented listener and an action-oriented listener, what we could have is a failure to communicate.

Many women favour people-oriented listening, while men are more action-oriented, which is one reason why some men don't appear to be good listeners when their wives are talking.

By recognizing our own listening preferences, we can adjust them to fit conversations and gain an advantage, Barker says.

"Listeners who are really doing their job have a lot more power," he says.

Barker offers an earful of practical tips and techniques to do that during conversations, from turning away from distractions, to leaning slightly forward and looking intent, to giving active feedback with eye contact and nods.

"There are certainly no eurekas," he says. "These things make sense, but the truth is most people don't stop and think about it."

Barker mentions men who pride themselves on being able to listen and read the newspaper simultaneously, but get no credit from women who need more feedback than an occasional grunt.

Just making an effort to look like a good listener goes a long way toward being one, he says.

"It's a physiological thing. These behaviours kick in the good listening habits automatically."

Rebecca Shafir, author of *The Zen Of Listening*, blames poor listening for such problems as high suicide rates and school violence to family breakups and drug abuse.

"There really seems to be a common thread that runs through many of the headaches and heartaches in our lives," says Shafir, a speech pathologist based in Winchester, Mass., who teaches communications seminars nationwide.

"If you interview teachers, business people, physicians and the saints that man the suicide and confession hotlines, you will find that poor listening is at the root of many of the tragedies."

Increasingly, we are bombarded with non-stop noise and distractions that make it hard to listen and comprehend, says Shafir.

Quoting advertising industry statistics, she says our average attention span is only about 22 seconds—which is why commercials are shorter and more repetitive than ever.

"We tend to do these things that interrupt the message, that cut it off, that keep us from getting the whole message," she adds.

Shafir says "internal distractions" include self-doubt, mind-wandering, prejudices, biases, even scatterbrained stuff like focusing on a speaker's green tie instead of his words.

"When your boss comes up to you, what's the first thing that comes into your mind? Do I have bad breath? Do I look all right? And all the while, we're not hearing what the boss is saying."

AFTER READING

Responding

1. a) Identify the two pieces of information that you found to be the most interesting in this article.
   b) With a partner, discuss each other's choices.
   c) Be prepared to report to the class on your choices and the reasons for them.

Understanding

2. Using information in this article, make a list of
   • reasons that account for poor listening skills
   • ways to improve listening skills
   • reasons for improving one's listening skills

3. Write a short **essay** explaining the relationship between attention span and commercials as described in the fourth-last paragraph of this article. Use examples to explain and illustrate the points in your essay.

Thinking About Language

4. Write the punctuation rule that explains the use of italics in this article.

Extending

5. Identify strengths and weaknesses in your own listening skills. Make a plan in writing for improving your listening skills.

6. With a partner, design a pamphlet or an audio or videotape for high-school students providing tips on "How to Improve Your Listening Skills for Better Learning." Visit the Web site of the International Listening Association <www.listen.org> to obtain additional information for your pamphlet.

For Conversation, Press #1

"Why is it that the more connected we get,
 the more disconnected I feel?"

MICHAEL ALVEAR

In your notebook, create a chart showing the pros and cons of pagers, cell phones, e-mail, voice mail, and the Internet.

A funny thing happened on the way to the communications revolution: We stopped talking to one another.

I was walking in the park with a friend recently. His cell phone rang, interrupting our conversation. There we were, walking and talking on a beautiful sunny day and—poof!—I became invisible, absent from the conversation.

The park was filled with people talking on their cell phones. They were passing other people without looking at them, saying hello, noticing their babies or stopping to pet their puppies. Evidently, the untethered electronic voice is preferable to human contact.

The telephone used to connect you to those absent. Now it makes people sitting next to you feel absent. Recently I was in a car with three friends. The driver shushed the rest of us because he couldn't hear the person on the other end of his cell phone. There we were, four friends, unable to talk to one another because of a gadget designed to make communication easier.

Why is it that the more connected we get, the more disconnected I feel? Every advance in communications technology is a setback to the intimacy of human interaction. With e-mail and instant messaging over the Internet, we can now communicate without seeing or talking to one another. With voice mail, you can conduct entire conversations without ever reaching anyone. If my mom has a question, I just leave the answer on her voice mail.

As almost every conceivable contact between human beings gets automated, the alienation index goes up. You can't even call a human being to get the phone number of another human anymore. Directory assistance is almost always fully automated.

Pumping gas at the station? Why bother saying good morning to the attendant when you can swipe your credit card at the pump and save yourself the bother of human contact?

Making a deposit at the bank? Why talk to a clerk who might live in the neighbourhood when you can insert your card into the banking machine?

Pretty soon you won't have the burden of making eye contact at the grocery store. Some supermarket chains are using a self-scanner so you can check yourself out, avoiding all those annoying clerks who look at you and ask how you are doing.

I'm no Luddite. I own a cell phone, a bank card, a voice-mail system and an e-mail account. Giving them up isn't an option — they're great for what they're intended to do. It's their unintended consequences that make me cringe.

More and more, I find myself hiding behind e-mail to do a job meant for conversation. Or being relieved that voice mail picked up because I didn't really have time to talk. The industry devoted to helping me keep in touch is making me lonelier — or at least facilitating my antisocial instincts.

So I've put myself on technology restriction: No instant messaging with people who live near me, no using the cell phone in the presence of friends, and no letting the voice mail pick up when I'm home.

What good is all this gee-whiz technology if there's no one in the room to hear you exclaim, "gee whiz!"?

AFTER READING

Responding

1. In your notebook, write your reactions to one of the points raised in this **article**.

Understanding

2. With a partner, reread the article and copy one sentence that represents the **thesis** of this article.
3. Explain how the Blondie comic strip reinforces the **theme** of Alvear's article.
4. List at least three methods of development the writer uses to argue his point. (See The Reference Shelf, pages 386–391.) With a partner, assess the effectiveness of each. Be prepared to explain your conclusions to the class.

Thinking About Language

5. Reread the article and record examples of each of the following:
   - punctuation used for stylistic effect
   - unconventional use of grammar for effect
   - a word based on an **allusion** to a historical movement

Extending

6. Create your own cartoon that pokes fun at new technologies. Post the cartoons for the class to see.
7. a) In a small group, discuss whether young people brought up with modern communication technology find it less alienating than older people who were brought up with fewer communications devices. From your discussion, design a thesis and create an oral **essay** to present to the class.
   b) As a class, evaluate the presentations based on a rubric you have designed. (See The Reference Shelf, page 404.)
   c) Update your Oral Communication Skills Action Plan using the class' feedback. (See The Reference Shelf, page 395.)

8. a) With a partner, plan and conduct a survey to help a technology company create and market a new communications device. From your research, create a **report** suggesting one type of product and at least one marketing strategy. Include visuals where possible and use a **layout** that is attractive and easy to read.
   b) Exchange your report with another group and give feedback on the questions they asked in their survey, the product they suggested, and how they applied the information in their surveys to a marketing strategy.

Life Line

"Please wait...please do not hang up the
phone. We appreciate your patience."

DOUGLAS CRAVEN

BEFORE **READING**

In a small group, discuss the most helpful and the most frustrating aspects of automated telephone answering or information services. Be prepared to report on the key points and most interesting examples from your discussion.

CHARACTERS:

a thin man
a voice mail service (male or female, a voice offstage)
another female voice
another male voice

Setting

The setting is simple. A thin man in a chair. Beside him is an end-table with a phone on it.

The man picks up the phone. We hear the dial tone. We hear as he dials. The phone rings three times.

Voice Mail Service: Hello, and welcome to the Good Samaritan Life Line. Are you in trouble? Do you need help? Are you alone?

If so, then we value your call. Please help us to direct you to the area where we can serve you best. If you are experiencing a personal crisis, press 1...now. If you have recently been through a personal trauma, such as divorce or bereavement, press 2...now. If you have twitches, shakes or lack of control over bodily functions, press 3...now.

The man hesitates.
If your problem is the inability to make decisions, please wait on the line and one of our representatives will be with you in a moment.

The man waits.
Please wait. [Long pause.] Please wait. [Long pause.] Transferring call. [Long pause.] Thank you for holding. All of our personal counsellors are busy serving other clients. Calls will be answered in sequence, so please do not hang up the phone. We appreciate your patience.

Jingly, twangly Musak begins to play.
Thank you for holding. All of our personal counsellors are busy serving other clients. Calls will be answered in sequen…

A click.
Hello? You have reached the office of [another voice] Marge Barrett, head psychologist in charge of hesitancy, indecision and impotence. [voice mail voice resumes] We are sorry, but [another voice] Marge Barrett, head psychologist in charge of hesitancy, indecision and impotence [voice mail voice resumes] is unable to come to the phone. Please stay on the line and you will be transferred. Please wait.

If your hesitation in life is the result of childhood trauma, please press 1.

He does.
If your brother or sister beat you up and stole your toys, press 1…now. If you accidentally walked in on your parents, press 2…now. If you had a bad experience with an electronic device, press 3…now. If your dog bit your…

He hits 3.
Please indicate which electronic device led to your bad experience. For personal computer, press 1. Now. For fishing sonar or other hardware relating to outdoor sports, press 2…now. For toaster, mixer or other kitchen appliance, press 3…now. For telephone, press 4…

He stabs the 4.
Your response was not understood. Please press the key firmly. For telephone, press 4…

He presses 4.
You have selected [pause] Fishing…sonar. Please press 8. *He does.* To confirm that you just pressed 8, please press 7. *He does.* Thank you. If you wish to cancel your selection… Fishing…sonar…please press 1.

He does, his finger hovering over the keys.
Please press…nothing. Please wait.

Please indicate which electronic device led to your bad experience. For personal computers, press…

He hits 4.
You have selected [pause] Telephone. Please hold the line. A representative will be with you shortly.

The Musak plays.
Please wait. [Long pause.] Transferring call. [Long pause.] Thank you for holding. All of our personal counsellors are busy serving other clients. Calls will be answered in sequence, so please do not hang up the phone. We appreciate your patience.

Thank you for holding. You have reached the office of [new voice] Wallace Ferktun, head of telephone and telecommunications psychology. [voice mail voice] We are sorry, but [new voice] Wallace Ferktun, head of telephone and telecommunications psychology, [voice mail voice] is not answering. Please press 1 to leave a message.

He does.
Your response was not understood. Please press the key firmly. [He does.] Please try again. [He does.] Your response was not understood. Please press [He does]. We are sorry, but your response was not

understood. Please hold the line. [Long pause. He moves to hang up.] Please do NOT hang up the phone. Transferring now. [Pause] Please press 9. Please press 2 to confirm that you just pressed 6 [Long pause.] or 9 to confirm that you just pressed 9. The first time. Thank you. Rerouting.

You have indicated that you have had a bad experience with [pause] the telephone. If your problem relates to the commercial or sexual misuse of telephone equipment, press 1 now. If it is the result of an electrical discharge from a telephone handset or an explosion of telephone equipment, press 2 now. If you were frightened of or intimidated by a telephone voice mail answering service, press 3 now.

He does.
You have selected…voice mail service intimidation as your reason for trauma. Push 1 to confirm your choice. If you think you have the guts.

He hesitates, considering this. Finally, he does.
Please hold the line. A representative from Good Samaritan Life Lines will be with you shortly. Transferring now. [Long pause.] Thank you for holding. All of our personal counsellors are busy serving other clients. Calls will be answered in sequence, so please do not hang up the phone. We appreciate your patience, you wimp. Go ahead and hang up, marshmallow. You can't can you?

He shakes the headset.
Please hold the line. A representative… Hello, you have reached the office of… Please hold the line. Transferring.
   Press 2…now.
He does.

Press 1…now. [He hesitates.] Press 1. Now. If you were frightened by the voice of a voice mail service because it sounded too much like your domineering mother, press 1 now. If you once heard a voice mail service say an extremely dirty word and it upset your sense of moral decency, press 2 now. If you fear being humiliated by a voice mail service, or are worried that you might be dominated by a voice mail service whose personality is stronger than your own…

He has his finger on the button. Long pause.
Please hold the line.

The Musak starts.
Please do not hang up. The representative …transferring. Hold. Seven-six-one-fourteen. Transferring. Do not hang up.

A strange noise emanates from the receiver.
That response is not understood by our system. Please press the Pound key.

An even stranger noise emanates from the receiver.
If you fear being humiliated by a voice mail service, or are worried that you might become dominated by a voice mail service whose personality is stronger than your own…and this is becoming just a wee bit scary…[long pause] Press 3… nnnnnnnn — Now.

He does.
You have selected a voice mail related angst as your trauma. If you are feeling trapped by this voice mail service, press 1. Now. [Does.] If you are feeling intimidated by this voice mail service, press 2. [Does.]

Please wait until I say now. [Pause.] Now. [He presses 3.] If you feel that this call has gone on too long, press 3. Now. If you think that it's stupid that the voice mail service would ask you if the call has gone on too long and thereby add time to the call, press 1...now. [Pause.] If you didn't quite follow that, press 2...now. [He does.] Press 1 if you didn't understand it because you are an idiot. Press 2 if you are a wimp. Press 3 if you are a snivelling, half-pint cry-baby who blubs his way through his limp, crayfishy existence, dreaming of a better life but never having the courage to seek it. [Pause.] Press 4 if you secretly know I was right about 3.

He presses 4.
To speak to a trained psychologist, press 1...now. [He does.] To speak to a priest, rabbi, minister or naturopath, press 2...now. [He does.] To speak to any other human being, anyone at all, press 3...now. [He does.]
Please hold.

The Musak plays. The man stabs all the numbers. Finally, in a supreme act of courage and strength, he moves to hang up.
Do not hang up your phone. Do NOT hang up your phone, I said.

But he does. Long pause. Finally, the phone rings. He lets it ring, but finally picks up.
If you are surprised that I'm calling you, press 1...now. [Pause.] Go on, I know you are. [He presses 1.] Good. If you thought you could get away from me that easily, press 2...now. [He does.] If you are beginning to feel like one of the characters in a Beckett play, press 3. [He

does.] If you really don't know what a Beckett play is, but you pressed 3 anyway, press 4. [He does.] If you are a moron, press 5. Now. [He does.] If you are a mucusy, lame, gutted, pigeony creature with the strength of a ten year old elastic, press 6. [He does.] Press 7 because I said so. [He does.] Now press 8. [He does.] Now 1. [He does. For each of the following numbers, he presses the key obediently.] 4 - 3 - 3 - 2 - 8 - 5 minus 3 — square root of 64. It's eight, you knob. Stop. Press 9 if you are becoming desperate. [He does.] If you are desperate enough to try anything to end this call, press the star. Now. [He hesitates...a trick? Finally, he does.] Okay, here's what I'm offering. One of the following choices leads to freedom, the other two lead to an eternity on this line. Please press 1, 2, or 3. Take your time. One means escape. The others...Choose. [We hear the strange screeching noise again...midnight radio squelch, oddly modulated.] No rush. Go ahead. Go on. Do something for a change.

He stabs the 3.
Damn it! All right. A deal's a deal! Please stay on the line, and an operator will assist you momentarily. Transferring, you lucky bastard.

Other Voice: Hello, how can I help you? If you would like to complain about the previous voice mail service, press 1 now. If you wish to register the pathos of your situation, press 2 now. To give up, press 3.

He does. Black out on the tone.

AFTER **READING**

Responding

1. Describe the two moments you found the funniest in this **play**. Give reasons why they are so funny.

Understanding

2. With a partner, make of list of examples of **satire** in this play. Include references to the play for each item in your list.

3. Research the following references in the play: Good Samaritan, Muzak, a Beckett play. Explain how each contributes to the satire in the play. How does knowing these references help you understand the play?

Thinking About Language

4. **Define** what is meant by a verb in the imperative mood. Explain why there are so many verbs in the imperative mood in this play.

Extending

5. a) In a pair, rehearse a performance of a part of this play.
   b) Present your rehearsed **scene** to the class live or on audio tape.
   c) After all pairs have performed their scenes, have a class discussion to assess the challenges involved in presenting this play on stage. Discuss whether a stage production of the play would be interesting and engaging for the audience.

6. a) Write a **script** for an automated information service for a local business.
   b) Practise reading your script out loud and, if possible, tape-record it. Listen to your own reading for ways to improve the tone and clarity of your voice.
   c) Present your script either live or tape-recorded to your classmates.

7. a) With a partner, create a shooting script for a television commercial for a company that is promising its customers "human" contact and service when they call. In your script, include the **dialogue** (if any), sounds, visuals, and camera angles.
   b) Present your shooting script to another pair for feedback, and revise as necessary.

For Reading Out Loud!

"...the most effective...way to foster in children a lifelong love of books and reading."

MARGARET MARY KIMMEL
AND ELIZABETH SEGAL

BEFORE READING

With a partner, describe memorable experiences of being read aloud to at home, in school, or elsewhere. Discuss whether you still enjoy being read to.

Many children today grow up with negative attitudes toward books and reading in any form. The media call it "a literacy crisis." The schools try new methods of teaching reading and test children more often, but nothing seems to cure the problem. Publishers bring out attractive books geared to poor readers, teachers report that these students are so turned off by books that the new formats don't entice them at all. Worried parents invest in expensive "teach your child to read" kits and high-powered electronic learning games, only to see their children growing up reading nothing on their own but an occasional comic book.

Meanwhile, research data have slowly been accumulating that suggest how we might resolve this crisis. Several studies of children from widely varied backgrounds who learned to read easily and remained good readers throughout their school years have revealed that they had something in common. They all had been read to regularly from early childhood and had as models adults or older children who read for pleasure.

In fact, reading aloud to children from literature that is meaningful to them is now widely acknowledged among experts to be the most effective, as well as the simplest and least expensive, way to foster in children a lifelong love of books and reading. The task now is to pass this word along to individual parents, school administrators, and classroom teachers.

Many of these adults understand the importance of reading aloud to a young child who can't yet read. But too often these same adults no more think of reading aloud to the child who has learned to read than they would continue to run alongside the child's first bicycle, steadying the vehicle, after the child had learned to ride alone.

This is a sad mistake. Reading aloud should continue all through the school years, for many reasons.

- *To stop the read-aloud sessions of the preschool years ends a rich shared experience.* A mother and father we know were concerned because their son's first-grade year was nearly over and he showed no signs of being able to read. They expressed their concern to his teacher and asked if she thought he needed special help to overcome a problem or disability. She stared at them in surprise: "Why, Jason reads quite well—and has been for several months now." It turned out that Jason had been keeping his new skill a secret, worrying that if his parents knew he could read to himself, they might stop reading him a bedtime story. Needless to say, Jason's parents reassured him that he could enjoy reading to himself *and* have his nightly story, too.

In many families now grown up, books read aloud together in childhood have become a treasured part of family history. "Remember when you read us *Five Children and It*, and we kids spent our entire week at the beach digging for a sand-fairy?" "I'll never forget when Mom was reading *Cheaper by the Dozen* in the car and Dad got laughing so hard that he had to pull over and stop."

In school, too, the shared experience that reading aloud provides creates a genuine bond in a group of diverse children that is unlikely to occur in any other way. As one teacher said after reading *A Bridge to Terabithia* to her class: "By the end of that story, we had been through so much together."

And this kind of communal experience is becoming rarer. In automobile assembly plants these days, many workers are plugged into the individual "walkaround" tape players. No doubt these help dispel the tedium of the job, but such gadgets cut off one worker from another; each is operating in his or her own world rather than sharing, as the cigar workers did, one fictional world.

- *Being read to promotes, rather than retards, children's desire to read independently.* Contrary to some parents' and teachers' fears, listening to stories doesn't make "lazy readers." Rather, what the children hear seems to whet their appetites to read that book or others like it for themselves. One school librarian told us that when she asks children to name their favourite book, they almost always name the book she or their teacher has most recently read to them.

We all know that film and television adaptations increase interest in a book. When *The Secret Garden* was telecast on *Once Upon a Classic*, copies of the book were scarce as hen's teeth in the libraries. (We know one little girl whose popularity shot up considerably as her classmates competed to borrow the copy she owned.) Reading a story aloud is another form of book promotion and is just as effective with the children it reaches as a *Star Wars* movie or an *Afterschool Special* on television. And it has the decided advantage that the individual parent or professional—not Madison Avenue or Hollywood—can choose what book to promote to a particular child or group of children.

One reason that reading a book or story works so effectively to motivate independent reading is that learning to read is difficult and often frustrating. Going on to read more and more challenging books means repeatedly risking failure. Hearing a first-rate story read aloud makes the rewards of sticking to it clear and tangible.

- *Being read to fosters improvement of children's independent reading skills.* Studies of first- and second-graders and fourth- through sixth-graders have demonstrated that children who are read aloud to on a regular basis over a period of several months show significant gains in reading comprehension, decoding skills, and vocabulary. The gains were greatest for disadvantaged students but not limited to them — all the children benefited significantly compared to the control groups, who were read to only occasionally or not at all.

Besides making children more eager to tackle the difficult tasks involved in learning to read, hearing stories read gets children used to the written language they will meet in books, which is different from spoken language.

- *All through their school years, young people can enjoy listening to books that would be too difficult for them to read on their own.* How exciting it is for the first-grader, who is struggling to read brief and perhaps insipid primer stories, to share the delights and dangers of a whole prairie year when the teacher reads a daily chapter from one of Laura Ingalls Wilder's books. Similarly, seventh-graders might find *The Wizard of Earthsea* beyond their ability or ambition for independent reading yet become totally absorbed in listening to an adult read it aloud.

Listening experiences like these are especially valuable for the student whose home language is not English and for children whose chief exposure to English comes from the television set.

- *Wonderful books that are "hard to get into" are more accessible when read aloud.* The first few pages of an unfamiliar book usually determine whether a child reading independently will go on or give up and look for another book. In some books the reader immediately knows what's going on and is almost instantly swept up in the events of the story. Fairy tales, for example, signal in the first few sentences who the characters are, whether they are good or bad, and what their predicament is. A formula story of a less exalted sort, like a Nancy Drew mystery or a Spiderman comic, also makes the reader feel right at home in familiar territory. But some of the richest, most rewarding books are the unconventional ones, the ones that don't fit a formula. Such books may defer gratification of the reader's curiosity in order to first establish a scene and mood; they are original rather than predictable. These books profit immensely from being read aloud. Your captive audience may be a bit restless until they get oriented, but they will soon be deep in the world of story with you if you have selected well.

- *For the poor student whose inability to read has barred her or him from access to stimulating material in every subject, including literature, there is no substitute for reading aloud.* The attempt of publishers to be responsive to the needs of poor readers by providing high-interest/low-level-of-difficulty books is praiseworthy, but the fact is that many literary experiences that would be moving and meaningful to a fifteen-year-old reading at a third-grade level simply cannot be conveyed in simple sentence structure and vocabulary. Reading aloud is a way to be sure these students aren't deprived of their rich literary heritage.

- *A significant number of children will always grasp material better through their ears than through their eyes.* When asked in a class, one student said he had no early memory of books. He didn't remember ever enjoying a book and doesn't read anything now except required assignments — not even the newspaper. He did recall with pleasure, however, records of stories that he owned as a child — folktales, Hans Christian Andersen stories, and the like. "Words on the page somehow come between me and the story" is the way he described his problem. He was envious of his classmates' memories of their parents reading to them. He was sure that would have been even better than the records.

There are others like this young man who may never find pleasure in reading, even if they have been read to in childhood. Is reading to such youngsters a waste of time, then? Not at all. Ideally, they should have occasional opportunities to listen to literature all their lives, so that they, too, can savor the unique pleasures of the written word.

- *Studies have shown that reading aloud to children significantly broadens their reading interests and tastes.* Children and adolescents who tend to limit themselves to one author's books or one type of book

in their independent reading — mysteries or sports stories or romances, for instance — will often be led to more challenging books and greater variety in their reading by hearing a book chosen by a knowledgeable adult.

- *Exposing children to good literature, presented for enjoyment, will increase the chances that their reading life doesn't end with high school graduation.* A major goal of the schools should be to turn out people who not only are able to read but find enough pleasure in reading that they will actually read a book now and then after they've left school. We know that many American [and Canadian] adults simply never read books; of these, only a small number are actually unable to read. In all likelihood, the adults who can but do not read books were once students who read only what was required of them at school. Once the assignments stopped, so did the reading. A few good books read aloud solely for the students' enjoyment could have made a difference.

- *Seeing adults reading with enjoyment increases the chances that children will become lifelong readers.* This means that the parent, teacher, librarian, grandparent, or other adult who finds time to read to a child and does it with enthusiasm is providing a model as well as a story. Observing adults who are eager to read and are engaged in reading is more effective in making readers of children than any number of lectures on the importance of reading.

And it's important to recognize that, though the parent makes a very effective model, children whose parents have never discovered the pleasures of reading need not be left out. Any adult or older child can fill this role. By providing regular reading-aloud sessions to children who do not get that experience at home, the school or day-care centre or library can break through the cycle of illiteracy that victimizes many young people. Then when these children who have enjoyed hearing stories grow up, they may very well pass on the pleasure by reading to the children in their lives.

AFTER READING

Responding

1. In a paragraph, explain why reading skills are important in today's society.
2. Identify experiences you have had and books you have read that are referred to in this **essay**. Write a **journal** entry explaining how those experiences and books contributed to your personal level of literacy or how having more of those experiences might have helped you attain a higher level of literacy.

Understanding

3. a) In your notebook, explain the three reasons for reading aloud provided in this essay that seemed most important to you.
   b) Explain what new information you have gained from reading this essay and how you can use that information in the future with your own children, or with the children of your friends or relatives.

Thinking About Language

4. "Publishers bring out attractive books geared to poor readers, teachers report that these students are so turned off by books that the new formats don't entice them at all" (paragraph 1). What punctuation mark would be better than the comma in this sentence? Name the error in the sentence as it appears in this essay.

Extending

5. In a small group, read aloud a section of a book, newspaper, or magazine **article** that you have recently enjoyed reading. After your reading, explain why you chose the selection you did.

6. a) With a partner, listen to part of a book read out loud on a tape.

   b) Brainstorm with your partner a list of reasons why taped books are becoming increasingly popular. Brainstorm a second list of literacy skills that are reinforced through listening to a taped book.

   c) Use ideas from your brainstormed list to write a short essay in praise of listening to taped books.

7. Design and make a poster to promote the importance of reading aloud to children. Identify the intended audience of your poster. Discuss some good locations for displaying your poster.

   Or

Visit a Web site that deals with parents and siblings reading to children. Prepare a **brochure** of helpful hints and advice for parents and siblings on how to read to very young children. Use a language **style** that is appropriate to your audience.

Murmel, Murmel, Murmel

"'...I can't take care of a baby.'"   ROBERT N. MUNSCH

BEFORE READING

Write a **journal** entry describing favourite books or stories you enjoyed hearing or having read to you as a child. If you can remember, explain why each appealed to you.

When Robin went out into her back yard there was a large hole right in the middle of her sandbox. She knelt down beside it and yelled, "ANYBODY DOWN THERE?"

From way down the hole something said, "Murmel, Murmel, Murmel."

"Hmmm," said Robin, "very strange." So she yelled even louder, "ANYBODY DOWN THERE?"

"Murmel, Murmel, Murmel," said the hole. Robin reached down the hole as far as she could and gave an enormous yank. Out popped a baby.

"Murmel, Murmel, Murmel," said the baby.

"Murmel yourself," said Robin. "I am only five years old and I can't take care of a baby. I will find somebody else to take care of you."

Robin picked up the very heavy baby and walked down the street. She met a woman pushing a baby carriage. Robin said, "Excuse me, do you need a baby?"

"Heavens, no," said the woman. "I already have a baby." She went off down the street and seventeen diaper salesmen jumped out from behind a hedge and ran after her.

Robin picked up the baby and went on down the street. She met an old woman and said, "Excuse me, do you need a baby?"

"Does it pee its pants?" said the old lady.

"Yes," said Robin.

"Yecch," said the old lady. "Does it dirty its diaper?"

"Yes," said Robin.

"Yecch," said the old lady. "Does it have a runny nose?"

"Yes," said Robin.

"Yecch," said the old lady. "I already have seventeen cats. I don't need a baby." She went off down the street. Seventeen cats jumped out of a garbage can and ran after her.

Robin picked up the baby and went down the street. She met a young woman in fancy clothes. "Excuse me," said Robin, "do you need a baby?"

"Heavens, no," said the woman. "I have seventeen jobs, lots of money and no time. I don't need a baby." She went off down the street. Seventeen secretaries, nine messengers and a pizza delivery man ran after her.

"Rats," said Robin. She picked up the baby and walked down the street. She met a man. "Excuse me," she said, "Do you need a baby?"

"I don't know," said the man. "Can it wash my car?"

"No," said Robin.

"Can I sell it for lots of money?"

"No," said Robin.

"Well, what is it for?" said the man.

"It is for loving and hugging and feeding and burping," said Robin.

"I certainly don't need that," said the man. He went off down the street. Nobody followed him.

Robin sat down beside the street for the baby was getting very heavy.

"Murmel, Murmel, Murmel," said the baby.

"Murmel yourself," said Robin, "what am I going to do with you?"

An enormous truck came by and stopped.

A truck driver jumped out and walked around Robin three times. Then he looked at the baby.

"Excuse me," said Robin, "do you need a baby?"

The truck driver said, "Weeeellll..."

"Murmel, Murmel, Murmel," said the baby.

"Did you say, 'murmel, murmel, murmel'?" asked the truck driver.

"Yes!" said the baby.

"I need you," yelled the truck driver. He picked up the baby and started walking down the street.

"Wait," said Robin, "you forgot your truck!"

"I already have seventeen trucks," said the truck driver. "What I need is a baby…"

"YOU can have the truck."

AFTER READING

Responding

1. With a partner, discuss your reactions to this children's **story**.

Understanding

2. Explain whether the illustrations in this story would help a child better understand the situations and ideas described in the words.

3. a) With a partner, read this children's story aloud.

   b) List the elements in the story that would be interesting and entertaining for a child.

   c) Make another list of lessons that a child could learn from this story.

4. Write a short **essay** explaining the extent to which this story presents "politically correct" ideas and values. Work with a partner to revise and edit your essays before submission. (See The Reference Shelf, page 393.)

Thinking About Language

5. Explain the purpose of capital letters used for whole sentences in this story. What does a similar use of capital letters in e-mails mean?
6. Assess whether the vocabulary and sentence structures in this story are suitable for very young children. Consider how the vocabulary and sentence structure in this children's story differ from those used in books for adults.

Extending

7. Prepare a reading of an appropriate children's book for students from Kindergarten to Grade 2. With the assistance of your teacher, arrange a visit to a local elementary school to read the story you have prepared to a class, to a small group of students, or to an individual student. Have fun! Your audience will love it and so will you.
8. a) With a partner, write and illustrate a story that would appeal to a child from Kindergarten to Grade 2. Create an imaginative plot with interesting but accessible vocabulary.
   b) Read your story to children in a class from Kindergarten to Grade 2.
   c) Make revisions to your children's book based on the response of the children you read it to.
9. a) Read at least two books written for children and prepare an **annotated bibliography** using proper bibliographic format for each book you read. (See The Reference Shelf, pages 378–379.)
   b) As a class, compile the entries into a booklet for parents. Include an introduction and graphics identifying the level of recommendation (e.g., 1 to 5 stars, with 5 being the highest recommendation) for each entry.

The Letter

"...I tried to forget you..."

SALLY MORGAN

BEFORE **READING**

Recall a situation from your experience (or from a novel, **play**, or film) where a letter has had a significant impact on someone's life.

The bus swayed back and forth making my tired old heart hurt even more.

Really, I wanted to cry, but no one cried on a bus. I glanced down sadly at the old biscuit tin sitting on my lap. Scotch Shortbreads, they weren't even her favourites, but she'd liked the colour of the tin so I'd given them to her.

I sighed and wiped away the tear that was beginning to creep down my cheek. She was gone, and I felt old and lonely and very disappointed.

My fingers traced around the lid of the old tin and slowly loosened it.

Inside was all she'd had to leave. A thin silvery necklace, some baby photos, her citizenship certificate, and the letter. I smiled when I remembered how it had taken her so long to write. She'd gone over and over every word. It was so important to her. We'd even joked about the day I would have to take it to Elaine. That day had come sooner than we both expected.

I've failed, I told myself as I lifted out the necklace. It'd been bought for Elaine's tenth birthday, but we hadn't known where to send it. Now we knew where Elaine lived but she didn't want the tin or anything in it.

I placed it back gently on top of the photo.

Elaine had said the baby in the photo wasn't her. She'd said it was all a silly mistake and she wished I'd stop pestering her.

It was the third time I'd been to see her and it looked like it would be the last. I picked up the letter. It was faded and worn. I opened it out carefully and read it again.

To my daughter Elaine,

I am writing in the hope that one day you will read this and understand. I suppose you don't want to know me because you think I deserted you. It wasn't like that. I want to tell you what it was like.

I was only seventeen when you were born at the Settlement. They all wanted to know who your father was, but I wouldn't tell. Of course he was a white man, you were so fair, but there was no love in his heart for you or me. I promised myself I would protect you. I wanted you to have a better life than me.

They took you away when I was twenty. Mr. Neville from the Aborigines Protection Board said it was the best thing. He said that black mothers like me weren't allowed to keep babies like you. He didn't want you brought up as one of our people. I didn't want to let you go but I didn't have any choice. That was the law.

I started looking for you when I was thirty. No one would tell me where you'd gone. It was all a big secret. I heard they'd changed your last name, but I didn't know what your new name was. I went and saw Mr. Neville and told him I wanted to visit you. That was when I found out that you'd been adopted by a white family. You thought you were white. Mr. Neville said I'd only hurt you by trying to find you.

For a long time I tried to forget you, but how could I forget my own daughter? Sometimes I'd take out your baby photo and look at it and kiss your little face. I prayed that somehow you'd know you had a mother who loved you.

By the time I found you, you were grown up with a family of your own. I started sending you letters trying to reach you. I wanted to see you *and my grandchildren, but you know all about that because you've sent all my letters back. I don't blame you and I don't hold any grudges, I understand. When you get this letter I will be gone, but you will have the special things in my tin. I hope that one day you will wonder who you really are and that you will make friends with our people because that's where you belong. Please be kind to the lady who gives you my tin, she's your own aunty.*

From your loving Mother.

My hands were shaking as I folded the letter and placed it back in the tin. It was no use, I'd tried, but it was no use. Nellie had always been the strong one in our family, she'd never given up on anything. She'd always believed that one day Elaine would come home.

I pressed the lid down firmly and looked out the window at the passing road. It was good Nellie wasn't here now. I was glad she didn't know how things had turned out. Suddenly her voice seemed to whisper crossly in my ear. "You always give up too easy!"

"Do not," I said quietly. I didn't know what to do then. Nellie was right, that girl was our own flesh and blood, I couldn't let her go so easily. I looked down at the tin

again and felt strangely better, almost happy. I'll make one last try, I thought to myself. I'll get a new envelope and mail it to her. She might just read it!

I was out in the yard when I heard the phone ring. I felt sure that by the time I got inside it would stop. It takes me a long while to get up the back steps these days. "Hello," I panted as I lifted the receiver. "Aunty Bessie?" "Who's this?" I asked in surprise. "It's Elaine." Elaine? I couldn't believe it! It'd been two months since I'd mailed the letter. "Is it really you Elaine?" I asked. "Yes, it's me. I want to talk to you. Can I come and see you?" "Ooh yes, any time."

"I'll be there tomorrow and Aunty… take care of yourself."

My hands shook as I placed the phone back on the hook.

Had I heard right? Had she really said, take care of yourself Aunty? I sat down quickly in the nearest chair and wiped my eyes.

"Well, why shouldn't I cry?" I said out loud to the empty room. "I'm not on the bus now!" Nellie felt very close to me just then. "Aah sister," I sighed. "Did you hear all that? Elaine will be here tomorrow?"

"Did you hear that sister? Elaine's coming home."

AFTER **READING**

Responding

1. Write a supported opinion **essay** on the following question: What importance does cultural background have when couples are having children or adopting children?

Understanding

2. Even though this **story** is fairly short, the events take place over a long period of time. Use a sequence chart or time line to trace the events of the story in chronological order, beginning with Elaine's birth.
3. Explain how each of the three women changes or develops in this story.
4. Based on your understanding of the story and the **characters**, suggest reasons for Elaine's decision to contact her aunt at the end of the story.

Thinking About Language

5. Suggest reasons for the unconventional punctuation of the **dialogue** in the telephone call from Elaine to Bessie near the end of the story.

Extending

6. With a partner, write a dialogue that might take place between Elaine and Bessie when Elaine comes to visit. Be prepared to perform your dialogue for the class.
7. In a small group, design a shooting **script** for the **scene** with Bessie on the bus. Use a **story-board** to help you decide where you would use long shots, medium shots, close-ups, zooms, high-angle shots, low-angle shots, and voice-overs. (See The Reference Shelf, page 425.) Write a revised draft of your shooting script to share with another group of students for comments and suggestions.
8. Write a short **biography** of an Aboriginal writer from Australia or New Zealand. Be sure to prepare a correctly formatted bibliography of the sources that you use for your research. (See The Reference Shelf, pages 378–379.)

Pyramus and Thisbe

BEFORE READING

As a class, brainstorm a list of names and stories from mythology that are still familiar names and stories today. Discuss how these names and stories are passed on from generation to generation.

The Story of Pyramus and Thisbe

OVID

"Next door to each other, in the brick-walled city
Built by Semiramis, lived a boy and girl,
Pyramus, a most handsome fellow, Thisbe,
Loveliest of all those Eastern girls. Their nearness
Made them acquainted, and love grew, in time,   5
So that they would have married, but their parents
Forbade it. But their parents could not keep them
From being in love: their nods and gestures showed it —
You know how fire suppressed burns all the fiercer.
There was a chink in the wall between the houses,   10
A flaw the careless builder had never noticed,
Nor anyone else, for many years, detected,
But the lovers found it — love is a finder, always —
Used it to talk through, and the loving whispers
Went back and forth in safety. They would stand   15
One on each side, listening for each other,
Happy if each could hear the other's breathing,
And then they would scold the wall: 'You envious barrier,
Why get in our way? Would it be too much to ask you
To open wide for an embrace, or even   20

Permit us room to kiss in? Still, we are grateful,
We owe you something, we admit; at least
You let us talk together.' But their talking
Was futile, rather; and when evening came
They would say *Good-night!* and give the good-night kisses   25
That never reached the other.
      "The next morning
Came, and the fires of night burnt out, and sunshine
Dried the night frost, and Pyramus and Thisbe
Met at the usual place, and first, in whispers,   30
Complained, and came—high time!—to a decision.
That night, when all was quiet, they would fool
Their guardians, or try to, come outdoors,

Run away from home, and even leave the city.
And, not to miss each other, as they wandered   35
In the wide fields, where should they meet? At Ninus'
Tomb, they supposed, was best; there was a tree there,
A mulberry-tree, loaded with snow-white berries,
Near a cool spring. The plan was good, the daylight
Was very slow in going, but at last   40
The sun went down into the waves, as always,
And the night rose, as always, from those waters.

And Thisbe opened her door, so sly, so cunning,
There was no creaking of the hinge, and no one
Saw her go through the darkness, and she came,   45
Veiled, to the tomb of Ninus, sat there waiting
Under the shadow of the mulberry-tree.
Love made her bold. But suddenly, here came something! —
A lioness, her jaws a crimson froth
With the blood of cows, fresh-slain, came there for water,   50
And far off through the moonlight Thisbe saw her
And ran, all scared, to hide herself in a cave,
And dropped her veil as she ran. The lioness,
Having quenched her thirst, came back to the woods, and saw
The girl's light veil, and mangled it and mouthed it   55
With bloody jaws. Pyramus, coming there
Too late, saw tracks in the dust, turned pale, and paler
Seeing the bloody veil. 'One night,' he cried,
'Will kill two lovers, and one of them, most surely,
Deserved a longer life. It is all my fault,   60
I am the murderer, poor girl; I told you
To come here in the night, to all this terror,
And was not here before you, to protect you.
Come, tear, my flesh, devour my guilty body,   65
Come, lions, all of you, whose lairs lie hidden
Under this rock! I am acting like a coward,
Praying for death.' He lifts the veil and takes it
Into the shadow of their tree; he kisses
The veil he knows so well, his tears run down
Into its folds: 'Drink my blood too!' he cries,   70
And draws his sword, and plunges it into his body,
And, dying, draws it out, warm from the wound.
As he lay there on the ground, the spouting blood

Leaped high, just as a pipe sends water spurting
Through a small hissing opening, when broken   75
With a flaw in the lead, and all the air is sprinkled.
The fruit of the tree, from that red spray, turned crimson,
And the roots, soaked with the blood, dyed all the berries
The same dark hue.
                "Thisbe came out of hiding,   80
Still frightened, but a little fearful, also,
To disappoint her lover. She kept looking
Not only with her eyes, but all her heart,
Eager to tell him of those terrible dangers,
About her own escape. She recognized   85
The place, the shape of the tree, but there was something
Strange or peculiar in the berries' color.
Could this be right? And then she saw a quiver
Of limbs on bloody ground, and started backward,
Paler than boxwood, shivering, as water   90
Stirs when a little breeze ruffles the surface.
It was not long before she knew her lover,
And tore her hair, and beat her innocent bosom
With her little fists, embraced the well-loved body,
Filling the wounds with tears, and kissed the lips   95
Cold in his dying. 'O my Pyramus,'
She wept, 'What evil fortune takes you from me?
Pyramus, answer me! Your dearest Thisbe
Is calling you. Pyramus, listen! Lift your head!'
He heard the name of Thisbe, and he lifted   100
His eyes, with the weight of death heavy upon them,
And saw her face, and closed his eyes.
                     "And Thisbe
Saw her own veil, and saw the ivory scabbard
With no sword in it, and understood. 'Poor boy,'   105
She said, 'So, it was your own hand,
Your love, that took your life away. I too
Have a brave hand for this one thing, I too
Have long enough, and this will give me strength
For the last wound. I will follow you in death,   110
Be called the cause and comrade of your dying.
Death was the only one could keep you from me,
Death shall not keep you from me. Wretched parents
Of Pyramus and Thisbe, listen to us,

Listen to both our prayers, do not begrudge us,   115
Whom death has joined, lying at last together
In the same tomb. And you, O tree, now shading
The body of one, and very soon to shadow
The bodies of two, keep in remembrance always
The sign of our death, the dark and mournful color.'   120
She spoke, and fitting the sword-point at her breast,
Fell forward on the blade, still warm and reeking
With her lover's blood. Her prayers touched the gods,
And touched her parents, for the mulberry fruit
Still reddens at its ripeness, and the ashes   125
Rest in a common urn."

Excerpts From *A Midsummer Night's Dream* — Pyramus and Thisbe

WILLIAM SHAKESPEARE

Philostrate: A play there is, my lord, some ten words long,
Which is as brief as I have known a play;
But by ten words, my lord, it is too long,
Which makes it tedious; for in all the play
There is not one word apt, one player fitted:
And tragical, my noble lord, it is;
For Pyramus therein doth kill himself.
Which, when I saw rehearsed, I must confess,
Made mine eyes water; but more merry tears
The passion of loud laughter never shed.
Theseus: What are they that do play it?
Philostrate: Hard-handed men, that work in Athens here,
Which never labour'd in their minds till now,
And now have toil'd their unbreathed memories
With this same play, against your nuptial.
Theseus: And we will hear it.
Philostrate: No, my noble lord;
It is not for you: I have heard it over,
And it is nothing, nothing in the world;
Unless you can find sport in their intents,
Extremely stretch'd and conn'd with cruel pain,
To do you service.

Theseus: I will hear that play;
For never anything can be amiss,
When simpleness and duty tender it.
Go, bring them in: and take your places, ladies.

. . .

Philostrate: So please your grace, the Prologue is address'd.
Theseus: Let him approach.   [*Flourish of trumpets.*]

[*Enter Quince for the Prologue.*]

Prologue:
If we offend, it is with our good will.
That you should think, we come not to offend,
But with good will. To show our simple skill,
That is the true beginning of our end.
Consider then we come but in despite.
We do not come as minding to content you,
Our true intent is. All for your delight
We are not here. That you should here repent you,
The actors are at hand and by their show
You shall know all that you are like to know.
Theseus: This fellow doth not stand upon points.
Lysander: He hath rid his prologue like a rough colt; he
knows not the stop. A good moral, my lord: it is not
enough to speak, but to speak true.
Hippolyta: Indeed he hath played on his prologue like a child
on a recorder; a sound, but not in government.
Theseus: His speech was like a tangled chain; nothing
impaired, but all disordered. Who is next?

[*Enter Pyramus and Thisbe, Wall, Moonshine, and Lion.*]

Prologue:
Gentles, perchance you wonder at this show;
But wonder on, till truth make all things plain.
This man is Pyramus, if you would know;
This beauteous lady Thisby is certain.
This man, with lime and rough-cast, doth present
Wall, that vile Wall which did these lovers sunder;
And through Wall's chink, poor souls, they are content
To whisper. At the which let no man wonder.

This man, with lanthorn, dog, and bush of thorn,
Presenteth Moonshine; for, if you will know,
By moonshine did these lovers think no scorn
To meet at Ninus' tomb, there, there to woo.
This grisly beast, which Lion hight by name,
The trusty Thisby, coming first by night,
Did scare away, or rather did affright;
And, as she fled, her mantle she did fall,
Which Lion vile with bloody mouth did stain.
Anon comes Pyramus, sweet youth and tall,
And finds his trusty Thisby's mantle slain:
Whereat, with blade, with bloody blameful blade,
He bravely broach'd his boiling bloody breast;
And Thisby, tarrying in mulberry shade,
His dagger drew, and died. For all the rest,
Let Lion, Moonshine, Wall, and lovers twain
At large discourse, while here they do remain.

[*Exeunt Prologue, Pyramus, Thisbe, Lion,*
and Moonshine.]

Theseus: I wonder if the lion be to speak.
Demetrius: No wonder, my lord: one lion may, when many asses do.
Wall: In this same interlude it doth befall
That I, one Snout by name, present a wall;
And such a wall, as I would have you think,
That had in it a crannied hole or chink,
Through which the lovers, Pyramus and Thisby,
Did whisper often very secretly.
This loam, this rough-cast and this stone doth show
That I am that same wall; the truth is so:
And this the cranny is, right and sinister,
Through which the fearful lovers are to whisper.
Theseus: Would you desire lime and hair to speak better?
Demetrius: It is the wittiest partition that ever I heard discourse, my lord.
Theseus: Pyramus draws near the wall: silence!

[*Re-enter Pyramus.*]

Pyramus: O grim-look'd night! O night with hue so black!
O night, which ever art when day is not!

O night, O night! alack, alack, alack,
I fear my Thisby's promise is forgot!
And thou, O wall, O sweet, O lovely wall,
That stand'st between her father's ground and mine!
Thou wall, O wall, O sweet and lovely wall,
Show me thy chink, to blink through with mine eyne!
       [*Wall holds up his fingers.*]
Thanks, courteous wall: Jove shield thee well for this!
But what see I? No Thisby do I see.
O wicked wall, through whom I see no bliss!
Cursed be thy stones for thus deceiving me!
Theseus: The wall, methinks, being sensible, should curse
again.
Pyramus: No, in truth, sir, he should not. "Deceiving me"
is Thisby's cue: she is to enter now, and I am to spy
her through the wall. You shall see, it will fall pat as I
told you. Yonder she comes.

[*Re-enter Thisbe.*]

Thisbe: O wall, full often hast thou heard my moans,
For parting my fair Pyramus and me!
My cherry lips have often kiss'd thy stones,
Thy stones with lime and hair knit up in thee.
Pyramus: I see a voice: now will I to the chink,
To spy an I can hear my Thisby's face.
Thisby!
Thisbe: My love thou art, my love I think.
Pyramus: Think what thou wilt, I am thy lover's grace
And, like Limander, am I trusty still.
Thisbe: And I like Helen, till the Fates me kill.
Pyramus: Not Shafalus to Procrus was so true.
Thisbe: As Shafalus to Procrus, I to you.
Pyramus: O kiss me through the hole of this vile wall!
Thisbe: I kiss the wall's hole, not your lips at all.
Pyramus: Wilt thou at Ninny's tomb meet me straightway?
Thisbe: 'Tide life, 'tide death, I come without delay.
            [*Exeunt Pyramus and Thisbe.*]
Wall: Thus have I, Wall, my part discharged so;
And being done, thus Wall away doth go.   [*Exit.*]
Theseus: Now is the mural down between the two
neighbours.

Demetrius: No remedy, my lord, when walls are so wilful to hear without warning.

Hippolyta: This is the silliest stuff that ever I heard.

Theseus: The best in this kind are but shadows; and the worst are no worse, if imagination amend them.

Hippolyta: It must be your imagination then, and not theirs.

Theseus: If we imagine no worse of them than they of themselves, they may pass for excellent men. Here come two noble beasts in, a man and a lion.

[*Re-enter Lion and Moonshine.*]

Lion: You, ladies, you, whose gentle hearts do fear
The smallest monstrous mouse that creeps on floor,
May now perchance both quake and tremble here,
When lion rough in wildest rage doth roar.
Then know that I, one Snug the joiner, am
A lion-fell, nor else no lion's dam;
For, if I should as lion come in strife
Into this place, 'twere pity on my life.

Theseus: A very gentle beast, and of a good conscience.

Demetrius: The very best at a beast, my lord, that e'er I saw.

Lysander: This lion is a very fox for his valour.

Theseus: True; and a goose for his discretion.

Demetrius: Not so, my lord; for his valour cannot carry his discretion; and the fox carries the goose.

Theseus: His discretion, I am sure, cannot carry his valour; for the goose carries not the fox. It is well; leave it to his discretion, and let us listen to the moon.

Moonshine: This lanthorn doth the horned moon present; —

Demetrius: He should have worn the horns on his head.

Theseus: He is no crescent, and his horns are invisible within the circumference.

Moonshine: This lanthorn doth the horned moon present; —
Myself the man i' the moon do seem to be.

Theseus: This is the greatest error of all the rest: the man should be put into the lanthorn. How is it else the man i' the moon?

Demetrius: He dares not come there for the candle; for you see, it is already in snuff.

Hippolyta: I am aweary of this moon: would he would change!

Theseus: It appears, by his small light of discretion, that he is in the wane; but yet, in courtesy, in all reason, we must stay the time.

Lysander: Proceed, Moon.

Moonshine: All that I have to say, is, to tell you that the lanthorn is the moon; I, the man in the moon; this thorn-bush, my thorn-bush; and this dog, my dog.

Demetrius: Why, all these should be in the lanthorn; for all these are in the moon. But, silence! here comes Thisbe.

[*Re-enter Thisbe.*]

Thisbe: This is old Ninny's tomb. Where is my love?

Lion: [*Roaring*] Oh——   [*Thisbe runs off.*]

Demetrius: Well roared, Lion.

Theseus: Well run, Thisbe.

Hippolyta: Well shone, Moon. Truly, the moon shines with a good grace.

                  [*The Lion shakes Thisbe's mantle, and exit.*]

Theseus: Well moused, Lion.

Lysander: And so the lion vanished.

Demetrius: And then came Pyramus.

[*Re-enter Pyramus.*]

Pyramus: Sweet Moon, I thank thee for thy sunny beams;
I thank thee, Moon, for shining now so bright;
For, by thy gracious, golden, glittering gleams,
I trust to take of truest Thisby sight.
                   But stay, O spite!
                   But mark, poor knight,
              What dreadful dole is here!
                   Eyes, do you see?
                   How can it be?
              O dainty duck! O dear!
                   Thy mantle good,
                   What, stain'd with blood!
              Approach, ye Furies fell!

> O Fates, come, come,
>
> Cut thread and thrum;
>
> Quail, crush, conclude, and quell!

Theseus: This passion, and the death of a dear friend, would go near to make a man look sad.

Hippolyta: Beshrew my heart, but I pity the man.

Pyramus: O wherefore, Nature, didst thou lions frame?
Since lion vile hath here deflower'd my dear:
Which is—no, no—which was the fairest dame
That lived, that loved, that liked, that look'd
with cheer.

> Come, tears, confound;
>
> Out, sword and wound
>
> The pap of Pyramus;
>
> Ay, that left pap,
>
> Where heart doth hop:

> [*Stabs himself.*]

> Thus die I, thus, thus, thus.
>
> Now am I dead
>
> Now am I fled;
>
> My soul is in the sky:
>
> Tongue, lose thy light:
>
> Moon, take thy flight;

> [*Exit Moonshine.*]

> Now, die, die, die, die, die.

Demetrius: No die, but an ace, for him; for he is but one.

Lysander: Less than an ace, man; for he is dead; he is nothing.

Theseus: With the help of a surgeon he might yet recover, and prove an ass.

Hippolyta: How chance Moonshine is gone before Thisbe comes back and finds her lover?

Theseus: She will find him by starlight. Here she comes; and her passion ends the play.

[*Re-enter Thisbe.*]

Hippolyta: Methinks she should not use a long one for such a Pyramus: I hope she will be brief.

Demetrius: A mote will turn the balance, which Pyramus, which Thisbe, is the better; he for a man, God warrant us; she for a woman, God bless us.

Lysander: She hath spied him already with those sweet eyes.

Demetrius: And thus she means, videlicent;—

Thisbe:
        Asleep, my love?
         What, dead, my dove?
      O Pyramus, arise!
         Speak, speak. Quite dumb?
         Dead, dead? A tomb
      Must cover thy sweet eyes.
         These lily lips,
         This cherry nose,
      These yellow cowslip cheeks,
         Are gone, are gone;
         Lovers, make moan:
      His eyes were green as leeks.
         O Sisters Three,
         Come, come to me,
      With hands as pale as milk;
         Lay them in gore,
         Since you have shore
      With shears his thread of silk.
         Tongue, not a word:
         Come, trusty sword;
      Come, blade, my breast imbue:

              [*Stabs herself.*]

         And, farewell friends;
         Thus Thisby ends:
        Adieu, adieu, adieu.

Theseus: Moonshine and Lion are left to bury the dead.

Demetrius: Ay, and Wall too.

Bottom: [*Starting up*] No, I assure you; the wall is down that parted their fathers. Will it please you to see the epilogue, or to hear a Bergomask dance between two of our company?

Theseus: No epilogue, I pray you; for your play needs no excuse. Never excuse; for when the players are all dead, there need none to be blamed. Marry, if he that writ it had played Pyramus and hanged himself in Thisbe's garter, it would have been a fine tragedy: and so it is, truly; and very notably discharged. But, come, your Bergomask: let your epilogue alone.

[*A dance.*]

The iron tongue of midnight hath told twelve:
Lovers, to bed; 'tis almost fairy time.
I fear we shall out-sleep the coming morn
As much as we this night have overwatch'd.
This palpable-gross play hath well beguiled
The heavy gait of night. Sweet friends, to bed.
A fortnight hold we this solemnity,
In nightly revels and new jollity.   [*Exeunt.*]

[*Enter Puck.*]

Puck: Now the hungry lion roars,
                   And the wolf behowls the moon,
                   Whilst the heavy ploughman snores,
                   All with weary task fordone.
                   Now the wasted brands do glow,
                   Whilst the screech-owl, screeching loud,
                   Puts the wretch that lies in woe
                   In remembrance of a shroud.
                   Now it is the time of night
                   That the graves, all gaping wide,
                   Every one lets forth his sprite,
                   In the church-way paths to glide:
                   And we fairies, that do run
                   By the triple Hecate's team,
                   From the presence of the sun,
                   Following darkness like a dream...

AFTER READING

Responding

1. a) In your notebook, make a list of other stories that the story of Pyramus and Thisbe reminds you of.

   b) Explain what elements in the story make it as relevant for today's readers as it was for Ovid's readers 2000 years ago.

Understanding

2. Rewrite the story of Pyramus and Thisbe in your own words. Compare it with a partner's version and correct your understanding, as necessary.

3. As a class, discuss the following:
   - four specific details that enhance Ovid's version of the story of Pyramus and Thisbe and what each of the details adds to the story
   - how Shakespeare has exploited details from the original myth to create humour in the version the labourers perform in *A Midsummer Night's Dream*

4. Explain how the labourer-actors have cast the play to match the real-life work and skills of the players.

5. Explain how each of the following is used as a source of humour in the **play**:
   - comments from the audience
   - misuse of language
   - **rhyme scheme**

Thinking About Language

6. With a partner, identify words and phrases in either version of the story that might be unfamiliar to a modern reader. Prepare a **glossary** of the terms you selected to assist readers.

Extending

7. As a class, rehearse and present the story of Pyramus and Thisbe from Shakespeare's *A Midsummer Night's Dream*.

8. Locate a filmed version of Shakespeare's *A Midsummer Night's Dream* and watch the **scene** on Pyramus and Thisbe. Write a **review** of the scene, explaining why it still appeals to audiences 400 years after it was written.

9. a) Research another pair of lovers from myth, legend, literature, or history, such as Hero and Leander, Guinevere and Lancelot, Romeo and Juliet, Abelard and Héloïse. Prepare an oral **report** of their story to present to the class.

   b) Consider using visuals and technology aids if appropriate.

   c) As a class, create an evaluation form to assess the report.

   d) Update your Oral Communication Skills Action Plan chart as necessary using feedback from your classmates. (See The Reference Shelf, page 395.)

Apples From the Desert

"...her heart already reconciled..."

SAVYON LIEBRECHT
TRANSLATED FROM THE HEBREW
BY BARBARA HARSHAV

BEFORE READING

Write about how young people differ from their parents and why these differences occur.

All the way from the Orthodox quarter of Sha'arei Hesed in Jerusalem to the great stretch of sand where the driver called out "Neve Midbar" and searched for her in his rearview mirror, Victoria Abravanel—her heart pounding and her fists clenched—had only one thing on her mind. She took some bread in brown paper and an apple with a rotten core out of her string bag and adjoined the blessing on the fruit to the prayer for travel, as prescribed. Her eyes were fixed on the yellowing landscape spread out in front of her—and her heart was fixed on her rebellious daughter Rivka, who had left the Orthodox neighborhood six months earlier and gone to live on a kibbutz of secular Jews. Now Victoria had found out from her sister Sara that Rivka was sharing a room with a boy, sleeping in his bed and living as his wife.

All through the eight-hour trip, she pondered how she would behave when she was face to face with her daughter: maybe she would cajole her as if she weren't angry with her, teach her about a girl's honor in a man's eyes, explain sensitive issues, one woman to another. Or maybe she would start out with cries of despair, shout out her grief, the disgrace that Rivka had brought down on their noble family, shriek like a bereaved mourner until the neighbors heard. Or maybe she would perform her mission stealthily, draw her daughter away from there with false news and then put her in her room under lock and key and obliterate all trace of her. Or maybe she would terrify her, tell her about Flora, Yosef Elalouf's daughter, who fell in love with some boy, gave up her virginity for him, and then he deserted her, so she lost her mind and wandered around the streets, pulling little children by the ear.

On the road from Beersheva, she came up with something new: she would attack the boy with her nails, rip off his skin and poke out his eyes for what he had done to this change-of-life daughter of hers. Her daughter would come back to Jerusalem with her, which was what she promised her sister: "I'll bring her back even if I have to drag her by the hair."

From her sister Sara, Victoria already knew that her daughter was sixteen when she met him. He was an army officer and was brought in to tell them about military service for Orthodox girls. Later on there was a fuss about letting people from the army come and poison the girls' hearts, but the venom had already worked on Rivka. Cunningly, he'd sent her letters through a friend even after he had returned to his kibbutz. And she, the fool, who was known for neither grace nor beauty—even when she was a baby, people would mistake her for a boy—she fell for it, and when she was eighteen she picked up and went to him in the desert.

The further Victoria got from Beersheva, the more her heroic spirit deserted her and the pictures in her imagination made her sigh. What if Rivka turned her back on her and threw her out? What if the boy raised his hand to strike her? How would she spend the night if they locked her out and the bus didn't leave till the next morning? What if they didn't get her message? She didn't know anything about traveling, hadn't been outside of the neighborhood since the barren Shifra Ben-Sasson of Tiberias gave birth four years ago.

But when the driver called out "Neve Midbar" again and found her in his mirror, she got off the bus, pulling her basket behind her. She stood there in the sand, the dry wind striking her throat. How could you leave the pure air and beautiful mountains of Jerusalem—and come here?

By the time she came to a path and found a woman to ask about Rivka, rivulets of sweat were streaming from her kerchief. Victoria plodded on, looking dizzily at a woman whose arms were laden with rows of pots, one inside the other, her bare legs in men's shoes and folded army socks. Coming toward them on the opposite path was a girl, also wearing pants, whose hair was cropped short. "Here's Rivka," said the woman. Just as Victoria was about to say, "That's not the one I meant," she recognized her daughter and burst into a shout that resounded like a sob. The girl put down the laundry basket she was carrying and ran to her, her head thrust forward and her eyes weeping.

"What's this...what's this?" Victoria scratched her nose. "Where are your braids? And those pants...that's how you dress...oy vey!" Rivka laughed: "I knew that's what you'd say. I wanted to get dressed but I didn't have time. I thought you'd come on the four o'clock bus. When did you leave home? Six? Come on. Enough of this crying. Here's our room. And here Dubi."

Stunned by the short hair, the frayed trousers with patches on the back, and the shoes spotted with chicken droppings, Victoria found herself squeezed in two big arms, a fair face close to hers, and a male voice said, "Hello, Mother." Her basket was already in his hand and she—not understanding herself, her hands suddenly light—was drawn after her daughter into a shaded room and seated on a chair. At once there was a glass of juice in her hand; her eyes looked but didn't know what they saw, and later on she'd remember only the double bed covered with a patchwork quilt and the voice of the giant with golden hair saying "Welcome, Mother." And as soon as she heard him say "mother" again, very clearly, she swallowed some juice that went down the wrong way and started choking and coughing. The two of them rushed to her and started pounding her on the back like a child.

"Leave me alone," she said weakly and pushed them away. "Let me look at you," she said after a moment. Once again she scolded Rivka: "What is this, those pants? Those are your Sabbath shoes?" Rivka laughed, "I'm working in the chicken coop this week. They brought in new hens. I usually work in the vegetable garden. Just this week in the chicken coop."

Weary from the journey, confused by what she was seeing, shaken by the vicissitudes of the day, and straining to repress her rage, which was getting away from her in spite of herself — and always remembering her mission — Victoria sat down with her daughter Rivka and talked with her as she had never talked with her children before in her life. She didn't remember what she said and she didn't remember when the boy who called her mother left, but her eyes saw and knew: her daughter's face looked good. Not since Rivka was a little girl had she seen her eyes sparkle like this. Even her short hair, Victoria admitted to herself, made her look pretty. Not like when she wore a skirt and stockings, with her broad shoulders, as if she were a man dressed up in women's clothes.

"You don't miss the neighborhood?"

"Sometimes. On holidays. I miss the Sabbath table and the songs and Aunt Sara's laugh. But I like it here. I love working outside with the animals...You, too, I miss you a lot."

"And Papa?" Victoria asked in a whisper into the evening light filtering in.

"Papa doesn't care about anybody. Especially not me. All day long in the store and with his books and prayers. Like I'm not his daughter."

"God forbid! Don't say such a thing," Victoria was scared — of the truth.

"He wanted to marry me off to Yekutiel's son. Like I was a widow or a cripple."

"Really?"

"Don't play games with me. As if you didn't know."

"They talked. You heard. We don't make forced matches. And anyway, Yekutiel's son is a genius."

"A pale, sick genius, like he sits in a pit all day long. And anyway, I don't love him."

"What do you think? You think love is everything?"

"What do you know about love?"

"What does that mean?" Victoria was offended and sat up straight. "This is how you talk to your mother around here?"

"You didn't love Papa and he didn't love you." Rivka ignored her and went on in the silence that descended: "I, at home... I wasn't worth much."

"And here?" Victoria asked in a whisper. "More."

A question began to take shape in Victoria's mind about Dubi, the fair-haired giant, but the door opened, a light suddenly came on, and he himself said, "Great that you're saving electricity. I brought something to eat. Yogurt and vegetables on a new plastic plate. That's okay, isn't it? Then,

Rivka, you should take Mother to Osnat's room. It's empty. She must be tired."

In the room that led out to the darkening fields, Victoria tried to get things straight in her heart. But years of dreariness had dulled her edge and yet she already knew: she wouldn't bring her daughter back to Jerusalem by her hair.

"Why did it take you half a year to come here?" Rivka asked.

"Your papa didn't want me to come."

"And you, you don't have a will of your own?" Victoria had no answer.

When Dubi came to take her to the dining hall, she poured all her rage on him, and yet she was drawn to him, which only served to increase her wrath.

"What's this 'Dubi'? What kind of name is that?" Anger pulled words out of her mouth.

"It's Dov, after my mother's father. The Germans killed him in the war."

"That's a good name for a baby, Dov?" She hardened her heart against him.

"I don't mind." He shrugged, and then stopped and said with comic seriousness, "But if you do—I'll change it tomorrow." She strained to keep from laughing.

In the evening, the two of them sat at the table with their eyes on Rivka as if she were all alone in the big hall, while she made the rounds with a serving cart, asking people what they wanted.

"You want something else to drink, Mother?" she heard him ask. She queried angrily, "You call me 'Mother.' What kind of mother am I to you?"

"I'm dying for you to be my mother."

"Really? So, who's stopping you?" she asked, and her sister Sara's mischievousness crept into her voice.

"Your daughter."

"How is she stopping you?"

"She doesn't want to be my wife."

"My daughter doesn't want to get married. That's what you're telling me?"

"Exactly."

As she was struggling with what he had said, he started telling her about the apple orchard he was growing. An American scientist who grew apples in the Nevada desert had sent him special seeds. You plant them in tin cans full of organic fertilizer and they grow into trees as high as a baby, with little roots, and sometimes they produce fruit in the summer like a tree in the Garden of Eden. "Apples love the cold," he explained as their eyes wandered after Rivka, "and at night, you have to open the plastic sheets and let the desert cold in. At dawn, you have to close the sheets to preserve the cold air and keep the heat out."

"Really," she muttered, hearing these words now and thinking about what he had said before. Meanwhile, somebody came to her and said, "You're Rivka's mother? Congratulations on such a daughter." And suddenly her heart swelled within her.

Then she remembered something that resurfaced from distant days and dimensions. She was fifteen years old. On Saturdays in the synagogue, she used to exchange glances with Moshe Elkayam, the goldsmith's son, and then she would lower her eyes to the floor. In the women's section, she would push up to the wooden lattice to see his hands that worked with silver and gold and precious stones. Something grew between them without any words, and his sister would smile at her in the street. But when the matchmaker came to talk to her about Shaul Abravanel, she didn't dare hurt her father, who wanted a scholar for a son-in-law.

At night, when Rivka took her back to her room, she asked, "You came to take me back to Jerusalem, didn't you?"

Her mother chose not to answer. After a pause she said, apropos of nothing, "Don't do anything dumb."

"I know what I want."

"Your aunt also knew when she was your age. Look at the kind of life she has now. Goes from house to house like a cat."

"Don't worry about me."

Victoria plucked up her courage: "Is it true what he told me, that you don't want to marry him?"

"That's what he told you?"

"Yes or no?"

"Yes."

"Why?"

"I'm not sure yet."

"Where did you learn that?"

"From you."

"How?" Victoria was amazed.

"I don't want to live like you and Papa."

"How?"

"Without love."

"Again love!" She beat her thighs with her palms until they trembled—a gesture of rage without the rage. They reached the door. Victoria thought a moment about the bed with patchwork quilt and heard herself asking, "And the special bedtime prayer, do you say that?"

"No."

"You don't say the prayer?"

"Only sometimes, silently. So even I don't hear it myself," said Rivka. She laughed and kissed her mother on the cheek. Then she said: "Don't get scared if

you hear jackals. Good night." Like a mother soothing her child.

Facing the bare sand dunes stretching soft lines within the window frame, as into the frame of a picture, Victoria said a fervent prayer, for both of them, her and Rivka. Her heart was both heavy and light, "...Let not my thoughts trouble me, nor evil dreams, nor evil fancies, but let my rest be perfect before Thee..."

And at night she dreamed.

In the dream a man approaches a white curtain and she sees him from behind. The man moves the curtain aside and the trees of the Garden of Eden are in front of him: the Tree of Life and the Tree of Knowledge and beautiful trees in cans of organic fertilizer. The man goes to the apple tree, laden with fruit, and the fruit drops off and rolls into his hands and, suddenly, the fruit is small and turns into stones. And Victoria sees handfuls of precious stones and gold and silver in his white fingers. Suddenly the man turns around, and it's Moshe Elkayam, the goldsmith's son, and his hair is in flames.

All the way back to Sha'arei Hesed she sat, her eyes still clutching at their rage but her heart already reconciled, her basket at her feet and, on her lap, a sack of apples hard as stones that Dubi gave her. She remembered her daughter asking, "You see that everything's fine, right?"—her fingers on her mother's cheek; and Dubi's voice saying, "It'll be fine, Mother."

All the way, she pondered what she would tell her husband and her sister. Maybe she would sit them down and tell them exactly what happened to her. When the bus passed the junction, she considered it. How could she describe to her sister, who had never known a man, or to her husband, who had never touched her with love — how could she describe the boy's eyes on her daughter's face? When the mountains of Jerusalem appeared in the distance, she knew what she would do.

From her sister, who could read her mind, she wouldn't keep a secret. She'd pull her kerchief aside, put her mouth up to her ear, like when they were children, and whisper, "Sarike, we've spent our lives alone, you without a husband and me with one. My little daughter taught me something. And us, remember how we thought she was a bit backward, God forbid? How I used to cry over her? No beauty, no grace, no intelligence or talent, and as tall as Og, King of Bashan. He wanted to marry her off to Yekutiel and they were doing us a favor, like Abravanel's daughter wasn't good enough for them. Just look at her now." Here she would turn her face to the side and spit spiritedly against the evil eye. "Milk and honey. Smart, too. And laughing all the time. Maybe, with God's help, we'll see joy from her."

And to her husband, who never read her heart, she would give apples in honey, put both hands on her hips and say, "We don't have to worry about Rivka. She's happy there, thank God. We'll hear good tidings from her soon. Now, taste that and tell me: apples that bloom in summer and are put in organic fertilizer and their roots stay small — did you ever hear of such a thing in your life?"

AFTER READING

Responding

1. A reader can often discover an author's **bias** by what happens to the main **characters** at the end of the **story**. Read the ending of this story and **hypothesize** about the writer's view of arranged marriage. In a series of paragraphs, show the pros and cons of arranged marriage, even if you have strong feelings for or against it. Compare your paragraphs with those of a partner, revising them as necessary.

2. Draw a **plot graph** of this story, labelling the parts. Typically a plot graph will show the following:

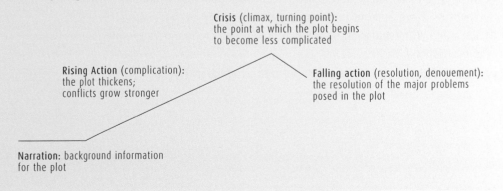

Crisis (climax, turning point): the point at which the plot begins to become less complicated

Rising Action (complication): the plot thickens; conflicts grow stronger

Falling action (resolution, denouement): the resolution of the major problems posed in the plot

Narration: background information for the plot

Understanding

3. With a partner, discuss the final paragraph of the story. Compare your ideas with those of another pair. Record the differences, if any, in your views and present them to the class.

4. In your notebook, answer this question with support from your personal knowledge or experience: "Could this story happen in any other culture?" Why or why not?

5. a) This story is told from a limited omniscient **point of view**: the readers can read the mother's thoughts. The writer could have shown the mother's thoughts by using the first person. With a partner, decide which point of view would have been more effective and why.

   b) With your partner, take one of the paragraphs showing the mother's thoughts and rewrite it from the first person point of view. Read the new version aloud to another pair of students.

   c) Individually, write a reflection on which version you prefer and why.

6. Write a **journal** entry from Victoria's point of view after she has returned from visiting her daughter. Focus on what she has learned from her journey.

Thinking About Language

7. Locate all the sentences in the story that contain ellipses. For each, explain why this punctuation is used.

Extending

8. Using print and/or electronic resources, research the various groups within Judaism (e.g., Orthodox, Reform, Conservative, etc.). As a class, discuss your findings, adding to your information when necessary.

9. Using print and/or electronic resources, research the apple as a **symbol** in literature from Judeo-Christian cultures. In a small group, explain how the writer has used the apple as a symbol in both the title and the body of the story. Create a visual representation (e.g., graphic organizer, annotated illustration) of your ideas and present it to the class.

10. a) With a partner, create a shooting **script** for a **scene** in the story. This shooting script should be designed for a made-for-television movie.

    b) Make a list of sponsors who might want to buy advertising time during this movie, explaining why these would be appropriate sponsors.

    c) Write a sales talk designed to sell advertising time for this program to these potential sponsors. Have another pair read it for content and persuasive techniques.

    d) Record your presentation on video or audiotape or create a computer-assisted presentation.

    e) As a class, prepare an evaluation form to assess this project.

Parents With Disabilities

"...not everyone has to be the same."

"Normal" Is Defined by Life Experiences

MARTIN PATRIQUIN

Stephen Little's life is happily average. He and his family live in Pickering, Ontario, at the foot of a leafy *cul-de-sac*, in a house with a manicured lawn identical to that of his neighbours. He enjoys the trappings of suburban splendour, right down to the fenced-in backyard strewn with his children's toys.

Average, that is, until you notice the wheelchair lift coming up the basement steps and Stephen Little emerging from his home office.

A car accident left Little paralyzed from the waist down in 1968. Over three years ago, his wife Tracy MacCharles gave birth to twins Travis and Genevieve. Thanks to the marvels of a new process in modern reproductive technology — a process only a decade old — they are his flesh and blood.

"From their perspective, this is just the way it is," says Little, 50.

Little drives with his hands. His arms power a special bike, his kids towed behind. Sports usually take place on the driveway, street or sidewalk, permitting Little to take part. They swim together at the cottage.

"I have limitations, but not things I won't do," says Little, national director of client services for the Canadian Paraplegic Association. "They see me being active to the point where there are no alarm bells on their part."

His only worry, he says, is his kids getting away from him. "For most able-bodied parents, there is nowhere the kids can go where they can't. With me, they can get physically get out of my reach and I can't do a thing about it."

So Little has a few variations on parental tricks, like having them push him when they go out together. This gives them something to do other than darting into traffic.

The kids only notice other people's wheelchairs, Little says. To them, their father is just that: He isn't diminished because of his disability, which is exactly what he wants to teach them.

"Normal is defined by life experiences," he says. "I can show them that not everyone has to be the same. They are going to have a broader appreciation of what it is like to be physically able."

Little decided he wanted kids shortly after the end of his first marriage, following what he calls "a rocking chair exercise." He imagined himself at 80, sitting on his porch, and pondered what he would regret most about his life.

That was the easy part. The couple considered every option (including donor sperm and adoption) before trying a new technique called intracytoplasmic sperm injection, which involved in vitro fertilization.

They hoped and prayed for the best, which came in the form of healthy twins in 1997.

The wonder of childbirth came with an accompanying shock. "I spent 45 years of my life without having any responsibilities for children whatsoever, and all of a sudden people are relying on me."

As for his disability, Little misses the little things like being able to jump into a lake unhindered or driving an honest-to-god sports car with manual transmission.

"These are small potatoes. I'm still healthy, I have a family that loves me and I'm employed," he says.

"The wheelchair is a reality that I have to deal with. I'm a good father. Does the chair make a difference? No."

All Parents Need a Helping Hand

HELEN HENDERSON

When Lisa Jones announced she was pregnant with her first child, some people were shocked that a woman in a wheelchair would consider becoming a mother.

"You can't even do things for yourself, let alone for any kids," they said.

When it became clear that Jones had thought things through very carefully, only one thing consoled her critics. "Don't worry," they told each other, "as soon as the baby is born, Children's Aid will take it away and give it to someone who can look after it."

Can a woman in a wheelchair be a good mother? Is nurturing a product of being able to walk or talk or see or hear? In a time and place where a 5-week-old baby boy can starve to death in the midst of plenty, why do we still put such store in the outward trappings of motherhood?

Jones, a health policy planner with the Halton Peel District Health Council, is a single mom. In a bright, two-bedroom apartment, filled with sunshine and laughter on a recent Sunday morning, she is raising her two daughters, Laural, 8, and Emily, almost 3, along with Laural's pet rabbit, Midnight.

Grinning at the kids' antics as a photographer captures them with their mother is

Janet Rondeau, a first-year nursing student at George Brown College. You might call Rondeau Jones' weekend executive assistant on the home front.

The technical term is nurturing assistant, a paid employee who helps parents with disabilities handle the physical tasks of raising a family. It's an important and complex role, involving everything from lifting and bathing to helping mothers cuddle and play with their kids. And if a project underway at the Centre for Independent Living in Toronto confirms its value, more parents with disabilities may be able to benefit from the process.

The relationship between parent and nurturing assistant is "very special," says Jones. "It's directed by the parent but it's also shared — and it's always evolving."

What works best? The Centre for Independent Living project is studying programs across Canada and around the world but it also wants to hear directly from parents and service providers.

"We're looking at the best ways of making things rewarding and cost-effective," says Mary Ocampo, project co-ordinator. Ultimately, the group wants to produce a how-to book for parents, prospective parents, workers and funding groups that might be interested in setting up nurturing assistance services.

As things stand now, parents who don't use attendant services for personal care are not usually eligible to get funding for nurturing assistance. "If we can show there's a need, we hope we can get that changed," says Ocampo.

Jones found her own ideas evolved as time went by. After Laural was born, she had a live-in nanny. But having an extra person permanently within the confines of the apartment proved stressful. So when she was expecting Emily, she went another route. "As your needs change, you change what you need," she says.

Although she has the use of her arms, she couldn't lift the baby in and out of her crib. So she needed someone overnight initially. Later, as Emily grew, Jones needed help only during the day. When her maternity leave ended and she returned to work, a different pattern evolved.

Mornings are the most hectic time. During the week, Jones has an assistant come in from 6:45 A.M. to 9:15 A.M. Her mother also helps out from about 7:30 A.M. on, eventually taking Emily to the babysitter as Laural leaves for school and Jones herself sets off to work.

"For a short time, we really need two extra people," she says.

In the afternoon, Laural goes to her grandmother's after school, but through the evening and overnight, Jones has the kids to herself.

Assessing needs and scheduling time within the funding allotted to families is one of the biggest issues in successful nurturing assistance, says Diane Duncan, manager of support services at Tobias House, which specializes in attendant care services and assisted living projects.

"Parents can't have assistance around the clock, so it's important to calculate the time when needs are most important."

Finding help from someone compatible, someone the children feel comfortable with and who has the right attitude toward disabilities, can also be a challenge, says Jones.

"You need someone who understands that when kids ask, 'Can I wear this tank top?' or 'Can I have a cookie?' the answer is: 'Ask your mom.'"

Even at the best of times, the parent may feel jealous, Jones says. "It's hard when you see someone swinging your kids around, doing things that you want to do but can't. You feel resentful. You have to deal with that."

Jones is uncomfortable with the term "nurturing" assistance. "Nurturing is really something spiritual; it's about love, and that's my role," she says.

But support and assistance for new mothers is crucial, she believes. "Everyone needs help. The need is just more visible when it comes to people with disabilities."

AFTER READING

Responding

1. Choose one of the people from these two **articles**. Make point-form notes about the person's life. Write about how you might feel if you were in the same situation.

Understanding

2. With a partner, reread "All Parents Need a Helping Hand" and make a list of the difficulties and rewards of having a "nurturing assistant" in the family. With another pair, compare your list.

3. Both articles are about the same topic, but each has different purposes. Describe the purposes of each of the articles using relevant points from each to indicate its purpose.

Thinking About Language

4. With a partner, compare the **tone** and the level of language in each article. (See The Reference Shelf, pages 349–351.) Use a chart to organize your ideas, copying down the words or phrases that support your points. Be prepared to compare your chart with those of your classmates.

5. In a paragraph, show that **inclusive language** has been used in the article titles. Explain why it is important to understand the effect of and to use inclusive language.

Extending

6. Research the job of "nurturing assistant" or "personal care attendant," and write a **report** on your findings. Be sure to include a job description, wages, work conditions, demands, etc. At the end of your report, write a paragraph explaining why you would or would not like a job such as this.

7. With a partner, create a television commercial supporting parents with disabilities. Brainstorm the messages you would like to send to your audience, choose the best, and create a shooting **script**. Write a short description of what you are trying to achieve with the commercial, and how you achieved it with your message and your visual and sound elements.

I'm Walking Out Of Your Jail Tonight

CHERRY NATURAL

On September 22, 1862, President Abraham Lincoln and Congress declared that all slaves in the United States were free from their owners, thereby abolishing slavery. This day came to be known as Emancipation Day and is still celebrated annually by Black Americans.

BEFORE READING

1. Read the above information on Emancipation Day and then predict what kind of jail the **narrator** of this **poem** is walking out of.

2. In a small group, read the poem aloud. Experiment with sounds and rhythms and be prepared to read the poem aloud to the class.

For Emancipation Day

Take a good look at me
Make a mental picture
capture all the details
Put them on your computer
I'm walking out of your jail tonight   5
Yes I'm walking out of your jail tonight
I'm gonna break those bars and set myself free
hire all the security that you can
Give them your weapon of destruction
that won't stop me   10
   I'm walking out of your jail tonight
Yes I'm walking out of your jail tonight
You have had your time and that's enough
I'm giving you back your man made rules
I'm giving you back your colonial attitudes   15
Take your laws out of my life
Your standards are not mine

If it is the last thing I be
I'm gonna be me
This spirit of mine must be free   20
so I'm walking out of your jail tonight
Yes I'm walking out of your jail tonight
I'm leaving the things you used to
control my mind, behind
You feed me with your hate, your jealousy,   25
Your greed, your guns and your drugs
Making me into the people's enemy
I say no more, I will take no more
I'm walking out of your jail tonight
Yes I'm walking out of your jail tonight   30
No amount of money can stop me
True wealth goes beyond possession
Call me insane, this time I won't complain
Madness has a way of freeing the soul
One more black woman is gonna be free   35
I'm walking out of your jail tonight, tonight, tonight

AFTER **READING**

Responding

1. In your **journal**, write a personal response to the poem. Did this poem affect you in any way? If yes, how so? If no, explain why.

Understanding

2. In your own words, tell the "story" of this poem. Include what has led up to the poem as well as what is happening in the poem.

3. In your notebook, answer the following questions: How does knowing the history of Emancipation Day help a reader understand this poem better? How might your interpretation of the poem be different without this knowledge? How could you access and use prior knowledge in the future when reading something new?

4. Describe the **atmosphere (mood)** of this poem. Explain the rhetorical techniques the poet uses to create the mood. (See The Reference Shelf, pages 366–367.)

Thinking About Language

5. a) In a small group, find the meaning of "colonial" (line 15). Look up the word "colonization," and come to an understanding of what it means to be "colonized." Explain the relationship between the two words, colonial and colonization.

   b) Using your understanding of both these words, explain what the narrator means in the line, "I'm giving you back your colonial attitudes." Present your ideas to the class.

6. This poem has little punctuation and lacks some expected capital letters. With a partner, list the reasons why you think the poet used this unconventional grammar and punctuation. Put your reasons on chart paper or on the board for the class to read and discuss.

Extending

7. a) In a small group, assign to each member a time period (e.g., 5 P.M.–7 P.M.) and a Canadian channel to watch on television. Have each person fill out a chart like the one below.

CHANNEL	ORIGIN	TIME PERIOD	PROGRAM	# BLACK PEOPLE	# BLACK WOMEN	ROLES OF THE BLACK WOMEN
Global	Canadian	5:00 – 5:30 P.M.	News	3	1	Reporter talking about germ-killing product

b) With the group, discuss the information on each chart. What **implicit meanings** and messages do television watchers get about Black people, specifically Black women? Based on your group's findings, create a **report** using charts, graphs, or other graphic elements to illustrate your points.

c) Present your report to the class, ensuring that everyone in the group contributes.

8. After reading this poem, write a list of questions for the poet. Combine your list with the other lists created in the class and choose five to ten questions that were most popular or most interesting. Find a contact address for Cherry Natural through the Canadian League of Poets or through the publisher of her poetry. (See Acknowledgements, page 448.) Write a letter to her with your questions, making sure to include your teacher's or a student's name and the school's correct address.

9. Research slavery in Canada and write a **research report** on one aspect of your research (e.g., the role of Harriet Tubman's underground railroad).

Shoes

SYLVIA HAMILTON

BEFORE READING

Using print and/or electronic sources, find out who Imelda Marcos is. Share your findings with the class.

When I finally
got her attention
"Size seven and a half, please"
as I reached for the shoe.

Contempt, veiled   5
as laughter:
"You can't afford those!"

At that moment
I resolved to try on
every size seven and a half   10
in the store.

Not that I would ever buy —
only that I would try.

She needed to know,
I had the right,   15
if I chose to
try and buy whatever
she had to show.

Very politely, "The grey pumps, please."
"The Almalfi in green."   20
(I hate green)
Canvas deck, why not.

When she was finally
surrounded by boxes,
her face truly red,   25
I left shoeless.
      Only Imelda would not be pleased.

AFTER READING

Responding

1. In your notebook, write your reaction to the **narrator**'s attitude in the shoe store and to the store clerk's attitude. Be prepared to discuss your reactions with the class.

Understanding

2. a) How did your research about Imelda Marcos help you understand the **poem** more fully?
   b) **Define** the word "**allusion**." Explain why writers use allusions in their writing. Why is this poet's allusion to Imelda Marcos effective?
3. a) In your notebook, write down a statement of **theme** for this poem.
   b) Write a series of well-developed paragraphs defending your interpretation of this poem, using **character**, narrative **voice**, figures of speech, or rhetorical devices to support your opinion.
4. With a partner, decide how the **setting** of the poem emphasizes its theme. Would other settings have worked just as well, and what would they be? Compare your ideas with those of another pair.
5. Explain why the poet might have chosen to organize the **stanzas** the way she did.
6. Make point-form notes on how the use of **direct speech** has affected the **tone** of this poem and its effect on the reader.

Thinking About Language

7. a) Reread the second stanza. With a partner, explain the meaning of the expression "Contempt, veiled as laughter." Describe what that would look and sound like if you were the person sitting in front of the sales clerk.
   b) Explain why the sales clerk's reaction to the customer is inappropriate.

Extending

8. Write an opinion paragraph on the following: "It is important to have general knowledge about history when you are studying literature." In a small group, read your paragraph aloud. Discuss the content of each paragraph and its organization and tone. Revise your paragraph.
9. a) With a partner, design and create a poster for the workplace, in which you cover one or more rules of workplace etiquette. Make a series of thumbnail sketches before you start and use your knowledge of design elements to create an effective visual presentation.
   b) Present your poster and discuss the design and how it emphasizes both the **implicit** and **explicit meanings** and messages of the poster.
10. In a small group, **roleplay** a situation that you or one of your group members has experienced in which you or they were unfairly labelled by another person. Your roleplay should include an appropriate way to react in a situation such as this.

Memoirs of a Really Good Brown Girl

"I lived a dual life..."   MARILYN DUMONT

BEFORE READING

Read the italicized print before the main text. As a class, discuss how this part of the text might relate to the title of the piece.

You are not good enough, not good enough, obviously not good enough. The chorus is never loud or conspicuous, just there.

Carefully dressed, hair combed like I am going to the doctor, I follow my older sister, we take the short-cut by the creek, through the poplar and cottonwood trees, along sidewalks, past the pool hall, hotel, variety store, the United Church, over the bridge, along streets until we reach the school pavement. It is at this point that I sense my sister's uneasiness; no obvious signs, just her silence, she is holding my hand like she holds her breath, she has changed subtly since we left home. We enter a set of doors which resemble more a piece of machinery than a doorway, with metal handles, long glass windows and iron grates on the floor, the halls are long and white, our feet echo as we walk. I feel as though I've been wrapped in a box, a

shoe box where the walls are long and manila gloss, it smells of paper and glue, there are shuffling noises I've never heard before and kids in the rooms we pass by. We enter a room from what seems the back door, rows of small tables lined up like variety cereal boxes, other small faces look back vacant and scared next to the teacher's swelling smile. (I have learned that when whites smile that fathomless smile it's best to be wary) I am handed over to the teacher. Later I will reflect upon this simple exchange between my older sister and the teacher as the changing of the guard, of big sister to teacher, and before that, when I was even younger, of mother to big sister.

This is my first day of school and I stand alone; I look on. Most of the kids know what to do, like they've all been here before, like the teacher is a friend of the family. I am a foreigner, I stay in my seat, frozen, afraid to move, afraid to make a mistake, afraid to speak, they talk differently than I do, I don't sound the way they do, but I don't know how to sound any different, so I don't talk, don't volunteer answers to questions the teacher asks. I become invisible.

I don't glisten with presence, confidence, glisten with the holiness of St. Anne whose statue I see every year at the pilgrimage, her skin translucent, as if the holy ghost is a light and it shines out through her fluorescent skin, as if a sinless life makes your skin a receptacle of light.

The other kids have porcelain skin like St. Anne too, but unlike her, they have little blond hairs growing out of small freckles on their arms, like the kind of freckles that are perfectly placed on the noses of the dolls I got each Christmas. In fact, the girls in my class look like my dolls: bumpy curls, geometric faces, crepe paper dresses, white legs and patent shoes.

My knees are scarred, have dirt ground in them from crawling under fences, climbing fences, riding skid horses and jumping from sawdust piles. I remember once, when I was a flower girl for my brother's wedding, I was taken home to the city by my brother's white fiancée and she "scrubbed the hell out of me." All other events that took place on that visit are diminished by the bathtub staging, no other event was given as much time or attention by her. I was fed and watered like a lamb for slaughter. I was lathered, scrubbed, shampooed, exfoliated, medicated, pedicured, manicured, rubbed down and moisturized. When it was over, I felt that every part of my body had been

hounded of dirt and sin and that now I, like St. Anne, had become a receptacle of light.

My skin always gave me away. In grade one, I had started to forget where I was when a group of us stood around the sink at the back of the class washing up after painting and a little white girl stared at the colour of my arms and exclaimed, "Are you ever brown!" I wanted to pull my short sleeves down to my wrists and pretend that I hadn't heard her, but she persisted, "Are you Indian?" I wondered why she had chosen this ripe time to ask me and if this was the first she'd noticed.

How could I respond? If I said yes, she'd reject me: worse, she might tell the other kids my secret and then they'd laugh and shun me. If I said no, I'd be lying, and when they found out I was lying, they'd shun me.

I said "No," and walked away.

I just watched and followed; I was good at that, good at watching and following. It was what I did best, I learned quickly by watching. (Some learning theories say that native kids learn best by watching, because they're more visual. I always knew that I learned by watching to survive in two worlds and in a white classroom.) I only needed to be shown something once and I remembered it, I remembered it in my fiber.

I lived a dual life; I had white friends and I had Indian friends and the two never mixed and that was normal. I lived on a street with white kids, so they were my friends after school. During school I played with the Indian kids. These were kids from the other Indian families who were close friends with my parents. At school my Indian friends and I would play quite comfortably in our own group, like the white kids did in theirs.

I am looking at a school picture, grade five, I am smiling easily. My hair is shoulder length, curled, a page-boy, I am wearing a royal blue dress. I look poised, settled, like I belong. I won an award that year for most improved student. I learned to follow really well.

I am in a university classroom, an English professor corrects my spoken English in front of the class. I say, "really good." He says, "You mean, really well, don't you?" I glare at him and say emphatically, "No, I mean really good."

AFTER READING

Responding

1. In your **journal**, write about a time when you acted differently with one group of people than with another. Explain why you acted the way you did and whether or not you would do things differently today.

Understanding

2. Use one word to convey the feeling the writer has about the school on her first day. Make a list of words under the headings "sight," "sound," and "smell" that help recreate the writer's feeling for the reader. Write your lists on the board.

3. Give four examples that indicate how the writer felt about her cultural background when she was in elementary school.

Thinking About Language

4. a) Look at the expression, "...I mean really good," in the last sentence of this **memoir**. Find the grammar rule that explains why this sentence is grammatically incorrect.

   b) The writer uses this incorrect grammar on purpose. With a partner, explain why the writer wants to use grammar unconventionally when speaking to the English professor.

5. Dumont uses both the terms "Indian" (page 229) and "native" (page 230) to refer to her cultural background. With the class, discuss the differences in these terms. Notice when Dumont uses each of the terms.

Extending

6. This piece of writing comes from a collection called *Poems.* In a small group, explain how this selection could be called a **poem**. Use The Reference Shelf (page 366) in this textbook and other reference books in your classroom to help you support your opinion.

7. In a small group, find out about the equity policies and procedures of your school board and school. Check the school board's Web site and the printed policies that are kept in the front office. Prepare an oral **report** of your findings on how your board and school help students from all cultures feel like part of the school and how the policies protect all students from harmful stereotypes and **bias**. Include visual aids to enhance your presentation and try to get the audience to participate. Be sure that all members of the group take an active part in the group's work.

8. Independently, using personal experience, the Internet, and other resources, research how Aboriginal Canadians are portrayed in the media. Using your findings, write an **essay** with a strong **thesis**. Be sure to include a properly formatted bibliography of all your sources. (See The Reference Shelf, pages 378–379.) Take your essay through all the stages of the writing process.

A Family Likeness

"...it could never be lost."   JACQUELINE ROY

BEFORE **READING**

In a small group, discuss the role played by support of friends and time in healing the painful emotions connected to great disappointment or loss.

"Livy, do you think you'll feel like coming out on Friday?" asked Melanie hesitantly. She'd been building up to asking for at least ten minutes, though she didn't know why she couldn't even ask a simple question anymore. Olivia didn't answer; she merely shook her head without bothering to look up. They continued to walk along the road in uneasy silence.

Melanie was getting tired of trying to get things back to normal. Patience didn't come naturally to her and she couldn't get used to having to think about every word and action in case Livy was upset by what she said or did. Yet she felt she had to try, because after all, they were best friends, and best friends stood by each other for better or for worse...Olivia's whole attitude said very clearly, leave me alone, just let me get on with it, and Melanie was often tempted to do just that. And the worst thing was, she was almost relieved that Livy wanted to be by herself so much, despite the efforts she was making to get her out. She wasn't exactly easy to get on with any more, and she looked so miserable that everybody round her felt miserable too—either that, or guilty because they *weren't* miserable. Sometimes Melanie wondered what it must feel like to have a parent just die on you as Olivia's father had died on her. But the subject was too big and too awful to be contemplated for any length, and Melanie could only push it to the back of her mind as one of those imponderables, like being put in prison for something you didn't do, or living through a nuclear war.

"I wish you would start coming out again," said Melanie, feeling the need to give it one last try. "There isn't any point in moping, he wouldn't have wanted you to..." Melanie faltered here; why did she have to mention Livy's father? She might cry or something, which would be awful. But Olivia's face didn't change, she just continued to plod homewards in the mechanical, uninterested way she'd adopted since the funeral last term...Melanie suddenly realized it had all been going on for at least three months. How long did the being miserable last? Maybe you never got over it.

Melanie became aware that Livy hadn't even attempted to respond to her question. "Aren't you going to say anything then?" she said crossly, though she wanted to be kind.

"Sorry," said Olivia. "I just don't want to come, that's all."

"OK, fair enough," said Melanie, but she tried to say it gently.

They fell into silence again. There was a limit to Melanie's ability to converse with someone who didn't want to talk back — or *couldn't* talk back perhaps. Vaguely, Melanie sensed there were things that Livy wanted to tell her but couldn't put into words. She'd been so silent since it happened, a silence that at times conveyed an angry hostility but at others held nothing but sadness. Melanie was barely able to deal with either. At fifteen, she was beginning to see just how complicated life could be and the idea of spending the next sixty or seventy years in a state of bewilderment was a daunting prospect. She hoped that age would bring wisdom but she had her doubts. Her mother, father and elder sister weren't showing much. Of course, she might manage to be different — wiser, more sensitive and more aware, but if her progress with Livy was anything to go by, she was doomed to a life of ignorance. If only Livy would let her do something, instead of shutting her out all the time...

They turned off the High Street and walked towards Olivia's gate. Livy began to fumble in her pocket for her keys. "Do you want to come in?" she said.

Melanie looked at her in surprise. Of late, Livy hadn't seemed able to wait to put the front door between them. "Yes, all right," she said, not really relishing the prospect. Her mother had said that Mrs. Everson's grief was such that she was cracking up under the strain. Melanie had never seen anyone cracking up and she wasn't sure she wanted to.

"You don't have to come," said Livy, clearly sensing her reticence.

"No, I'd like to, thanks."

The house hadn't changed, that was something. It was full of nice things, books, plants, pottery and pictures — sketches mostly, done by Livy's dad. She wondered if it hurt Livy to see them on the walls. It would have hurt her had she been in Livy's shoes...

Perhaps that was the trouble — up until then their lives had been similar; so similar that they'd been drawn to one another since their first day of school. They'd spotted each other across the playground at the age of just five because they looked so much the same; each had short curly hair and golden coloured skin and later they'd discovered they each had one black parent and one white, that they lived two streets apart and that they both had a birthday in the last week of August. They'd always felt like twins — until last term, that is. Melanie was beginning to realize that if Livy's father could die, then hers could too, that nothing was safe or certain. That was why she felt afraid...Why had it been Livy's father and not hers? It could so easily have been her own father who'd died in that accident. Who or what decided things like that? Did it make it better or worse to believe in God?

"Would you like something to drink?" said Livy. "There's cola in the fridge."

"They put teeth in a glass of that stuff and they just disintegrated."

"Does that mean no?"

Melanie smiled. "I guess it does. Have you got any fruit juice?"

"Orange or grapefruit?"

"Orange please."

They sat and looked at each other across the kitchen table, aware that just now, in choosing drinks, they'd almost had a normal conversation.

"Where's your mother?" asked Melanie.

"She'll be back later. She said she'd get some shopping."

"Is she OK?"

"Why shouldn't she be?"

Melanie shrugged. They both knew the answer to that, but perhaps it was better to avoid it.

"Would you like a sandwich?" said Olivia.

Melanie wasn't hungry but Livy had lost so much weight that you could get two people into her jeans. Maybe if she agreed to have a sandwich, Livy would have one too. "What have you got?"

"Ham, cheese, banana, liver pâté..."

"Cheese. I'm thinking of becoming a vegetarian."

"Are you?" said Livy. "I tried it once but I only managed to keep it up for a few days. Mum got sick of cooking three separate meals, one for her, one for me and one for dad...Cheddar or Edam?" she said briskly, drawing the subject away from her father as if she'd moved there inadvertently and had been stung by the memory.

"Edam," said Melanie, "it's less fattening. I've decided I'm going to have a healthy body—do you know how many people die of heart disease each year?" She stopped abruptly. How crass could you get? She just

had to talk about dying. It was rather like needing to laugh in church; the more you didn't want to do something like that, the more you just had to do it. She'd be discussing the cost of funerals next.

Livy began to butter some bread. Melanie noted with satisfaction that she was doing two lots. She looked around the kitchen and her eyes rested on the wall opposite. There was a portrait of Livy's father there—a self-portrait, she supposed. Some time before his death, he'd been hailed as the most outstanding black painter and sculptor of his generation. There was a book about him and he'd been on television.

"Mum put that painting up," said Livy. "I know she thinks of him a lot but she won't talk about him. I wish she would."

"It's a nice picture," said Melanie. It was an inadequate thing to say but she couldn't think of anything more. She focused her attention on her sandwich, chewing steadily. Livy finished hers.

"Would you like to see the others—the other paintings?"

No I wouldn't like, thought Melanie almost fiercely, but she sensed that an honour was being bestowed on her and that it was important to Livy. It was also the first gesture of friendship to come for some time, so she grasped it quickly. "Yes, all right," she said.

The studio was at the top of the house. They went upstairs slowly. "I haven't been in here since he died," said Livy, and Melanie couldn't think of an answer.

The room was light and airy—a window spanned one wall. All around were the trappings of an artist: easels, paints, brushes. There was a black plastic bin full of hardening clay and a powdery dust on the plain

"How do you mean?"

"Do you see yourself as black or white?"

"I don't know. Neither, I suppose. No, *black.*"

Olivia nodded. "Me too. That's why what he did was so important."

Melanie knew what she meant. Part of her own sense of herself was somewhere in these paintings and sculptures. How much more was it there for his daughter?

"I wish I was like him," Livy said.

"You are like him. Everybody says so."

"Not just to look at. I want to do what he did."

"Paint?"

"Paint and sculpt."

"Why shouldn't you? You're the best in the school at art—even better than the sixth form."

"Did you know that his father—my grandfather—was a carver too? And his father before him, and back as far as you can imagine."

Melanie nodded.

"Then it's up to me to carry on or the whole thing will be broken."

"Then carry on," said Melanie quietly.

"I'm not his son."

"What does that matter? You're his daughter."

Olivia was crying; Melanie was trying not to look but she could see it through the corner of her eye. "You're his daughter, Liv, that counts."

"It's always sons."

"He didn't have any sons. Besides, even if he had had them, it would still have been you because you've got the talent—anyone who's seen your paintings would know that."

"But you see, Melanie, I want to do it in order to be part of a tradition, but as a

wooden floor. As they walked, their footsteps were imprinted on it. Some of the paintings were six feet high. Melanie felt awed by their stature and vibrance. And everywhere, black figures surrounded them, with elongated necks and large heads—heads large enough to house the spirit; Melanie remembered the description from the programme.

Olivia wandered around, and Melanie watched her with anxiety; what loss was she feeling now? Yet she seemed more relaxed than she'd been for some time; the room seemed to hold something that eased the pain.

"How do you see yourself?" Olivia asked suddenly.

daughter, I can't be part of it, I can only break with it."

Melanie felt out of her depth. She sat on a chair without a back by the window. It was covered with spots of dried paint; it looked like a palette. "Did he say you couldn't do it?"

"No. We didn't discuss it. You see, I couldn't ask him to teach me in case he said no, and he never suggested it. I watched him though, and tried to learn that way. He liked me to be here."

"Perhaps he was waiting until you were old enough to be shown properly."

"I wish I knew. I'm not sure whether he would have shown me or not. I want to do it though."

"Then do it, Livy. Go to art school—do whatever you have to do."

"It won't be the way it should be."

"Nothing ever is. Look, things have changed. Even traditions change—they adapt to suit the times. For your father's father, and all those fathers before him, daughters were for cooking and cleaning, just as for the white slave owners, blacks were for picking cotton and harvesting bananas or whatever it was. It can all be changed once people realize that it can be...Oh hell, I don't know how to put this, I can't think how to get it across. But I know I'm right. Your father would want you to be a carver and a painter—he'd probably expect it of you. He wouldn't think you were less able or less important just because you're a daughter rather than a son. Livy, just look at his work. It goes beyond men and women; it even goes beyond black and white."

Olivia looked again. As a small child, she'd watched her father chipping and smoothing rough edges, making something live through the large, shapeless slabs. Figures had appeared as if by magic: men and women and children with long necks and large oval heads, masks with angry, scary faces, horses and strange birds from ancient African mythologies. She'd wanted to emulate him, to carve and paint as he did. Her father had shown her each of the figures he'd created, and told her all the stories. She knew about Anansi and Nyankapon, the First Pinci and Brer Rabbit. Since his death, she'd gone over all the legends in her mind, preserving them as the only link she now possessed with her past—her history. She had been born of a Jamaican father and an English mother, she was British but she was also black, and she'd been afraid that an important part of that identity had been buried with her father. Now she was coming to realize that it could never be lost, just as the spirit of her father could never be lost either; it lived on in the work he'd left behind him and it lived on in her.

Olivia walked round, remembering all her father had taught her, how each piece of wood, each stone held an image waiting to be freed; how the carver simply let it out. She touched each one of the shapes she saw, felt its roughness or its smoothness in her fingertips. She too could free the animals and birds and children trapped in their inanimate materials. And all around the walls, figures looked down at her in paint, in wood, in stone; timeless forms, the spirits of her past brought to life. She saw and felt their colours and was soothed.

She was her father's daughter; she had the right to inherit his skills.

AFTER READING

Responding

1. In your notebook, identify the qualities that make Melanie a better-than-average friend to Olivia.

Understanding

2. With a partner, discuss the significance of the following lines from the **story**:
   - "They fell into silence again." (page 233)
   - "Did it make it better or worse to believe in God?" (page 233)
   - "She'd be discussing the cost of funerals next." (page 234)
   - "No, *black.*" (page 235)
   - "It's always sons." (page 235)

   Be prepared to report to the class on the significance of any one of the quotations.
3. In a paragraph, state one **theme** of this story and provide reasons to support your choice. Be prepared to read your paragraph to the class. How many supportable themes does this story have?

Thinking About Language

4. In the third–last paragraph, the **narrator** tells us the story takes place in England. Identify language clues in the earlier part of the story that indicate the story is British.

Extending

5. a) This short story could be scripted and turned into a fine short film. Write an **essay** explaining the challenges involved in raising money to film and market a short story like this. Use an appropriate method of development to organize your essay. (See The Reference Shelf, pages 386–391.)
   b) Exchange your essay with a partner to revise and edit each other's work.
   c) Update your Writing Skills Action Plan as necessary. (See The Reference Shelf, page 395.)
6. a) With a partner, using print and/or electronic sources, research and write a **report** on the kinds of discrimination children of mixed parentage sometimes suffer.
   b) Before beginning your research, create a research plan with a list of questions to identify your information needs.
   c) Consider including charts and graphs, if appropriate, that will enhance the presentation of the information in your report.
   d) In the final draft of your report, include a correctly formatted bibliography of all the sources that you use. (See The Reference Shelf, pages 378–379.)

Race and Ethnicity

"...a child should be able to 'identify' with all of his or her heritage."

1. As a class, brainstorm a list of hyphenated Canadians, such as Italian-Canadians, Japanese–Canadians, etc.

2. The Canadian Census asks people about their sociocultural background including ethnic origin. As a class, discuss whether this is a good idea.

The following two selections were written in response to news of a custody case between Kimberly Van de Perre, a white woman, and a Black NBA player, Theodore "Blue" Edwards. They went to court over custody of their son, Elijah.

The Debate on Ethnicity

ALISON BLACKDUCK

...

I think about miscegenation regularly.

As the child of a Canadian woman of European descent and an indigenous man, I often felt pressured to either justify to others, including my indigenous peers, why I identify myself as an indigenous per-son, or explain why having a Canadian mother didn't make me Canadian. (Today, I don't bother explaining myself because it's nobody's business and I'm recognized as a member of my father's nation by the leadership and the community.)

Fortunately, I'm dark-haired, dark-skinned and dark-eyed, so I didn't have to explain physical ambiguities such as green eyes or red hair as do many other people of mixed indigenous/non-indigenous descent. As I've matured into adulthood, my dark features no longer appear as distinctly "Indian" as they did during childhood.

(Not surprisingly, most people guess that I'm Asian because they're ignorant of the fact that indigenous people form various nations, each with unique, distinguishing physical characteristics. I can spot the dif-ference between a Mohawk and a Dogrib in the same intuitive way that many Israeli Jews can identify which of their fellow Jews are Sephardic and which are Ashkenazi.)

I'm an adult now and sometime during my adulthood I'd like to have children. But I don't know if I'll have children with an indigenous man or a non-indigenous man.

If I have children with an indigenous man, our children won't be torn about who they are. If I have children with a non-indigenous man, I know that our children will be concerned about their identity and so will I.

In the latter case, I won't identify my children as indigenous like me, but I won't identify them as non-indigenous either.

I worry that my hypothetical non-indigenous partner won't understand why my children and I are concerned about who they are.

Last week, I started thinking about miscegenation again after reading newspaper stories about the Supreme Court custody dispute between Kimberly Van de Perre and Theodore Edwards over their 4-year-old son, Elijah.

Edwards and his wife Valerie, both of whom are black Americans, argue that Elijah's mother, a Canadian of European descent, is incapable of teaching Elijah how to survive and thrive as a black person in a world dominated by white people.

Therefore, the Edwards believe that's one reason, though not the only one, why Elijah should be entrusted to their custody.

Elijah's mother, Van de Perre, stated publicly that she understands why her ex-lover and his wife are concerned about Elijah's upbringing. She says she's never been discriminated against because of her appearance, so she knows Elijah will have many life experiences she won't relate to.

However, she is his mother, and she is white; therefore, she argues, Elijah is black and white — which is true.

But now the debate isn't about Elijah's mixed ethnicity, it's about our — and I mean white and non-white people — judgment of miscegenation.

It's also about who holds sexual power in a relationship between two people from two visibly distinct ethnicities (I am loath to use the word "race" because "race" is an arbitrary term that describes nothing but the differences in colour between people) and how that balance, or in some cases, imbalance, of power is influenced by the larger outside community.

The Whole Idea of Race Is Meaningless

MARI RUTKA

Re *Race cannot be ignored in custody case*, Opinion, June 25, 2000.

As a person whose ancestors came from many different countries, I am very much aware of racist attitudes. Sometimes people's racist comments and attitudes stem from deliberate ill will. More often, these comments and attitudes stem from ignorance and are a product of the particular era and place in which a person grew up.

While I find the former category of actions intolerable, I mostly find the

latter amusing. As much as possible, I try to gently educate those whose actions stem from ignorance by presenting them with a different perspective. It doesn't always work, but at least most of the time some progress is made. For example, I have not infrequently been asked: "What are you?" I know the person asking wants me to recite my ethnic origins, but I will sometimes respond to the question of "what" I am by saying, "I'm human."

This response, I find, usually produces a thoughtful silence. I like to hope that each thoughtful silence is a little gain toward a day when we will truly judge each person for their merits and their merits alone and not prejudge others on the basis of their appearance.

I think making the issue of race paramount in the Elijah Van de Perre custody case works directly against this. In an unfortunate case where a child cannot grow up with both parents, both parents would do well to draw upon their love for their child to do what is best for that child. I do not believe, however, that claiming one or the other parent's ethnic background "identifies" the child should be given consideration when determining who should finally raise that child. Love is more important.

To be sure, a child should be able to "identify" with all of his or her heritage. This is a wonderful thing and I know I am very proud of all the intrepid individuals who journeyed so far at so many times and from so many places to come together to be my family. But I think assuming that a child cannot have access to his or her heritage because one parent is not of that heritage is, in itself, a racist assumption.

As with other racist assumptions, those who think this way are prejudging a person's motivations, sensitivity and abilities based solely on their ethnic background. Although my mother was often asked if I was adopted because I looked "different" from her, I feel she did a very good job of acquainting me with the backgrounds of all my ancestors and the customs of their lands. My parents also helped me to see the humour in sometimes-awkward racist situations, and for that I thank them. In the end, I would say the most important factor in helping me to adjust to a world that doesn't always know what to make of me has been that my parents love me. That love is more important than the place of origin of any of my ancestors. That love should be the most important consideration in what happens to Elijah. Letting a determination of what Elijah "is" only demonstrates and perpetuates

the kind of categorizing thinking that results in racism in the first place.

As we progress into the 21st Century, there are, and likely will be, more and more individuals who are like Elijah, like me and like many others who have multiple ethnicities in their backgrounds. It seems to me that people who worry over whether someone is "black" or "white" or "Asian" or whatever label is being attached, are worrying in vain.

Genetic research is demonstrating ever more clearly that the whole idea of race is meaningless. The genetic variation existing between individuals who are tagged as being of the same "race" can be as great, or greater, than the variation that exists between two individuals of different so-called "races."

The national census that has just been conducted reflects a certain and mildly racist tardiness in attempting to label us by our parts. I had to laugh when I saw there were only four boxes into which we could put the ethnic origins of our ancestors. That was way too few for my family, and, I suspect, for many other families, as well. What is most important for this nation is loving the diversity that we represent. Learning from our diversity and taking all the best from our ancestors gives Canada a strength and potential from which we can and will only benefit.

AFTER READING

Responding

1. Alison Blackduck writes, "...I identify myself as an indigenous person." (page 238)
   Mari Rutka writes "Love is more important." (page 240)
   In a **journal** entry, explain whether or not the idea of race is meaningless or meaningful to you and your sense of your identity.

Understanding

2. Based on the information available in these two selections, identify the details of the custody case that prompted the writers to express their opinions on race and ethnicity.

3. In your notebook, fully explain the following:
   • the distinction between the concerns Alison Blackduck feels she and her hypothetical children will experience if their father is indigenous or non-indigenous
   • the distinction between "the former" and "the latter" that Mari Rutka makes in the second paragraph of her letter to the editor
   Be prepared to discuss your ideas with the class.

4. a) With a partner, analyze the arguments of both writers using a chart like the one below. Explain the extent to which each relies on facts, personal experience, insults, and/or emotions to make her case.

	BLACKDUCK	RUTKA
Facts		
Personal Experience		
Insults		
Emotions		
Other		

   b) After completing your analysis, explain which writer's ideas you most agree with and why.

Thinking About Language

5. Look up the word "miscegenation" in several dictionaries. Explain whether the **definitions** provided suggest any negative connotations for the word.

Extending

6. Read or reread the **story** "A Family Likeness" (pages 232–236). Explain whose view—Blackduck's or Rutka's—the two young women in the story would agree with most. Give reasons for your decision.

7. a) With a partner, using print and/or electronic sources, research current information on what genetic research is revealing about racial differences and differences between individuals.

   b) Using your findings, prepare an illustrated written or oral **report** with appropriate charts, graphs, and photos. Be sure to include a correctly formatted bibliography of all the sources that you use. (See The Reference Shelf, pages 378–379.)

8. **Debate** the following resolution: Be It Resolved That Young People Should Be Raised by People of Their Own Cultural Background. (See The Reference Shelf, page 401.) You may need to do research to prepare your arguments.

Love in the Classroom

AL ZOLYNAS

— for my students

Afternoon. Across the garden, in Green Hall,
someone begins playing the old piano —
a spontaneous piece, amateurish and alive,
full of simple, joyful melody.
The music floats among us in the classroom.   5

I stand in front of my students
telling them about sentence fragments.
I ask them to find the ten fragments
in the twenty-one-sentence paragraph on page forty-five.
They've come from all parts   10
of the world — Iran, Micronesia, Africa,
Japan, China, even Los Angeles — and they're still
eager to please me. It's less than half
way through the quarter.

They bend over their books and begin.   15
Hamid's lips move as he follows
the tortuous labyrinth of English syntax.
Yoshie sits erect, perfect in her pale make-up,
legs crossed, quick pulse minutely
jerking her right foot. Tony,   20
from an island in the South Pacific,
sprawls limp and relaxed in his desk.

The melody floats around and through us
in the room, broken here and there, fragmented,
re-started. It feels mideastern, but   25
it could be jazz, or the blues — it could be
anything from anywhere.
I sit down on my desk to wait,
and it hits me from nowhere — a sudden
sweet, almost painful love for my students.   30

"Never mind," I want to cry out.
"It doesn't matter about fragments.
Finding them or not. Everything's
a fragment and everything's not a fragment.
Listen to the music, how fragmented,   35
how whole, how we can't separate the music
from the sun falling on its knees on all the greenness,
from this movement, how this moment
contains all the fragments of yesterday
and everything we'll ever know of tomorrow!"   40

Instead, I keep a coward's silence.
the music stops abruptly;
they finish their work,
and we go through the right answers,
which is to say   45
we separate the fragments from the whole.

AFTER READING

Responding

1. In your **journal**, describe how reading this **poem** makes you feel.

Understanding

2. In your notebook, explain the following:
   - the causes of the teacher's "sudden sweet, almost painful love" for the students
   - the meanings and significance of "the fragments" and "the whole" in this poem
3. Identify a point in the poem where the **tone** changes. Explain how the shift in tone helps develop the ideas expressed in the poem.

Thinking About Language

4. a) With a partner, write **definitions** of quarter, tortuous, labyrinth, and syntax, as they are used in this poem. Add any new or unfamiliar words you have defined to your personal word list.

   b) Explain to your partner whether the difficult vocabulary is appropriate in this poem or not.
5. Find the two sentence fragments in this poem. Are they appropriately placed in the poem?

Extending

6. Write a well-constructed letter to a favourite teacher explaining three reasons why you admire or appreciate what she or he has done for you. If possible, send the signed letter to the teacher.

7. a) This poem depicts a classroom with students who originated from various parts of the world. With a partner, create a poster promoting cultural diversity and sensitivity in your school.

   b) As a class, create an evaluation form to assess the impact of each poster, focusing on the message and the use of font, colour, and other design elements.

   c) Present your poster to the class, explaining the production choices that you made.

Hand Painting

"It was like magic."   PADDY FAHRNI

I turned from winter window, the cold damp already tensing my bones. The class was over. We women milled about, collecting coats and bags. Somebody grabbed my hand. The old woman Abado. She wanted to give me a gift.

We had talked about henna decoration before, and I had seen the women's exquisite painted hands. Abado had noted my interest and now offered to paint my hands. The familiar, mundane duties of my afternoon brought refusal to my lips, but Abado, now joined by Shamis, enticed me.

And it was evident that Abado had gone to some trouble.

"The dry powder in the shops is no good," said Shamis. "We make our henna fresh, from leaves. We mix it—we use it in one day."

Soon we were sitting around my kitchen table. Under the kitchen light our roles transformed. Abado shed her frustrations at being hampered by age and strangeness

and became the gracious expert. Resourceful, outspoken Shamis became the deferential handmaiden. And as the painting progressed, I, stolid and middle-aged, felt increasingly pampered and young—like an innocent bride. Abado pulled a plastic bag from her purse. Inside was a small baggie filled with the olive-black mud. She opened the baggie and mashed the henna around, remixing. An organic odour, at once alluring and awful, filled the room.

"Haa," sighed Shamis, sniffing in happy recognition. "Henna!"

Abado demanded, "Batricia, what you want? What!"

"Make Somali designs."

"Maybe not nice for you."

"No, Abado. I like them. Do the same as for you."

Shamis spoke in Somali—some discussion.

"Really, Abado. Make Somali designs."

With a sigh, Abado undid a big safety pin from the folds of her dress. I hadn't noticed it before. She must have pinned it there that morning, or maybe she always wears it, like men with their multitools ever ready on belt or in pocket. With the pin, she carefully made a tiny hole in a corner of the baggie, picking at it and testing the squeezed line of henna on her own hand until she was satisfied.

"Open your hand THIS!"

Hand thrust out flat and stretched. I did so. Without a moment's thought or planning, Abado took my hand, turned it palm up, and began to squeeze the henna onto my fingers.

Without a moment's planning, but with a lifetime's experience. How many times had she sat among a bride's party? Abado squeezed out a median line down my fingers, palm to tip. She added fronds out from the midline. My palms were drawn with organic shapes—symmetry not important. The drawings sat happily in my hand with a human, not geometric, symmetry.

While Abado worked intently, Shamis used any spilled henna to apply to her nails. Reapply, that is. For a wedding party two weeks ago she had hennaed her hands—and now took the opportunity to refresh the colour. We three gossiped softly in simple English. Abado spoke in Somali to clarify meaning and exclaim properly. She demanded names and explanation of objects and the layout of the house. She thought about my responses and then, in the light of her culture, recommended various improvements. The right of a senior woman. My kitchen is suited for hurried individuals, grabbing a quick bite. It's only on the weekend we relax and cook together. In Abado's kitchen, I imagine large pots simmering, many voices at the table.

The backs of my hands were drawn more delicately—perhaps by tradition or perhaps because Abado was conserving the henna supply. One line down the middle of my hand continuing to the end of the middle finger. A line from wrist to thumbtip. A line down each finger. Then with looping lines she accented this exoskeleton tracery—with special attention to the index finger. These simple lines resonated a time and place at once exotic and familiar.

Abado's hands were steady and careful. If she made a mistake she wiped the wet henna first with her finger, then onto a cloth. The dark, olive-black, wet henna is put on lumpen and heavy, like mud. It sits for twenty to forty minutes, sinks in, and dries to a mid-olive. The hands must be kept rigid and flat as it dries.

"SO," said Abado, thrusting her wrinkled brown hand.

Moving the hand results in the henna running down the folds in the skin, ruining the image.

We breathed the stringent, earth-scented air. Abado picked off the dry henna, letting it fall to the floor, to reveal the richest red-brown lines. Parts of the design she retraced with wet henna for a deeper tone. The women were interested in the henna on white skin, more noticeable on the back of the hand and especially on the fingernails. Henna was meticulously reapplied to my nails, but not to Abado's satisfaction. She shook her head and tutted. At times Abado cradled one of my hands in one of hers, using her other hand to retrace, leaning over so our heads were close while Shamis held my other hand, her fingers scratching and rubbing off the dry henna. This attention was almost overwhelming — so soothing.

After several hours I was truly decorated. My hands were covered with organic designs. I had a long flower or insect up the underside of one arm. On the other arm was an uncertain looking heart with an arrow through it — awkward next to the vibrant flowers. But my hands and arms were aching. Three hours and only my hands were finished! Abado and Shamis talked down their work modestly. They hadn't had enough time. The hands, arms, feet, legs would take a group of women a day.

"Your husband wash dishes tonight," Abado said. She warned me not to use a lot of water on my hands tonight, but to rub in cream several times tonight and tomorrow.

"Put cream come very beautiful."

I looked down at my hands. They seemed magical, intense. I looked at Abado. This old woman, struggling in a strange cold country, had given me a gift of warm attention, a gift resonating with a thousand pair of hands.

Going up the stairs that night, my hands flew ahead of me like exotic birds. Hands against the white wall. Against my black sweater. Up by my face in the mirror. Pulling through my hair. Against my white nightgown. The silkiness of the hennaed skin.

"You will have beautiful dreams the first night. I always have beautiful dreams the first night," Shamis had smilingly confided.

I laid down into the pillow, feeling langorous and content, enveloped by the warm scent. I believed I had been touched as if I was a valuable being.

Over the next weeks, I noticed the henna. The deep red against the green lettuce I held under the kitchen tap, the spirals on my hand matching the curl of my husband's hair, my hands on the steering wheel, on the pen. The scent lasted into the second week. Each night I inhaled it as I fell asleep. It was like magic. Each time I saw my hands, I felt the hands of my friends.

But, over the next few days, it was in reaching for money — palm up — that my hennaed hands triggered the biggest reactions. The cashier at McDonald's drive-thru gave me my change and smiled, exclaiming, "Oh, you've been to a wedding! My girlfriend does that!"

The blonde postal clerk at Safeway was in fine form — tired, but joking with the customers, "Henna! I know that. My neighbours from India had a big party. I was up all night! I had such a good time!"

"Oh, is that henna?"

"I like your henna."

"Oh yeah, that henna stuff."

Cashiers all over the city remarked. Well, younger cashiers. Older female cashiers either ignored my hands ("Nothing can surprise me anymore") or asked about it in a straightforward way. As did the other mothers at the hockey games.

"What's that all over your hands?"

They'd be interested to hear my by now abridged description. Openly curious, they'd ask practical questions—if it lasted long, if it came off on clothes. They'd mention a friend they knew. They'd give their opinions.

"That's not for me!"

"I thought your hands were dirty!"

"I might try something small."

"Do you know somebody who can do it?"

The kids—well, the kids knew it all.

"That stuff!" said the eleven-year-old boy. "Yeah, I saw it in a magazine."

"Cool henna," the twelve-year-old girl remarked. "I saw a show on TV."

"My friend's sister did some on me last summer."

Two little girls took a felt from their mother's purse and imitated my henna on their hands.

The men reacted differently.

"You have *mehndi*?" the Indian Subway employee questioned me disapprovingly. The combination of my face and hands was jarring for him. We all know it well: what is familiar is comfortable. Unfamiliar, uncomfortable.

The white men, silent and suspicious, were uneasy with the dark markings.

"What's that voodoo stuff?"

They eyed my hands as if they were dirty.

Weeks passed. The henna markings slowly faded, and so did my memories of that afternoon. It was as if comforting hands slipped slowly from my skin. The classes have finished now. Somebody said Abado moved away.

Outside, the winter grey continues. We have just passed the longest night of the year. Lonely, I remember and long for the special kindness of the handpainting afternoon.

AFTER READING

Responding

1. In a small mixed-gender group, discuss whether this **story** appeals equally to males and females. Be prepared to report to the class on interesting points in your discussion.

Understanding

2. In a paragraph, state one **theme** of this story and provide reasons to support your choice. Be prepared to read your paragraph to the class. How many supportable themes does this story have?

3. a) Reread the description of the process of applying the henna. Is the description positive or negative?
   b) Select the words and phrases that create the reader's impression of the process.
   c) In a paragraph, explain how the words and phrases create the impression.

4. "The class was over." With a partner, discuss what kind of class this might have been where the women met. Be prepared to support your choice or choices to the class.

5. Make a chart (using the template below) of the various reactions of the people who saw the **narrator's** hands.

PERSON	REACTION	UNDERLYING CAUSE OF THE REACTION
cashier at McDonald's	knowing smile	thought she had been to a wedding
the narrator herself		
white men		

Thinking About Language

6. The author of this story does not always identify the speaker of a quotation. Describe when the author does and does not identify the speaker. Explain why the reader is always able to determine who the speaker is.

Extending

7. a) Using print and/or electronic sources, do research on henna, mehndi art, and Somali culture. Prepare an oral report on one interesting aspect of the results of your research.
   b) Use visuals and technology aids, if appropriate, to enhance your presentation.
   c) As a class, create an evaluation form to assess each presentation, focusing on content, organization, and use of visuals and technology (if appropriate).
   d) Using the feedback from your classmates, update your Oral Communication Skills Action Plan. (See The Reference Shelf, page 395.)

Stop or Go

"Trust is our first inclination."

As a class, discuss the following: Have you ever gone through a red light (or considered doing it)? Be sure to explain all the circumstances surrounding the situation.

In and of Ourselves We Trust

ANDY ROONEY

Anecdotal start or example to illustrate the main point of the essay

Last night I was driving from Harrisburg to Lewisburg, Pennsylvania, a distance of about 80 miles [128 km]. It was late, I was late, and if anyone asked me how fast I was driving, I'd have to plead the Fifth Amendment to avoid self-incrimination.

At one point along an open highway, I came to a crossroads with a traffic light. I was alone on the road by now, but as I approached the light, it turned red, and I braked to a halt. I looked left, right, and behind me. Nothing. Not a car, no suggestion of headlights, but there I sat, waiting for the light to change, the only human being for at least a mile in any direction.

I started wondering why I refused to run the light. I was not afraid of being arrested, because there was obviously no cop anywhere around and there certainly would have been no danger in going through it.

Thesis or main point

Much later that night, after I'd met with a group in Lewisburg and had climbed into bed near midnight, the question of why I'd stopped for that light came back to me. I think I stopped because it's part of a contract we all have with each other. It's not only the law, but it's an agreement we have, and we trust each other to honour it: We don't go through red lights. Like most of us, I'm more apt to be restrained from doing something bad by the social convention that disapproves of it than by any law against it.

It's amazing that we ever trust each other to do the right thing, isn't it? And we do, too. Trust is our first inclination. We have to make a deliberate decision to mistrust someone or to be suspicious or skeptical.

It's a darn good thing, too, because the whole structure of our society depends on mutual trust, not distrust. This whole thing we have going for us would fall apart if we didn't trust each other most of the time. In Italy they have an awful time getting any money for the government because many people just plain don't pay their income tax. Here, the Internal Revenue Service makes some gestures toward enforcing the law, but mostly they just have to trust that we'll pay what we owe. There has often been talk of a tax revolt in this country, and our government pretty much admits that if there were a widespread tax revolt here, they wouldn't be able to do anything about it.

We do what we say we'll do. We show up when we say we'll show up.

I was so proud of myself for stopping for that red light. And inasmuch as no one would ever have known what a good person I was on the road from Harrisburg to Lewisburg, I had to tell someone.

A Traffic Light Is a Brainless Machine

DAVID SCHOENBRUN

It was midnight in Paris and we were rolling along the Quai d'Orsay toward the Avenue Bosquet, where I live, on the left bank of the river Seine. As we came to the Pont Alexandre III, the cab slowed down, for the traffic light was red against us, and then, without stopping, we sailed through the red light in a sudden burst of speed. The same performance was repeated at the Alma Bridge. As I paid the driver, I asked him why he had driven through two red lights.

"You ought to be ashamed of yourself, a veteran like you, breaking the law and endangering your life that way," I protested.

He looked at me, astonished. "Ashamed of myself? Why, I'm proud of myself. I am a law-abiding citizen and have no desire to get killed either." He cut me off before I could protest.

"No, just listen to me before you complain. What did I do? Went through a red light. Well, did you ever stop to consider what a red light is, what it means?"

"Certainly," I replied. "It's a stop-signal and means that traffic is rolling in the opposite direction."

"Half-right," said the driver, "but incomplete. It is only an automatic stop signal. And it does not mean that there is cross traffic. Did you see any cross traffic during our trip? Of course not. I slowed down at the light, looked carefully to the right and to the left. Not another car on the streets at this hour. Well, then! What would you have me do? Should I stop like a dumb animal because an automatic, brainless machine turns red every 40 seconds? No, monsieur," he thundered, hitting the door jamb with a huge fist. "I am a man, not a machine. I have eyes and a brain and judgment, given me by God. It would be a sin against nature to surrender them to the dictates of a machine. Ashamed of myself, you say? I would only be ashamed of myself if I let those blinking lamps do my thinking for me. Good night, monsieur."

Is this bad, is this good? Frankly I no longer am sure. The intellectual originality of the French is a corrupting influence if you are subjected to it for long. I never doubted that it was wrong to drive through a red light. After more than a decade of life in Paris, however, I find my old Anglo-Saxon standards somewhat shaken. I still think it is wrong to drive through a stop signal, except possibly very late at night, after having carefully checked to make sure there is no cross traffic. After all, I am a man, not a machine.

AFTER READING

Responding

1. In your notebook, take the side of either Andy Rooney or the French cab driver. Defend the side you take, referring to both the **essays** and your personal experiences.

Understanding

2. With a partner, look at the organization of each of the essays. (See The Reference Shelf, pages 386–391, for a brief description of various types of essay organization.) Point out one aspect of organization the two have in common and one way in which they differ.

3. Show how David Schoenbrun's opinion changes from the beginning to the end of the essay "A Traffic Light Is a Brainless Machine."

4. With a partner, create and **roleplay** a discussion between Andy Rooney and the French cab driver. Be prepared to present your roleplay to the class.

Thinking About Language

5. a) Identify the meaning of the phrase "social convention" in the following: "Like most of us, I'm more apt to be restrained from doing something bad by the social convention that disapproves of it than by any law against it" ("In and of Ourselves We Trust," page 253).

   b) Put this sentence into plain language.

   c) Is the **style** of this sentence representative of the rest of Andy Rooney's essay? Support your answer using examples from the essay.

Extending

6. a) With a partner, find an advertisement (print, television, or radio) that promotes safe driving. Assess the advertisement in terms of the target audience (age, gender, socio-economic level, cultural groups), production decisions made (see The Reference Shelf, pages 428–429), and effectiveness of the message.
      Present your findings to the class using a computer and presentation software, if possible.

   b) As a class, create an evaluation form for the presentations and complete a peer evaluation on each presentation.

7. a) Invite a local police officer into your class to talk about the *Motor Vehicle Safety Act* and the reason we have traffic rules and regulations. Prepare and send a series of questions ahead of time so the officer can be prepared to address your interests and concerns.

   b) While the officer is in your class, take notes on the information given. After the presentation, compare your notes to those of the rest of the class.

   c) Discuss note-taking strategies that helped you get the information, and strategies that did not work as well.

Hedge-hopping

"...now he looks like a soul in the
clutches of the Devil."

RAÚL TEIXIDÓ
TRANSLATED BY JAMES GRAHAM

*for the writer and cinéaste Alfonso Gumucio
Dragón*

A beige suit, maroon shoes, lightweight
straw hat made for the warm weather: He
was dressed almost the same as the last
time. "I hope you had a good rest," Don
Aurelio said with an obliging smile. Guests
like Mr. John lent the place class.
Moreover, the elegant stranger seemed the
same as always, cautious, following his
habits to the letter: A Campari, newspapers
he'd bought at the kiosk in the plaza,
which he read later on over dessert....You
could count on him not forgetting to leave
a juicy tip.

The photographer Balthazar, nodding
out in his seat, his ancient camera next to
him, half opens his eyes and watches the
man in the light suit walk over to
Salustiano's kiosk. A limber step, good
looking, the photogenic type. In fact he
would like to take Mr. John's portrait and

was looking for an angle that would take
in the whole scene: A solitary tourist in his
neat and crisply ironed summer suit, hat
tilted at a sharp angle to ward off the sun;
the single file of trees around the edge of
the central area, with the church tower in
the background — everything contributing
to a splendid composition on a postcard.
On the flip side it would read: *Santa María
del Camino, Plaza de la República*, putting it
that way so it would be clear that, despite
the lethargy common to the epoch, this
peaceful city also possessed an international flavor of its own, thanks to the people
from far away who passed through and
even, like the anonymous stranger, stayed
a few days.

On days he didn't go out, Mr. John
came down to the dining room around
five; sitting in his usual spot, he reviewed
his notes or wrote something in quick little
letters while taking sips from a drink that
calmed his stomach...a relaxed man, all

activities aimed at undermining the constitutional government, in collusion with local elements. He should be watched discretely during his stay in this locality, while waiting for other instructions that may come from headquarters.

The man with the bushy mustache watches the street from the window, occasionally wiping the sweat off his face, his eye on the single thing moving on the deserted sidewalk: The dull white and drooping figure of the water vendor's donkey, earthen jars on either side of its back tied by leather straps, and the man walking behind keeping pace with the animal through a long row of shuttered doorways.

In the office a small fan sitting on top of the file cabinet isn't enough to break up the block of stale air. Captain Gómez calls for a subordinate, hands him a few folders, and then returns to his observation point. The donkey and his owner have disappeared, and the skinny line of shade that the roofs cast at the foot of the houses strikes him as little more than the fine line drawn by a pencil over the surface of old ashen debris.

"Mr. John always stays here actually, but I don't know a thing about what he does. Well, I think he has business with the government. In any case he doesn't talk much. And no, he doesn't receive visitors. When he doesn't go out, he sits at that table to work. I suppose he feels lonely in his room. He's a guest who keeps to himself—well mannered, I can tell you that. Yesterday by chance I saw him writing a letter to his wife in the United States. Her name is Linda. He went out early

his affairs in order. As he takes the cup away, Don Aurelio manages to make out the name at the top of the letter that Mr. John was writing: Linda. *Of course, a man has to keep in touch with his family*, he thinks, fanning himself with the napkin.

John Talbott, North American.

Business agent.

Employed by the firm of Campbell & McGregor (agricultural supplies).

Previous visits to the country: November 1969 and April 1970, for authorized stays of one to two weeks.

Memo (urgent and confidential) to police authorities:

Apparently John Talbott, a citizen of the United States, has made visits to our country for reasons very different than stated, presumably illicit political today, I think in order to get the most out of the morning, before it gets too hot…" Don Aurelio looks at Captain Gómez's sweaty forehead and his bushy mustache, as rough as the brush on a hog.

"We already know the gringo isn't here now. Give me the key." Two men hang around the bar while the search is carried out. Don Aurelio asks himself what would happen if Mr. John walked in at that moment, and he breathes a sigh of relief when Captain Gómez brings the search to a close.

"Absolutely routine, as you can see. But be careful about spoiling things by squealing to the gringo, because I'll find you out…" he warns, wagging a dirty and blistered finger in a vague circling gesture that takes in the counter and the shelves, making it clear that indiscretion could cost Don Aurelio those items and much more. He then yanks his hat on with both hands, nods, and goes out. Don Aurelio sets about cleaning the counter, a worried look on his face.

Later that night Don Aurelio goes down to the kitchen for a cold beer. He thinks he sees something moving behind the service entrance, perhaps the stray dogs, who at that hour are accustomed to knocking the garbage cans over. He jumps when he sees Mr. John's silhouette moving toward the lighted part of the service area.

"Ah, it's you."

Don Aurelio would have preferred not to see Talbott until the next day at least, as if by then Captain Gómez's visit could be considered in the far past and, more than anything else, not worth mentioning. In any case Don Aurelio is certain Mr. John doesn't know about the search. Apparently his guest couldn't sleep on account of the heat. "Me neither, as you can see. Come in and sit down. Let's have something to drink."

They both drink a beer while chewing the fat. Mr. John lives with his wife and two sons in Boston; he has been with the company for many years and is familiar with several Spanish-speaking countries. "When I retire, I'll settle down in a South American country," Mr. John says. Don Aurelio likes this gringo; despite his reserve, he inspires trust. What's more, anyone could see that he was a man with class. But why is he always on the road like an ordinary traveling salesman, when he seems capable of so much more? Even worse, the police have their eyes on him now: Captain Gómez had cast doubt on the legitimacy of his business dealings. Given such a hypothesis, what is Mr. John's occupation? Contraband liquor or cigarettes? He could let Don Aurelio have a few cartons, at a friendly price. Aurelio laughs at his own joke. His shirt sticks to his chest and his throat is parched all over again. The dogs start to make a racket with their hungry growls. He stays where he is and listens to them for a while, unable to get back to sleep.

"And what if we detain him until we can verify our suspicions?"

"Mr. Talbott isn't formally accused of anything and there are no charges against him. We are only investigating. You didn't read the memo?"

"Perhaps we could…"

"In twenty-four hours our intelligence service will give us definitive confirmation. Your superiors appreciate your professional zeal, Captain, but they ask you to hold on a little while. Let's not forget that Mr. Talbott is a citizen of a friendly country."

"And if it turns out that there is evidence he is one of the contacts for the subversives? At this moment I've got the guy in Santa María, within my grasp. It may not be the same later."

"He doesn't know we're watching him, and we already know he's staying for a few days. In any case if for any reason he tries to take off before, you have the authority to put him in preventive detention."

Which means they don't approve of a precautionary arrest, Captain Gómez thinks….*As if we couldn't excuse ourselves later if something goes wrong. Even if I'm not in the political branch, my nose tells me this guy is a subversive agent. It wouldn't be the first time…*

He wipes the sweat from his face and goes through John Talbott's file one more time: passport, identity card, working papers, visa — everything as it should be. Nothing in his room gave him away: there were only catalogs, client lists, magazines in English and Spanish, paperback novels: The guy was as clean as the Easter bunny. *No, sir, this one wasn't going to get away with it.*

Captain Gómez's persistent calls to headquarters always drew the same response: *You must limit yourself to waiting for the urgent communiqué that could be coming at any moment.* And in fact that moment arrives just when he is midway in his route between the desk and the window looking out onto the street, the window where he was going to position himself and get a handle on his impatience. The suspicions of the political branch in respect to the true nature of John Talbott's activities in the country have been fully confirmed. As a consequence his arrest and solitary confinement are authorized until such time that government agents arrive in Santa María to take him to the capital.

"That mechanic — is he coming or not!" Pablo drags his tail a bit before making his appearance. He shows up just as Captain Gómez arrives looking for him, so the two men almost crash into one another. "Where were you, man! Come over here and listen to what I have to say." The captain accepts a cold drink courtesy of the house, leans against the counter, and, drawing close to Don Aurelio and Pablo in a confidential manner, takes care of business with an important air: "I'm not going to repeat what I say, so pay attention. Bear in mind that I stand for the government and am the maximum authority in this town — that's the condition under which I speak. Everybody knows Mr. Talbott. He's been to our town many times, he's considerate, keeps to himself, never causes problems, et cetera, et cetera. All right, then, you must know that our secret service has been investigating him, and they say he's a conspirator — in other words, an undesirable element. He's to be arrested and put in the hands of competent authorities. That's why I'm here: I'm asking for your help. By no means can we allow the gringo to slip through our hands — understand? At this moment he doesn't suspect anything, but we have to take precautions. You — Pablo or whatever your name is — this guy rented the car he uses to get around from you, isn't that so? Okay, then; drive the car to the garage tonight. Tell him you need to tune it up and you'll bring it back early tomorrow morning — just so you won't make him suspicious.

Above all, I don't want him to have any means of transportation available should he decide to take off ahead of time and catch us sleeping. And look, if he tries to take off by some other means or you notice anything, Mr. Aurelio, any kind of unusual movement by your guest, get in touch with me immediately. If you don't, I can accuse you of obstructing the work of the authorities." Captain Gómez leaves without saying good-bye. Don Aurelio stays put, looking over the empty dining room. The gringos have always financed the government; it was even said that they choose the candidates, removing or putting in office those who serve their interests. But it was clear there were other kinds of gringos; gringos who sympathize with the opposition, who go up against the ruling puppets and make a commitment to the dangerous task of changing the rules of the game. It seemed that Mr. John belonged to this rare species.

After dinner Mr. John mentions that Pablo has taken the car to the shop, something Don Aurelio already knows all too well. And he adds that in any case he only needs the car one more time for the trip to the station, because he is being forced to cut his stay short for family reasons. "Nothing serious, I hope," Don Aurelio says, disguising his reaction. "What I want to say is…well, there are always problems, the point is to find a solution for them." He feels as if he is assisting involuntarily in a dangerous scheme whose inner workings have brought about Captain Gómez's visit. Breathing deeply, he swallows some saliva and decides that he, too, will run the risk: "Look here, Mr. John, I have something to tell you." Looking concerned, his audience

gets ready to hear him out. "I believe you are a good person, Mr. John," Don Aurelio goes on, "which is why I don't want to be an accomplice to an injustice. In the first place you should know that the police searched your room and…you already knew! It's better that way. I didn't dare to say anything about it to you last night, please understand, because the Captain threatened to close my business if anything leaked out. But that isn't the important thing: Captain Gómez has orders to arrest you. The car repairs are just a trick meant to keep you from leaving before midday. He was here a little while ago, he said so in those very same words." Mr. John stares at him for a few seconds through his dark glasses and nods in gratitude. Don Aurelio despairs of asking him how he thinks he will elude the blockage that has begun to fence him in, but only manages to get out a few words about his own safety: "If there's trouble, whatever else you do, Mr. John, don't let anybody know I ratted — it could cost me my hotel, and even my skin!"

"They won't have a chance to talk to me," Mr. John says in a serious tone. "And you, friend, keep this. You've earned it," he adds, pushing a wad of bills into the top pocket of Don Aurelio's jacket. Don Aurelio gestures a refusal, which Mr. John ignores.

On the way to his room, Mr. John tips his hat in a gesture of greeting…or farewell.

"Good luck, gringo," Don Aurelio replies. Music from the jukebox fills the room.

Mr. John drums his fingers nervously after dialing the number. There is the silence of a broken connection, the emptiness of space at the other end of the line while his call's invisible projectile makes a path through darkness and distance until at last it reaches its goal. When it is time to speak, Mr. John inquires in a neutral voice: "Is this the Marechiaro Inn?"

"Yes, it is," a voice replies. "Specializing in all types of food and lodging."

"Pay attention: I wish to cancel an order, number twenty/twenty-seven. The family won't be able to meet on the day we have chosen, and as of now, we have canceled the party. Please tell Enrique that I need his trailer as soon as possible, as soon as the sun comes up—is that clear?" Mr. John repeats his message's code words, and then the entire text word for word to make certain they have received it correctly. He stays in the phone booth a few moments after he's hung up the phone.

Captain Gómez smoothes his mustache and lays out his plan with undisguised pleasure. "Three men with me, in the jeep. A second car behind for cover. You two watch the main door and the service entrance, and you go with me when I go in. Have your rifles ready and keep your eyes open!" His gaze, lively and nervous, seems fixed on an invisible victim. "I've got him, he had to fall to earth right here in Santa María," he thinks, adjusting the holster of his revolver. "'And now what, mister? Are you ready to come with us to the station?' I can just see his face! And let it be clear that if he's looking for it, I'll finish him off right there—pow! Pow! After all it's only a question of an enemy agent, and, in this type of war, aliens…don't matter at all. I'll be laughing when I see what the press says about it later."

Mr. John sees the jeep coming his way, and he hides behind Salustiano's kiosk; nevertheless one of the cops notices him and tells him to freeze. The vehicle comes to a sudden stop and guns can be heard cocking, readying to fire. In a split-second reaction even the most attentive observer could not have predicted, Mr. John lifts his right arm, hurls a solid object toward the jeep, and dashes at full speed toward an unguarded street, like a fox who races through the bushes in flight from his pursuers. A huge blast rends the air and the window in Don Aurelio's restaurant shatters in a terrific shower of glass flying in all directions. A thick cloud of smoke rises up into the trees. Captain Gómez, pulling himself together quickly, steps over the body of one of his agents on the ground, and orders everyone else to follow him.

Don Aurelio is standing on the sidewalk, astonished by the damage. "Holy Jesus, Captain! What the Devil?"

"The bastard had a grenade," the captain snarls. "Call an ambulance at once. There's a man badly hurt." And with his guard in tow, he runs toward a second car, waiting for him a few yards away.

Mr. John is a courteous and quiet man, never in a hurry, but now he looks like a soul in the clutches of the Devil. He tears out of Santa María like a wild man, leaving behind the steaming heap of a police jeep, its occupants tossed about like marionettes, and bursts into Pablo's garage, pistol in hand. He forces Pablo behind the wheel and orders him to drive full speed for the outskirts of town, making him an unintentional hostage. The surprised mechanic doesn't pay attention to anything but the dusty road. Pressing the gun against Pablo's temple, Mr. John makes it clear that he shouldn't let up on the accelerator, while he clutches his hat with his free hand, keeping an eye out for any tricky maneuvers or unforeseen obstacles that God knows how they could have avoided.

Pablo's nightmare concludes as quickly as it began, as Mr. John jumps out of the car at the edge of a clearing, yelling at Pablo to keep going, to throw his pursuers off his scent. He couldn't say what the stranger did afterward; as is only logical, Pablo had made every effort to follow instructions, without saying a word, because his life was in danger. But yes, as he stops the car, he notices the outline of a small plane behind some bushes, very similar to the kind used in crop dusting. "What else could I do — that nut was off his rocker, with a revolver to boot!" he would plead later on — sitting under the withering stare of Captain Gómez, while over in the Plaza de la República, unusually crowded with curiosity seekers, Don Aurelio wondered just how much it would cost him to replace the glass in the window. *Crazy gringo! What else did he have up there? A bazooka?*

The hard jolts come fast and furious as the airplane increases its speed. The tiny cabin vibrates as if at any moment it will break in pieces. Mr. John feels he is about to witness an imminent explosion. The dry ping of bullets can be heard, as insistent as curses that don't reach their target.

After running the last several feet of the rocky terrain, the small plane makes its takeoff, tracing a wide semicircle before climbing in altitude. Before his eyes Mr. John sees the tilted plane of a familiar landscape — corn fields, an irrigation canal, humble dwellings, and granaries — slipping slowly into the distance as if swallowed by a toboggan. The pilot, up until that moment absorbed in his work, gives Mr. John a conspiratorial look and flashes a thumb's up. Mr. John smiles back at him, wondering over his hat, lost in the last stretch of the getaway, and the paperback novel he'd left in his room at the hotel. He had forgotten it on the night table: *The Wonderful Country.*

Little by little the small craft straightened its course, rising up toward a clear and luminous July sky.

AFTER READING

Responding

1. Reread the first paragraph of the story and what you wrote for the "Before Reading" activity. Describe additional meanings and **foreshadowing** you are now aware of in the first paragraph.

Understanding

2. In a few paragraphs, describe Don Aurelio's attitude(s) toward Mr. John. Provide reasons from the story to support the attitude(s) you describe.

3. a) Explain the **irony** in the title of the paperback novel Mr. John left in his room at the hotel.
   b) Explain the significance of the title of this story.

4. With a partner, list all the implied charges against Mr. John mentioned in the story. Using your list, write a formal government **report** describing the suspicions and potential charges the government has against Mr. John. Read your report to the class.

5. a) This story is dedicated to a filmmaker and is told in a series of episodes or vignettes, which create **suspense**. In a small group, discuss
   - the influence of cinematic storytelling on the structure of the story
   - ambiguous elements in the story that the reader must interpret
   b) As a class, discuss each group's observations.

6. Imagine that Mr. John arrives home and has to write a report to his employer. Write Mr. John's report on the events of this story to his employer.
   Or
   From the perspective of a newspaper reporter in the Latin American country or Mr. John's home country, write a newspaper account of the events in this story.

Thinking About Language

7. With a partner, look up the word "gringo" in the dictionary. What is the **connotation** of the word? Discuss how knowing the connotative meanings of the word adds to the reader's understanding of this story.

8. As a class, discuss what a **cliché** is and when to use or avoid using it. Locate three clichés used in this story. Explain whether the use of clichés weakens or enhances this story.

Extending

9. In a small group, prepare a **proposal** for a film production company, explaining why this story would be an excellent movie. Present your proposal to the class.

10. Think about the effect the first paragraph of this story had on you when you read it to do the "Before Reading" activity. Write an introductory paragraph to a story in which you foreshadow aspects of the plot, **character**, **setting**, and tone for the reader.

Trifles

"...a sheriff's wife is married to the law."   SUSAN GLASPELL

CHARACTERS

Sheriff Peters

County Attorney Henderson

Mr. Hale, a farmer

Mrs. Peters, the sheriff's wife

Mrs. Hale

Scene:

The kitchen in the now abandoned farmhouse of John Wright, a gloomy kitchen, and left without having been put in order—the walls covered with a faded wall paper. Down Right is a door leading to the parlor. On the Right wall above this door is a built-in kitchen cupboard with shelves in the upper portion and drawers below. In the rear wall at Right, up two steps is a door opening onto stairs leading to the second floor. In the rear wall at Left is a door to the shed and from there to the outside. Between these two doors is an old-fashioned black iron stove. Running along the Left wall from the shed door is an old iron sink and sink shelf, in which is set a hand pump. Downstage of the sink is an uncurtained window. Near the window is an old wooden rocker. Center stage is an unpainted wooden kitchen table with straight chairs on either side. There is a small chair Down Right. Unwashed pans under the sink, a loaf of bread outside the breadbox, a dish towel on the table—other signs of uncompleted work. At the rear the shed door opens and the Sheriff comes in followed by the County Attorney and Hale. The Sheriff and Hale are men in middle life, the County Attorney is a young man; all are much bundled up and go at once to the stove. They are followed by the two women—the Sheriff's wife, Mrs. Peters, first; she is a slight wiry woman, a thin nervous face. Mrs. Hale is larger and would ordinarily be called more comfortable looking, but she is disturbed now and looks fearfully about as she enters. The women have come in slowly, and stand close together near the door.

County Attorney: (*At stove rubbing his hands.*) This feels good. Come up to the fire, ladies.

Mrs. Peters: (*After taking a step forward.*) I'm not — cold.

Sheriff: (*Unbuttoning his overcoat and stepping away from the stove to right of table as if to mark the beginning of official business.*) Now, Mr. Hale, before we move things about, you explain to Mr. Henderson just what you saw when you came here yesterday morning.

County Attorney: (*Crossing down to left of the table.*) By the way, has anything been moved? Are things just as you left them yesterday?

Sheriff: (*Looking about.*) It's just the same. When it dropped below zero last night I thought I'd better send Frank out this morning to make a fire for us — (*sits right of center table*) no use getting pneumonia with a big case on, but I'd told him not to touch anything except the stove — and you know Frank.

County Attorney: Somebody should have been left here yesterday.

Sheriff: Oh — yesterday. When I had to send Frank to Morris Center for that man who went crazy — I want you to know I had my hands full yesterday. I knew you could get back from Omaha by today and as long as I went over everything here myself —

County Attorney: Well, Mr. Hale, tell just what happened when you came here yesterday morning.

Hale: Harry and I had started to town with a load of potatoes. We came along the road from my place and as I got here I said, "I'm going to see if I can't get John Wright to go in with me on a party telephone." I spoke to Wright about it once before and he put me off, saying folks talked too much anyway, and all he asked was peace and quiet — I guess you know about how much he talked himself; but I thought maybe if I went to the house and talked about it before his wife, though I said to Harry that I didn't know as what his wife wanted made much difference to John —

County Attorney: Let's talk about that later, Mr. Hale. I do want to talk about that, but tell now just what happened when you got to the house.

Hale: I didn't hear or see anything; I knocked at the door, and still it was all quiet inside. I knew they must be up, it was past eight o'clock. So I knocked again, and I thought I heard somebody say, "Come in." I wasn't sure, I'm not sure yet, but I opened the door — this door (*indicating the door by which the two women are still standing*) and there in that rocker — (*pointing to it*) sat Mrs. Wright. (*They all look at the rocker.*)

County Attorney: What — what was she doing?

Hale: She was rockin' back and forth. She had her apron in her hand and was kind of — pleating it.

County Attorney: And how did she — look?

Hale: Well, she looked queer.

County Attorney: How do you mean — queer?

Hale: Well, as if she didn't know what she was going to do next. And kind of done up.

County Attorney: (*Takes out notebook and pencil and sits left of center table.*) How did she seem to feel about your coming?

Hale: Why, I don't think she minded—one way or other. She didn't pay much attention. I said, "How do, Mrs. Wright, it's cold, ain't it?" And she said, "Is it?"—and went on kind of pleating at her apron. Well, I was surprised; she didn't ask me to come up to the stove, or to set down, but just sat there, not even looking at me, so I said, "I want to see John." And then she—laughed. I guess you would call it a laugh. I thought of Harry and the team outside, so I said a little sharp: "Can't I see John?" "No," she said, kind o' dull like. "Ain't he home?" says I. "Yes," says she, "he's home." "Then why can't I see him?" I asked her, out of patience. "'Cause he's dead," says she. "*Dead?*" says I. She just nodded her head, not getting a bit excited, but rockin' back and forth. "Why—where is he?" says I, not knowing what to say. She just pointed upstairs—like that. (*Himself pointing to the room above.*) I started for the stairs, with the idea of going up there. I walked from there to here—then I says, "Why, what did he die of?" "He died of a rope 'round his neck," says she, and just went on pleatin' at her apron. Well, I went out and called Harry. I thought I might—need help. We went upstairs and there he was lyin'—

County Attorney: I think I'd rather have you go into that upstairs, where you can point it all out. Just go on now with the rest of the story.

Hale: Well, my first thought was to get that rope off. It looked…(*stops, his face twitches*)…but Harry, he went up to him, and he said, "No, he's dead all right, and we'd better not touch anything." So we went back downstairs. She was still sitting that same way. "Has anyone been notified?" I asked. "No," says she, unconcerned. "Who did this, Mrs. Wright?" said Harry. He said it business-like—and she stopped pleatin' of her apron. "I don't know," she says. "You don't *know*?" says Harry. "No," says she. "Weren't you sleepin' in the bed with him?" says Harry. "Yes," says she, "but I was on the inside." "Somebody slipped a rope 'round his neck and strangled him and you didn't wake up?" says Harry. "I didn't wake up," she said after him. We must 'a' looked as if we didn't see how that could be, for after a minute she said, "I sleep sound." Harry was going to ask her more questions but I said maybe we ought to let her tell her story to the coroner, or the sheriff, so Harry went fast as he could to Rivers' place, where there's a telephone.

County Attorney: And what did Mrs. Wright do when she knew that you had gone for the coroner?

Hale: She moved from the rocker to that chair over there (*pointing to a small chair in the corner*) and just sat there with her hands held together and looking down. I got a feeling that I ought to make some conversation, so I said I had come in to see if John wanted to put in a telephone, and at that she started to laugh, and then she stopped and looked at me—scared. (*The County Attorney, who has had his notebook out, makes a note.*) I dunno, maybe it wasn't scared. I wouldn't like to say it was. Soon Harry got back, and then Dr. Lloyd came, and you, Mr. Peters, and so I guess that's all I know that you don't.

County Attorney: (*Rising and looking around.*) I guess we'll go upstairs first—and then out to the barn and around there. (*To the sheriff.*) You're convinced that there was nothing important here—nothing that would point to any motive?

Sheriff: Nothing here but kitchen things. (*The County Attorney, after again looking around the kitchen, opens the door of a cupboard closet in Right wall. He brings a small chair from Right—gets up on it and looks on a shelf. Pulls his hand away, sticky.*)

County Attorney: Here's a nice mess. (*The women draw nearer.*)

Mrs. Peters: (*To the other woman.*) Oh, her fruit; it did freeze. (*To the Lawyer.*) She worried about that when it turned so cold. She said the fire'd go out and her jars would break.

Sheriff: (*Rises.*) Well, can you beat the women! Held for murder and worryin' about her preserves.

County Attorney: (*Getting down from the chair.*) I guess before we're through she may have something more serious than preserves to worry about.

Hale: Well, women are used to worrying over trifles. (*The two women move a little closer together.*)

County Attorney: (*With the gallantry of a young politician.*) And yet, for all their worries, what would we do without the ladies? (*The women do not unbend. He goes below the center table to the sink, takes a dipperful of water from the pail and pouring it into a basin, washes his hands. While he is doing this the Sheriff and Hale cross to cupboard, which they inspect. The County Attorney* starts to wipe his hands on the roller towel, turns it for a cleaner place.) Dirty towels! (Kicks his foot against the pans under the sink.) Not much of a housekeeper, would you say, ladies?

Mrs. Hale: (Stiffly.) There's a great deal of work to be done on a farm.

County Attorney: To be sure. And yet (with a little bow to her) I know there are some Dickson County farmhouses which do not have such roller towels. (He gives a pull to expose its full length again.)

Mrs. Hale: Those towels get dirty awful quick. Men's hands aren't always as clean as they might be.

County Attorney: Ah, loyal to your sex, I see. But you and Mrs. Wright were neighbors. I suppose you were friends too.

Mrs. Hale: (Shaking her head.) I've not seen much of her of late years. I've not been in this house — it's more than a year.

County Attorney: (Crossing to the women.) And why was that? You didn't like her?

Mrs. Hale: I liked her well enough. Farmers' wives have their hands full, Mr. Henderson. And then —

County Attorney: Yes —?

Mrs. Hale: (Looking about.) It never seemed a very cheerful place.

County Attorney: No — it's not cheerful. I shouldn't say she had the homemaking instinct.

Mrs. Hale: Well, I don't know as Wright had, either.

County Attorney: You mean that they didn't get on very well?

Mrs. Hale: No, I don't mean anything. But I don't think a place'd be any cheerfuller for John Wright's being in it.

County Attorney: I'd like to talk more of that a little later. I want to get a look at things upstairs now. (He goes past the women to where steps lead to a stair door.)

Sheriff: I suppose anything Mrs. Peters does'll be all right. She was to take in some clothes for her, you know, and a few little things. We left in such a hurry yesterday.

County Attorney: Yes, but I would like to see what you take, Mrs. Peters, and keep an eye out for anything that might be of use to us.

Mrs. Peters: Yes, Mr. Henderson. (The men leave by door to stairs. The women listen to the men's steps on the stairs, then look about the kitchen.)

Mrs. Hale: (Crossing to the sink.) I'd hate to have men coming into my kitchen, snooping around and criticizing. (She arranges the pans under sink which the Lawyer had shoved out of place.)

Mrs. Peters: Of course it's no more than their duty. (Crosses to cupboard.)

Mrs. Hale: Duty's all right, but I guess that deputy sheriff that came out to make the fire might have got a little of this on. (Gives the roller towel a pull.) Wish I'd thought of that sooner. Seems mean to talk about her for not having things slicked up when she had to come away in such a hurry. (Crosses to Mrs. Peters at cupboard.)

Mrs. Peters: (Who has been looking through the cupboard, lifts one end of a towel that covers a pan.) She had bread set. (Stands still.)

Mrs. Hale: (Eyes fixed on a loaf of bread beside the breadbox, which is on a low shelf of the cupboard.) She was going to put this in there. (Picks up loaf, then abruptly drops it. In a manner of returning to familiar things.) It's a shame about her fruit. I wonder if it's all gone. (Gets up on the chair and looks.) I think there's some here that's all right,

Mrs. Peters. Yes—here; (*holding it toward the window*) this is cherries, too. (*Looking again.*) I declare I believe that's the only one. (*Gets down, jar in her hand. Goes to the sink and wipes it off on the outside.*) She'll feel awful bad after all her hard work in the hot weather. I remember the afternoon I put up my cherries last summer. (*She puts the jar on the big kitchen table, center of the room. With a sigh, is about to sit down in the rocking chair. Before she is seated realizes what chair it is; with a slow look at it, steps back. The chair which she has touched rocks back and forth. Mrs. Peters moves to center table and they both watch the chair rock for a moment or two.*)

Mrs. Peters: (*Shaking off the mood which the empty rocking chair has evoked. Now in a businesslike manner she speaks.*) Well, I must get those things from the front room closet. (*She goes to the door at the Right, but, after looking into the other room, steps back.*) You coming with me, Mrs. Hale? You could help me carry them. (*They go in the other room; reappear, Mrs. Peters carrying a dress, petticoat and skirt, Mrs. Hale following with a pair of shoes.*) My, it's cold in there. (*She puts the clothes on the big table, and hurries to the stove.*)

Mrs. Hale: (*Right of center table examining the skirt.*) Wright was close. I think maybe that's why she kept so much to herself. She didn't even belong to the Ladies' Aid. I suppose she felt she couldn't do her part, and then you don't enjoy things when you feel shabby. I heard she used to wear pretty clothes and be lively, when she was Minnie Foster, one of the town girls singing in the choir. But that—oh, that was thirty years ago. This all you was to take in?

Mrs. Peters: She said she wanted an apron. Funny thing to want, for there isn't much to get you dirty in jail, goodness knows. But I suppose just to make her feel more natural. (*Crosses to cupboard.*) She said they was in the top drawer of this cupboard. Yes, here. And then her little shawl that always hung behind the door. (*Opens stair door and looks.*) Yes, here it is. (*Quickly, shuts door leading upstairs.*)

Mrs. Hale: (*Abruptly moving toward her.*) Mrs. Peters?

Mrs. Peters: Yes, Mrs. Hale?

Mrs. Hale: Do you think she did it?

Mrs. Peters: (*In a frightened voice.*) Oh, I don't know.

Mrs. Hale: Well, I don't think she did. Asking for an apron and her little shawl. Worrying about her fruit.

Mrs. Peters: (*Starts to speak, glances up, where footsteps are heard in the room above. In a low voice.*) Mr. Peters says it looks bad for her. Mr. Henderson is awful sarcastic in a speech and he'll make fun of her sayin' she didn't wake up.

Mrs. Hale: Well, I guess John Wright didn't wake when they was slipping that rope under his neck.

Mrs. Peters: (*Crossing slowly to table and placing shawl and apron on table with other clothing.*) No, it's strange. It must have been done awful crafty and still. They say it was such a—funny way to kill a man, rigging it all up like that.

Mrs. Hale: That's just what Mr. Hale said. There was a gun in the house. He says that's what he can't understand.

Mrs. Peters: Mr. Henderson said coming out that what was needed for the case was motive; something to show anger, or—sudden feeling.

Mrs. Hale: (*Who is standing by the table.*) Well, I don't see any signs of anger around here. (*She puts her hand on the dish towel which lies on the table, stands looking down at table, one-half of which is clean, the other half messy.*) It's wiped to here. (*Makes a move as if to finish work, then turns and looks at loaf of bread outside the breadbox. Drops towel. In that voice of coming back to familiar things.*) Wonder how they are finding things upstairs. I hope she had it a little more red-up up there. You know, it seems kind of *sneaking.* Locking her up in town and then coming out here and trying to get her own house to turn against her!

Mrs. Peters: But, Mrs. Hale, the law is the law.

Mrs. Hale: I s'pose 'tis. (*Unbuttoning her coat.*) Better loosen up your things, Mrs. Peters. You won't feel them when you go out. (*Mrs. Peters takes off her fur tippet, goes to hang it on chair back left of table, stands looking at the work basket on floor near window.*)

Mrs. Peters: She was piecing a quilt. (*She brings the large sewing basket to the center table and they look at the bright pieces.*)

Mrs. Hale: It's a log cabin pattern. Pretty, isn't it? I wonder if she was goin' to quilt it or just knot it? (*Footsteps have been heard coming down the stairs. The Sheriff enters followed by Hale and the County Attorney.*)

Sheriff: They wonder if she was going to quilt it or just knot it! (*The men laugh, the women look abashed.*)

County Attorney: (*Rubbing his hands over the stove.*) Frank's fire didn't do much up there, did it? Well, let's go out to the barn and get that cleared up. (*The men go outside.*)

Mrs. Hale: (*Resentfully.*) I don't know as there's anything so strange, our takin' up our time with little things while we're waiting for them to get the evidence. (*She sits in chair right of table smoothing out a block with decision.*) I don't see as it's anything to laugh about.

Mrs. Peters: (*Apologetically.*) Of course they've got awful important things on their minds. (*Pulls up a chair and joins Mrs. Hale at the table.*)

Mrs. Hale: (*Examining another block.*) Mrs. Peters, look at this one. Here, this is the one she was working on, and look at the sewing! All the rest of it has been so nice and even. And look at this! It's all over the place! Why, it looks as if she didn't know what she was about! (*After she has said this they look at each other, then start to glance back at the door. After an instant Mrs. Hale has pulled at a knot and ripped the sewing.*)

Mrs. Peters: Oh, what are you doing, Mrs. Hale?

Mrs. Hale: (*Mildly.*) Just pulling out a stitch or two that's not sewed very good. (*Threading a needle.*) Bad sewing always made me fidgety.

Mrs. Peters: (*With a glance at the door, nervously.*) I don't think we ought to touch things.

Mrs. Hale: I'll just finish up this end. (*Suddenly stopping and leaning forward.*) Mrs. Peters?

Mrs. Peters: Yes, Mrs. Hale?

Mrs. Hale: What do you suppose she was so nervous about?

Mrs. Peters: Oh—I don't know. I don't know as she was nervous. I sometimes sew awful queer when I'm just tired. (*Mrs. Hale starts to say something, looks at Mrs. Peters, then goes on sewing.*) Well, I must get these things wrapped up. They may be through sooner than we think. (*Putting apron and other things together.*) I wonder where I can find a piece of paper, and string. (*Rises.*)

Mrs. Hale: In that cupboard, maybe.

Mrs. Peters: (*Looking in cupboard.*) Why, here's a bird cage. (*Holds it up.*) Did she have a bird, Mrs. Hale?

Mrs. Hale: Why, I don't know whether she did or not—I've not been here for so long. There was a man around last year selling canaries cheap, but I don't know as she took one; maybe she did. She used to sing real pretty herself.

Mrs. Peters: (*Glancing around.*) Seems funny to think of a bird here. But she must have had one, or why would she have a cage? I wonder what happened to it?

Mrs. Hale: I s'pose maybe the cat got it.

Mrs. Peters: No, she didn't have a cat. She's got that feeling some people have about cats—being afraid of them. My cat got in her room and she was real upset and asked me to take it out.

Mrs. Hale: My sister Bessie was like that. Queer, ain't it?

Mrs. Peters: (*Examining the cage.*) Why, look at this door. It's broke. One hinge is pulled apart. (*Takes a step down to Mrs. Hale's right.*)

Mrs. Hale: (*Looking too.*) Looks as if someone must have been rough with it.

Mrs. Peters: Why, yes. (*She brings the cage forward and puts it on the table.*)

Mrs. Hale: (*Glancing toward door.*) I wish if they're going to find any evidence they'd be about it. I don't like this place.

Mrs. Peters: But I'm awful glad you came with me, Mrs. Hale. It would be lonesome for me sitting here alone.

Mrs. Hale: It would, wouldn't it? (*Dropping her sewing.*) But I tell you what I do wish, Mrs. Peters. I wish I had come over sometimes when *she* was here. I—(*looking around the room*)—wish I had.

Mrs. Peters: But of course you were awful busy, Mrs. Hale—your house and your children.

Mrs. Hale: I could've come. I stayed away because it weren't cheerful—and that's why I ought to have come. I—(*looking out window*)—I've never liked this place. Maybe because it's down in a hollow and you don't see the road. I dunno what it is, but it's a lonesome place and always was. I wish I had come over to see Minnie Foster sometimes. I can see now—(*Shakes her head.*)

Mrs. Peters: Well, you mustn't reproach yourself, Mrs. Hale. Somehow we just don't see how it is with other folks until—something turns up.

Mrs. Hale: Not having children makes less work—but it makes a quiet house, and Wright out to work all day, and no company when he did come in. (*Turning from window.*) Did you know John Wright, Mrs. Peters?

Mrs. Peters: Not to know him; I've seen him in town. They say he was a good man.

Mrs. Hale: Yes—good; he kept his word as well as most, I guess, and paid his debts. But he was a hard man, Mrs. Peters. Just to pass the time of day with him—(*Shivers.*) Like a raw wind that gets to the bone. (*Pauses, her eye falling on the cage.*) I should think she would 'a' wanted a bird. But what do you suppose went with it?

Mrs. Peters: I don't know, unless it got sick and died. (*She reaches over and swings the broken door, swings it again, both women watch it.*)

Mrs. Hale: You weren't raised around here, were you? (*Mrs. Peters shakes her head.*) You didn't know—her?

Mrs. Peters: Not till they brought her yesterday.

Mrs. Hale: She — come to think of it, she was kind of like a bird herself — real sweet and pretty, but kind of timid and — fluttery. How — she — did — change. (*Silence; then as if struck by a happy thought and relieved to get back to everyday things. Crosses to cupboard, replaces small chair used to stand on to its original place.*) Tell you what, Mrs. Peters, why don't you take the quilt in with you? It might take up her mind.

Mrs. Peters: Why, I think that's a real nice idea, Mrs. Hale. There couldn't possibly be any objection to it, could there? Now, just what would I take? I wonder if her patches are in here — and her things. (*They look in the sewing basket.*)

Mrs. Hale: (*Crosses to right of table.*) Here's some red. I expect this has got sewing things in it. (*Brings out a fancy box.*) What a pretty box. Looks like something somebody would give you. Maybe her scissors are in here. (*Opens box. Suddenly puts her hand to her nose.*) Why — (*Mrs. Peters bends nearer, then turns her face away.*) There's something wrapped up in this piece of silk.

Mrs. Peters: Why, this isn't her scissors.

Mrs. Hale: (*Lifting the silk.*) Oh, Mrs. Peters — it's — (*Mrs. Peters bends closer.*)

Mrs. Peters: It's the bird.

Mrs. Hale: But, Mrs. Peters — look at it! Its neck! Look at its neck! It's all — other side to.

Mrs. Peters: Somebody — wrung — its neck. (*Their eyes meet. A look of growing comprehension, of horror. Steps are heard outside. Mrs. Hale slips box under quilt pieces, and sinks into her chair. Enter Sheriff and County Attorney. Mrs. Peters stands looking out of window.*)

County Attorney: (*As one turning from serious things to little pleasantries.*) Well, ladies, have you decided whether she was going to quilt it or knot it?

Mrs. Peters: We think she was going to — knot it. (*Sheriff crosses to stove, lifts stove lid and glances at fire, then stands warming hands at stove.*)

County Attorney: Well, that's interesting, I'm sure. (*Seeing the bird cage.*) Has the bird flown?

Mrs. Hale: (*Putting more quilt pieces over the box.*) We think the — cat got it.

County Attorney: (*Preoccupied.*) Is there a cat? (*Mrs. Hale glances in a quick covert way at Mrs. Peters.*)

Mrs. Peters: (*Turning from window takes a step in.*) Well, not *now*. They're superstitious, you know. They leave.

County Attorney: (*To Sheriff Peters, continuing an interrupted conversation.*) No sign at all of anyone having come from the outside. Their own rope. Now let's go up again and go over it piece by piece. (*They start upstairs.*) It would have to have been someone who knew just the — (*Mrs. Peters sits down left of table. The two women sit there not looking at one another, but as if peering into something and at the same time holding back. When they talk now it is in the manner of feeling their way over strange ground, as if afraid of what they are saying, but as if they cannot help saying it.*)

Mrs. Hale: (*Hesitatively and in hushed voice.*) She liked the bird. She was going to bury it in that pretty box.

Mrs. Peters: (*In a whisper.*) When I was a girl — my kitten — there was a boy took a hatchet, and before my eyes — and before I could get there — (*Covers her face an* *instant.*) If they hadn't held me back I would have — (*catches herself, looks upstairs where steps are heard, falters weakly*) — hurt him.

Mrs. Hale: (*With a slow look around her.*) I wonder how it would seem never to have any children around. (*Pause.*) No, Wright wouldn't like the bird — a thing that sang. She used to sing. He killed that, too.

Mrs. Peters: (*Moving uneasily.*) We don't know who killed the bird.

Mrs. Hale: I knew John Wright.

Mrs. Peters: It was an awful thing was done in this house that night, Mrs. Hale. Killing a man while he slept, slipping a rope around his neck that choked the life out of him.

Mrs. Hale: His neck. Choked the life out of him. (*Her hand goes out and rests on the bird cage.*)

Mrs. Peters: (*With rising voice.*) We don't know who killed him. We don't *know.*

Mrs. Hale: (*Her own feeling not interrupted.*) If there'd been years and years of nothing, then a bird to sing to you, it would be awful — still, after the bird was still.

Mrs. Peters: (*Something within her speaking.*) I know what stillness is. When we homesteaded in Dakota, and my first baby died — after he was two years old, and me with no other then —

Mrs. Hale: (*Moving.*) How soon do you suppose they'll be through looking for the evidence?

Mrs. Peters: I know what stillness is. (*Pulling herself back.*) The law has got to punish crime, Mrs. Hale.

Mrs. Hale: (*Not as if answering that.*) I wish you'd seen Minnie Foster when she wore a white dress with blue ribbons and stood up there in the choir and sang. (*A look around the room.*) Oh, I *wish* I'd come over here once in a while! That was a crime! That was a crime! Who's going to punish that!

Mrs. Peters: (*Looking upstairs.*) We mustn't — take on.

Mrs. Hale: I might have known she needed help! I know how things can be — for women. I tell you, it's queer, Mrs. Peters. We live close together and we live far apart. We all go through the same things — it's all just a different kind of the same thing. (*Brushes her eyes, noticing the jar of fruit, reaches out for it.*) If I was you I wouldn't tell her her fruit was gone. Tell her it *ain't*. Tell her it's all right. Take this in to prove it to her. She — she may never know whether it was broken or not.

Mrs. Peters: (*Takes the jar, looks about for something to wrap it in; takes petticoat from the clothes brought from the other room, very nervously begins winding this around the jar. In a false voice.*) My, it's a good thing the men couldn't hear us. Wouldn't they just laugh! Getting all stirred up over a little thing like a — dead canary. As if that could have anything to do with — with — wouldn't they *laugh*! (*The men are heard coming downstairs.*)

Mrs. Hale: (*Under her breath.*) Maybe they would — maybe they wouldn't.

County Attorney: No, Peters, it's all perfectly clear except a reason for doing it. But you know juries when it comes to women. If there was some definite thing. (*Crosses slowly to above table. Mrs. Hale and Mrs. Peters remain seated at either side of table.*) Something to show — something to make a story about — a thing that would connect up with this strange way of doing it — (*The* women's eyes meet for an instant. Enter Hale from outer door.)

Hale: (*Remaining by door.*) Well, I've got the team around. Pretty cold out there.

County Attorney: I'm going to stay awhile by myself. (*To the Sheriff.*) You can send Frank out for me, can't you? I want to go over everything. I'm not satisfied that we can't do better.

Sheriff: Do you want to see what Mrs. Peters is going to take in? (*The Lawyer picks up the apron, laughs.*)

County Attorney: Oh, I guess they're not very dangerous things the ladies have picked out. (*Moves a few things about, disturbing the quilt pieces which cover the box. Steps back.*) No, Mrs. Peters doesn't need supervising. For that matter a sheriff's wife is married to the law. Ever think of it that way, Mrs. Peters?

Mrs. Peters: Not—just that way.

Sheriff: (*Chuckling.*) Married to the law (*Moves to the other room.*) I just want you to come in here a minute, George. We ought to take a look at these windows.

County Attorney: (*Scoffingly.*) Oh, windows!

Sheriff: We'll be right out, Mr. Hale. (*Hale goes outside. The Sheriff follows the County Attorney into the other room. Then Mrs. Hale rises, hands tight together, looking intensely at Mrs. Peters, whose eyes make a slow turn, finally meeting Mrs. Hale's. A moment Mrs. Hale holds her, then her own eyes point the way to where the box is concealed. Suddenly Mrs. Peters throws back quilt pieces and tries to put the box in the bag she is carrying. It is too big. She opens box, starts to take bird out, cannot touch it, goes to pieces, stands there helpless. Sound of a knob turning in the other room. Mrs. Hale snatches the box and puts it in the pocket of her big coat. Enter the County Attorney and Sheriff, who remains Down Right.*)

County Attorney: (*Crosses to door facetiously.*) Well, Henry, at least we found out that she was not going to quilt it. She was going to—what is it you call it, ladies?

Mrs. Hale: (*Standing facing front, her hand against her pocket.*) We call it—knot it, Mr. Henderson.

CURTAIN

AFTER READING

Responding

1. In a small group, read the **play** aloud. Make a list of strategies that members of the group used to make the meaning of the words clear and dramatic.

2. In your notebook, write your reactions to the ending of this play.

Understanding

3. With a partner, reread the play and list all the facts that can be considered clues that help to explain the mystery behind John Wright's death. Compare your list with those of your classmates.

4. In a small group, discuss and explain the following:
   - the significance of the title of this play
   - the **irony** in the line "I wish if they're going to find any evidence they'd be about it." (page 271)
   - why Mrs. Hale and Mrs. Peters do not reveal their discoveries
   - whether Mrs. Hale and Mrs. Peters are doing the right thing at the end of this play

   Ensure that each member contributes to the discussion and takes notes.

Thinking About Language

5. With a partner, write **definitions** of the following words: crafty, abashed, reproach, covert, close, red-up, and facetiously as they are used in the **context** of this play. Add any new or unfamiliar words you have defined to your personal word list.

6. Copy two sentences from the play that are colloquialisms and two that are in dialect. (See The Reference Shelf, page 351.) For each sentence, explain how you know the words are colloquialisms or dialect. Be prepared to explain the difference between colloquialism and dialect.

7. Explain why the word "center" is spelled one way in this play, while in some other selections it is spelled "centre."

Extending

8. In a short **essay**, explain how this play can be interpreted as an observation on male/female equality.

9. As a class, **roleplay** the trial of Mrs. Wright. Some members of the class will take the parts of the **characters** in the play, while others will play the parts of Mrs. Wright's lawyer, witnesses, reporters, and members of the jury. All information presented at the trial must be consistent with the facts presented in the play.

10. Create a poster for a production of "Trifles" by your school's Drama Club. Be prepared to explain how you designed your poster to appeal to the students in your school.

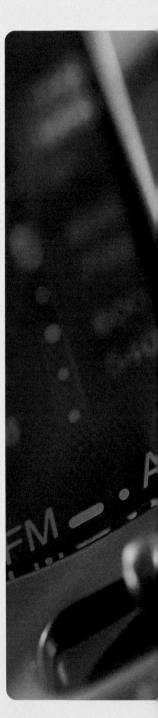

UNIT 3

> Media

united colours of benneton

AMUNA BARAKA-CLARKE

BEFORE READING

As a class, brainstorm a list of memorable advertisements by Benetton. Discuss what makes them so memorable and controversial.

what a gwan benneton
what a gwan wid benneton

when i taking dih train
i see dem ads at every stop & i cry out in pain
becuz the images   5
of i & i
perpetuate all dem
white lies

dem seh blk is bad & white is right
all whitey look like gold   10
all we is blk as nite
but dat nuh right
dis sight of oppression
so stop all of dis exploitation
cuz it nuh right dese signs if downpression   15
mih nah 'low dem fih dis fih we blk nation

what a gwan wid benneton...

everywhere i turn
& everywhere i look
i see dem clothing ads wid jah people   20
scattered all aroun babylon neighbourhood

i see white goldilocks
& a blk child fox
for dat picture dem need a good box

i see blk ooman   25
ah nurse white baby
& dem ave dih nerve fih seh dem end slavery

& dere's a white wolf
ready fih nyam blk sheep
lawd how dem love depict we as enemy   30

& mih nuh understand
how dem so presumptuous
fih show a white man ah grab mih fih mek mih im love

what a gwan wid benneton...boycott haffi go on!

AFTER READING

Responding
1. Write an explanatory paragraph for each of the following:
   - what is upsetting the **narrator** of this **poem**
   - why it is upsetting the narrator
   - whether you think the narrator has something to be upset about

Understanding

2. In your notebook:
   - identify the "white lies" referred to in the second **stanza**
   - explain what the narrator means when she refers to "dis exploitation" and says "dem ave dih nerve" and "dem so presumptuous"
   - explain whether or not you think Benetton will change its advertising campaign due to the boycott mentioned in the last line of the poem
3. Prepare an oral reading of this **dramatic monologue** to present to a small group of students in your class.
4. Rewrite this poem using your own speech patterns.

Thinking About Language

5. With a partner, prepare a **glossary** to help readers with the dialect used in this poem. (See The Reference Shelf, page 351.) Discuss the impact of the use of dialect in this poem.

Extending

6. a) Write your own **poem** or **essay** in response to another memorable or controversial series of advertisements by a company. Describe the advertisements and the social or political issues they raise. Take a position on the advertising campaign.
   b) Exchange your work with a partner for revision and editing feedback, focusing on effectiveness of arguments and evidence for support.

7. a) Using print and/or electronic sources, research the use of boycotts to bring about a policy change by a business. Select one boycott to research in detail and prepare a **report** to present to the class on its purpose, duration, and results. If appropriate, use visual and technology aids to present your report.
   b) As a class, create an evaluation form to assess the presentations. (See The Reference Shelf, page 404.)
   c) Using feedback from your classmates, update your Oral Communication Skills Action Plan as necessary. (See The Reference Shelf, page 395.)

Turn of the Scrooge

BEFORE READING

As a class, discuss what you know of Charles Dickens' **character** Ebenezer Scrooge either from reading *A Christmas Carol* or from seeing a film or television version.

In A Christmas Carol, *Dickens describes Ebenezer Scrooge as "a squeezing, wrenching, grasping, scraping, clutching, covetous, old sinner!" In other words, hardly a likely candidate for a TV pitchman. But that's exactly what Scrooge has been for Canadian Tire since 1982, thanks to a gradual revamping of his image. Here,* Saturday Night *examines the miser's make-over.*

1982: THE DEBUT

In the depths of the early-eighties recession, Canadian Tire's advertising agency, Doner Canada, proposed a Christmas concept: Santa Claus converts the penny-pinching Scrooge to the yuletide spirit, thanks to Canadian Tire's low prices. Actor John Davies won the role of Scrooge and made his first appearance in November, 1982, in an ad featuring the now-famous slogan, "Give like Santa. Save like Scrooge." Davies continues in the part to

this day. In order to protect the Scrooge mystique, Canadian Tire doesn't allow him to do interviews about the character.

1987: SANTA'S STAND-INS

"After a few years, we found that the 'Save like Scrooge' concept was so strong, we didn't really need Santa," says Karl Bruenjes, Canadian Tire's director of broadcast advertising. But there was a catch: market testing showed that Scrooge was less likeable when he acted too miserly. So Santa was gradually phased out and replaced with a new foil: the ghosts of Christmas. (In one memorable ad, Jacob Marley's spirit appears, chained to all the overpriced gifts he's ever purchased.) The ghosts facilitate Scrooge's image make-over: with Santa he played the bad guy, but with the dour spirits, he's transformed into a good guy, dispensing money-saving wisdom.

| 1982 | 1987 | 1989 | 1992 | 2000 |

1989: SCROOGE GOES SOLO

To help Scrooge's transition from cantankerous geezer to affable curmudgeon, Canadian Tire produces a public-service announcement in which Scrooge asks Canadians to donate to charity with a plaintive "Please give…" Around this time, the concept of Scrooge Approved Pricing is unveiled and becomes a mainstay of the campaign. From here on out, Scrooge appears both alone and with other characters; his sidekick, Santa, makes a comeback in the mid-nineties.

1992: THE QUEBEC PROBLEM

"The Scrooge campaign was an established success in English Canada," says Bruenjes. "But Dickens's story has little resonance among French-speaking Quebecers." To solve the dilemma, Canadian Tire creates Gratteux, Santa's stingy elfin accountant. "Gratteux" literally means "scratcher," a colloquial reference to instant lotteries and scratch-and-save tickets; in common usage, a *gratteux* is a cheapskate. Aside from his miniature size, Gratteux, portrayed by

Richard Lalancette, looks, sounds, and acts just like Canadian Tire's Scrooge — and is now as strongly identified with the company in Quebec as Scrooge is in the rest of the country.

TODAY: SCROOGE AS LOGO

The latest ads feature whimsical images like grown men in a snowball fight. Scrooge only appears at the end to deliver the slogan. More than eighty commercials later, he's essentially the equivalent of a company logo. "That's what you strive for in advertising," says Bruenjes. "Something that's yours, that no one else can have." But while the slogans are copyrighted, the Scrooge character is not: he remains in the public domain, and the company must use him continually, so that he's identified with their brand. "There's now an entire generation who've grown up with our Scrooge," says Bruenjes. "They may not even be aware of Dickens or *A Christmas Carol*. To them, Scrooge is a Canadian Tire icon, period."

AFTER READING

Responding

1. With a partner, discuss whether or not the use of the character of Scrooge was a good choice for this series of advertisements. List your arguments.

Understanding

2. In your notebook, write a one-paragraph **summary** of the information contained in "Turn of the Scrooge."

3. Look closely at the dates and the content of each advertisement described. Explain what the differences tell us about how Canadian consumers have changed.

Thinking About Language

4. Use a dictionary to verify the meaning of the following words as used in this selection: foil, dour, cantankerous, geezer, affable, and curmudgeon.

5. Account for the writer's use of past and present verb tenses throughout this selection.

Extending

6. Identify other commercials or advertising campaigns in which a human character has become "essentially the equivalent of a company logo." Discuss whether the character has changed over the years. Explain the impressions of the company or of the product that are identified with the character.

7. In a small group, view film and video versions or adaptations of *A Christmas Carol*. Write a critical **review** comparing the portrayal of Scrooge (or the Scrooge-like character) by actors such as Allistair Sim, Albert Finney, Bill Murray, Henry Winkler, etc. Work with a partner to revise and edit your review, and then update your Writing Skills Action Plan as necessary. (See The Reference Shelf, page 395.)

8. In a small group, identify another advertising campaign that would benefit from a makeover. Suggest ways new life could be created in the campaign. Create a **storyboard** for one of your suggested advertisements.
   Or
   In a small group, create your own commercial using the Scrooge character.

Could Scrolling Ads in the Hallways Be Next?

"'If the corporate world wants to come into my classrooms...and help improve the delivery and quality of education...I'm all for it.'"

BEFORE READING

As a class, discuss the pros and cons of running advertisements of large companies in schools.

Imagine walking down the hallway at your high school and seeing ads for Nike, McDonald's and the Gap scrolling away on fancy displays.

You might expect that kind of advertising at a sports arena or mall. But some say it could soon appear at cash-strapped schools.

Colin Ruck, a businessman from Kelowna, B.C., approached his local school district three years ago with an offer to pay $510 000 a year to run ads for large corporations.

Parents objected because they didn't want students to be exposed to commercialism in schools.

"Corporations are interested in that age group because they're about to become spenders and they certainly influence their parents and their spending habits," Ruck says.

"I haven't talked to a school board that isn't interested—they're always looking for money," he says, adding that U.S. high schools are more open to advertising.

Ron Rubadeau, superintendent of the Kelowna school district, says some trustees are still interested in the idea.

"The issue's not dead," Rubadeau says.

Most of the money the school would get from allowing the advertising would go to extracurricular activities such as sports that in past years used to be free but now cost a bundle, he says.

"Do you want to pay a thousand bucks to play basketball?" asks Rubadeau, referring to money needed for coaches, referees, scoreboards, uniforms and transportation.

Ruck says that if parents are so concerned about advertising in schools, they shouldn't allow Coke and Pepsi vending machines or scoreboards in the gym with those corporations' names on them.

Leslie Carter, director of strategy and innovation at Pepsi Cola Canada, says the company makes deals with schools because they need the money.

"We operate in a really competitive industry and we keep that information confidential," Carter says when asked about deals.

She says Pepsi is concerned about the effects of commercialism and has recently reduced the size of its branding on vending machines to make it less prominent.

Ed Arnott, principal of Bishops College, a high school in St. John's, Nfld., says his school sells Pepsi because that's the only way to get needed funding.

"I would sell my soul, not to get more money, but to improve the delivery of education in this building," Arnott says.

"The reality is that education in my province is under-resourced and under-funded. If the corporate world wants to come into my classrooms and into my building and help improve the delivery and quality of education that we are providing to our children, I'm all for it."

However, he says, the product must be appropriate and he would want to retain

control over the type of advertising he'd allow in the school.

Joe Panunto, spokesperson for the Commission scolaire de Montréal (Montreal school board), says his board would never sign a contract with a cola company, although some schools in other parts of Quebec have done so.

Panunto says such a deal wouldn't fly because the school board has spent $500 000 to promote a nutrition program.

WHAT'S ONLINE?
Want to learn more? Check out these Internet sites:
www.policyalternatives.ca/eduproj Canadian Centre for Policy Alternatives, a non-profit research organization
www.media-awareness.ca/eng/med/class/teamedia/adtopics.htm Media Awareness Network
www.commercialfree.org U.S. site on commercialism in schools

AFTER READING

Responding

1. One school principal said that the products advertised in schools must be appropriate. In your notebook, write about the advertisements you think are appropriate for a school, and explain your choices.

Understanding

2. Identify the **bias** in this **article**. Make point-form notes on the cues that helped you identify the bias.

3. With a partner, explain how some advertisements that might be seen in a school may convey messages that go against the school's values. Compare your responses with those of another pair of students.

4. In a clearly written paragraph, using ideas from the article and from your own knowledge, explain why corporations want to advertise in schools. Discuss your paragraph and those of your classmates with the class.

Thinking About Language

5. In paragraph 12, the pronoun "they" could refer to more than one group. Identify the two things it could refer to. Rewrite the sentence so there is no confusion about which antecedent the pronoun is referring to.

6. A new paragraph begins every time a quotation is introduced. Write the grammar rule that explains why the writer has followed this format.

Extending

7. a) Leslie Carter says Pepsi is concerned about commercialism within schools, so Pepsi has reduced the size of its "branding" on its machines. What does "branding" mean as used in this sentence?

   b) Write a letter to the company responding to this action. Explain whether or not you believe that Pepsi is serious about commercialism in schools.

8. In a small group, using print and/or electronic sources, research the codes that govern the advertising of cigarettes and alcohol. Based on your research, could alcohol or tobacco companies ever advertise in a school? Explain your answer, referring to the research you have conducted.

9. a) If your school has advertising, decide whether it should have more. If your school doesn't have advertising, decide whether you should have some. In a well-organized **essay**, defend your position. You may wish to do more information gathering before you write your essay.

   b) Take your essay through the writing process, focusing on the quality of your arguments and the organizational patterns used throughout. (See The Reference Shelf, pages 386–391.)

Ads Talkin' About Your Generation

"'Generational mindsets and feelings...
determin[e] what and how consumers buy.'"

BOB DART

BEFORE READING

With a partner, discuss how you can identify advertisements aimed at your generation and advertisements aimed at your parents', guardians', or grandparents' generation. Be prepared to report to the class on points raised in your discussion.

Depression Babies. The Silent Generation. The Swing Generation. The Greatest Generation. Baby Boomers. Generation Jones. Baby Busters. Echo Boomers. Generation X. Generation Y. Millennials.

Why do we have such a generation glut?

Longer life spans are part of the explanation. But a bigger reason is the eagerness of demographers and sociologists to slice and dice the marketplace into thinner and more precise segments.

"Generational mindsets and feelings are major factors in determining what and how consumers buy," explains Ann Fishman, president of Generational Targeted Marketing Corp. in New Orleans.

"Every individual is shaped by the history he or she lived through during the formative years," she says. "These distinct historical experiences create characteristics that stay with people throughout the rest of their lives."

If you lived through the Great Depression, you are apt to be thrifty, Fishman says. For others, coming of age during the Vietnam War shaped their view of authority.

Members of a generation "share common core values and experiences," agrees Walker Smith, president of Yankelovich Partners and co-author of *Rocking The Ages*, a book on generational marketing.

But generational generalizations are a bit like astrology. Saying that gen-Xers are slackers or baby boomers are obsessed with youth is a lot like saying that Leos are egomaniacs or Scorpios are suspicious.

While age cohorts share some characteristics, they are divided by even more differences, says Stephen Roulac, CEO of the Roulac Group, a business strategy and financial consulting firm in San Rafael, Calif.

As a marketing device, generational targeting is "a real blunt instrument," he says.

Still, even skeptics agree that assigning personalities to generations has become embedded in the popular culture as well as in market research. The real disagreement comes on definitions.

For example, baby boomers are generally defined as the people born from 1946 through 1964, years when the number of births soared.

"If you were born in 1945, your first-grade classroom was probably not crowded. If you were born in 1946, when you went to first grade, you probably didn't have place to sit," explains Smith.

Because of their sheer numbers, boomers "were always competing more," he says.

But some boomers born in 1946 had children of their own before 1964, putting two generations within one. Some boomers were in college, while others were in kindergarten.

"Clearly, they had very different sets of formative experiences," says Jonathan Pontell, a sociologist who created a new generation for North Americans born from 1954 through 1964. "They came of age in the '60s. We came of age in the '70s.

Pontell, 42, named this group "Generation Jones." "Jones" refers to a large, nearly anonymous group, and also is a slang word meaning an intense longing.

"Jonesers feel that we belong between the boomers and gen-Xers," says Pontell.

But Pontell is not the first to subdivide the giant baby boom generation. In a study last year, Yankelovich, a pioneer in generational marketing, listed characteristics of the older "Leading Boomers," central "Core Boomers" and younger "Trailing Boomers."

So, what is a generation, anyway?

The word once applied mainly to families, says Roulac. Grandparents, parents and children made up three generations.

"But now generation is a code word for a demographic or marketing target," says Robert Thompson, president of the International Popular Culture Association and a professor at Syracuse University. "What is really happening now is an attempt to name cohorts and, slowly but surely, to narrow the range of years that each cohort will include."

There are distinct differences between even the two youngest generations, demographers say.

Generation Y, born after 1977 and also called echo boomers, the digital generation or millennials, are the biggest population bulge since the baby boomers. And, having grown up in the best over-all economy ever, they are materialistic, optimistic and affluent.

Generation X, born between 1965 and 1977, is a smaller and far more cynical group that grew up in an age of divorce and two working parents, and entered the workplace during a recession. They believe older generations have made a mess of things, says Fishman.

"We tend to define the entire generation on images attached to a small group within it," Thompson notes.

While sometimes called the "Woodstock Generation," not many boomers were actually at Woodstock or were even devotees of the hippie lifestyle.

But because "generations" are so much a part of the popular culture, many North Americans identify with their age cohort. Some even shape their self-perception to fit the generational image.

"Certainly baby boomers think of themselves as a baby boomer. It's kind of a group you feel that you belong to," says Smith. "Baby boomers are accepting of that."

Not so the next generation. That's partly because "gen-Xer is a label attached by boomers," he explains.

AFTER READING

Responding

1. Describe one advertisement you have seen that you feel is aimed at one of the "generations" identified in this **article**.

Understanding

2. Create a chart like the one below to identify the formative years and key historical events that shaped individuals in each of the generations listed in the first paragraph of this article. You may need to do additional research to complete the chart.

GENERATION	FORMATIVE YEARS	KEY HISTORICAL EVENTS
Depression Babies		
The Silent Generation		
The Swing Generation		
The Greatest Generation		
Baby Boomers		
Generation Jones		
Baby Busters		
Echo Boomers		
Generation X		
Generation Y		
Millennials		

3. What name is given to your generation? Write a short **essay** to explain the generalizations and characteristics associated with your generation and whether they are true.

4. Most companies want to sell their products to as wide a demographic range as possible. In your notebook, explain why and how a company would target an advertising campaign to a particular generation.

5. With a partner, identify reservations expressed in this article about the value of generational targeting in advertising. Name specific products and explain why generational targeting would or would not be an effective strategy.

Thinking About Language

6. Distinguish between the two **definitions** of "generation" presented in this article.

Extending

7. With a partner, research a company that markets the same product in two different ways to two different generations of consumers. Brainstorm a list of reasons why the company thought the double campaign was worth the extra cost involved. Be prepared to present a **report** to the class on your findings. If possible, bring the advertisements to school and show them to the class.

8. Find an advertisement that targets a particular demographic audience. Adapt the advertisement to appeal to a different demographic.

9. **Debate** the following resolution: Be It Resolved That Advertising Makes Life Better for Everyone. (See The Reference Shelf, page 401.) You may need to do research to prepare your arguments.

Why Is "YKK" Stamped on My Zipper?

"...the herald of an intensely private zipper company..."

PHILIP PREVILLE

BEFORE READING

Look up the following words and write the **definitions** in your personal word list: insignia, enigmatic, pedigree, skittish, oblique, mantra.

Chances are, if you pull an item of clothing from your closet right now and look at its zipper, you'll see the letters "YKK" stamped on the pull tab. The mysterious letters carry the air of a secret-society insignia — akin to a two-headed eagle or a one-eyed pyramid. And, in a sense, that's appropriate, because YKK is the herald of an intensely private zipper company that stretches around the globe.

To understand this enigmatic order, one must understand the history of the zipper itself. Contrary to popular myth, the zipper was not invented by a Canadian. The credit goes to an American named Whitcomb Judson, who patented a "Clasp Locker" in 1891 and started a company, Universal Fasteners, to manufacture it. But his invention didn't really catch on — mostly because it didn't work particularly well. It wasn't until 1917, when a Swedish-born employee of Universal Fasteners named Gideon Sundback received a patent for the "Separable Fastener," that the device became practical. Universal Fasteners promptly established subsidiaries in Canada, the United Kingdom, and elsewhere. Sundback himself moved north to run the Lightning Fastener Company of Canada, which is probably the source of the misunderstanding about the zipper's pedigree.

In 1934, Yoshida Kogyo Kabushikikaisha founded his own zipper company in Tokyo, which quickly grew to become one of the world's largest. Today, Yoshida's YKK Group is made up of ninety-one affiliates and subsidiaries in fifty-seven countries, including Universal Fasteners (which YKK bought in 1987) and YKK Canada Inc., which produces zippers in a suburban Montreal plant. YKK employs 35 749 people worldwide,

anchor the pocket stitching on jeans), hook-and-loop fasteners (Velcro), and aluminum architectural products.

Little else is known about YKK. The company remains privately owned by the Yoshida family and is extremely secretive in its business affairs, shying away from most journalistic inquires. "Though they operate around the world, everything is controlled from Tokyo," says historian Robert Friedel, author of *The Zipper: An Exploration in Novelty*. "They are very skittish." In typically oblique fashion, the website for YKK America features a link to employment opportunities, which curtly instructs job-seekers to "please contact the department of labour for the state which the YKK company of your choice is located."

Though it may be a stretch to compare YKK with a secret society or a religious sect, it's worth nothing that Mr. Yoshida runs his company according to a Zen-like mantra he calls The Cycle of Goodness, which holds that "no one prospers unless he renders benefit to others." As a company, YKK emulates the zipper itself: it's so ubiquitous that no one ever thinks about it.

churns out over two million kilometers of zippers per year, and rings up sales of more than 500 billion yen annually (approximately $7.3 billion). They also manufacture buttons, rivets (those metal pimples that

AFTER READING

Responding

1. a) If you were a person looking for a job with YKK, how would reading this **article** prepare you for a job **interview** with this company?

b) Based on the information in this article, write a short explanation of why you would or wouldn't want to work for YKK.

Understanding

2. In your notebook, write two **explicit meanings** and two **implicit meanings** from this article. As a class, compare your observations.

3. In a small group, decide whether the writer of this article presents a neutral view or a **bias** for or against the company. Support your opinion with specific words and phrases chosen from the article.

4. Reread the introduction and the conclusion of this article. Make a point-form list of the ways the writer has tied the introduction to the conclusion and how he has unified the article with these elements. Be prepared to defend your ideas to the class.

5. Divide the article into sections, creating subtitles for each section. Be prepared to discuss the following question with the class: "Would the inclusion of subtitles improve the article or not?"

6. "No one prospers unless he renders benefit to others." Compare the Yoshida philosophy to the philosophies of other employers you know.

Thinking About Language

7. a) In your notebook, explain why "YKK" is in quotation marks in the title but nowhere else in the article. Explain as well why the title is in the form of a question. Is the question form used effectively?

b) Share your thoughts with the class and take notes from the full class discussion.

Extending

8. a) Choose a company that makes a product that we use every day but that we don't pay much attention to. Research the history of that company and write a **report**. Be sure to create a research plan before you begin and record the bibliographical information of all your sources. (See The Reference Shelf, pages 378–379.)

b) With a partner, revise your report, focusing on content, organization of information, and integration of quotations from your research. (See The Reference Shelf, page 393.)

How to Make a Demo CD

"A good demo package is important for
every musician and performer."

JIM CARRUTHERS

BEFORE READING

As a class, identify new recording artists who have arrived on the scene in the last year. Discuss
what the class knows about how each artist got his or her start.

Note: If you decide to create your own
demo CD, we highly recommend that you
do more research aside from reading this
selection. Be sure to check the credibility
of bookers, reviewers, and anyone whom
you contact.

Working at a record company years ago, I
was often asked how to make sure a
demo tape would attract attention. The
answer was simple: Make sure to use a
top-quality high-bios, C-90 brand-name
cassette; don't punch out the recording
tabs; and don't mark the insert or cassette
shell. That way we'd have a stock of good
tapes to record something we liked. These
days a demo cassette wouldn't even get
you that far.

A good demo package is important for
every musician and performer. Bookers,
radio shows, reviewers, publishers and
record labels all form their impressions
from your demo. Producing and copying a
good CD demo is better quality and now
cheaper than cassette.

There are several steps to putting
together a good demo.

PUBLISHING AND COPYRIGHT

Secure the ownership of your original
material, and get clearance to use other
people's material. You can set up your own
publishing company, or go through a music
publisher — it's not difficult. An important
resource is SOCAN (the Society of
Composers, Authors and Music Publishers
of Canada). Even if you don't intend to
make money with your demo, you should
protect your rights — remember what happened to George Michael?

RECORDING

Most newer computers can handle CD
quality sound: 16 bit sampling rate, 44khz
stereo. You will need about 1 gigabyte of
hard-drive space for an album, mixes and

edits. A good pair of headphones will make a big difference in your final results. For software, there is a wide range of freeware, share ware and commercial recording and editing software. Save your final mixes as AIFF files with no compression. You can use these to burn your demo CD, and also convert them to MP3s for online use.

CD BURNING

The best way to get a CD burner is to borrow one from the office. Some local printing shops will burn you one if you ask, but this can get expensive for multiples, and a good burner can cost as little as $300. Sequence your tracks, set a consistent space between them, and then, using the CDR software included with your CD writer, create a disc image if you are planning on running several copies. Doing a simulated run first will cut down on the number of drink coasters you create.

PACKAGING

Smart-looking, well designed packages don't help so much with getting your music heard by a record label, but are definitely required if you are going to send your demo out to bookers, radio stations and reviewers — these people get a lot of material and will be more inclined to open CDs from bands who look "professional." It's also a good practice if you decide to have your own record label, like Ani Difranco (who has been able to make a lot of money without selling a million records simply by doing it all out of her garage).

Follow a template (in Quark or Photoshop, for example) for the packaging you want to use (jewel box, insert card, CD tray, etc.) and prepare your packaging with some graphics and text — or better yet, get a designer to prepare the files for printing. As an alternative, get Adobe Acrobat files (.pdf) prepared as well to accompany any MP3 distributions you do. Small runs of CDs can be burned on a home computer, and then labeled and packaged using a colour printer. Longer runs of discs and inserts can be prepared by graphics houses from a master disc and ready-to-print files.

GETTING IT OUT THERE

The truth is, there's no substitute for playing live and getting a "following." Bookers and record labels want to know you already have "fans" before they sign you up. So make sure you have CDs available at shows, and to send to the music press prior to a gig. Some record stores — even HMV — will take a few well packaged indie CDs on consignment, and this can help you build that "buzz" that is so crucial to the majors.

---

www.insound.com/machine
(Simple Machines Mechanic's Guide)

www.socan.ca
(SOCAN is a performing rights society run by Canadian composers, lyricists, songwriters and music publishers)

www.mp3.com

www.farmdub.com
(upload your music and others can vote on it)

AFTER READING

Responding

1. Explain why the information in this selection is or is not important to you.

Understanding

2. Identify the intended audience for the information in this selection.
3. Invite an AV technician to the class to explain any applications, acronyms, or points in this informational text that the class has difficulty understanding.

Thinking About Language

4. With a partner, rewrite this informational text as a set of instructions in a "plain language style." (See The Reference Shelf, page 352.) Feel free to re-categorize or add to the information in the **article**. Compare and discuss your rewrite with that of another pair.
5. Write **definitions** of the following words as used in this informational text: burner, template, following, gig, indie, and buzz.

Extending

6. Research a local band that is trying to release or has already released a recorded version of its work. Share your findings with a small group.
7. a) In a small group, use these instructions to burn a CD. You might record a school or local band on your demo CD or read aloud versions of some of the **poems** in this textbook. Some members of the group could design and create the CD cover.
   b) Present your CD and cover to the class, explaining your production choices.

The Maytag Repairman

"The new Maytag apprentice is a 'curious and intense character...'"

BEFORE READING

Some advertisements and commercials are part of a "story" about the characters using a product. In a small group, brainstorm a list of such "story commercials" and assess the effectiveness of each. Be prepared to report on your list and assessments to the class.

Maytag Repairman Enters 21st Century

PETER GODDARD

Now we *really* know it's a whole new millennium out there.

Old Lonely, the Maytag repairman, has a partner. The guy's young and — wait for it — he wants to fix stuff.

In the fantasy world of TV ad-dom, this is like Mr. Whipple needing a helper to squeeze the Charmin.

The original Maytag spots had Canadian roots. First heard on Quebec radio in the 1950s, they featured a French-speaking repairman who couldn't find anything to repair.

In the first of the new Maytag spots, which debut Thursday in Canada after several weeks on American TV, the hotshot apprentice (played by chisel-jawed American character actor Mark Devine) does his best to stain his spanking new Maytag uniform to test out the new Maytag "stain machine."

He's dragged belly-first by a windblown parachute along a stretch of lawn to pick up some nasty old grass stains. He then sweats it out with some old geezers in a sauna to soak up perspiration.

That's just the beginning. In a grandiose gesture of self-smudging, the young apprentice grabs Old Lonely's coffee and pours it down the front of his own uniform.

"Uhhhhh," he winces.

But, hey. Old Lonely (played for the last 11 years by Gordon Jump from *WKRP in Cincinnati*) couldn't give a flying Kenmore. He's appeared in more than 100 Maytag spots. He's reading *Retire* magazine. He's out of there soon.

"At least the new kid is keeping busy," the old boy says, shaking his head.

The new Maytag apprentice is a "curious and intense character," says Mark Faulkner of Leo Burnett, the Chicago ad agency that has been hustling Maytags since 1955.

He's not going to sit around like old Maytag repair-duffers do. He's not waiting for something to break. No way. He's going to be out there, "testing new products and exploring the boundaries," Faulkner says.

There are boundaries to be explored in the washing-machine business? Doesn't this run contrary to the whole idea of the Maytag repairman—to go nowhere where some man has gone before him?

Well, the new guy "is still bored," says Trent Roth, head of marketing for Maytag Canada. "But he's young. He has to keep busy. He's trying to find a way to foil Maytag."

In fact, the first TV Maytag Man (played by Jesse White, a well-regarded veteran of Broadway and Hollywood) originally had apprentices.

Old Lonely first appeared on North America TV in 1967 during *The Today Show*. In the spot, he showed a group of young Maytag repair guys how to while away their time when all the Maytags out there were *not* breaking down.

Soon enough these spots, in their unruffled, understated way, became some of the most radical commercials on television— just one guy not doing much while complaining about the product he's selling because of what *it* wouldn't do.

Anticipating *Seinfeld*—the "show about nothing"—the Maytag spots also showed Old Lonely sitting there just snoring or filling up the empty hours by teaching a parrot how to speak. These non-events have

since gone off to make for the longest-running TV campaign with a real character.

But viewers could see Old Lonely's old loneliness was getting to him. Maytag could see that too, and in recent spots provided him with a basset hound named Newton (after Newton, Iowa, the Maytag headquarters).

But before Old Lonely hangs up his unused Maytag wrench, the company needed to introduce the next Old Lonely.

It could be the start of something old.

The Maytag Man Gets Busy

8/1/99

Company
Maytag Corp., Newton, Iowa

Reason for Redesign
Maytag wanted to change the site's look (www.maytag.com) so that it would be in sync with non-Web advertising campaigns.

Designer
Giant Step LLC, Chicago

What's New
Back-end integration makes site easier to maintain; customer service section helps users troubleshoot problems before they call for service; dealer locator includes maps.

MAYTAG CORP. STRIVES TO MAKE consumers equate its brand with dependability. But the metaphor around which it had designed its inaugural Web site—the home of dependability—had grown increasingly limiting since the site's October 1995 launch, according to Stan Sturtz, Maytag's manager of brand management administration. "Every time there was something new, we were adding things to the front door of that house," Sturtz says. Content was hard-coded rather than backed by a database, making the site difficult to update. And the site's cartoon image of the Maytag Man was out of step with the rest of Maytag's advertising, which had started portraying the world's loneliest repairman as a helpful guide.

For less than $500 000, Giant Step LLC (creators of the initial site) came up with a sophisticated redesign, using active-looking photos of the actor who plays the Maytag Man. Screened images of household and kitchen scenes use warm colors similar to other Maytag ads. Appliance descriptions are drawn directly from Maytag's product database. Literature requests and product registrations are integrated with back-end systems so that customer support reps do not need to rekey them. Giant Step still hosts the site, but Maytag can now remotely update promotions and contests.

Maytag had outgrown its October 1995 Web site and needed a more flexible design.

NAVIGATION BAR is repeated on interior pages, so users can quickly move from one area of the site to another.

DROP-DOWN MENUS let customers click right to product information.

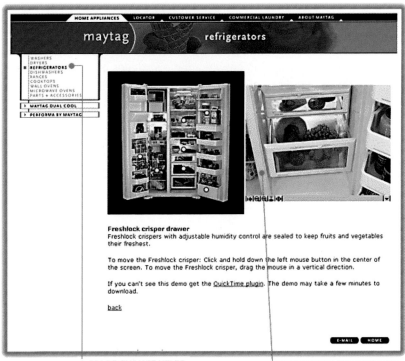

| COLOR CHANGE HELPS
users see where they
are on the site

"HOT SPOTS" LET CUSTOMERS
test special product features

AFTER READING

Responding

1. If you have seen Maytag commercials, write about what you like or dislike about them. If you have never seen commercials for Maytag, describe a commercial you have seen and what it is you like and dislike about the commercial.

Understanding

2. List the main reasons identified in this **article** for the most recent change in the Maytag repairman commercials. Add any other reasons you can think of to the list. In a paragraph, explain which reason on the list you think is the most important.

3. The last line of the article says "It could be the start of something old." Write the **cliché** that this statement is based on and explain what the writer means by this statement.

Thinking About Language

4. This article has short sentences appropriate for a **newspaper article**. See how many sentences you can combine into one grammatically correct sentence, and see who in your class can combine the most sentences into one. In a small group, discuss the impact of combining sentences on the **style** of the writing and its impact for readers.

Extending

5. Look for current Maytag advertisements (either print or electronic) and be ready to discuss what has happened to the new character in these advertisements.

6. In a small group, role-play a meeting between the executives of an advertising agency and a company that you are aware of that uses "serial commercials." In the roleplay, have the advertising agency suggest a radical change to the commercials. Be prepared to present your roleplay to the class.

7. a) With a partner, design a series of commercials for a product. Present the proposal as a sales talk to the class, who will decide whether or not to send the commercials into production. (See The Reference Shelf, page 402.)

   b) As a class, assess the presentations using a rubric that you have created. (See The Reference Shelf, page 404.)

8. **Debate** the following resolution: Be It Resolved That Product Placement Advertisements Should Replace Commercial Messages During and Between Television Programs. (See The Reference Shelf, page 401.) You may need to do research to prepare your arguments.

Excerpts from **The Straight Story**

"'...I'm not dead yet.'"

MARY SWEENEY AND
JOHN ROACH

BEFORE READING

1. In your notebook, describe how elderly people are usually depicted in the films or television shows you watch.

2. As a class, discuss why a cross-country journey continues to be the basis for many films.

1   EXT. — NIGHT SKY
Autumn evening FULL of STARS. Music plays over as credits roll.
   DISSOLVE TO:

2   EXT. — DAY LAURENS, IOWA
It is a hot day in early September in Laurens, a small rural community in north central Iowa. The main drag, all of four blocks, is bookended by a giant grain elevator and a John Deere dealership. No cars on the road.
   CUT TO:

3   EXT. — DAY SMALL HOUSE & NEIGHBORING HOUSE
At the neighboring house, DOROTHY, a rather large woman, 50ish, with bleached blond, cropped hair is sunbathing in a chaise lounge. She is wearing bermuda shorts, a tank top and eye protectors over her eyes. Next to her is a small table with a plate on it. Out of the other house, which has chipped siding and faded, peeling window frames, comes ROSE (late 30s, brown hair in a pixie cut, stocky, in jeans and a cotton shirt). The door slams and Rose heads down the walk. Dorothy doesn't move a muscle or remove her eye protectors.

DOROTHY
   Hey Rose.
Rose doesn't break stride but yells over...

ROSE
    Hey Dorothy.

Rose exits and we remain on the two houses and Dorothy sunbathing. After a moment, Dorothy reaches over and feels the plate next to her. She lifts the protectors and checks out the table…sees she's out of treats, gets up, grabs the plate and heads into her house. As the screen door slams shut behind her we slowly move in on the house Rose came from. We might be hearing footsteps as we move closer. The sound leads us slowly toward the rear of the house. As we continue moving closer we hear a short peel of rubber followed by a thudding sound and a sound like a stick dropping. We hold on the house in silence.

CUT TO:

4   EXT. — DAY HOUSE AND NEIGHBORING HOUSE

As before. Dorothy comes back out carrying the plate now filled with treats. Munching all the while she settles back into the chaise lounge and resumes sunbathing.

5   EXT. — DAY LATER — SMALL TOWN BAR IN LAURENS

A small brick storefront bar. Two windows with neon beer signs are on either side of a red door with a window in the shape of a tilted martini glass. The door opens and BUD, a stocky 70ish man in jeans, a cotton shirt and construction boots emerges. He looks down the street. Not seeing anyone he turns and sticks his head back in the door of the bar and yells in…

BUD

   I'm goin' over there.

He lets the door close and heads off down the street. Another man, SIG, late 60s, 6'0", 265 lbs., in bib overalls and a seed cap, comes out the bar door holding a long-neck beer bottle and watches Bud walk away.

SIG

   We're waitin'.

       CUT TO:

6   EXT. — DAY LAURENS RESIDENTIAL STREET

Bud is striding down the street past small and weatherbeaten houses. The yards are mowed and dotted with lawn chairs and picnic tables. He approaches the house we saw earlier. He turns up the walkway, reaches the front door and starts knocking somewhat angrily.

BUD

   Alvin! Alvin Straight!

       CUT TO:

7   EXT. — DAY THE NEIGHBOR'S YARD

Dorothy doesn't move a muscle when she hears the knocking. She yells across the yard to Bud.

DOROTHY

   Rose left a couple of hours ago.

       CUT TO:

8   EXT. — DAY SMALL HOUSE

Bud jumps. He hadn't seen Dorothy until she spoke.

BUD

   Did you hear me hollerin' for Rose? I'm not looking' for Rose.

DOROTHY

   I ain't seen Alvin today.

BUD

   Did I ask...

Bud stops for a look at Dorothy who still has the eye protectors on. He shakes his head in exasperation. He resumes knocking on the door.

BUD

   Straight...you're late!!

Not getting any response he heads around to the backyard and finds no one. He goes up to the back door and starts knocking.

BUD (cont'd)

Alvin?!

CUT TO:

9   INT.—DAY KITCHEN

From inside the darkened kitchen we see Bud through the door window, knocking.

BUD

What the hell Alvin!

At a break in his knocking on the door we hear an off-camera voice.

ALVIN

Come on in Bud.

Bud, startled, reaches down, opens the door and enters. He stands blinking and flustered, letting his eyes adjust to the darkened room.

BUD

Where the hell are you Alvin? I can't see a damn thing.

ALVIN

I'm right here Bud...watch your step.

Bud's eyes adjust and he follows the sound of Alvin's voice to the kitchen floor right at his feet. ALVIN STRAIGHT is stretched out on the floor. He is in his 70s, a lean man, weathered face, bald with a full, scruffy white beard. He is wearing a plaid cotton shirt, worn jeans and black cowboy boots. There is a wooden cane lying on the floor next to him.

BUD

What the hell's goin' on? What in god-damn hell are you doin' on the floor Alvin? What'r ye nuts? You're supposed to be down at Davmar's one hour ago.

At this point a shadow falls on them and Dorothy fills the door frame.

DOROTHY

What's going on...

She sees Alvin on the floor.

DOROTHY (cont'd)(panicking)

Oh my god Alvin!

ALVIN

(with resignation)

Hey there Dorothy.

Dorothy makes a beeline for the phone, and picks it up.

BUD

What the hell are you doin'?

DOROTHY
(breathlessly)
   What's the number for 911?

Bud rolls his eyes.

ALVIN
(with authority)
   Dorothy, put that phone down.

She doesn't move. Her face flushed, bosom heaving, she looks back and forth between Alvin, Bud and the phone. Bud strides over to her and yanks the phone out of her hand.

BUD
   I gotta call the bar and tell them we're not comin'.

Dorothy grabs the phone back, wild-eyed.

DOROTHY
   Bud Heimstra are you crazy? We have stricken man here.

   Bud hesitates and looks over at Alvin, assessing his condition.

BUD
   You stricken Alvin?

Dorothy starts dialing.

ALVIN (cont'd)
   Dorothy, PUT THAT PHONE DOWN!

Dorothy hesitates. Bud tries to wrestle the phone from her. We hear the front door slam and Dorothy and Bud freeze. Rose enters the kitchen from the front of the house.

ROSE
   Dad? What's all the...yelling?

She stops short. She takes in the scene...Bud and Dorothy at the phone and her dad on the floor.

ROSE (cont'd)
   What have you...done to my dad?

BUD
   Oh for cry aye.

ROSE
   Dad?...are you...?

Rose starts to cry.

ALVIN
(exasperated but forcefully)
   I just need some help gettin' up.

CUT TO:

10 EXT.—DAY PARKING LOT

We see Rose helping Alvin get out of the passenger side of their car. Once standing, Alvin won't move. Rose is tugging on his arm. He is not budging and he's shaking his head.

ALVIN

  I'm not goin'.

ROSE

  Dad...

ALVIN

  I'm not goin'.

ROSE

  Dad...you promised me.

After a pause Alvin nods.

ALVIN

  Alright Rosie.

They slowly make their way across the hot parking lot to the Doctor's office.

          CUT TO:

OMIT SCENES 11, 12, & 13.

          CUT TO:

14 INT.—DAY EXAMINING ROOM

The nurse and Alvin enter the examining room. She turns to him and hands him a robe.

NURSE

  O.K. Mr. Straight, you need to take off all your clothes except your underwear and put this robe on.

ALVIN

(gruffly)

  Just bring me the doctor.

          CUT TO:

15 INT.—DAY DOCTOR'S RECEPTION, LATER

Rose is standing in front of a series of bird paintings.

ROSE

  I see you like birds. I build...birdhouses...for bluebirds.

NURSE

  Oh, that's nice.

ROSE

  Yah...Pete sells my birdhouses...at the...Ace.

NURSE

  Oh...I'll look for them next time I'm in.

CUT TO:

16   INT.—DAY   EXAMINING ROOM

Alvin leans against the examining table as he pulls his pants to a close and fastens his belt. He is shirtless. His skin hangs loosely off his rib cage. He has a serious farmer's tan: lily white chest and shoulders and arms with nut brown face, neck and hands. A middle-aged DOCTOR GIBBONS is standing looking over some notes.

DOCTOR GIBBONS

   So you're not sure just how long you were on the floor?

ALVIN

(shaking his head)

   I remember my cane slippin'...and losing my balance...

(he pauses, concentrating)

   ...next thing I knew Bud Heimstra was banging on my kitchen door.

The doctor nods at this account and writes something in his notes. Alvin sits on the examining table and looks around. He takes in the foreign room: bright fluorescent lights, slick pastel Formica surfaces, matching pastel framed art, bio-hazard warnings and medical equipment. He looks back to the Doctor and catches the man watching him with a look of concern on his face.

ALVIN (cont'd)

   Somethin' the matter Doc?

The Doctor switches to an attempt at a smile.

DOCTOR GIBBONS

   Listen Alvin, sometimes it's my job to tell people things they don't want to hear. I'm concerned about you. I think you need an operation on those hips.

ALVIN

   No operations.

DOCTOR

   Well...this morning you fall and can't get off the floor...that's your hips Alvin. You'll have to use a walker to get around now.

ALVIN

(barks)

   No walker.

DOCTOR

   Fine...a second cane then. You say you're not seeing too well. That could be a diabetes-related problem. I would like to run some...

ALVIN

   No!

The doctor looks back down at his notes and up at Alvin.

DOCTOR GIBBONS

    I can see and hear that you smoke. I would guess you're in the early stages of emphysema. And Alvin you have circulation problems. I worry about your diet and unless you change some things quick, there will be some serious consequences.

Alvin doesn't say anything. He just stares at the Doctor.

        CUT TO:

17   INT. — DAY KITCHEN

ALVIN sits at the kitchen table and takes a deep drag off a Swisher Sweet. Two canes are propped up against the table. Rose looks on. She stands in the middle of the kitchen holding a birdhouse, fretfully watching Alvin. She holds the birdhouse out to him.

        CUT TO:

ROSE (cont'd)

    It has a...red roof.

Alvin looks at the birdhouse and smiles at Rose.

ALVIN

    That's another pretty one Rose.

He continues smoking. Rose, pleased at his response, turns smiling to do a few dishes. She sets the birdhouse down.

ROSE (cont'd)

    I want to paint the...next roof...(she blurts)...blue.

Alvin smiles again.

ALVIN

    That's a good idea.

Rose turns to the window and thinks for a while with a smile on her face. As she reflects, her smile begins to fade.

ROSE (cont'd)

    What did the...Doctor say?

Alvin puts out the Swisher Sweet.

ALVIN

    Said I'm goin' to live to be a hundred.

Rose smiles at this. Alvin stands, puts on a cream-colored Stetson and heads to the back door.

ALVIN (cont'd)

    Time to cut the lawn.

ROSE (cont'd)

    I can...cut it for...you...Dad.

Alvin is navigating the door with his two canes in hand. Says gently back over his shoulder.

ALVIN

    I got it sweetheart.

Rose turns, clears the table and takes dishes over to the kitchen sink. Out the window over her shoulder we see Alvin cross the backyard and mount a Rehds riding mower. She sets the dishes in the sink, then gets distracted by the birdhouse.

                CUT TO:

18   EXT. — DAY ALVIN'S BACKYARD

Alvin tries to start the mower. No luck. He performs a slow, painful, laborious dismount. Then in a quick move he turns and bangs the mower with his cane.

ALVIN

    Damn!

                CUT TO:

19   INT. — DAY LAURENS ACE HARDWARE

A group of locals are in the store. SIG, BUD, PETE, mid-60s, 6'0", lean, gray and wearing slacks and a red Ace vest, and APPLE, early 60s, short, bald and talkative. He is wearing a short-sleeve shirt and a tie. He's concentrating on his right boot. He frowns as he works it up and down with his toes. His attention is split between working the shoe and watching the Weather Channel which is on the television over the counter.

APPLE

(all the while stomping his foot)

    Looks like another low comin' out of the panhandle of Texas. That's where they all come from. You know in the winter that's where we get all our big dumps.

PETE

    Apple I doubt very much if we'll be getting snow this week.

Sig giggles.

SIG

    And here comes Alvin Straight. He's not movin' too well.

PETE

    Well he took that bad fall.

BUD

    An hour late! I found the darn fool on the kitchen floor.

SIG

    He looks like he ain't gonna make it to the door. If he was a horse they'd shoot 'im.

PETE
(scolding)
    How old are you now Sig?
Apple has his shoe off and is digging inside of it with his hand. He looks
up at Pete's remark.
APPLE
    He's 70 in September..."Oh the days dwindle down to a precious few..."
SIG
    You can shut up any time Apple.
Alvin enters. They turn their heads, nod hello. Bud scowls.
PETE
    Mornin' Alvin. What can I do for you?
Alvin approaches the counter and opens his mouth to speak but is inter-
rupted by...
APPLE
    Local forecast!
            CUT TO:

20   INT. — DAY HARDWARE STORE TELEVISION
The Weather Channel. The local forecast runs with the accompanying
music. Conversation stops abruptly and they all turn to watch the local
forecast together. There is the potential for thunderstorms later in the day
with a possible tornado watch.
PETE
    And what can I do you for Alvin?
ALVIN
    Plugs for the Rehds. Won't start.
            CUT TO:

21   EXT. — LATE DAY ALVIN'S BACKYARD
Alvin is changing the plugs, smoking Swisher Sweets. Rose is sitting on
aluminum lawn chair painting the roof of her birdhouse blue. A storm is
moving in. Alvin looks up to the sky.
ALVIN
    Storm comin'...not mowin' today.
            CUT TO:

22   INT. — NIGHT ALVIN'S LIVING ROOM
Alvin and Rose are watching Storm Watch on the Weather Channel.
CUT TO:

23   INT. — NIGHT THE TELEVISION IN ALVIN'S LIVING ROOM
WEATHER PERSON
    Severe thunderstorm warning and tornado watch continue until 9 P.M.
    for all of west central Iowa. The National Weather Service advises seek-
    ing shelter in basement rooms. Avoid all windows...

CUT TO:

24 INT.—NIGHT ALVIN'S LIVING ROOM
Rose and Alvin sit by the window watching the lightning. A big bolt cuts
through the sky to the ground.

ALVIN
   I love a lightning storm.

ROSE
   Me...too Dad.

The phone rings. Rose is reluctant to leave the show at the window and
lets it ring 3 or 4 times. Finally she gets up and leaves the room to answer
the phone in the kitchen.

ROSE
(off camera)
   Hello...this...is Rose.
   Yah...yah...Uncle...Lyle?

Alvin's expression changes to a frown as the light of the TV plays off his
face. He does not turn his head or speak but he is listening and reacting to
Rose's conversation.

ROSE (cont'd)
   Oh...no. When? O.K. Ah...ah...I'll tell him. Yah. O.K. bye.

Rose comes back in and sits down. She doesn't say anything and neither
does Alvin for a bit. We see another big crack of lightning out the window.
The Storm Watch continues off screen.

WEATHER PERSON
(voice over)
   A tornado has been sited in Ida County. Sac, Calhoun and Pocahontas
   Counties are all under tornado watch...

ROSE (cont'd)
   That was Bobby...Uncle Lyle had a...a...ah...stroke.

On the word "stroke," a bolt of lightning brilliantly illuminates Alvin's
face. Then he sits stonefaced in darkness looking out the window. He
doesn't respond.

ROSE (cont'd)
   Dad?

CUT TO:

25 EXT.—NIGHT ALVIN'S HOUSE
Alvin's house is being buffeted by a fierce midwestern electrical
storm.

CUT TO:

26 EXT.—DAY ALVIN'S YARD
Alvin is mowing the lawn.

27 INT. — DAY ALVIN'S HOUSE, KITCHEN

Rose is standing at the kitchen window talking on the phone. Over Rose's shoulder Alvin crosses back and forth through the window frame riding the mower. Rose is talking to one of her brothers.

ROSE

No Bobby he...didn't say much...They both been so...stubborn. No...no it was longer. I remember...It was July 7, 1988. Bobby, I always remember...the dates.

Through the window we see Alvin stop the mower. He sits and stares. He lights up a Swisher Sweet.

ROSE (cont'd)

I...don't know...what....he'll do.

Rose hangs up and looks back out at Alvin sitting on mower.

CUT TO:

28 INT. — NIGHT ALVIN'S LIVING ROOM

Rose is sitting in the dark looking out the window at the freshly mown lawn. She hears a noise and turns. There is Alvin, with two canes, silhouetted in the doorway to the kitchen.

ALVIN

Rose honey, why don't you come in here and join your dad for a cup of coffee.

Rose looks puzzled. This is not a common invitation from Alvin.

ROSE

Dad...we're not going to move again are we? You always set me down for a coffee when you tell me we are going to move again.

Alvin laughs a little. Rose is clearly wary.

ALVIN

No honey...we're not breaking camp.

Rose sighs in relief and smiles. Alvin pauses, clearly uncomfortable.

ALVIN (cont'd)

Unless you make so many bluebird houses we run outa room.

ROSE

(taking her father seriously)

Dad...oh jeez...I can stop making them...

ALVIN

Easy honey. Your pa was just makin' a joke.

Rose is relieved. Alvin pauses and draws a breath.

ALVIN (cont'd)

Rose. I'm goin' to get back out on the road. I'm going to go see Lyle.

ROSE

But Dad...how are you...?

Alvin turns and starts to hobble toward the kitchen.

ALVIN

I haven't quite figured that out yet.

He moves off into the kitchen.

CUT TO:

29   EXT. — DAY ALVIN'S BACKYARD

From around the side of the house comes Rose hauling a large piece of aged plywood. She talks as she wrestles with the large board. She is speaking to Alvin who is on the back stoop with a wrench and a ball joint. She is also reasoning aloud with herself.

ROSE

One...Your eyes are bad...That is why you don't drive your car because you cannot see the signs anymore.

Rose turns and looks directly at Alvin. He is letting her vent.

ROSE (cont'd)

One...Your eyes are bad.

Rose walks back around the corner of the house and returns with another large piece of old plywood. As Rose enunciates her reasons she ticks them off on her fingers.

ROSE (cont'd)

Two...Lyle is in Wisconsin which is 317 miles away. You can't take any bus straight to Mt. Zion. You'd have to stay overnight in Des Moines...and...then there's no bus to Zion.

Rose eyes Alvin again. She vanishes around the corner one more time. Alvin continues working on the ball joint, adding oil to loosen the bolt. Rose comes around the corner again.

ROSE

Three...Your hips. You can't hardly stand for two minutes and when you do stand up after you are sitting down this is the sound you make when you stand..."aaaaaraaaaarrrrhhgggg." That is your arthritis sound.

Alvin chuckles at her impersonation of him. She is almost finished with her tasks. Her talking slows as she gets to the last of her rant.

ROSE (cont'd)

Four...You are 73 years old. You were born when Calvin Coolidge was President of America.

Rose sits down next to Alvin on the stoop. She is hot, tired, worried and upset. Her voice almost breaks as she finishes her speech.

ROSE (cont'd)

You are 73 years old...And I can't drive you there.

ALVIN

    Rosie...darlin'...I'm not dead yet.

This subdues Rose. Alvin looks at her for a beat, turns and moves to a stool with the wrench and ball joint. He begins screwing the ball joint to a beam.

ROSE

(tired and exasperated)

    What are we building?

            CUT TO:

30   INT. — NEXT DAY GROCERY STORE

Rose is pushing a grocery cart down the aisle. She checks a list in her hand.

ROSE

    Coffee.

Rose places eight large cans of Folgers into the cart. She counts as she deposits them.

ROSE (cont'd)

    One...two...three...four...five...six...seven...eight.

She checks list again.

ROSE

    Wieners...

Rose places several large packs of wieners in the cart.

ROSE (cont'd)

    One...two...three...four...five...six.

She reaches back into the cold meat case.

ROSE (cont'd)

    Braunschweiger.

Rose makes faces in incremental disgust as she counts.

ROSE (cont'd)

    One...two...three...four...

She hates braunschweiger. She checks her list again. She moves down the aisle and into the next one. She pauses before a display.

ROSE (cont'd)

    Bug juice.

Rose throws insect repellent into the cart.

ROSE (cont'd)

    One.

She checks her list and nods in satisfaction, heading to the checkout counter.

            CUT TO:

31   INT. — DAY GROCERY STORE CHECKOUT COUNTER

Rose is loading her purchases onto the counter. BRENDA the checkout girl looks on with a curious expression. Brenda is 20ish, cute, a little hefty. Very cheerful.

BRENDA
(a statement)
 Havin' a party.

Rose looks at her blankly.

ROSE
 Oh...Jeez I love parties.

BRENDA
 Yah, me too.

ROSE (cont'd)
 So where's it at?

Brenda is confused.

BRENDA
 Where's what at?

ROSE
 Your party.

BRENDA
 I'm not havin' a party. I thought you're havin' a party.

ROSE
 I am?

BRENDA
 Well yah...look at all that braunschweiger.

ROSE
 Yah it's a lot of braunschweiger.

Brenda starts to ring up the braunschweiger.

ROSE
 It's for my dad...for his...trip. My dad...He...is going to...Wisconsin.

CHECKOUT GIRL
 Oh Wisconsin! A real party state.

Rose is keeping an eye on her items. She makes a "yuk" face.

ROSE
 I hate braunschweiger.

Brenda, still checking, nods in assent and makes a sour face.

CUT TO:

32 EXT.—DAY ALVIN'S BACKYARD

Rose comes walking out of the house with groceries. She sets them on the picnic table and heads back into the house. Alvin loads the groceries into the now finished trailer. The back door of the house opens and a big sheet of foam rubber flies out the door followed by Rose. She hauls it over to the trailer and sets it in. She fusses over its arrangement.

CUT TO:

33   INT. — DAY ACE HARDWARE

Pete, Sig, Apple and Bud are in the store. They are watching the Weather Channel. Sig has a toothpick in his mouth. Apple is sitting on a stool. Alvin and Rose enter.

PETE

    Morning Alvin. How are you today Rose?

Alvin nods. Rose smiles.

ROSE (BLURTS)

    My...dad...is going to see...his...brother. I keep askin' him how...he's goin' to get there...but he doesn't say...nothin'.

Alvin throws a look at Rose. She smiles.

PETE

    Your bluebird houses are selling well Rose. I'm gonna need some more from you.

SIG

    Taking a trip Alvin eh?

ALVIN

    Yup.

Apple is sitting on a stool with one shoe off. His hand is inside the shoe.

APPLE

    Well if you're traveling by car you know my wife'll get those AAA trip tix. Those babies'll tell you where every piece of construction is all along the "I" system.

PETE

    I don't suspect Alvin'll be takin' your wife along with him Apple.

ALVIN

    Oh Lord.

BUD

    You can take my wife.

Alvin chuckles and then sets one cane against the counter. With his other cane he makes his way down the store aisle to the gas cans. He grabs one 5-gallon container and heads back to the counter.

SIG

    Where's your brother at Alvin?

Alvin sets the can on the counter. He turns to walk back down the aisle.

ROSE

    Mt. Zion. Sixty-three miles east of the Missi...ssippi.

PETE

    Sixty-three miles, eh Rose?

APPLE

Did you know that the Mississippi...the old mighty Mississipp...is the single most profitable waterway in the world? Did you know that the Japanese harvest pearls outta the river down to Prairie du Chien...pearls!

SIG

And carp.

PETE

And walleye...need help there Alvin?

ALVIN

No thanks, Pete.

Pete and Sig exchange a glance and look at Rose. She smiles. Alvin picks up another 5-gallon gas can.

SIG

What's doin' at your brother's Alvin? The Straight family reunion?

Alvin gives Sig a look.

ALVIN

You could say that.

Alvin puts the other gas can on the counter.

SIG

(goading Alvin)

Alvin you got three 5-gallon cans. Fifteen gallons of gas there. Just what you gonna do with that much gas?

Rose is getting nervous with Sig's prying ways. She knows that this is a sensitive area for Alvin. She looks to the TV.

ROSE

Local forecast!

The whole gang stops and watches as the Weather Channel gives the local forecast.

CUT TO:

34 INT.—DAY THE TV SCREEN

The local forecast runs and the radar is looking clear.

CUT TO:

As soon as it is over they look at each other to remember where they were in conversation.

SIG

Ahh...so what you need so much gas for Alvin?

Alvin returns to the counter. This time he has two medium-sized Styrofoam coolers. Alvin stops and looks long at Sig.

ALVIN

Sig, you are one nosy sonofagun.

BUD

    You got that right.

Sig clamps his jaw. Alvin turns back to Pete.

ALVIN (cont'd)

    Pete, I'd like to buy that from you.

Alvin points to a contraption used in hardware stores to grab things on high shelves. Pete sees what he's pointing to and gets a possessive jolt. He turns to Alvin.

PETE

    Jeez Alvin.

ALVIN

    Well?

Pete eyes the grabber. He looks down the aisle to the other end of the store where he's got another grabber hanging.

PETE

    I do have two of them...I guess I could sell you that one.

ALVIN

    Five bucks would seem about right.

PETE

(puzzled)

    Those things are hard to come by Alvin. It would take me two months to get another one on order. That's a damn good grabber. Jeez...I can't let that grabber go for less than.....jeez.....$10.00.

ALVIN

(considering, not too happy)

    O.K. Ring her up.

Pete pulls down the grabber and longingly works it a few times and sets it reluctantly down on the counter. Alvin smiles. Pete starts ringing up Alvin's items.

PETE

    Three 5-gallon gas cans at $9.89. Two Styrofoam coolers...

The beautiful bells and clicks and hammers of the old cash register are the only sounds in the room.

PETE

    Two coolers, 99 cents and one...one...Alvin...

ALVIN

    Ring it up Pete.

PETE

    With tax that's $44.25.

Alvin fishes out a large black wallet held to his belt by a chain. He pulls out two twenties and a five and hands them to Pete.

SIG

What you need that grabber for Alvin?

Alvin turns to him.

ALVIN

Grabbin'.

Apple has his arm up to his elbow digging in his boot. Suddenly he feels something.

APPLE

Hah! It's a nail!

CUT TO:

35 EXT. — DAY ALVIN'S BACKYARD

Alvin and Rose are in the backyard. Alvin takes a can of W-2 lubricant. He sprays the hitch holder on the trailer. Then he laboriously makes his way across the lawn to the riding mower. He sprays the hitch ball on the mower. Rose is confused. Alvin then mounts the lawn mower. He begins backing it up to the trailer. Awareness finally crosses Rose's face. Her jaw drops.

ROSE

Oh...jeeez Dad. Oh jeez...Dad.

CUT TO:

36 EXT. — NIGHT ALVIN'S BACKYARD

Alvin is seated on a chaise lounge smoking a Swisher Sweet. He is looking at his mower/trailer rig. A mosquito coil burns beside him, casting a warm glow on the scene. Rose is lying on the ground on a blanket looking up at the stars. It is a beautiful autumn evening.

ROSE (cont'd)

...that trailer is too heavy for that...it's a lawnmower. You are going to...drive...a lawnmower to...another state.

ALVIN

Now Rose you gotta cease with your worryin'. You get that from your mother.

ROSE

But Dad...you...can't.

ALVIN

Rose..."can't" doesn't live here.

Alvin takes a puff of cigar.

ALVIN

It's gonna be fine Rose.

ROSE

Dad...please. I will find someone to drive you to Wisconsin. Pete...you like Pete...Pete...he is a good driver.

ALVIN

Now, Rose, sweetheart...

Rose is starting to tear up. She is so worried about what he is doing. He reaches down and takes her hand.

ALVIN (cont'd)

I been on the road plenty. Didn't your mom and I haul you kids all around the country?

Rose nods, close to tears. She counts.

ROSE

One, Wisconsin...Two, Minnesota...Three, Wyoming but not long... Four was Oregon. We had goats. Five...New Mexico and.....six... good old...Iowa.

ALVIN

Remember when we traveled...you and your sister and brothers...

Rose nods and the reminiscence makes her happy.

ALVIN (cont'd)

We sure saw a lot. We all liked travelin'.

ROSE

Yeah.

(smiling at first but then the worry returns)

But this is different Dad.

ALVIN

It is Rose...it's easier...I'm not luggin' seven kids in the back.

Rose nods. Her emotions are confused.

ROSE

But Dad...you will be all alone. Won't you be lonely?

ALVIN

Rosie...sometimes a man likes bein' a little lonely.

Rose ponders this notion. A new anxiety creeps in.

ROSE

I will be alone...here...

This stops Alvin. He realizes he hadn't really thought about that and it makes him feel both bad and a little worried. He hides his concern.

ALVIN (cont'd)

And you're going to be just fine. Dorothy is next door and she can't keep her nose out of our business. She'll be over here seven times a day.

Rose laughs.

ROSE

Wait 'til she hears about...this Dad.

They both share a laugh.

ALVIN (cont'd)
Rose I got to go see Lyle. I got to make this trip on my own. I know you
understand that.
ROSE
I guess so....
ALVIN
Look at that sky Rose...full of stars tonight.
                    CUT TO:
37   EXT. — NIGHT ALVIN'S BACKYARD
POV a sky full of stars.
                    CUT TO:
38   INT. — DAY GROCERY STORE
Dorothy is at the checkout counter. Brenda is checking her out.
BRENDA
One bag of potato chips, two boxes of powdered donuts, one bag of corn
nuts, six pack of Coca-Cola, two Snickers, three Hostess Sno-Balls...
DOROTHY
Give me a couple of packs of Salem lights will ya hon?
Dorothy glances out the window of the store just in time to see Alvin
passing on his mower hauling the trailer.
DOROTHY
Well...I don't believe my eyes.
Brenda looks up and glances out the window. She sees Alvin passing on
the mower. She doesn't miss a beat in her checking.
BRENDA
Oh yah. He's goin' to visit his brother in Wisconsin.
DOROTHY
On a lawnmower?!?!
BRENDA
Yah...
DOROTHY
Great party place, Wisconsin.
                    CUT TO:
39   INT. — DAY HARDWARE STORE
The Weather Channel is STILL on. Pete, Sig and Apple are watching. As
they watch they hear a noisy engine approach out front. They turn to the
storefront window. Alvin pulls into frame hauling the trailer behind his
riding lawn mower.

SIG

(stunned)

　Crimenetto.

All three exit the hardware store after Alvin.

CUT TO:

40　EXT.—DAY　LAURENS MAIN STREET

The three hardware regulars trot alongside Alvin as he passes out of town.

APPLE

　Alvin just what are you settin' out to do here?

BUD

　Oh for da cry eye Alvin.

APPLE

　Alvin you are gonna get blown right off the road is what I'm afraid.

SIG

(running out of breath and stopping, bending over,

hands on knees, wheezing)

　Oh...(puffing)...jeez Alvin.

All three stop and watch as Alvin moves slowly out of town.

PETE

(to no one in particular)

　He'll never make it past the Grotto.

CUT TO:

41　EXT.—DAY　IOWA COUNTY HIGHWAY 314

Tight shot of very, very slow yellow center line moving through frame to the tune of Steppenwolf's "Born to Be Wild" à la Easy Rider.

CUT TO:

42　EXT.—DAY　IOWA COUNTY HIGHWAY 314

Wide shot from behind and then beside Alvin which takes in expansive landscape. A beautiful sunny day. America at five miles an hour.

. . .

FADE IN:

82　EXT.—DAY　HIGHWAY 18

Alvin going down the road. He sees a small figure up ahead. A car whizzes past Alvin. The figure ahead sticks out a thumb. The car passes by. Alvin approaches the figure, sees it's a young, tough-looking girl CRYSTAL. She has dark hair under a baseball cap. Somewhere between 13 and 17 years old. Heavy eye makeup, bad tattoo on her shoulder. She is wearing a tank top, cut-offs, high-top sneakers with tiger-striped laces, and a backpack. Alvin nods in acknowledgment as he passes her. She coldly returns his gaze.

CUT TO:

83   EXT. — NIGHT ALVIN'S CAMPSITE

Alvin is eating a raw hot dog. He has built a campfire.

CUT TO:

84   EXT. — NIGHT SAME HIGHWAY WIDE SHOT

Crystal is walking along.

CUT TO:

85   EXT. — NIGHT SAME HIGHWAY CRYSTAL'S POV

Crystal spies Alvin's campfire in the field along the road. The lawnmower and trailer are clearly visible and she remembers him from the road.

CUT TO:

86   EXT. — NIGHT SAME HIGHWAY

Crystal considers. Her face is unreadable…her intentions are unclear. She cuts off the road into the field and heads toward the campsite.

CUT TO:

87   EXT. — NIGHT ALVIN'S CAMPSITE

Alvin barely looks up as Crystal walks into range of campfire light. Neither of them say anything for some time.

CRYSTAL

   I couldn't get a ride.

Alvin nods his head. Doesn't say anything for a bit.

ALVIN

   Hungry?

CRYSTAL

   Whatya got?

ALVIN

   Wieners.

CRYSTAL

   Wieners?

ALVIN

   Grab a stick and cook one.

He points to the fire. She hesitates…looks at Alvin for a bit longer. Alvin just keeps looking at the fire. Finally she looks around, finds a stick and leans toward Alvin to take a hot dog. She hunkers down holding the stick with the hot dog over the fire. She casts occasional glances at Alvin. More silence. She looks over to the mower and trailer. Her expression darkens.

CRYSTAL (cont'd)

   What a hunk of junk.

ALVIN

   Eat your dinner missy.

Startled a bit at his abruptness she falls silent. She nibbles on her hot dog and then realizing how hungry she is she begins to eat faster. She polishes off the hot dog. Alvin notices this.

ALVIN (cont'd)
    Get yourself another.

She's relieved at this offer and gets another hot dog, puts it on the stick and holds it over the fire. They sit, not speaking, listening to a chorus of crickets and peepers.

CRYSTAL
    How long you been out on the road?

ALVIN
    I've traveled just about all my life.

CRYSTAL
    I like being out on the road.

ALVIN
    It's different for a girl alone.

CRYSTAL
(defensively)
    It doesn't have to be different for a girl.

Alvin just nods his head. Doesn't speak or look at her.

CRYSTAL (cont'd)
    Where you from?

ALVIN
    Laurens.

She nods, and sits quietly.

CRYSTAL
    You got a wife back there?

ALVIN
    Nope.

CRYSTAL
    Kids?

ALVIN
    My wife Frances brought fourteen kids into the world. Only seven
    made it...My daughter Rose lives with me.

No comment for a while.

ALVIN (cont'd)
    Frances died in '81.

Quiet for time.

ALVIN (cont'd)
    Where's your family?

Now she's not talking.

ALVIN (cont'd)
>   You runnin' away?

She still doesn't answer. Alvin leans back and draws on his cigar. He looks at the girl.

ALVIN (cont'd)
>   How far along are you?

Crystal looks away from the fire into the darkness.

CRYSTAL
>   Five months.

Alvin nods. More quiet. Alvin gets up, walks out of firelight with his grabber and comes back with a log. He throws it on the fire and works the embers for a bit.

ALVIN
>   My daughter Rose that lives with me...she's what some people would call a little slow. But she's not. She's got a mind like a bear trap for facts and keeps everything organized around the house. She was a real good mom...had four kids.

He pauses looking into the fire. Crystal watches him expectantly.

ALVIN (cont'd)
>   One night...someone else was watchin' the kids...

>>   DISSOLVE TO:

88   INT. — NIGHT ALVIN'S KITCHEN

We see the shot of Rose sitting alone in the kitchen that we saw before. She is at the kitchen table smoking a cigarette and thinking.

ALVIN
(continuing in voice over)
>   There was a fire. Her second boy got burned real bad. Rose didn't have nothin' to do with it.

He pauses.

ALVIN (cont'd)
(continuing in voice over)
>   ...but...because of the way Rose is...the state said she wasn't comp'tent to care for the kids and took them all away.

>>   DISSOLVE TO:

89   EXT. — NIGHT ALVIN'S CAMPSITE

ALVIN
>   Not a day passes she doesn't pine for those kids.

Crystal looks away from him into the fire. He looks back to the fire, coughs.

ALVIN
>   Well, I'm headin' to see my brother Lyle.

CRYSTAL

Huh?

ALVIN

I said I'm goin' to visit my brother Lyle in Mt. Zion.

CRYSTAL

Where's that?

ALVIN

In Wisconsin. Just over the state line.

CRYSTAL

(nodding)

Oh...Cheddar Heads.

Alvin laughs at this and Crystal smiles, too.

ALVIN

Aren't those just about the dumbest things you ever saw a person put on their head?

She nods and laughs.

CRYSTAL

I hear that's a real party place, Wisconsin. Guess I'll never get to find out.

They sit in silence. Alvin looks away from the fire.

ALVIN

I haven't seen my brother in ten years.

Alvin picks up the hot dogs and takes one out of the pack. He proceeds to eat it raw.

CRYSTAL

You're eatin' a raw hot dog!

ALVIN

(smiling)

I like 'em straight up.

Crystal makes a face. Alvin munches slowly.

CRYSTAL

Ten years is a long time.

Crystal shivers with a chill. Alvin notices this.

ALVIN

There's a blanket in the trailer.

Crystal leaves firelight. She rustles about in the trailer.

CRYSTAL

(offscreen)

What the hell kind of boom box is this?

ALVIN

Eight track stereo...watch your god-damned language.

CRYSTAL
(offscreen)
   Are these videotapes or what?
ALVIN
   That's music girlie.
CRYSTAL
   They're huge!...I never seen anything like this.
We hear some rattling and the sound of the tape going in. A sweet Patsy
Cline ballad floats out of the trailer and into the night air. Smiling, Crystal
comes back into the light with a blanket around her shoulders.
CRYSTAL (cont'd)
   Figured it out.
ALVIN
   Good girl.
They sit for a while and listen to the music.
CRYSTAL (cont'd)
   Your brother.
ALVIN (cont'd)
   Lyle and I had a falling out.
CRYSTAL
   Over what?
ALVIN
   I can't say as I recall.
CRYSTAL
   Well that's pretty stupid. You haven't seen him in ten years because of a
   fight and you can't remember what the fight was about?
ALVIN
   You got some rude habits girl.
Crystal is taken aback. She is quiet, thinking.
ALVIN (cont'd)
   Maybe I do recall.
Quiet for a while.
ALVIN (cont'd)
   People do lots of stupid things, knowing they're stupid.
He looks at her. She looks up.
CRYSTAL
   Sorry.
They both stare into the fire for a while.
CRYSTAL
   So why are you going to see him now?

ALVIN
  He's sick.
Crystal is poking the fire with the stick. Alvin picks up another stick and he starts poking the fire.
CRYSTAL
  My family hates me. They'll really hate me when they find out...
ALVIN
  You didn't tell them?
CRYSTAL
  No...no one knows...not even my boyfriend.
ALVIN
  Well that doesn't strike me as fair treatment of your people.
CRYSTAL
  I can take care of my own problems.
There is a pause as they watch the fire. Then Alvin speaks.
ALVIN
  Don't let pride make you dumb. I should know.
She's listening.
ALVIN (cont'd)
  They may not be happy. But not so much that they want to lose you... or your little problem.
CRYSTAL
  I don't know about that.
ALVIN
  Well a course neither do I but a warm bed and a roof sounds a mite better than this...eating hot dogs on a stick with an old geezer traveling on a lawn mower.
She giggles a bit and then falls silent. After a moment, Alvin stirs.
ALVIN (cont'd)
  When my kids were young I played a game with them. I'd give each of them a stick. One for each of 'em, and I'd tell them to break it. They'd do that easy. Then I'd tell them to make one bundle of all the sticks and try to break that. A course they couldn't. I used to say that was family, that bundle.
Crystal listens in silence.
ALVIN (cont'd)
  Sleep in the trailer if you want. I'll be just fine here in my chair.
CRYSTAL
  No, I'll be fine sleeping out here. Looking at the stars helps me think.
Alvin nods. He begins to struggle to his feet. Crystal stands to help him. After a moment of hesitation Alvin accepts her arm. He stands, nods,

smiles and moves slowly to the trailer. Crystal sits down alone to watch the fire. We hear the sounds of Alvin settling into the trailer. A bit of silence.

ALVIN
(from offscreen)
    Sweet dreams.

        CUT TO:

90   EXT. — NIGHT ALVIN'S TRAILER
Alvin's trailer door is open to the night air. We slowly push into the dark rectangular opening of the trailer.

        FADE IN:

91   EXT. — SUNRISE
A wide establishing shot of the Iowa landscape at sunrise.

        CUT TO:

92   EXT. — SUNRISE ALVIN'S CAMPSITE
Alvin crawls out of the trailer. Crystal's gone. Next to the cold campfire is a bundle of sticks bound with a tiger-striped shoelace.

AFTER READING

Responding

1. In a paragraph, explain why you would or would not like to see the film based on this screenplay.

Understanding

2. In your notebook, explain the purpose of the three opening shots of this screenplay.
3. Describe the kind of music you would select to play during the first shot of this screenplay. Explain why you would make that choice.

4. With a partner, divide this screenplay into **scenes**. For each scene, describe the contribution it makes to **plot** and **character** development. (See The Reference Shelf, page 368, for a discussion on purposes of **acts** and scenes.)

5. In a small group, discuss the following questions:
   - Is the underlying premise of this screenplay believable?
   - Why would audiences more likely accept a premise like this in a film than in a book?
   - To what extent has the screenwriter attempted to provide reasonable explanations for the premise?
   - Why would the screenwriter include the scenes with Crystal in the film?
   - Do you admire Alvin Straight? Why?
   - Do you think Alvin eventually reaches his brother Lyle in the film? Why?
   Be prepared to report your ideas and observations to the class.

6. a) Create a list of characters that appear in these segments of the screenplay.
   b) For each, explain which actor you would cast in the part.
   c) Check the credits for this film and see who actually played each part.

Thinking About Language

7. Explain one reason for the irregular number of ellipsis dots used occasionally in this screenplay.

8. With a partner, explain what you can tell of the characters from the language that they use. Be prepared to discuss your ideas and observations with the class.

Extending

9. With a partner, using the format of this screenplay, write an additional scene for this film. Work with another pair to revise and edit your scene. Be prepared to read your scene aloud to the class.

10. Read the complete screenplay and write an **essay** on an aspect that you found most interesting. Use an appropriate method of development to organize your essay. (See The Reference Shelf, pages 386–391.) With a partner, take your essay through the writing process before submission and, using feedback from your partner, update your Writing Skills Action Plan as necessary. (See The Reference Shelf, page 395.)

A Man, a Lawnmower, an Open Road

BEFORE READING

Read the title of this **review**. Predict whether it will be positive or negative. Explain the basis for your prediction.

The Straight Story is a film dedicated to the memory of Alvin Straight, a man who drove from Iowa to Wisconsin to see his sick brother. He made the journey of hundreds of miles on his lawnmower. Yes, it's all true.

Richard Farnsworth stars as Alvin. This is the story of a man nearing the end of his life, and all that life represents, which happens to be plenty. Alvin lives with one of his daughters (played by Sissy Spacek). When the news comes that his brother has had a stroke, Alvin needs to see his brother and fix up the quarrel that left them estranged years before.

Not so healthy himself and no longer able to drive, Alvin undertakes the trip on a John Deere sit-down mower. *The Straight Story* is really a collection of vignettes held together by breathtaking cinematography.

Along the way, Alvin meets people—from a runaway teen to a preacher to another WWII vet to complete strangers

who take him in—and what they talk about together is what this film is all about. It takes a while to shake off what the movies have led us all to expect and just fall into Alvin's story; no monsters, no untoward events, no secretly villainous people pop up. Just folks.

Given the hokey/stupid/right-wing crazy way the American heartland is often depicted in films, this one should be required viewing for all big-city residents.

You could see *The Straight Story* as a head-on collision between tense modern life and the old ways. At one point, Alvin meets up with a crazed woman who has tried and failed to stop hitting deer on the highway as she commutes madly each day to work. There's an obvious nature-versus-man-made chaos thing happening here; as for Alvin, he quietly cooks and eats the deer.

Farnsworth, who carries the entire movie, is a mesmerizing presence on the screen. When people ask him if he's not frightened to be travelling the highways alone, he says, "I fought in the trenches in WWII—why would I be scared of an Iowa cornfield?"

He explains what it means to be a brother. He goes over a repair bill with some mechanics and politely shames them into making it fair. What a guy.

In just under two hours, *The Straight Story* summarizes an almost-lost generation of people, their values and a certain way of life. This is charming fare, and you could bring your granny to see it with you. Make that charming and rare.

AFTER READING

Responding

1. After reading this review, decide whether it is a positive or negative review of the film. Use specific points made in this review to support your position.

Understanding

2. With a partner, discuss the following questions.
   - Does Liz Braun give away too much of the **plot** or story line of the film in her review?
   - Does the film reviewer adequately support her claim that this film "should be required viewing for all big-city residents"?

   Be prepared to present your answers to these questions to the class.
3. Read the **scenes** from *The Straight Story* printed in this textbook on pages 303 to 331. Explain whether the description of the film in this review is an accurate description of the screenplay.
4. Who is the intended audience of this review? Explain how three sentences from this review helped you to identify the intended audience.
5. Account for this review's lack of technical terms used in filmmaking.

Thinking About Language

6. Select three interestingly worded ideas in this film review. Explain whether each is appropriate to the intended audience of the review and the nature of the film being reviewed.

Extending

7. How would this review have to be different for each of the following audiences?
   • students studying film-making techniques
   • sports fans
   • 13 year olds

8. Locate three reviews for a recently released film. Analyze the reviews under these headings: focus of each review, helpfulness of the review to a consumer. Consider creating your analysis of the reviews in an appropriately designed and labelled chart.

9. Watch a video or movie (on television or at the theatre) and write a review for the movie, using one of the reviews you have read as a model. Exchange your review with a partner and give your partner suggestions for ways to improve the content, organization, and **voice** of the review.

UNIT 4

> The Reference Shelf

The English Language

Note: For a more detailed discussion of grammar, punctuation, research, and writing, and for additional examples and exercises, students and teachers should refer to *The Harcourt Writer's Handbook* (Toronto: Harcourt Canada, 1999).

PARTS OF SPEECH

A noun names a person, place, or thing. Nouns are commonly classed as common (desk, chair), proper (Canada, Maria), collective (herd, class), concrete (pen, paper), and abstract (anger, honesty).

A pronoun takes the place of a noun. Pronouns agree with their antecedents (the words to which pronouns refer) in number and gender but take the case of the role they play in a sentence. Pronouns can be classed as possessive (my, her, your) or relative (that, which, who, whom, whose).

An adjective describes a noun or pronoun. Adjectives can be positive (good, fast, beautiful), comparative (better, faster, more beautiful), or superlative (best, fastest, most beautiful).

An adverb describes the how, when, or where of a verb, adjective, or another adverb. Examples:

She will sing proudly. (how) She will sing tomorrow. (when) She will sing here. (where)

A verb identifies the action or state of being in a sentence. Verbs can be classed as transitive, intransitive, and linking or copula.

Transitive verbs express an action toward an object (person or thing). Example:

Mary *revised* the essay. (The action "revised" is directed toward "essay.")

Intransitive verbs express action or tell something about the subject without directing the action toward a receiver (object). Example:

John *walked* for fifteen minutes. (The action "walked" is not directed toward an object or receiver.)

Copula verbs link or connect the subject with a noun, pronoun, or adjective in the predicate of a sentence. They express a state of being or becoming, rather than an action. Examples:

Rita *is* a good athlete. (Rita = good athlete)

Pierre Trudeau *remained* popular even after he retired from political life. (Pierre Trudeau = popular)

Grandma *seemed* happy and contented. (Grandma = happy, contented)

A **verb tense** tells when the action occurs. The three most commonly used tenses in English are **present**, **past**, and **future**. Do not change needlessly from one tense to another. When writing about events that take place in the present, use verbs in the present tense. Similarly, when writing about events that occurred in the past, use verbs in the past tense.

Verb voice can be active or passive. **Active voice** expresses an action that is done by its subject. Example:

Jason *ate* the cake. (The subject "Jason" performs the action "ate.")

Passive voice expresses an action that is done by its subject. Example:

The cake *was eaten* by Jason. (The subject "cake" receives the action "was eaten.")

The passive voice is also used when the doer of the action is unknown or not important to the context. Example:

An announcement *was made* over the P.A. system. (The doer of the action is unknown.)

The active voice tends to be more direct, hard-hitting, and forceful; however, the passive voice is often used effectively to create an objective tone and clarity in reports, manuals, and scholarly essays.

Some Specific Verb Forms

An **infinitive** is a verb form preceded by the preposition "to." It can be used as a noun, adjective, or adverb. Examples:

To know your strengths and weaknesses is *to understand* yourself. (Both "to know" and "to understand" are infinitives. As nouns, they act respectively as subject and subjective completion of the copula verb "is." As verbs, they express action or emotion and have an object "your strengths and weaknesses.")

The subject *to study* is English. ("To study" is an infinitive. As an adjective, it modifies the noun "subject.")

Ready *to go*, we loaded the car. ("To go" is an infinitive. As an adverb, it modifies the adjective "ready.")

A *gerund* is a verb form usually ending in "ing." Gerunds are verb forms used as nouns. Like other nouns, they can be modified by adjectives. Like verbs, they can also be modified by adverbs. Example:

Walking briskly fifteen minutes a day is good exercise. ("Walking" is a gerund. Like a noun, it is the subject of the predicate verb "is"; as a verb, it is modified by the adverb "briskly.")

A *participle* is a verb form. It can be in the present tense (ending in "ing") or in the past tense (often ending in "d" or "ed"). Participles are used as adjectives. Like other adjectives and verbs, they can be modified by an adverb. Examples:

Looking at the camera, Samantha smiled. ("Looking" is a present participle. As an adjective, it modifies "Samantha," the noun subject of the sentence; as a verb, it has an object, the prepositional phrase "at the camera.")

Freshly *baked* cookies are delicious. ("Baked" is a past participle. As an adjective, it modifies the noun "cookies"; as a verb, it is modified by the adverb "Freshly.")

Infinitive phrases include the infinitive form of a verb and its object or modifier. They can be used as nouns, adjectives, or adverbs. Examples:

To express your ideas clearly is important. (In this sentence, "To express your ideas clearly" acts as the noun subject of the verb "is." Within the infinitive phrase, "To express" has an object, the noun "ideas," and is modified by the adverb "clearly.")

She is the player *to watch in the next game.* (Here, "to watch in the next game" acts as an adjective modifying the noun "player." Within the infinitive phrase, the prepositional phrase "in the next game" acts as an adverb modifying the infinitive "to watch.")

At noon, Brian went to the cafeteria *to buy himself some lunch.* (Here, the infinitive phrase "to buy himself some lunch" is used as an adverb modifying the verb "went." Within the infinitive phrase, the infinitive "to buy" has both a direct object, "lunch," and an indirect object, "himself.")

Gerund phrases include the gerund form of a verb and its object or modifier and are used as nouns. Examples:

The gentle pattering was as welcome as the rain that caused it. (The gerund phrase "The gentle pattering" acts as a noun because it is the subject of the verb "was." Within the gerund phrase, "gentle" is an adjective modifying the noun part of the gerund "pattering.")

I feared *sleeping in the dark.* (The gerund phrase is used as the object of the verb "feared." The gerund "sleeping" is modified by the adverb phrase "in the dark.")

Participial phrases include the participle form of a verb (ending in "ing") and its object or modifier. They are used as adjectives. Example:

Seeing the cat, the dog barked loudly. (The participial phrase "Seeing the cat" acts as an adjective modifying "dog," the noun subject of the sentence. Within the participial phrase, "cat" acts as an object of the verb part of the participle "Seeing.")

Conjunctions

A conjunction is a word that joins words or groups of words used in the same way. Common conjunctions are *and, but, or, so, for, when.* A conjunction can also be a group of words: *as though, except that, in order that, so that, not only...but also.*

Conjunctions can be divided into two classes: coordinating and subordinating.

CONJUNCTION TYPE	DESCRIPTION	EXAMPLES
coordinating	combines words or groups of words used in the same way (principal clauses)	and, but, nor, or, so I was hungry, *so* I ate the sandwich. He wasn't angry *or* sad. She lost the match, *but* she didn't feel disappointed.
subordinating	combines a main idea (principal clause) and a secondary or less important idea (subordinate clause)	although, if, provided that, whenever, because, unless, while, though *Whenever* she can't sleep, she reads a book.

Other common parts of speech include prepositions and interjections.

OTHER PARTS OF SPEECH	DESCRIPTION	EXAMPLES
preposition	relates a noun or pronoun to some other words in the sentence	at, behind, by, in, into, near, of, on, to, through, under, with
interjection	refers to a word or words that express emotion or thought, but are not essential to the sentence	alas, hey, oh dear, oops, ouch, well, wow

PARTS OF SENTENCES

Words need to be joined together to make sense. Joined together, they are called sentences. It is easy to recognize a sentence: it begins with a capital letter, it ends with a period (or other end punctuation), and it contains at least one verb.

Sentences come in a variety of forms. Some sentences are simple; some are complex. All sentences have a subject and a predicate. Sentences may also include such elements as an object, a subjective completion, prepositional and participial phrases, and principal and subordinate clauses.

SENTENCE PART	DESCRIPTION	EXAMPLES
subject	indicates who or what performs the action of the predicate	*Marie* was furious. Her *brother* spilled coffee all over her new dress.
predicate	indicates what is said about the subject; the key word in the predicate is the verb	Janice *is* tired. The stranger *knocked* on the door.
object	receives the action of a transitive verb	The banging of the door startled *the dog.*
subjective completion	describes the subject after a linking or copula verb	Ben is the *leader.* Megan feels *happy.*
prepositional phrase	begins with a preposition followed by a noun or pronoun (the object of the preposition) and any adjectives modifying that object	The dog *in the pound* is rabid.
prepositional adjective phrase	modifies a noun or pronoun	The members *of the union* want to negotiate. (The adjective phrase "of the union" modifies the noun "members.") None *of us* had money. (The adjective phrase "of us" modifies the pronoun "none.")

(continued)

SENTENCE PART	DESCRIPTION	EXAMPLES
prepositional adverb phrase	modifies a verb, adjective, or adverb	She asked *for water.* (The adverb phrase "for water" modifies the verb "asked.") Paul is good *at physics* but better *at geography.* Is the water warm enough *for swimming*? (The adverb phrase "for swimming" modifies the adverb "enough.")
principal clause (independent clause)	refers to the main idea and makes sense on its own	*She did not go out.*
subordinate clause (dependent clause)	refers to the secondary idea and does not make sense on its own	She did not go out *because she had homework to do.*

Types of Subordinate Clauses

Adjective clauses are subordinate clauses used to modify a noun or pronoun. Examples:

This is the book *that I wanted.* ("That I wanted" is an adjective clause modifying the noun "book.")

This dress, *which my mother bought,* is the prettiest one that I own. "Which my mother bought" is an adjective clause modifying "this dress." (Note: Clauses that provide additional rather than essential information to the sentence are set off by commas.)

Adverb clauses are subordinate clauses used to modify a verb, adjective, or adverb. Examples:

After she read the letter, she tore it. ("After she read the letter" is an adverb clause modifying the verb "tore.")

Her health is better *than it ever was.* ("Than it ever was" is an adverb clause modifying the adjective "better.")

Noun clauses are subordinate clauses used as a noun. Examples:

Kelly felt *that she had been cheated.* ("That she had been cheated" is a noun clause acting as the object of the verb "felt.")

Whoever baked this cake certainly likes raisins and walnuts. ("Whoever baked this cake" is a noun clause and the subject of the sentence.)

SENTENCE VARIETY

In order to create variety in your writing, you need to know about different sentence types and orders.

SENTENCE VARIETY	DESCRIPTION	EXAMPLES
Type of Sentence by Purpose:		
assertive	makes statements	The prime minister is addressing the country today.
interrogative	asks questions	Who took my pen?
imperative	makes commands	Watch out!
exclamatory	expresses emphatic or emotional utterances	Oh, be quiet!
Type of Sentence Structure:		
simple	has one principal clause with a subject and predicate	My mother is the best cook.
compound	has two or more principal clauses, which need connecting words	Mei Lin felt sad, but Suk Ying was happy to be leaving.
complex	has one principal clause and one or more subordinate clauses, which need a connecting word to relate the subordinate clause(s) to the principal clause	I was late because I missed the appointment and had to wait an hour before the doctor was free.

(continued)

(continued)

SENTENCE VARIETY	DESCRIPTION	EXAMPLES
compound-complex	contains two principal clauses and at least one subordinate clause. This is the most unwieldy and difficult sentence structure to use correctly. However, the ability to combine ideas and subordinate some of the ideas is a skill that demonstrates a sophisticated control of language and ideas, and it allows for subtle and precise emphasis on certain ideas in a piece of writing.	When Daniel left he locked the door, but he forgot to turn off the lights. ("He locked the door" and "he forgot to turn off the lights" are both principal clauses; "When Daniel left" is a subordinate clause.)
SENTENCE ORDER		
natural	places the subject before the predicate	The rabbit hopped away.
inverted	places the predicate before the subject	Behind the social persona lurked an evil mind.
split	places part of the predicate before the subject (or between the subject and the verb) for emphasis or effect	Tony, when he learned the news, was disappointed.

SENTENCE STRUCTURES

Using Parallel Structures

Parallel structure (the same grammatical structure for all items that have the same function) is used in speeches, poetry, and other forms of writing for rhetorical effect. The repetition of words and phrasing reinforces parallelism and balance, emphasizing ideas and creating a persuasive case for each.

In instructions or manuals, parallel structure may be used to help the reader understand and follow a series of directions. In reports, parallel structure may be used for clarity when creating headings. Example:

Report: How a Designer Creates an Effective Layout

HEADINGS USING NOUNS	HEADINGS USING THE PARTICIPLE FORM OF THE VERB
Titles	Choosing Titles
Fonts	Varying Fonts
White Space	Creating White Space
Graphics	Using Graphics

In each case, the report writer has used parallel structure in the headings. All the headings have the same grammatical structure.

In a résumé, the writer might describe a particular volunteer position using action verbs. Example:

VOLUNTEER EXPERIENCE

Credit Island Retirement Home
Read to blind residents
Planned recreational activities
Watered plants
Arranged flowers
Recorded memoirs for residents'
  anthology

Using Sentence Structures to Show Relationships Between Ideas

Compound Sentences

If two ideas are of equal importance in a sentence, a compound sentence structure should be used. The connecting words are like a fulcrum on a teeter-totter when two people of equal weight are sitting on either side.

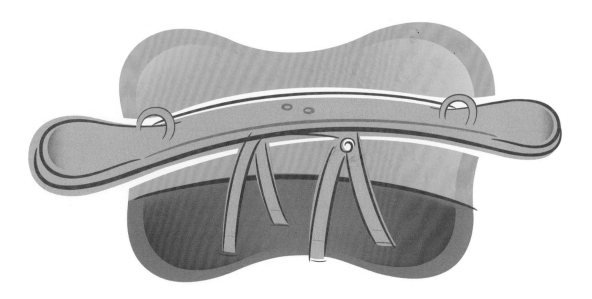

Example: Lee went skiing and broke his leg.

Both ideas carry the same weight. They are both important in the sentence.

Complex Sentences

If one idea is more important than another idea in a sentence, a complex sentence should be used. The idea in the principle clause is more important than the one in the subordinate clause. If two people of significantly different weights sat on the ends of a teeter-totter, the heavier person would weigh down the teeter-totter.

Example: Although Lee went skiing, he hated the cold and the wet.

The main idea is that Lee hated the cold and wet. The idea that he went skiing is not as important as his strong feelings against the weather.

SENTENCE ERRORS

Writers often make errors. The following table lists some common sentence errors and shows how they can be corrected.

SENTENCE ERROR	DESCRIPTION	EXAMPLES	HOW TO FIX IT
fragment	a group of words, punctuated as a sentence that lacks either a subject or a complete verb	Desperately running to catch the bus.	Maya was desperately running to catch the bus.
run-on	too many complete sentences or thoughts joined together as a single sentence	I got a lot of work done today I finished the reading and I went to the library and I started my assignment but I didn't fill in the chart because I couldn't find it.	I got a lot of work done today. I finished the reading, and I went to the library. I started my assignment, but I didn't fill in the chart because I couldn't find it.
comma splice	a comma is used to separate two main clauses or two complete thoughts that are not connected by a connecting word	I liked the story by Isaac Asimov, it deals with education in the future.	I liked the story by Isaac Asimov. It deals with education in the future.
subject-verb disagreement	the rule that singular subjects take singular verbs and plural subjects take plural verbs is broken	Jean and Maxine is starting a business. The distance between the two bus stops are two kilometres.	Jean and Maxine *are* starting a business. The distance between the two bus stops *is* two kilometres.
pronoun-antecedent disagreement	pronouns do not agree with their antecedents in gender (masculine, feminine, or neuter), number (singular or plural), or person (first person, second person, or third person)	Everyone must do their part. One of the women had lost their job.	Everyone must do *his or her* part. One of the women had lost *her* job.

LANGUAGE AND STYLE

Tone and Purpose

Language will change with the purpose and audience of your writing. The language you choose for a piece of writing helps create the tone or attitude, also known as voice, in your written work. Your language can range from very formal to informal.

The table below shows the characteristics of three levels of language: formal, moderate, and informal.

LEVELS OF LANGUAGE	FORMAL	MODERATE	INFORMAL
Vocabulary	• longer, less common words • few colloquialisms, popular phrases • little slang • few or no contractions • avoids the use of the pronouns *you* and *I*	• long and short words • more popular language • some contractions • occasional use of the pronouns *you* and *I*	• shorter, simpler, everyday words • some slang, more popular words and phrases • contractions • frequent use of the pronouns *you* and *I*
Sentence and Paragraph Structure	• longer and more complex sentences and paragraphs	• combination of simple, compound, and complex sentences; average-length sentences and paragraphs	• shorter, simpler sentences and paragraphs
Tone	• academic and impersonal, often instructional	• varies, depending on purpose and audience	• conversational and casual—sounds like everyday speech

Depending on the purpose of your work, you may choose the form and the level of language that is most suitable. The following table shows some forms, their purposes, and the appropriate level of language used.

FORMS OF WRITING	PURPOSE	LEVEL OF LANGUAGE
Personal Writing: • diaries • journals • logs • lists • letters/notes	• reflect on activities, events, or experiences • record personal thoughts • communicate to self, and others	• informal; short, simple, everyday words • may use colloquial language or slang • may use contractions • may use pronouns *I* and *you* • shorter and simpler sentences and paragraphs; unity and coherence may not always be present
Imaginative Writing: • autobiographies • letters • lyrics • monologues • poetry • scripts • stories	• amuse, entertain, evoke emotions, and provoke thought and reflection • self-expression • communicate personal ideas and feelings with others	• may range from informal to formal, depending on the tone the writer wants to achieve • verbs are generally more vivid and vigorous (less use of the verb *to be*) • nouns are more concrete and specific • the number and variety of modifiers (adjectives and adverbs) increases • figures of speech and other literary devices may be used
Informational and Academic Writing: • analyses • biographies • business letters • charts • editorials • essays • instructions	• record and report observations, research, and analysis • interpret information, sometimes using graphics	• may range from informal to formal depending on the purpose and audience • sentences and paragraphs are

(continued)

(continued)

FORMS OF WRITING	PURPOSE	LEVEL OF LANGUAGE
Informational and Academic Writing: • lab reports • news articles • plans • reports • reviews • summaries • surveys • textbooks • travelogues	• describe how to assemble or create • summarize information • inform • argue and persuade	generally moderate in complexity • some subject-specific language, but mostly familiar vocabulary • some of this writing may be in point form

Levels of Language

Slang is very informal (and often quickly outmoded) vocabulary and language patterns used by particular groups or in special informal contexts. It is usually not appropriate to use slang in formal written work, but it is often used in fiction to show character and create mood.

A **colloquialism** is also an informal, conversational expression that is often inappropriate to use in formal written work. Many dictionaries will tell you whether an expression is considered slang or colloquial.

Jargon is specialized vocabulary used by a profession, trade, or group. It must be used carefully in oral and written work because it can all too easily obscure meaning or mislead or exclude non-specialists.

Good writing uses simple, clear language—called Plain Language Style (see below)—and avoids the use of slang, colloquialisms, and jargon.

Dialect is a local version of a language, with its own vocabulary and sentence structure.

We use **Standard Canadian English** in our schools. This is the oral and written English used by a broad range of Canadian society (including government, medicine, law, science, business, and the media). Standard Canadian English follows accepted rules and practices of grammar, usage, spelling, and punctuation.

Language for Electronic Communication

With the increased use of e-mail and on-line chat has come a new level of language. The immediacy and speed of electronic communication, especially live chats, demands short bursts of thought, abbreviated spelling (e.g., "u" for "you"), and shorthand symbols known as "emoticons" to express emotions and reactions (e.g., :-) for "smile").

A writing style suitable for speedy electronic communication is not suitable for writing reports, essays, business letters, or reviews, which require more formality and development of thought. Writers need to be aware of their purpose and audience and have the flexibility to write in a variety of ways appropriate to the situation.

Style

Using Variety for Rhetorical Effect

In fiction and poetry, writers use different words that refer to the same person, place, or thing to explore shades of meaning. Similarly, in advertisements, poetry, and fiction, spelling and grammar are sometimes used incorrectly to catch the reader's interest or to make a point. For instance, "night" appears as "nite" on some signs and posters. In the excerpts from *The Straight Story*, dialogue that is grammatically incorrect is used to imitate the everyday speech of people, thus making the characters more realistic.

Plain Language Style

When to Use a Plain Language Style

Plain Language Style is used when the clear and accurate communication of information is the main goal of the writing. This is especially important in media such as reports, instructions, recipes, warnings, and policies.

In reports and instructions (e.g., see the instructions for "How to Make a Demo CD," pages 295–296), writers try to use the same word consistently to refer to the same person, place, or thing so that the reader does not become confused. The consistent use of the same word for the same thing in reports and instructions is one of the aspects of a Plain Language Style.

Some rules of using a Plain Language Style:

- Use words that your reader is likely to know. Keep technical words and jargon to a minimum. Provide a definition of any word the reader is not likely to be familiar with.
- Omit unnecessary words.
- Organize the information you are communicating in a logical manner.
- Use parallel structures in a list of instructions to make them easier to follow.
- Use a clear layout, icons, and illustrations to make your document clear and easy to read.

You can find out more about "Plain Language Style" by using the phrase to create an Internet search.

SPELLING

Good spelling is important to communicate ideas and information clearly and accurately. Incorrect spelling will distract your reader from the ideas you are expressing. In some cases, it may even confuse the reader about what is being referred to or said.

Following is a list of common sources of spelling errors in people's writing:

- differences in American and Canadian spelling (e.g., *color* is American; *colour* is Canadian)
- new and unfamiliar technical, business, and literary terms
- names that have different spellings (Mckay, MacKay, etc.)
- homophones (there, their, and they're)
- frequently confused words (accept, except)
- correct placement of apostrophes (do'nt for don't)

How to Improve Your Spelling*

One way to improve your spelling is to look for spelling patterns. There are three common sets of spelling patterns in English:

- **Sound Patterns:** Look for words, or parts of words, that sound alike: **sh**ip, **sh**ore, **sh**ampoo; br**ead**, h**ead**.

---

* Excerpted from Lynn Archer, Cathy Costello, and Debbie Harvey, *Reading and Writing for Success* (Toronto: Harcourt Brace & Company, Canada, 1997), pages 225–226.

- Meaning Patterns: Look for words that share similar or related meanings: **two**, **twice**, **twins**; **visible**, **vision**, **visual**. These are sometimes called word families.
- Function Patterns: Look for words that are the same part of speech. For example, you add "*ed*" to most verbs to make the past tense, no matter how the ending is pronounced: load**ed**, call**ed**, jump**ed**.

If there is a word that you always have trouble spelling, see if it fits a spelling pattern that will help you remember the correct spelling.

TECHNOLOGY TIP

Computer spell checkers have made it easier to pick up obvious spelling errors that may slip by when you proofread your writing. But a spell checker does not know when you have used **there** instead of **their**, or **right** instead of **write**.

Keep a list of the words you misspell. Look them up in a dictionary and write them correctly in an alphabetical list. Then use your list for reference when you are writing. If you put a check mark beside a word in your list each time you find that you have spelled it correctly without looking it up, you will have a record of how your spelling is improving.

Make up your own memory aids. Sentences, poems, or phrases about spelling patterns and odd ways of pronouncing words can help you remember how to spell difficult words. Try this memory aid:

"**i** before **e** except after **c** or when sounded like **a** as in **neighbour** and **weigh**."
Common exceptions: **neither**, **height**, **weird**, **either**, **seize**, **ancient**, **foreign**, **leisure**, **forfeit**.

If you are not sure how to spell a word, follow these steps.

1. Think about the way the word looks. Write it down the way you think it might be spelled. If it does not look right, try again.
2. Look up your best version of the word in the dictionary. Some sounds can be spelled in more than one way. If you cannot find a word in a dictionary, there may be a different way to spell one of the sounds in the word. See the following chart:

Sound (consonants)	Different Spellings
f	fish, physical
sk	skip, scare, school
s	soft, civil, psychology
sh	ship, chef
k	kick, candy, chemistry, quiche
r	roof, wrinkle
n	now, knife, gnome, pneumonia, mnemonic

Sound (vowels)	Different Spellings
a (as in cave)	trace, train, day
e (as in me)	these, team, see, key
o (as in go)	bone, coat, toe, low

3. When you have found the word in the dictionary, check the pronunciation and read the definitions. Knowing more about the word may help you remember it.
4. Practise spelling the word: look at it spelled correctly, and then cover the word and write it down. Check to see if you spelled it correctly.

PUNCTUATION

End stops such as the period (.), the question mark (?), and the exclamation mark (!) are used to end a sentence. Other punctuation marks (commas, dashes, and so on) perform different functions.

A comma (,) is used after an introductory word, phrase, or clause; to separate items in a list; after the introduction to direct speech; and to make the meaning of the sentence clear.

A dash (—) is used before or around a definition or clarification of a word, phrase, or idea. For example:

In a democracy, a premise of jurisprudence—the science or philosophy of law—is that everyone is equal before the law.

A colon (:) is used to introduce a list, an example, a quotation, or an explanation. The colon is also used in dramatic dialogue to indicate that a character begins speaking.

A semicolon (;) is used to join principal or independent clauses in a sentence. This use is sometimes referred to as a "soft" period. It is used in this way with some transitional words and phrases. Examples:

Patty likes to act; her sister gets stage fright. (The semicolon here replaces a period because the two ideas are very closely connected.)

Sonya felt angry; however, she soon calmed down. (There are several transitional words and phrases like "however" that usually require a semicolon when used.)

Alana, Eric, and Tina went shopping; Claude, Francine, and Alison stayed home. (The use of commas in the two principal clauses makes the semicolon useful for clarity.)

The semicolon is also used between items in a series when the items themselves contain commas. Example:

My painting class will meet on Monday, October 16; Tuesday, October 24; Monday, October 31; and Friday, November 1.

A hyphen (-) is used to combine words or parts of words to form an expression that needs to be seen as one word. Examples:

ex-ballplayer, run-on sentence

Quotation marks (" ") are used to indicate direct speech and the titles of short poems, stories, and articles. Direct speech requires quotation marks; indirect speech does not. Examples:

Direct: "Do you have a loonie?" Dad asked. "I need one for the parking meter."

Indirect: My dad asked me for a loonie for the parking meter.

Italics or <u>underlining</u> are used to indicate the titles of books, full-length plays, newspapers, and magazines. Example:

We read an article called "The Will to Win" in *The Toronto Star.*

Parentheses ( ) are used around a word, phrase, or idea that could be left out without destroying the sense of the writing. These words, phrases, or ideas are sometimes called "parenthetical." They are also used around references and notes inserted into a text. Examples:

My favourite season is spring (just before the heat sets in).

Many British novelists have dealt with the theme of social inequities (see Austen, Dickens).

Ellipsis dots (…) are used by writers to show that part of a quotation has been left out or to indicate a pause in dialogue. Examples:

The prime minister, who was in China at the time, said the report was nonsense.

with ellipses becomes

The prime minister...said the report was nonsense.

VAN HELSING: So...Three transfusions...And the effect?

SEWARD: She rallied after each. The color returned to her cheeks, but the next morning she would be pale and weak again. She complained of *bad dreams*. Ten days ago we found her in a stupor from which nothing could rouse her. She...died. (from *Dracula*, page 38)

Reading and Researching

READING STRATEGIES

Backgrounds of Readers and Writers Influence the Interpretation and Meaning of Texts

With some texts (e.g., a bus schedule), every reader will get the same information and understanding. With most texts, however, readers will not get exactly the same meaning because of differences in personal experiences and prior knowledge. For instance, a student who has had similar experiences of prejudice will understand "Memoirs of a Really Good Brown Girl" by Marilyn Dumont (page 228) in a different way than will a student without that experience. Readers' personal experiences and prior knowledge affect their understanding of and preferences for texts. Because class and group discussions of texts draw on a wide range of experience and knowledge, they can help to refine your comprehension of what you have read.

Similarly, each writer writes from his or her own personal experience and knowledge. Shakespeare could not write about airplanes because they were not part of his experience. An author's view of people, emotions, and values will reflect his or her own experience and knowledge. For this reason, it is always important that you read critically in order to evaluate the information and ideas in a text. In some cases, you may alter your ideas in light of new information in a text; in other cases, you may disagree with a text because it does not seem valid in light of your experience.

Using Prior Knowledge and Experiences

You can bring prior knowledge and experiences from your own life, from personal reading, and from your previous studies to help create both interest in and understanding of what you read. You might bring previous knowledge about

- the subject of the piece
- the issues in the piece
- the author
- the author's style and themes
- the setting (both time and place)
- subject-specific information (science, mathematics, history, geography, another language, technology, art, music, drama)
- vocabulary

Predicting

Predicting is a skill that makes you think ahead before you read. Whether or not your predictions are correct doesn't matter as much as the interaction you are having with the text. Once again, this kind of activity can increase your interest in what might, at first, seem to be a boring text.

Before Reading

- Use the title to predict the content of the text and its purpose.
- Look at any illustrations or graphical elements to establish possible events (fiction) or points the writer is making (non-fiction).
- Read a summary or cover blurb to predict what might happen, who is involved (fiction), or the writer's point of view (non-fiction).
- Use the vocabulary in the first few lines to predict the author's style, the time in which the piece is set, the difficulty of the piece (fiction and non-fiction), or the specific subject matter to be discussed (non-fiction).
- Read the first one or two paragraphs to predict the narrator's tone, the initial problem in the story, something about the characters (fiction), the audience for whom it was written (fiction and non-fiction), and the thesis or point of view (non-fiction).

During Reading

- Predict what decisions the characters will make (fiction).
- Forecast how the setting might change and the effect this could have on the action (fiction).
- Try to foresee changes in the direction of the plot (fiction).
- Predict what arguments or details a writer might use to support important points (non-fiction).

After Reading

Questioning can help you create and maintain interest in what you are reading. Wondering on paper (which is really what questions are) also helps you decide what you need and want to know. You can use questions at any time before, during, or after your reading to help you predict.

Questions are useful to help you recall, restate, reflect on, and analyze what you have read.

Questions to help you recall might include the 5Ws and 1H: who, what, where, when, why, and how (the same questions that are used for creating a news report).

To restate, try using one of the following to start your question:
How could I
- rephrase?
- reword?
- explain?
- illustrate?

To help you reflect, think about some of the following question starters:
- What would happen if…?
- What would I have done…?
- What else could have happened…?
- If I could choose one part that makes me feel…what would it be?
- Which character do I most identify with?
- I wonder if the writer…?
- How is this like…?

You could use some of the following questions to help you analyze:
- What evidence do I have that…?
- What conclusions can I draw…?
- What reasons are there for…?
- What can I infer from…?
- What arguments can I select…?
- How do I know that…?
- What proofs do I have that…?
- What do I need to find out about…?

READING FOR UNDERSTANDING

Understanding Strategies Used in Writing Prose and Poetry

Writers are often asked, "Did you mean to...?" Yes, writers do think of symbols, image patterns, metaphors, irony, contrasts, and a host of other things when they write. Some start their work with an image or symbol at the core; others bring it in as they draft and redraft their work.

For readers to draw out the greatest meaning from a text, it is important that they be aware of how writers use the tools of their trade and notice the writers' techniques and how their writing has been crafted.

Following are some tools that writers use for both prose (ordinary language or literary expression not marked by rhythm or rhyme) and poetry (a form of writing divided into lines and stanzas):

- Syntax is the structure of a sentence or the way a sentence is put together.
- An allusion is a reference to a well-known character, place, or story or to another literary work. For example, "The young player threw the baseball with Herculean strength." The allusion is to the great strength of the Greek hero Heracles. (Note: Hercules is the Roman name for Heracles.)
- An oxymoron juxtaposes (places side by side) two opposites to create a vivid image. Examples: "crashing silence," "loving hate," "bittersweet."
- Contrast is used to show how two or more characters, objects, or ideas are different.
- Hyperbole is a fancy name for exaggeration. It can be used seriously to create in a reader's mind a picture "larger than life," or it can be used comically to make a reader laugh.
- Understatement is the opposite of hyperbole. It shows something as much less important than it is. The effect of understatement is often irony or sarcasm.
- Three types of irony are verbal irony, dramatic irony, and situational irony. Verbal irony occurs when the real or intended meaning of a word, phrase, or sentence is different from what the speaker of that word, phrase, or sentence intended. A different kind of irony, occurring in fiction and drama, is dramatic irony. This takes place when the reader or viewer shares knowledge with the writer that a character does not have. The character will then say or do something that foreshadows what the audience knows will happen but that the character has no idea about. The character speaks more truly than he or she can possibly know. Situational irony occurs when what actually happens is different from what is expected by the reader or viewer.
- A symbol is an object, person, or action that is used to represent some other idea, principle, object, theme, or character. A country's flag is the symbol of

that country; each hockey team has its symbol on its jersey. Many names are symbolic. Many of those names are also allusions to famous people.

Reading Prose (Narrative, Drama)

Plot

Plot does not always drive a piece of fiction. A story may be character driven or thematically driven. No matter what drives a story, there is always some kind of plot, however thin.

Jack Hodgins, a famous Canadian novelist, identifies six things a plot-driven story must have:
- a main character (protagonist) we care about or are interested in
- knowledge that this character has a goal and a strong reason for achieving it
- obstacles that stand in the way of the character's goal
- a sense that each event is somehow the cause of the event that follows
- conflicts that intensify to the point where something has to break, which then causes the main character's life to turn a corner
- a resolution that allows the reader to feel the story has come to a satisfying end*

The ways writers approach story writing are as varied as the writers themselves. A writer may outline the whole story before it is written, or a writer may develop a story from an idea about a character, a theme, or a situation.

Setting versus Scene

The word setting is most often used by students to mean the place or time in which a story is set. Writers, however, often use the word to describe a writing technique, that is, "telling about" a story. The word scene means "showing" the story. Most writers agree that "showing" is more effective than "telling."

To "show" a story
- use description
- appeal to the five senses
- include dialogue or internal monologue
- include action

Example

The weather is perfect for shinny. Cold enough to make the ice hard and fast, but windless, so your face doesn't freeze solid. On a night like tonight, I can play for hours and feel like I'm on a beach in Florida.

---

* Jack Hodgins, "Specialized Tool: Fiction," in *A Passion for Narrative* (Toronto: McClelland & Stewart, 1993), page 126.

The Game is just starting. Everybody is dropping their sticks in a pile in the center of the ice, getting ready to choose teams. I don't bother going inside the shack beside the rink. I sit on the snowbank surrounding the rink boards, tear off my boots and put on my Bauer Supreme Custom Flo-Fit 4000 skates. They aren't top of the line like the pros use, but I've worked them in until they're so comfortable they feel like a part of my body—peeling leather, frayed ballistic nylon, chipped plastic feet. Only the blades look new, glossy and dangerous under the rink lights, honed to thumbnail narrowness by hundreds of sharpenings. (from "Johnny B," page 146)

ACTIVITIES

1. How does the example above "show" the story rather than "tell about" it?
2. Look back at one of the stories you have read from this anthology. Examine the plot of the story using Jack Hodgins's six aspects of plot. When you have looked at each point, decide whether the story you have examined is plot driven. What aspects of a plot-driven story does it have? What is it missing?

Characters

As readers, how do we learn about character?
- the narrator tells us
- the main character tells us herself or himself
- other characters tell us
- the character's own behaviour tells us

What makes one character different from another?
- appearance
- speech (level of language, dialect, speech rhythms, pet words)
- action (physical reactions to things; body language; facial expressions; habits like a cough, throat clearing, giggling, talking constantly when nervous)
- thoughts and opinions

ACTIVITY

Choose one story you have read from this anthology. Make a four-column chart with headings: "What the narrator tells us," "What the character tells us," "What other characters tell us," "What the character's behaviour tells us." Fill in the chart for one main character in the story. (Note: You may not be able to find something for every column. If you can't fill in every column, explain why not.)

Narrative Point of View

There are five main points of view a writer can use in fiction.

NARRATOR	DESCRIPTION	COMMENTS
first person involved	the narrator is the main character in the story	• a very personal type of narration that makes the reader feel involved with the character who is telling the story • the reader should be clear about the amount of time that has passed between the events and the telling of them • the reader should be able to decide whether the narrator has changed or developed since the events took place • the reader must decide over the course of the story whether the narrator is trustworthy (whether everything he or she is saying is the truth)

(continued)

NARRATOR	DESCRIPTION	COMMENTS
first person observer	the narrator may be a minor character in the story and have some role to play in the plot, or he or she may be observing the action from a distance, unknown to the characters in the story	• the writer creates some distance between the reader and the events by using this type of narrator • the reader must question whether this narrator is telling the truth about the events as he or she saw them or was involved in them
third person omniscient	the narrator knows all, sees all, and tells all	• this type of narrator is the most reliable since he or she can see inside and tell us, the readers, about every character's thoughts
third person limited	the narrator tells the story from the perspective of one or two main characters, but does not tell the thoughts of anyone else	• this narrator has the same effect as the first person narrator since we feel very close to the character whose story is being told • at times we feel as if we are inside that character's head, but the narrator can also step back from the character or action • this narrator is less reliable as a source of total information than the omniscient narrator
third person reporter	the narrator tells the facts, without going into any of the characters' heads	• the reader feels very distanced from this narrator as he or she cannot get into the heads of any of the characters and the reader can hear only what is being reported. This limits our understanding of motivations and emotions. • this narrator is only as reliable as his or her observations. Remember, he or she can't be in every place at one time, and so we might be missing some details.

Story Forms

There are many story forms. Some have become so popular that they are considered genres. Examples of genres are

- science fiction
- fantasy
- detective fiction

- romance
- historical fiction

Some other story forms include

- adventures
- parodies
- quests
- tall tales
- legends
- myths
- fairy tales

- fables
- parables
- sequels
- prequels
- humour
- choose-your-own-adventures

Reading Poetry

Types of Poetry

A narrative poem tells a story and may take the form of a ballad. It is generally organized in stanzas with a regular rhythm and rhyme scheme.

A lyric poem conveys strong emotions and impressions. Although words to songs are called lyrics, lyric poetry is not necessarily set to music.

Blank verse, used frequently by Shakespeare, has a regular metrical pattern and does not have a regular rhyme scheme.

A free-verse poem has very few restrictions and has no set rhyme, rhythm pattern, or line length.

A prose poem is written in prose but uses poetic devices like rhythm, images, and figures of speech to convey a single idea.

The haiku is a type of traditional Japanese poetry. The haiku
- consists of three unrhymed lines: five syllables in the first, seven syllables in the second, and five in the third
- has a final line that resonates with more than one level of meaning
- is often about nature and the passage of time

Concrete poetry is arranged in a shape that enhances or reflects the topic.

Imagistic poetry tends to be fairly short, focusing on one or two central images.

Haiku is a type of imagistic poetry (although it was invented long before the imagist writers popularized imagistic poetry).

Sound

Authors use many devices to manipulate the sounds of their writing. Here are some devices you should know. (Note: These are all elements of rhetoric; they are tools you can use not only when analyzing reading but also when you are doing your own writing.)

- Dialect, such as a patois, is an effective tool for characterization but, like accents, must be used sparingly to avoid stereotyping.
- Imitating an accent from a different culture can be an effective way to distinguish one character from another or to denote a feeling, mood, or culture. Be careful, though; overuse of an accent can make a character laughable or can perpetuate stereotypes.
- Alliteration is the repetition of the initial sound in a series of words (luscious lying lips). The words do not have to be in sequence but should be relatively close to each other to sustain an effect.
- An echo effect can be set up with the repetition of a word or series of words. If an entire stanza is repeated, it is called a refrain or chorus. (Watch that you don't overuse repetition; it can get tiresome and trite.)
- Rhyme is an obvious way of drawing attention to sound. End rhyme and internal rhyme are both effective ways to echo sounds.

Line Divisions

There are many reasons for dividing lines, other than rhythm and rhyme. When you are reading or writing a poem, consider these reasons for grouping words into a line:

- to contain a complete thought
- to set off a strong image
- to emphasize a word or phrase
- to complete a thought started in a previous line
- to use to advantage a grammatical structure (phrase or clause)
- to create irony or a reversal of expectation

Purposes of Acts and Scenes

The purposes of acts and/or scenes in dramas are to
- introduce the setting (time and place)
- introduce the conflict
- give background information
- further plot/build conflict
- add a plot twist
- resolve the conflict
- introduce character(s)
- build characters
- introduce a central image or symbol
- create a pattern of an image or symbol
- build an analogy
- introduce a turning point
- create a climax

Differences in Types of Drama

FILM	TELEVISION	STAGE	RADIO
Acts and Scenes			
Acts and scenes are rarely delineated or obvious; although changes of setting and cuts, and changes in the central character in a scene are clues.	Acts and scenes are similar to film, but they may correspond to commercial breaks.	Acts and scenes may be indicated by a scene change and intermission breaks.	Acts and scenes may be indicated by musical interlude or commercial.
Screenplay writers will include scenes and perhaps acts, but they are not obvious to the audience.		Shakespeare's plays did not originally have acts and scenes. These were written in later versions of his plays.	

(continued)

(continued)

FILM	TELEVISION	STAGE	RADIO
Plot			
Generally, actions of characters speak for themselves.	Generally, actions of characters speak for themselves.	May have a chorus or narrator to tell about the action in addition to the action of the characters.	May have a chorus or a narrator (who might be a character) to tell about the action. Actors take on more responsibility to tell the audience what is happening since the audience cannot see the action.
Actors			
Actors can range from "real" to animated and digitized. Actors get many opportunities to perfect their performances with multiple takes.	Actors can range from "real" to animated and digitized. Actors get many opportunities to perfect their performances with multiple takes.	Actors are real. They get one opportunity to make the performance the best it can be.	Actors are real. There may be many opportunities to perfect their performances.
Special Effects			
Unlimited special effects.	Unlimited special effects.	Limited special effects. The sophistication of the technical/computerized apparatus will vary.	Special effects limited to sound and dialogue.
Dialogue			
Dialogue is enhanced by action, facial expressions, use of voice, camera work, sound, location, and special effects.	Dialogue is enhanced by action, facial expressions, use of voice, camera work, sound, location, and special effects.	Dialogue is enhanced by movement of characters, facial expressions, use of voice, sound, and interaction with props and sets.	Dialogue is enhanced by sound, use of voice, and sound effects.

(continued)

(continued)

	FILM	TELEVISION	STAGE	RADIO
Setting, Time, and Place				
	Flexible setting. Time and space can be easily manipulated through camera shots and editing.	Flexible setting. Time and space can be easily manipulated through camera shots and editing.	Although there is some flexibility on the set, it is less than in a film or on television. Some plays have only one setting. Time and space are less easily manipulated.	Flexibility in setting, but the change in setting must be indicated through sound and dialogue. Time and space are easily manipulated as both are limited only by the imagination of the listener.
Imagination				
	Little room for imagination. The thinking is done for the viewer through picture and sound elements.	Little room for imagination. The thinking is done for the viewer through picture and sound elements.	More room for imagination as fewer concrete details are provided than on film or television. Fewer special effects and the limitations of the stage allow the viewer to imagine more.	Most room for imagination.

Methods of Development in Drama

A dramatist may use many devices to organize a play. Some of them are defined below.

Chronological Order

The events in the play take place in the order that they happened in time. The drama starts at the beginning and moves to the end.

Flashback

The drama moves from the present to the past, with flashbacks filling in what has happened prior to the present. Flashbacks can be the distant past or the recent past. The drama may move between the past and present several times throughout.

Transitions

Transitions take place between acts and scenes and allow the viewer to understand the relationship between characters, setting, and action. Transitions can take many forms:
• characters and setting remain the same between scenes
• the same character is mentioned by people in scenes that follow one another
• the location remains the same but the characters change between scenes
• the location changes but characters remain the same between scenes
• a dialogue is started in one scene and continued in another
• the topic of dialogue in one scene is picked up in the next scene

Sometimes a playwright may want to show dislocation between scenes and acts, and will introduce all new characters in a new location without plot ties. At some point these seemingly disjointed scenes will tie into the events in the drama and will make sense in the context.

Close Reading of a Text

The demand for the analytical reading of texts increases as you progress through your schooling. It is important that you know how to read a text closely in order to discover details in it that you might miss in a cursory reading.

When reading literature, one of the most important concepts to establish is the theme of the piece. A theme is different from a subject. The subject is what the piece is about; the theme is what the author is saying about the subject. There may be more than one theme in a piece of writing.

You can use sets of questions (heuristics) such as the following to help you establish the theme:
• What is the text about?
• What is the author saying about that subject?
or
• Who wins?
• Who loses?

- What is won?
- What is lost?
- Whose side is the author on?

Examining the answers to these questions may help you to discover the meanings and ideas the author is conveying through his or her work.

Creating a Theme Statement

When creating your theme statement, put your ideas about the theme in complete sentences. A single word can often capture the subject of a piece of writing, but not the theme. Try starting your sentence with "The author is saying that...."

ACTIVITY

As a class, read one drama, poem, or short story in this textbook. Using one of the sets of questions above, come to an understanding of what the author is saying to his or her audience. In a small group, discuss your ideas about the theme and come to a consensus. Present your theme (and any differing opinions) to the class. Discuss the similarities among the themes that various groups have identified.

Additional Tools for Close Reading

Some elements appear in all types of literature. Much like the elements of design in visual arts, these elements are tools writers use to emphasize or develop the theme. Following is a list of these elements.

Figures of speech — including simile, metaphor, alliteration, and onomatopoeia

Rhetoric — imagery, word choice, sentence structure, and diction

Structure — the way the writing is put together

Prose
- chapters
- divisions within chapters
- sequence of events

Poetry
- stanzas
- typographical layout
- line divisions
- groups of stanzas (sometimes called "chapters," "books," or simply given numbers)

Setting

Time
- era
- time of year
- time of day

Space
- real or fantasy world
- country or city
- dark or light
- enclosed or open space

Character
- what the character does and says about himself or herself and others
- what others say about him or her
- how the character reacts to others and to a variety of situations
- what the narrator says about him or her
- his or her physical features and psychological makeup
- what motivates him or her

Perspective — the type of narration (in novels, short stories, and poems) and the way we see the action (in drama)

You can create your own heuristic by asking yourself, How does any single design element or combination of design elements help emphasize or develop the theme?

BIAS

Detecting Bias

Unintentional bias is often present in written or media works. When you are reading or viewing these works, you can detect bias by watching for stereotypes, determining what interests are being served, and identifying the underlying assumptions and values behind the ideas and information presented.

In a small group, choose from this textbook a piece of literature that you have not previously studied. Answer the following questions:

- Which one or two elements are the most evident in the author's work?
- How do these elements develop and change throughout the work?
- What pattern(s), if any, emerge(s)?
- How does each of these elements support or emphasize the theme of the writer's work?

Write a thesis about the work based on the theme and the elements you have identified.

Avoiding Bias

To avoid bias in your own work

- use inclusive language (e.g., firefighter instead of fireman)
- use current terminology (e.g., Aboriginal peoples rather than Indians)
- avoid stereotypes
- do not be afraid to identify the assumptions or values you bring to the work

RESEARCH STRATEGIES: GENERATING IDEAS

In ancient times, speakers would be given a topic on which they would be expected to speak convincingly without notes. One useful technique they all knew was called the classical topoi. These were simple questions the speakers asked themselves to help them first to think about their topics and then to generate and organize their ideas. These questions are

- What is it?
- What is it like?
- What is it unlike?
- Where did it come from?
- What can come of it?
- What has been said about it?

Before you visit the library or surf the Internet, figure out what you already know about your subject and what you need to know. Using the classical topoi, you can generate even more questions to help you narrow and refine your research focus.

Choose one of the following topics and, using as many questions as you can think of, make a list of what you already know about the topic. Make another list of what you would like to find out. Organize your notes in a way that will be useful when you have to go back and reread them.

infatuation   perogies   Special Olympics   pow wow   Ottawa
generation gap   Scrabble   snowboarding   music videos

How to Find "Good" Information

     Find   **Assess**   **Toss**   **Record**

Find

- Make a list of things you want to find out.
- Start with very general resources, such as dictionaries, encyclopedias, atlases, indexes (any or all of these could be electronic sources, depending on your library). Then move to more specific sources, such as books, magazines, periodicals, newspapers, CD-ROMs, non-print resources (videotapes, audiotapes, artwork, and so on), and other electronic resources.
- If using books, skim tables of contents and indexes to find out whether your topic is listed.
- Scan articles for titles, illustrations, subtitles, and captions that include references to your topic.
- Skim read to establish the amount and usefulness of the available information.
- Save resources that look as if they will have the information you need.

Assess

- Look for information that is verified in several sources. Assessing is particularly important for information that comes from the Internet.
- Decide whether the information is useful, given the topic you've chosen.
- Ask yourself whether the resource presents a complete view or a one-sided view of your topic.
- Search out information that is clear, understandable, and at a level appropriate for you.
- Check whether the information is up-to-date.

Toss

- Discard information that can be found in only one source and for which you cannot find support anywhere else.
- If the author is not reliable, do not use his or her information. (Ask a librarian, teacher, or other experts if you don't know about the author's reliability.)
- Do not include anything that suggests racism, sexism, homophobia, or other forms of prejudice and bias.
- Discard information from old research or outdated sources.
- Do not include vague or overgeneralized information.
- Avoid personal opinion pieces that don't contain facts.

Record

- Record information in an organized way (on cue cards, in a special notebook, in an electronic file).
- Keep accurate records (including page numbers) of quotations you have used or ideas you have paraphrased.
- Put ideas in your own words to guarantee that you understand them, but be sure you document their source. *Do not plagiarize.*

RESEARCH USING THE INTERNET*

More and more students are turning to the Internet when doing research for their assignments, and more and more instructors are requiring such research when setting topics. However, research on the Internet is very different from traditional library research, and the differences can cause problems. The Internet is a tremendous resource, but it must be used carefully and critically.

---

* This section is adapted from Erindale College, University of Toronto. "Research Using the Internet." <http://www.erin.utoronto.ca/3lib/publ/evaluate/webevalu.htm> (15 Aug. 2001).

Anyone can put anything on a Web site — there is no review or screening process, and there are no agreed-upon standard ways of identifying subjects and creating cross-references. This is both the glory and the weakness of the Internet — it's either freedom or chaos, depending on your point of view, and it means that you have to pay close attention when doing research on-line. There are many solid academic resources available on the Internet, including hundreds of on-line journals and sites set up by universities and scholarly or scientific organizations. Using material from those sources is no problem; it's just like going to the library, only on-line. It's all the other stuff on the Internet that you have to be cautious about.

Here are a few basic guidelines to remember:
- **Don't rely exclusively on Internet resources.** Sometimes you will be able to do all of the research for your assignment only on the Internet, but usually your teachers will expect you to make use of both Internet and library resources. Cross-checking information from the Internet against information from the library is a good way to make sure that the Internet material is reliable and authoritative.
- **Narrow your research topic before logging on.** The Internet allows access to so much information that you can easily be overwhelmed. Before you start your search, think about what you're looking for, and if possible formulate some very specific questions to direct and limit your search.
- **Know your subject directories and search engines.** There are several high quality peer-reviewed subject directories containing links selected by subject experts. Bubl Ink/5:15, Infomine, InfoSurf, and Scout Report Signpost are good examples. These are excellent places to start your academic research on the Internet.

    Search engines differ considerably in how they work, how much of the Internet they search, and the kind of results you can expect to get from them. Learning what each search engine will do and how best to use it can help you avoid a lot of frustration and wasted time later. Because each one will find different things for you, it's a good idea to always use more than one search engine. The library at the University of California, Berkeley has an excellent site, How to Choose the Search Tools You Need, that covers similar information for different directories and search engines.
- **Keep a detailed record of sites you visit and the sites you use.** Doing research on the Internet inevitably means visiting some sites that are useful and many that are not. Keeping track is necessary so that you can revisit the useful ones later, and also put the required references in your paper. Don't just rely on your browser's History function, because it retains the Web addresses of all the sites you visit, good or bad, and the memory in the History file may be erased at the end of your computer session. It's better to

write down or bookmark the sites you've found useful, so that you'll have a permanent record.

- **Double-check all URLs that you put in your paper.** It's easy to make mistakes with complicated Internet addresses, and typos will make your references useless. To be safe, type them into the Location box of your browser and check that they take you to the correct site.

RESEARCH DOCUMENTATION

To avoid *plagiarism* (using someone else's work and claiming it as your own), it is necessary to cite the sources of information and ideas in your work.

If you summarize or paraphrase someone else's ideas in your writing, do not use quotation marks around the reference, but do indicate the source of the idea, either in a parenthetical note following the reference or in a footnote or endnote.

The Canadian Encyclopedia reports that Pierre Elliott Trudeau was born in...

If you use a direct quotation from someone else in your writing, integrate it into your text with an introductory sentence or phrase, and use quotation marks around the exact words of the person you are quoting. For example:

We see Calpurnia's fear for Caesar's safety when she says, "You shall not stir out of your house today." (II, ii, 9)

The Canadian Human Rights Act gives each of us "an equal opportunity to work and live without discrimination."

If you need to change the punctuation of the original to suit the context in your own writing, put square brackets around any changes you made. For example:

Caesar responds that any harm that might come his way will dissipate "when they shall see [t]he face of Caesar." (The square brackets show that the "t" on "the" was a capital in the original because it started a new line of poetry.)

In general, quotations should be kept short and relevant. If your quotation goes on for several sentences, it is best double indented (from both margins) and single spaced. For example:

The exact language of the report in this section reads:

> The mayor's taskforce found that residents wanted frequent and reliable garbage pickup at least twice a week in the summer and once in the winter. The additional summer service was requested due to concerns about odours and animals.

If there is a grammar or spelling error in the original, the word "sic" in square brackets indicates that you are aware of the error but have left the original intact. For example:

The witness was quoted as saying, "I never seen [sic] the man before."

At the end of a research report, provide your reader with all the sources you consulted in preparing the report. Sources are listed on a final page titled Bibliography, Works Cited, or References. Following is the format for a few typical sources. (Note: If you don't have a computer or are handwriting your work, underline all book titles and magazine or newspaper names that you might otherwise put in italics.)

Books

Author's last name, First name. *Title*. City of publication: Publisher,
    Year of publication.
Munsch, Robert N. *Munschwork 2: The Second Munsch Treasury*. Toronto: Annick Press Ltd., 1990.

Newspaper Articles

Author's last name, First name. "Title of article." *Name of Newspaper*
    Full date: Page(s) of article.
Oldenburg, Don. "Now Hear This." *The Toronto Star* 1 April 2001: E6.

Magazine Articles

Author's last name, First name. "Title of article." *Name of Magazine*
    Full date: Page(s) of article.
Bhattacharjee, Shikha. "Remembrances of Calcutta." *SAMAR* Fall/Winter 2000: 38.

Encyclopedia Entries

Author's last name, First name. "Title of entry." *Name of Encyclopedia*.
    Year of publication.
Randall, Mary. "The Ozone Layer." *New Encyclopaedia Britannica*. 2002.

The Internet

Author's last name, First name. "Title of Work." Year or full date (if applicable) of publication. <Internet address> (Date of retrieval).
Ledes, Richard. "Housing Construction: The Challenges of Building Interactive Narrative." 1996. <http://www.intelligent-agent.com/aug_building.html> (20 Aug. 2002).

or

Name of organization. "Title of Work." Year or full date (if applicable) of publication. <Internet address> (Date of retrieval).
Canadian Broadcast Standards Council. "Canada Deals with Media Violence." <http://www.cbsc.ca/english/canada.htm> (13 Oct. 2002).

Writing

MAKING AN OUTLINE

An outline helps you organize information before you write your first draft. It can help save you time, even though, at first, it may seem like an extra step. When you plan your writing with an outline, you will have a solid foundation for your composition.

Outline Headings

Use topics for your headings. Keep them short. If you are going to write a report on renting an apartment, your topic headings might look like this:

I.   Introduction
II.   Deciding what you want
III. Sharing or living alone
IV.   Researching neighbourhoods
V.   Using the want ads
VI.   Using other sources
VII. Interviewing the landlord
VIII. Signing a lease
IX.   Moving in
X.   Conclusion

GRAPHIC ORGANIZERS

To help you organize your information before you write, you can also use graphic organizers. Following are examples of the types of organizers that you can use.

Time Lines

Time lines help you to organize events in chronological order. For example, you might assemble a time line like the one in "Food Issues Through the Ages" (page 14).

Clustering

Clustering is a special form of representing-to-learn using a kind of graphic outlining. Put a key concept, term, or name in a circle at the centre of a page and then free-associate, jotting down all the words that occur to you in circles around the central idea in whatever pattern "seems right." Often, clustering reveals connections and relationships among pieces of information.

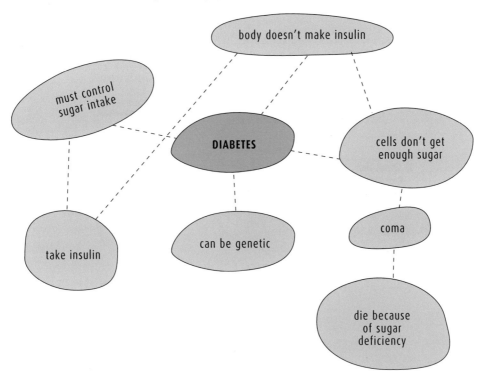

Drawing and Sketching

This is the graphic equivalent of freewriting. Create original drawings to illustrate ideas found in your reading, discussions, and inquiry.

Story Maps

Story maps are diagrams or maps of the events in a story or narrative, often done chronologically. They can apply both to literature and to historical narrative.

Pyramus and Thisbe

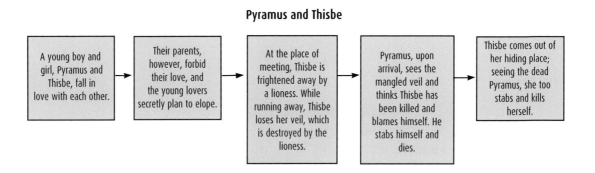

Venn Diagrams

When subjects—books, concepts, people, countries, and so on—have certain attributes that are *alike* and others that are *different*. You can use two or three interlocking circles to display the contrasts and similarities.

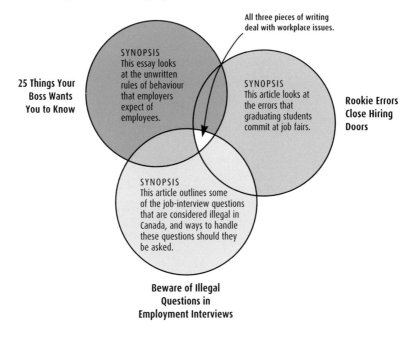

SUMMARIES

In today's busy world, many documents are prepared in two versions: a full, detailed version and a summary, a short version of the original document. A good summary captures the main ideas and supporting details of the original accurately and clearly in as few words as possible.

Following are some tips for writing a summary:
• Use a highlighter to identify key concepts in the original.
• Stick to the key concepts in your summary.
• Try to keep the structure, tone, and style of the original intact.
• Leave out unnecessary words, examples, and information.
• Use one general word to replace several specific words.
• Use one example to represent a series of examples.

Executive Summary

Sometimes people in business and in post-secondary education need to discover whether or not a report or research paper has the information they need to support an argument or a proposal. The executive summary is created to provide readers with the key points of the report or paper and may include some or all of the following:
• purpose of the research/report
• how the information was gathered
• brief summary of the findings
• conclusion

The executive summary also allows readers with little time to quickly read the essential information.

ACTIVITY

Having read the definition of both regular and executive summaries, explain how an executive summary differs from a regular summary in its purpose and its form.

ORGANIZING YOUR EXPOSITORY WRITING

Essays

The word essay comes from the French word essayer, which means "to try." In an essay, a writer takes a position or a point of view and presents that point of view with proofs to convince his or her audience.

Three main types of essays you will be writing include the personal essay, the primary source essay, and the full research essay. Below is a chart that shows the differences among them.

PERSONAL	PRIMARY SOURCE	FULL RESEARCH
Resources		
• a writer might use only her or his personal knowledge and experience; however, the writer may also use outside sources to support his or her thesis	• the writer uses only the primary source he or she is working from • if a writer is working on a thesis about "Dracula" (pp. 35–67), he or she would use only that play for his or her research	• the writer uses a variety of high-quality resources both print and electronic
Organization		
Introduction		
• may or may not contain a thesis • introduces the topic • "hooks" the reader into the essay • may include anecdotes, quotes, questions	• contains a thesis and reference to the main points that will be developed in the essay • longer essays have longer introductions often including background information	• contains a thesis and reference to the main points that will be developed in the essay • longer essays have longer introductions often including background information

(continued)

(continued)

PERSONAL	PRIMARY SOURCE	FULL RESEARCH
Body		
• contains main arguments supported by details, facts, statistics, etc. • may be ordered in a variety of ways: definition, chronology, problem/solution, cause/effect, classification, induction/deduction, process analysis	• contains main arguments supported by details, facts, statistics, etc. • may be ordered in a variety of ways: definition, chronology, problem/solution, cause/effect, classification, induction/deduction, process analysis	• contains main arguments supported by details, facts, statistics, etc. • may be ordered in a variety of ways: definition, chronology, problem/solution, cause/effect, classification, induction/deduction, process analysis
Conclusion		
• may contain thesis • may summarize points • may make a recommendation for action	• summarizes ideas • explains why the information in the essay is important for the reader to know	• summarizes ideas • explains why the information in the essay is important for the reader to know
Tone		
• may range from informal to formal	• generally formal • written from the point of of view of the writer without the use of "I" or "we" • could use very formal "one" but may sound stilted	• generally formal • written from the point of view of the writer without the use of "I" or "we" • could use very formal "one" but may sound stilted

Reports

Some reports, such as laboratory and science reports, require specific headings. If headings are not given, use the same format as an essay: introduction, body, conclusion.

Introductory Paragraph: This opening paragraph defines your topic and explains the purpose of the report.

Body: This central section develops the topic in a series of paragraphs, and it quotes experts or uses quotations from a variety of sources. Quotations must be accurate, and footnotes must be used to show where the quotations came from. Visuals such as charts are often used to explain the information.

Conclusion: This summarizes findings and refers back to the introduction.

Bibliography: The bibliography lists all the sources that were used. (See pages 378–379.)

METHODS OF DEVELOPMENT

Although this section reviews seven ways to develop individual paragraphs, reports, and essays, no matter which method you use, you must provide details. Details add credibility and substance to your writing and are essential for creating convincing expositions, narratives, and descriptions. Different types of paragraph development also increase the readability of your exposition.

Development by Deduction/Induction

Deductive reasoning is based on a premise (an assumption that is considered true because it can be proven). The major form of deductive reasoning follows this order:

Major premise: All humans need water to survive.
Minor premise: A teenager is a human.
Conclusion: Therefore, a teenager needs water to survive.

In inductive reasoning, facts or proofs are used to support a generalization. The major form of inductive reasoning follows this order:

Generalization: Brand X is an exceptional product.

Proofs:
- Many studies have been conducted that show that the product does what it claims to do.
- I have used the product for 10 years and have been satisfied with its performance.
- I have used other products that claim to do the same thing, but they have not performed as well.
- A survey was conducted of 10 000 people who compared Brand X with Brand Y. Of those people, 9998 thought Brand X was better.

With a partner, examine two essays in this textbook and determine whether they use deductive or inductive reasoning. Share your ideas with the class.

Process Analysis

Some writing done in college and in the workplace demands an analysis of the process of an activity or a procedure. When a writer uses process analysis to organize ideas, he or she works through the steps of a process, explaining how and why each step is carried out.

You might use process analysis in a report in which you analyze, for example, a group project you have completed. Below is an example of point-form notes that might have been taken in preparation for this report. The writer has used "How to Find Good Information" (page 375) to organize the report.

Find
- *our group decided what information we needed to do the project*
- *asked to go to the library — had a problem because there were too many people in the library*
- *2 of the group stayed and worked with computers*
- *2 of the group signed out books and went back to class*
- *all made notes*
- *used the bibliography pages we were given in class to make sure we listed the books and Web sites*
- *one person in the group didn't do any note-taking*
- *we had a meeting and talked with that person about the problem*
- *M said he couldn't find any information*

Assess
- *looked at the notes with group*
- *wasn't enough for the project*
- *wanted to kick M out of group*
- *said we'd meet at library tonight*
- *M can't come*

From these notes, you can see that not only is the writer talking about the process, he or she is also analyzing the process, evaluating the different stages. From the notes, the writer can then create his or her report—either individual or group.

Instructional manuals, cookbooks, and many science textbooks use process analysis. With a partner, locate one or two examples of these types of books. Choose a section that uses process analysis. Does the use of process analysis help or enhance the reader's understanding of the information? Share your books and observations with the class.

Development by Definition

Developing an essay by definition is the process of explaining what is meant by a term, an idea, or an object. When developing a definition, start with a general statement; for example, "A hero performs an act that puts the welfare of others before that of himself or herself."

With each new example, start a new paragraph.

ACTIVITY

Choose a character from one of the stories you have read in this textbook, and, using definition, write a paragraph to prove that he or she is one of the following: dependent, a victim, a hero, courageous, ignorant.

Development by Chronology

Chronology is the order in which a series of events takes place. A personal essay may focus on a series of events leading up to an incident such as a car accident that has been preceded by several near misses. A news report may discuss the incidents leading up to an important event, such as decreases in budgets and reductions in staff resulting in an increased health risk for workers.

Caution: Using a chronological approach when writing about literature may lead to retelling the story instead of examining the various literary aspects of the story.

ACTIVITY

For one of the stories or novel excerpts in this textbook, write a newspaper report in which at least one paragraph is developed by using chrono-logical order.

Development by Problem/Solution

Many writers use problem/solution as a method of organizing. This type of organization is particularly effective when writing a persuasive essay about a problem that may have a solution (e.g., a shortage of summer jobs for students, young children finding inappropriate sites on the Internet, violence on television).

As with cause and effect, the problem is posed (see below), its history or background is discussed, and a solution is proposed. Several solutions can be offered, but each should be accompanied by an explanation of its benefits and drawbacks.

When offering possible solutions, a writer must mention a solution's negative aspects because readers will often have already considered what the writer is proposing and will know the strengths and weaknesses of the arguments beforehand. The writer loses credibility if he or she does not acknowledge these weaknesses. It is up to the writer, then, to prove that the strengths far outnumber the drawbacks.

ACTIVITY

With a partner, research and discuss the pros and cons of genetically modified foods. Choose one of the major problems related to this issue (e.g., people not understanding the benefits of these new foods, businesses not appearing to care about the long-term effects these foods might have). Write a persuasive essay on the problem and the solutions you have found.

Development by Cause and Effect

Discussions of cause and effect are concerned with the reasons why something happens. Questions to ask about cause and effect include

- What has caused it?
- Where has it come from?
- Where is it going?
- What will happen to it?
- What is it used for?
- How does it fit into the larger scheme of things?
- What would happen if it didn't exist?
- Why does it exist?
- Could it be changed?

When organizing cause-and-effect paragraphs, you can either

- start with a cause and show or try to predict its effect (e.g., If handgun ownership is not regulated, more handgun-related deaths will occur.)

   or

- start with an effect and try to explain its cause (e.g., Fewer secondary schools offer classes in auto mechanics because of the expense of the program.)

Remember: The fact that one event follows another does not necessarily mean that the first event is the cause of the second. Examples:

I wore my red socks when I won my first tennis match.

Wearing those red socks did not necessarily cause my win.

I wrote two exams with the same pen and got over 80 percent on both exams.

Using that pen did not cause my success.

ACTIVITIES

Read the following paragraph.

Aerobic exercise improves the capacity of your body tissues to extract oxygen from red blood cells, transport it to the inside of the cells, and use it for energy production. Although your red blood cells are always saturated with more oxygen than your body requires at any given moment, the ability of the tissues to pick up this oxygen can vary greatly from one person to the next. An aerobically fit person picks up oxygen from the bloodstream about 25 percent more efficiently than someone who is unfit. And the more oxygen your tissues can pick up, the less stressful it is for your heart to deliver adequate quantities of oxygen to your tissues. (from Barry Simon and James Meschino, *The Winning Weigh: Seven Steps to Healthier Living*)

1. List the cause and effect in this paragraph.
2. With a partner, create a list of five other causes and effects. Individually, choose one and write a short paragraph showing the relationship of the two events.

Development by Classification

Classification is used to show how something fits into a category or how it differs from a category. Some questions you might ask yourself are

- What other things are like it?

- What kinds of it are there?
- What is it part of?
- What goes along with it?
- How does it differ from others like it?
- What connects it to all the other things in the category?

If developing a paragraph or essay using classification
- Be sure you have an adequate and accurate definition of the category.
- Ask yourself why it is important to look at the issue or idea as part of a category.
- Include both similarities to and differences from the category to create more interest.
- Make sure there is a point to considering your subject as part of a category.
- If the category is a literary genre, research that genre for accurate information.

ACTIVITIES

1. a) Work with a partner. For each of the following subjects, list 20 items that could be included in that category.
   - volunteer work
   - insects
   - world conflicts
   - Canadian literature
   - professional sports

   b) Break each of the lists you've made into subcategories, creating a subtitle for each.
2. Examine your categories and subcategories. Create a topic sentence for an expository paragraph you could write on one of these categories or subcategories.

TRANSITIONS

In order for your writing to flow logically from one sentence to the next sentence —one point to the following point—you need to include transitions. Transitions connect your ideas, helping your readers to follow the logic of your argument. Transitions can be used between sentences in the same paragraph or as a logical bridge between paragraphs. They come in many forms.

Repetition

Repetition of a word or phrase from one sentence or paragraph to the next will signal a continuation of the same topic. Example:

While Grade 12 students are often very good at writing short stories, they sometimes find *writing essays* difficult. *Essay writing* challenges students' ability to think and write logically.

Remember, however, that overusing this technique can result in a repetitive or monotonous voice.

Substitution (Pronouns, Synonyms)

Substituting a pronoun or a synonym for the subject in your previous sentence connects the two ideas. Example:

Doing science is more exciting than just *reading* about science. *The former* shows students how scientific principles work; *the latter* tells students how the scientific principles work.

Be sure the antecedent of the substituted word(s) is clear. (For example: "Students like doing science, not just reading about science. *It* is exciting." The second sentence is unclear. What does the word "it" refer to: the doing or the reading?)

Transitional Words or Connectives

Transitional words or connectives show relationships between ideas. Here are examples of relationships and the kinds of transitional words that are used in each:

- to add ideas: *and, moreover, furthermore, further, similarly, too, likewise, again, in the same way, besides*
- to show cause and effect: *accordingly, therefore, as a result, consequently, hence, thus, for this reason, it follows that*
- to compare: *similarly, likewise*
- to contrast or introduce a limiting thought: *but, nevertheless, otherwise, on the other hand, conversely, on the contrary, however, yet, still*
- to introduce examples: *for example, for instance, such as*
- to indicate order: *next, in the second place, to begin with, first* (not *firstly*), *second, in conclusion*
- to show a relationship of time: *then, now, currently, at present, somewhat later, thereupon, thereafter, eventually, at the same time, meanwhile, presently (soon)*
- to show a spatial relationship: *to the right, in the distance, straight ahead, at the left, above, below, in between*

Example:

Many students love to study French; *furthermore*, they understand the value of learning to speak and write a second language.

REVISING YOUR WRITING

Whether revising your own or someone else's work, practise using a simple memory device, or mnemonic: RADS. RADS will help you decide whether or not your ideas are complete and in the best possible order. Use RADS to help you examine your entire composition, including each paragraph and sentence.

R Reorder

❏ Are my ideas in the best possible order?

❏ Have I considered alternative orders (chronological, sequential, climactic)?

❏ Does one idea flow logically into another?

❏ Are there any ideas out of place?

A Add

❏ Do I have enough ideas to make my work convincing?

❏ Do I need to add more details?

❏ Do I need to add some more examples?

❏ Have I used enough description, including adjectives, adverbs, and interesting verbs?

❏ Will my audience be convinced?

❏ Could I add some imagery, similes, or metaphors to create a stronger effect?

❏ Could I add some transition words to help link my ideas?

D Delete

❏ Do I have any ideas that don't support my main idea?

❏ Do I have ideas that don't add to the point I am trying to make?

❏ Do I have some ideas that clutter up my work?

❏ Is my language too flowery or descriptive for the tone I want to set?

❏ Have I repeated ideas?

S Substitute

❏ Are there other ideas I have gathered that might be better than the ones I have?

❏ Do I have one weak idea? Should I continue my research to find a better one?

❏ Are there words that don't capture the feeling I want to create?

❏ Should I use a thesaurus to help find better words?

❏ Are there some linking words that are not working?

❏ Have I used the appropriate language for my audience?

Proofreading and Editing Your Writing

Good ideas are hard to read if a writer has not proofread and edited his or her work. Check the following before writing your final draft.

Sources

- ❏ Have I used quotation marks around any words or phrases I have borrowed from other sources?
- ❏ Have I named the source of those words?
- ❏ When I have used ideas from other sources, have I given credit to that author?
- ❏ Have I created a bibliography of all my sources?

Grammar and Usage

- ❏ Have I checked and corrected any sentence fragments, comma splices, and run-on sentences? (See pages 347–348.)
- ❏ Have I included a variety of sentence types (simple, complex, compound), sentence lengths, and sentence orders (natural, inverted, split)? (See pages 344–347.)
- ❏ Do all my verb tenses agree?
- ❏ Do all my pronouns agree with their antecedents in number and gender?
- ❏ Have I used a consistent point of view (not switching from *I* to *you* or *one*)?
- ❏ If I have used a thesaurus, have I checked the dictionary to be sure the connotation of my new word is correct?
- ❏ Have I written in the active voice and used the passive only when appropriate? (See page 339.)
- ❏ Have I written sensitively, avoiding racist, sexist, and homophobic language?

Spelling

- ❏ Have I checked my work for unintended errors, such as leaving out letters?
- ❏ Have I checked all my homophones, such as *their/there/they're; know/no?*
- ❏ Have I checked all my plurals?
- ❏ Have I used apostrophes correctly?
- ❏ Have I capitalized the correct words (especially in dialogue, scripts, and poetry)?
- ❏ Have I checked the spelling of specialized vocabulary?
- ❏ Have I used a dictionary or a spell-check program on my word processor?

Punctuation

❏ Have I used end stops and capitalization appropriately and correctly?
❏ Have I used commas, dashes, and colons appropriately and correctly?
❏ Have I used quotation marks for direct speech and quotations from sources?

ACTION PLANS

You should keep a log on how you can improve the work you are doing in each of these areas: reading, writing, oral communication, and media literacy.

These action plans do not need teacher input to make them valid, although after each returned assignment, you should enter your teacher's remarks. Your action plan should be updated every time you receive feedback from either your teacher or peers.

Below is one way to set up an action plan for writing. You may use this template to create action plans for your work in reading, writing, oral communication, and media studies.

Writing Skills Action Plan

Assignment: Sept. 12: in-class editing of analytic essay based on Rooney's essay

Feedback	Action Plan
• Increase the depth of my argument by more references to the story.	• Take more time to write the essay.
• Reorder points — start with the third paragraph, followed by the second.	• Reread the essay for logic.
• Show that there is another viable point of view, but that isn't pertinent to my position.	• Do some more outside reading to familiarize myself with what others have said about the issue.

Oral Communication Skills

PURPOSE OF GROUP WORK

In college and in the workplace, you will be required to work in groups with classmates or colleagues. Teachers and employers expect you to use the group skills that you have been developing throughout your education.

GROUP WORK IS USED FOR:

- extending the ideas of others
- adding information to current knowledge and experience
- exploring possibilities

- drawing conclusions
- assessing ideas and arguments
- understanding and using business or technical concepts

AS A GROUP MEMBER, YOU SHOULD BE ABLE TO:

- contribute to and lead discussions within the group
- suggest directions for the group to move
- solve problems
- connect ideas, information, and arguments to prior knowledge

- summarize ideas and information
- record ideas and information
- report on the process and the product of the group
- fulfill a variety of roles in the group, moving between roles as necessary

ORAL PRESENTATIONS

Just as it is important to listen while someone else speaks, whether in a formal or an informal group setting, so it is important that you speak well to convey your message effectively. As a student, you require good speaking skills for various oral activities, including

- debates
- demonstrations
- dramatic and/or choral readings
- group work
- independent study presentations
- performances—role plays, readings, storytelling
- symposia

- interviews
- meetings
- reports
- seminars
- speeches
- video presentations
- sales talks

A formal oral presentation is one of the most common activities that you will be involved in. Here are some suggestions to help you plan an effective oral presentation.

Planning Your Oral Presentation*

Know Your Purpose

What do you want to accomplish with your oral presentation?
- to inform
- to persuade
- to motivate
- to entertain

Know Your Audience

- their age groups
- their interests in your topic
- the reason they are listening to your presentation

Planning Your Content

Know Your Subject

- read—books, articles, electronic information
- talk—personal or phone interviews, discussions
- view—movies, documentaries, interviews
- record—on tape, on cue cards, in your notebook, on your computer
- organize

---

* Based on S. Carlile Clark and Dana V. Hensley, *38 Basic Speech Experiences* (Topeka, Kansas: Clark Publishing, 1999).

- discard information that is not adding to your presentation
- add information where you find you have gaps
- replace weak information with stronger points
- order your information in the most logical order, starting with a hook to get your audience interested and ending with a powerful conclusion
- think of ways to get your audience involved

Some General Tips for Presenting

- get the audience's attention
- make them want to hear what you have to say
- make it clear to the audience why the material is important to them
- if appropriate, involve your audience
- ask your audience to take some action (further study, a comparison with something they already know)
- appeal to their emotions and needs (love, wealth, self-preservation, nationalism, loyalty, religions, political beliefs, desire for recognition, desire for adventure)
- be sincere and enthusiastic
- use humour (words, anecdotes, body language, gestures, props) where appropriate
- incorporate visuals such as board work, posters, overheads, slides, electronic devices, presentation software

Avoiding Stress in Formal Presentations

Being nervous before speaking in public is not uncommon. The extra rush of adrenaline you get when you're nervous can work in your favour to keep your speaking energized and exciting.

Signs of Stage Fright

Those of you who have "stage fright" *may* experience one or more of these symptoms of stress:

- your breathing becomes faster
- your heart rate speeds up
- you perspire more
- you feel fidgety or as if you have butterflies in your stomach
- you feel nauseated or faint
- your mouth gets dry
- your knees feel weak

Getting Past Stage Fright

You can help to calm your nerves and get past your stage fright by doing the following things:

- *Speak in front of an audience as often as possible:* Start with small groups and move up to increasingly larger audiences.
- *Pick a topic that interests you:* If you are participating in a debate or making a presentation, choose ideas that will hold your attention. If you're not enthusiastic about your topic, you will not feel confident because you might feel the audience will not be interested either.
- *Prepare:* Most students who get stage fright are afraid they won't do a good job. Research thoroughly, create an outline, write out your oral presentation or speech, and try it out, first in front of the mirror or into a tape recorder, then on your family or friends. Say the speech as many times as possible. Of course, this means you can't be writing your speech the night before it is due! While you are rehearsing, visualize yourself in the room where you will be presenting, in front of your audience.
- *Memorize:* If you have to memorize your presentation, use mnemonics to help you remember the order of your points or key words in your presentation. Mnemonics are memory aids. One useful mnemonic is creating an acronym, a word in which each of the letters stands for another word. You probably already know some acronyms to help you remember. MRS VANDERTRAMP is an acronym for the irregular verbs in French. BEDMAS is an acronym for the order of operations in mathematics.
- *Think of the audience:* The speech isn't about you — it's about them! You are trying to persuade, entertain, or inform *other* people, not yourself. Focus on them. Some experts suggest imagining your audience in their underwear!
- *Move:* Facial expressions and some hand gestures keep you relaxed and use up some of that excess energy you feel. You can physically move around if it is appropriate to the type of oral presentation you are giving.
- *Wear appropriate clothing:* You don't want to be worried about the length of your skirt or the need for a tie. Think about your audience. Think about the formality of the occasion. Decide on your clothing ahead of time. Wear it while you are practising your speech at home.

ORAL REPORTS

Oral reports are similar to written reports. They are organized by subtopic. When presenting an oral report, it is a good idea to have visuals to accompany your presentation.

Overheads

Here are a few reminders about using overheads.
- Plan ahead. Do not ask your teacher for an overhead projector at the last minute.
- Be sure you have the right kind of markers for overheads.
- The font size on your overheads should be large enough for the audience to see. (Do not expect regular-sized type from a word-processed document on an overhead to be read by anyone but you.)
- If you are hand writing an overhead, be sure to leave margins on all sides so that your handwriting will fit the image size.
- Colour provides interesting contrasts, if you can manage it.
- Be sure there are no errors on your overhead.

Posters

You can create eye-catching posters on Bristol board or chart paper to accompany your report.
- Put only a small amount of information on each poster.
- Make the poster's lettering large enough to be seen from the back of the room.
- Plan your layout so that you have large borders and so that your lettering is uniform in size and fits into the space on the page.
- Check all the text to ensure that there are no errors on your poster.

Blackboard

As old-fashioned as the blackboard may seem, you can use it as effectively as you can any other visual aid.
- Prepare your board work in advance, if possible.
- Write in large letters that can be seen from the back of the room.
- Use colours, if they are available.
- Print, rather than write.
- Check all the text to ensure that there are no errors in your board work.

Computer-Assisted Presentations

When planning a computer-assisted presentation, remember to
- Plan each of your slides to provide you with enough information to speak about the topic, but not all the information that you will convey to your audience.
- Add some graphics, if appropriate.
- Use a background that does not interfere with the information on your screen.
- Check all the text to ensure that there are no errors on your slides.

DEBATING

Debate Procedure

The Chair introduces the topic, introduces the speakers, explains the time limits, and announces the judges' decisions. It is up to the Chair to maintain the tone of the debate.

The First Speaker for the Affirmative   4 minutes

Give a brief introduction to the topic, define any necessary terms, note any points agreed on by all debaters, note any issues to be excluded, state clearly and briefly all the affirmative points, and prove the point you have chosen to deal with.

The First Speaker for the Negative   3 minutes

State agreements and disagreements with the interpretation of the topic by the first speaker, state the arguments for the negative side, indicate who will prove each argument, refute briefly the arguments of the first speaker, and present your own arguments.

The Second Speaker for the Affirmative   3 minutes

Refute the arguments of the first speaker for the negative and state your own arguments and proof.

The Second Speaker for the Negative   4 minutes

Refute any arguments for the affirmative as yet unanswered, state your own arguments and proof, and sum up the arguments for the negative side.

The First Speaker for the Affirmative   1 minute

Do not introduce any new arguments; refute arguments already made and sum up the affirmative arguments.

Debate Terminology

refute: to prove a statement or argument to be wrong or false
point of order: a question to the Chair regarding proper following of rules
point of personal privilege: a question to the Chair regarding a misrepresentation of your argument

THE SALES TALK*

A sales talk is a speech in which you try to persuade an audience to buy a product or service from you.

To sell any product you must be
• completely familiar with the product
• confident in the product and in yourself

Materials that you should have at the sales talk:
• order forms
• pens and pencils
• receipts
• business cards

Presenting the Sales Talk

Introduction

• Introduce yourself by name (have business cards available).
• Give some background information:
    • about you (your education, qualifications, history with the company, or other companies like it)
    • about your company (how long it's been in business, its reputation for quality, how it stands behind its products)

Demonstration

• Explain the purpose of your product.
• Show its advantages, special features, improvements over other similar products or over previous models, dependability, beauty, ease of use, and economy.
• Be clear and concise—too much information just overwhelms people.
• Mention any endorsements you have—what others (especially if they have a relationship to your audience) have said about the product.
• Tailor what you say to your audience and their needs.

---

* Based on S. Carlile Clark and Dana V. Hensley, *38 Basic Speech Experiences* (Topeka, Kansas: Clark Publishing, Inc., 1999), pages 74–76.

How to Order

- where and when they can purchase what you are selling
- cost (make sure you say that taxes and shipping are extra or included, depending on how you have figured out the price)
- how they can pay (cash, personal cheque, certified cheque, debit card, credit card)
- whether there are special prices if ordered on the spot
- when they can expect delivery or whether they can take it with them from the sales meeting

Question Period

- Answer openly and honestly.
- If by chance you don't know the answer to a question, be sure to get that person's number and phone him or her immediately with the answer.

Conclusion

- Thank the audience for their attention.
- Express an interest in speaking to them individually and tell them where you will be located for further questions.

Special Tips

Here are some tips you may want to keep in mind for the sales talk:
- Look good; dress smartly. Remember this is the business world.
- Smile.
- Be confident, but avoid slipping into sounding boastful.
- Keep your language simple, descriptive, and vivid but avoid jargon and technical terms.
- Use visuals whenever possible — these could be on overhead, poster board, handouts, with a computer program or, if small enough, the product itself.
- Do not criticize competitors. Praise their products but show yours is better.

ACTIVITY

Think about a product you really know about and believe in. Create a business presentation for that product. You can fabricate the background information if you cannot find information on the company that manufactures the product.

RUBRIC

You will often be involved in evaluating the work of your classmates. You may use the following rubric to help you create an evaluation form. Note that although this rubric is specific to oral presentation, it may be adapted to evaluate other types of activities, such as writing and media works.

ORAL PRESENTATION — DEBATES, SPEECHES, SALES TALKS, AND SYMPOSIUMS

ACHIEVEMENT CATEGORIES	BELOW 49% (R)	50–59% (LEVEL 1)	60–69% (LEVEL 2)	70–79% (LEVEL 3)	80–100% (LEVEL 4)
KNOWLEDGE • understanding the relationship between ideas	• ideas and purpose are unclear	• ideas and purpose are recognizable but not clearly developed	• ideas and purpose are recognizable but simple	• ideas and purpose are clear and straightforward	• ideas and purpose are clear, focused, and well developed
THINKING • critical and creative thinking skills	• facts, ideas, and events, if present, are unrelated	• facts, ideas, events, and details are limited and may have some inaccuracies	• facts, ideas, events, and details are accurate but may not be connected	• facts, ideas, events, and details are plentiful and coherently connected	• facts, ideas, events, and details are accurate and clearly connected
COMMUNICATION • logical organization	• minimal logic in plan and sequence	• weak plan and sequence	• adequate plan and sequence	• logical plan and sequence	• thoughtful and logical plan and sequence
APPLICATION • oral conventions and techniques	• oral skills do not engage the audience	• uses oral skills with limited effectiveness to engage the audience	• uses oral skills with some effectiveness to engage the audience	• uses oral skills effectively and with confidence to engage the audience	• uses oral skills creatively and effectively to engage the audience

TELEPHONE COMMUNICATION

Whether you are using the telephone to request information or to have an interview, you need to be clear. You may have a "face that launched a thousand ships," but even the beauty of Helen of Troy would not be able to influence an unseen person on the other end of the telephone. No one can see your facial expressions or your gestures. Content is the key to clear and effective telephone communication.

Asking for Information

Before Calling

1. Write down the kinds of information you want to know.
2. Record the names and telephone numbers of the places where you think you can get the information.
3. Have paper and pencil ready to record information given to you.

On the Telephone

1. Identify yourself (name, where you are calling from).
2. Explain the reason for your call.
3. Ask for the person most likely to be able to help you.
4. Once you are speaking to the most appropriate person, make sure you take down his or her name.
5. Identify yourself again, and thank the person for taking time for your questions.
6. Ask your questions. Record the answers.
7. If necessary, ask the person to repeat any information you might have missed.
8. If the person cannot help you, ask if he or she knows who might be able to help.
9. Thank the person once again.

Interviewing Over the Telephone

Sometimes you will call about a job and suddenly find that you are being interviewed over the telephone.

Before Calling

1. Be prepared with your résumé.
2. Think about what questions you might be asked in an interview and prepare answers for them.

On the Telephone

1. Explain why you are calling, and ask for the correct person if a name has been given to you.
2. If you do not know whom to speak to, explain why you are calling and ask for the name of the appropriate person. Jot it down.
3. Ask to speak to that person.
4. Introduce yourself and explain why you are calling.
5. Ask any questions you have. (Hint: It is always easier to ask about pay and benefits over the telephone.)
6. If the person starts to ask you questions, ask if this is an interview or if another interview will be scheduled. If the person says it is an interview, put your best interviewing skills into play.
7. If you are not being interviewed, and if you are still interested in the job, ask if there will be interviews and request an appointment.
8. Thank the person by name and assure him or her that you will be at the appointed place at the appointed time. (Hint: If you do not know the location of the interview, get directions.)

ACTIVITY

In a group of three, set up a situation in which information is needed or a job interview is being conducted on the telephone. Two members of the group can role-play the situation while the third person takes notes on how well the person seeking the information or the job is doing.

Transmitting Information

In the workplace, you may be required to use the telephone to transmit information to a supplier or to a client. Accuracy is the key to successful transmission. Here are some pointers:
- Write down the information you have to transmit.
- Be sure the information is accurate; double check with your employer.
- Find out who the person is that you are to speak to (contact).
- Find out if you can leave the information with an administrative assistant.

- If you are leaving your information with someone other than your contact, be sure to ask for the name of the person with whom you have left the information.
- When you are leaving the information, make sure you leave your name and the name of the person you are calling for.
- Relay the information slowly and clearly.
- Ask if details need to be repeated.
- Take any message that needs to be given in return.
- Thank the person for his or her time.
- Record in a log the date and time you called and to whom you spoke.
- E-mail a message to your employer with the date and time the call was made, the name of the person to whom you spoke, and any message given in return (this leaves a "paper" trail that could be traced if something untoward happens in the future).

The Business of Life

INTRODUCTION TO COMMUNICATION

In college and in the workplace, you will be expected to communicate with teachers, colleagues, employers, older people, younger people, and people from different backgrounds. Your communication will be spoken, written, and non-verbal, including body language and facial expressions. You need to be effective at all types of communication in order to be successful.

Why is good communication important? It is good for

- building better relationships
- sharing what we know, think, and feel with others
- learning from others
- resolving problems, disagreements, and complaints in a way that will do us the most good
- avoiding misunderstandings
- responding to others without hurting them or getting hurt
- showing ourselves in the best light possible and bringing out the best in others

Good communication is

direct: Mean what you say; say what you mean. Don't "drop hints" or "beat around the bush."

specific: Give all the information needed to get your message across.

tactful: Be polite. Think about the other person's feelings and rights before you speak. You want to avoid saying things accidentally that will hurt them or harm you. Remember, once words are out of your mouth or down on paper, they can't be taken back.*

---

* Herta A. Murphy, Charles E. Peck, and Sheila A. O'Neill, *Effective Business Communications* (Toronto: McGraw-Hill Ryerson Ltd., 1983), page 89.

clear: Use details to describe how you feel.

honest: Say what you really feel. Make sure what you say matches the facts.

LETTERS

As you get older and your experiences broaden, especially in the workplace, you will probably need to write a letter to a person you don't know or a business you have not dealt with before. You may be sending this letter by post or by e-mail. Whichever method you choose, the content and message of the letter will be the same, though the format of the e-mail may be less formal.

Business Letter Format

A letter with a full block format
- is justified left,
- has no indentations for paragraphs, and
- has one line space between paragraphs.

In an open punctuation format, there are no punctuation marks at the end of any line that is above the message (e.g., return addresses, dates) or below the message (e.g., the closing). There is an exception to the rule: if the last word in the line is an abbreviation (e.g., Blvd.), it should be punctuated with a period.

Wording

The most important part of writing a letter is your choice of words. Even if you are angry at a person or company, you must choose words that are calm and non-threatening. Yelling—in person, on the phone, or in a letter or e-mail—is rarely effective.

Often, when you write a business letter, you want something: information, a refund, a job, a sale. Sometimes, however, a business letter is what we call a "goodwill" letter—a letter of thanks or acknowledgement. Whatever your reason for writing, the basic principles of letter writing are the same.
- Be clear.
- Be concise.
- Provide details.
- Tell the truth.
- Be courteous.

Reference Letters

Whether you are asking for a letter of reference or writing one, you should keep the following in mind:

- The letter must be addressed to a specific person or position.
- Use a "To whom it may concern" salutation only if you do not know the specific person to whom you should address the letter. Try to find out the name of the person you are writing to.
- The introductory paragraph should state what position is being applied for (a brief description will suffice). It should also include the reason you are writing the letter.
- The body of the letter should summarize the applicant's skills.
- The content should be specific, pointing out specific examples of the applicant's skills.
- The conclusion should include a general comment about the applicant (i.e., would you hire the person?) and your contact information.

RÉSUMÉS

Résumés should be
- limited to one page (if possible)
- complete
- accurate
- a good representation of who you are
- an accurate summary of what you can do

Sample Résumé

Roberta Smith
120 Victoria Avenue West
Winnipeg, MB
R3Z 6H6
(H) (204) 555-0295
(B) (204) 555-2879
roberta_smith@young.ca

Skills

Management	• Shift manager for fast-food restaurant in charge of five employees per shift
Cash	• Familiar with both ABC Model 5200 and XYZ Model 2280
Customer Service	• Served food in fast-food restaurant • Worked as a telemarketer selling storm windows
Group Leadership	• In charge of organizing the equipment and food for a group of 15-year-olds on a school-sponsored canoe trip
Teaching	• Responsible for creating Sunday School lessons and teaching ten 5-year-olds each Sunday

Work Experience

June 2000 – present
Shift Manager
Eat at Joe's Hamburger Emporium
Supervisor: Viveen Mallon
Phone: (204) 555-0345

January 1999 – present
Sunday School Teacher
Advent United Church
Supervisor: Maleen Worth
Phone: (204) 555-4782

. . . 1

Name
Address

Home phone
Business phone
E-mail address

In the skills section, highlight the types of skills you have acquired through the work you have done or the experiences you have had in school or in your community.

In this section, include your work history.

(continued)

(continued)

2/

March 1999 – May 2000
Telemarketer
Freezies Storm Windows
Supervisor: Elgin Felcone
Phone: (204) 555-3967

Education   1998
Graduated from Terry Fox Collegiate,
Brandon, Manitoba

Extracurricular   Soccer; choir; skateboarding
Interests

References on Request

If you wish to list your references, you can. (This section is optional.)

The **skills résumé** is the most popular and currently thought to be the most effective way to present yourself on paper. Remember to tailor your résumé to suit the requirements of each potential job or employer. If possible, keep your résumé in an electronic file, where you can revise it easily and at short notice.

The skills résumé has several distinct parts, as shown in the sample on these past two pages.

Applying for a Promotion

A résumé is a flexible document. It should be customized to the job you are applying for, emphasizing relevant skills or experiences. Similarly, if you are applying for a promotion, your résumé should be written to show that you have the skills and the experiences to succeed in a higher-level job. All of the skills you list on your résumé have to show that you are the most suitable candidate.

If you are applying for a promotion in your current workplace, you will likely have to compete with other people from within your workplace as well as others from outside. Be sure to emphasize what you have done for the company already. Demonstrate your understanding of how the company works. Think of things you will bring to the company in the future. If you have a great idea for a change in the way things are done, it could be an opportunity to bring it up, especially if the new position would allow you to have some influence on how things work.

Also be ready to work with the successful candidate, if it is not you. Often, employers will ask the following question in the interview: "If you don't get this position, but one of your colleagues does, how will you deal with that?" Have an answer ready.

If you are applying for a promotion outside your current workplace, be sure you have researched the company and the position. Be prepared to reflect your research in your covering letter, your résumé, and your interview.

If you do not get the job, ask for a follow-up interview. Find out why you didn't get the position. This information could help you improve your résumé, covering letter, or interview for the future.

Building a Work Portfolio

Many of you have created portfolios, collections of your best work. Similarly, you should create a professional work portfolio. Such a portfolio can be kept in a folder, a binder, or in an actual portfolio. When you are starting to work, your résumé may not reflect all of the things you have actually done. A portfolio can help fill those gaps. A portfolio that you would use for a job early in your work career could include

- your résumé
- letters of recommendation
- brochures describing places or programs for which you have volunteered

- a few of your best school assignments
- pictures of artwork or the products of a technological project that you created
- any certificates you've earned inside or outside school
- awards
- thank-you letters

As you move forward in your career, your portfolio will change, reflecting your more recent job and life experiences and achievements.

PERFORMANCE REVIEWS

School is not the only place where your performances are judged. In almost every job you have, your supervisor will want to know how well you are doing. If you become the supervisor, you will want to know how the people who work for *you* are doing *their* jobs.

Some performance reviews will determine whether or not you will get a raise. Other performance reviews will determine whether you will become a permanent worker at the company. Still others will determine whether or not you will keep your job. The following performance review guidelines are based on the skills that employers have identified as the most important to success in the workplace. They are also a good indicator of how well you work within your classes.

You can use these guidelines to evaluate your own performance on a project or a group activity, or to evaluate the performance of your peers. Your teacher may use these guidelines to evaluate your performance in class, in group work, or on a project.

Performance Review Guidelines

When you are completing your performance review, consider some of the following points. Not all of them will be appropriate for each project you undertake, and you may wish to add some things that you feel are important.

Communication Skills

- listening to understand and learn from others
- reading, understanding what you read, and using written materials (e.g., graphs, charts, visual material) to complete the job successfully
- writing clearly and effectively in the required format so that others can understand what you have written

- voicing opinions clearly without overpowering others
- applying your understanding of the sender/receiver communications model

Thinking Skills

- thinking critically, acting logically
- evaluating situations, using good judgement, and applying effective decision-making skills when faced with a problem
- using technology and information systems effectively
- applying any specialized knowledge that you have to the project

Learning Skills

- learning independently
- learning something new from the project
- improving on skills learned during previous projects

Attitudes and Behaviours

- completing the project with confidence
- feeling a sense of self-esteem from working through the process and completing the project
- having honesty and integrity
- having a positive attitude toward personal learning and growth
- persisting with the project in order to complete it

Responsibility

- setting goals and priorities and working toward them
- planning and managing time effectively
- being accountable for your actions

Adaptability

- recognizing and respecting the differences and talents of others
- identifying and suggesting new ideas and ways to get the job done—displaying creativity

Working With Others

- understanding the project and working as a group member toward completing it successfully
- understanding the dynamics of the group and working effectively within it
- planning and making decisions with the group and taking responsibility for outcomes (both positive and negative)

- respecting the thoughts and opinions of others
- having a give-and-take attitude within the group to achieve results
- working as a group member when appropriate and as an individual within the group when appropriate
- taking various roles in the group (leader, recorder, reporter, worker, decision maker) when appropriate

Sample Performance Review (Based on a Group Project)

I think that our "Communication Styles" performance was not half as good as it could or should have been.

We, as a group, did not really work well together. When creating our script there was a clash of ideas and some of the members did not quite understand what was required. These two things resulted in a lot of lost, valuable time. Our group should have listened when instructions were given, recognized the deadline, and planned and managed our time much more effectively. I personally did not work as well and as quickly as I can, due to a lot of talking and distractions. Although we had to rush the day before, we still got our script done, memorized and presented.

When creating our script there were many ideas, some that were similar and some that weren't. Everyone was trying to express ideas and opinions about what we should do and fortunately we listened to each other, compromised and combined ideas to create a finished product. I can honestly say that a couple of times I overpowered the group with strong comments and ideas that I thought were good (e.g., when brainstorming I wrote down many of my own situations and read them to my group); thankfully, they weren't mad or frustrated with me.

Our presentation group was different from many others. From the second day on, one of our members decided she was not going to attend class for the next couple of days. Although we were a group minus a member, we kept on going. On the last day we persisted with the script in order to get it completed for the next day's per-

formance. I feel that in this group, particularly, I found it hard to persist with the brainstorming and the starting of the project. But I have to say that we pulled it off pretty well with the help of sweet Tiffany! (Thanks.)

I did recognize the differences and talents of other people in my group and, yes, I respected them. I feel that we all did. Just by working with each other we could tell what each others' weaknesses and strengths were and we attempted to work around or with them.

When faced with a problem, we did evaluate the situation using good judgement. For example, when we found out we were to present the next day and our script was not even complete, we made the decision to work hard and meet with each other between different periods to practise and copy the script.

All members were accountable for their own actions. If one was not there, then they would suffer and we would go on. If group members did something wrong or did not practise or even copy down their lines until the last minute it was that person's fault and they were accountable for their own actions.

We did not clearly understand the dynamics of the groups but worked well within it. We had different personalities and work habits, which caused us to be less successful than we could have been. The group did not recognize the need to work harder.

By Tanny Hart

The Media

ANALYZING VISUAL AND MEDIA WORKS

Elements of Visual Production: Television, Video, Film*

People who make television programs, videos, films, and other visual productions must deal with two main things: picture elements (what the production looks like) and sound elements (how the production will sound).

Picture Elements

- original live-action or dramatized footage
- stock footage: archival footage or footage from other films
- interviews
- re-enactments
- still photos
- documents, titles, headlines, cartoons, other graphics
- blue screen (for special effects)
- special effects

Sound Elements

- sound recorded at the same time as visuals (on-the-street interviews, at a live concert)
- sound recorded on its own and dubbed onto the film or tape
- voice-over: voices or commentary recorded separately from filmed visuals and then dubbed onto the film or tape

---

* Information based on Arlene Moscovitch, *Constructing Reality: Exploring Issues in Documentary* (Montreal: National Film Board of Canada, 1993).

- narration: scripted voice-over spoken by narrator, filmmaker, or participant
- sound effects
- music
- silence
- ambient noise (background noise)

Camera Terms

As you make storyboards (see pages 425–426) and prepare for filming, you will find the following camera terms helpful. These terms should help you to be very specific, so that others can understand exactly what you mean.

Camera Angle

- high: sometimes called the bird's-eye view. The camera is placed well above normal eye level. Viewers feel that they are looking down on the subject and many consequently feel superior to it, or the subject may give the impression of being overwhelmed and/or alone.
- low: sometimes called the worm's-eye view. The camera is placed below eye level. Viewers feel that they are looking up at the subject. This may make the viewers feel that the subject is more powerful than they are or that the subject is in control.

Camera Movement

- tilt up: the camera moves upward (from low angle to high)
- tilt down: the camera moves downward (from high angle to low)
- pan: the camera moves from right to left or left to right across an imagined horizon or panorama
- dolly: the camera moves in toward (dolly in) or out from (dolly out) the subject in a straight line. In this case, the camera is mounted on a tripod with wheels or on a makeshift dolly. The camera can be hand-held.
- truck: the camera moves right or left in a straight line and is usually mounted
- zoom in or out: the camera lens focuses in on or back from the subject (from wide angle to close-up and vice versa)

Camera Distance

- extreme close-up: a detailed shot of a very small area
- medium close-up: a shot that might include the head and shoulders of the subject
- close-up: a shot taken a short distance from the subject

- medium shot: a shot midway between a close-up and a long shot
- medium long shot: a shot that would have the subject in full view
- long shot: a shot in which the camera is placed far away from the subject
- extreme long shot: a shot that would have the subject in the distant background

HOW MEDIA MANIPULATE THE EMOTIONS AND THOUGHTS OF THE VIEWER/LISTENER

	TV	FILM	PRINT	RADIO
PICTURES				
Camera Angles Worm's Eye View • the camera looks up at people or objects • the object in front of the camera looks bigger • can be used to produce a threatening effect (e.g., a negative character or object seems larger than life, overwhelming, and frightening) • if the camera is seeing the world from the point of view of a character, that character may be feeling inadequate	✓	✓	✓	
Bird's Eye View • the camera looks down on people or objects • it makes the person or object seem smaller • if the camera is seeing the world from the point of view of a character, that character may be feeling powerful or invincible • if the camera is looking down on a character, the character may be feeling small or powerless	✓	✓	✓	
Eye Level • the most neutral camera angle • may imply that the character is feeling all right about himself or herself or the situation • if two characters are talking to each other and each is shown at eye level, this may suggest that they are being straightforward	✓	✓	✓	
CAMERA DISTANCE				
Close-ups (Extreme, Medium, Regular) • exclude details of the background • can show reactions of the character, influencing the audience's response to the character • can be used for suspense (e.g., an enemy is sneaking up on the character; the character is about to walk into a bad situation)	✓	✓	✓	

(continued)

420 UNIT 4 · THE REFERENCE SHELF

(continued)

	TV	FILM	PRINT	RADIO

CAMERA DISTANCE

Medium and Long Shots   ✓ ✓ ✓
- include more of the body and the background
- capture actions
- used when things happening around the character
  are important

CUTS/EDITING

If a filmmaker includes everything that happened in
"real time," it would make a film very long. The
filmmaker must then decide what is important for the
audience to see with cuts and editing, thus manipulating
how we see and interpret events.

Delaying Time   ✓ ✓
- filmmaker makes an event, which takes a short time in
  real time, take a long time, adding to suspense and
  lengthening an emotion
- slow motion is one technique to delay time
- alternative technique is to use cut-aways: many shots
  between the beginning and end of an action causing
  the action to take much longer than it would in real time

Example: Below is how a filmmaker might delay time for a
scene in which a man has to shoot a horse he doesn't
want to kill:

Camera Shot	Distance
1. finger on trigger	Extreme close-up
2. horse's head and neck	Close-up
3. man's face, chewing gum rapidly and staring at the horse, squinting	Medium close-up
4. finger on trigger as it starts to pull	Extreme close-up
5. reaction of man's two children secretly watching him	Close-up

In real time, pulling the trigger would take a split second.
In the film, this moment takes much longer, building
suspense and allowing the audience to feel what
the man and his children feel.

Speeding Up Time   ✓ ✓
- can capture the breathlessness of a scene
- generally done with cuts and edits that bring two
  moments in time closer together

(continued)

	TV	FILM	PRINT	RADIO
CONTENT OF SHOT	✓	✓	✓	

- who or what is in the shot
- relationship between people or objects in the shot
- dominant colours
- actions of the characters in the shot

	TV	FILM	PRINT	RADIO
LIGHTING	✓	✓	✓	

- creates mood (e.g., harsh lighting — everything is exposed; soft lighting — romantic, gentle, something hidden)
- the filmmaker can create a dramatic effect by using lighting that creates a mood and then shattering it with action that is the opposite of that mood

	TV	FILM	PRINT	RADIO
SETTING (WEATHER, TIME OF DAY, SEASON, URBAN/RURAL)	✓	✓	✓	

- mood, action, and characters may be reflected by the conditions or may contrast with the conditions
- can become a cliché (e.g., a funeral takes place in the middle of a rain storm; a dreadful event happens on a cold, dark, windy, and rainy night)

SOUND

	TV	FILM	PRINT	RADIO
Music • foreshadows events • complements events • contrasts with events	✓	✓		✓
Sound Effects/Ambient Noise • support the actions • sound effects that go against can foreshadow events or create dissonance (discomfort)	✓	✓		✓
Voice-Over • explains or comments on what is on the screen	✓	✓		
Silence • creates suspense or tension • provides a contrast to a noisy scene • foreshadows an event	✓	✓		✓

	TV	FILM	PRINT	RADIO
ACTORS/BROADCASTERS	✓	✓	✓	✓

- facial expressions
- body language
- tone of voice

MEDIA WORKS AND AUDIENCE

In the media, the audience is perhaps the most important factor that television program and movie creators have to keep in mind. Being able to draw a large audience means success. But how do the creators find out which programs or movies will be successful with audiences?

Measuring Television Audiences

In order to ensure that they carry programs that will attract a large audience, television networks have to find a way to measure the number of viewers who watch their programs. Neilsen Media Research is a company that provides television networks and program producers with an estimate of the number of viewers and a profile of the viewers (e.g., age group, gender). Using a sample population, Neilsen installs a meter on every television set in a participating household. The meter is connected to a central "black box," which receives the vital market information.

With such feedback, television networks and program producers can decide on what kinds of programs to carry or make. Popular programs will attract advertisers, who buy airtime to run their commercials and reach a large viewing audience. These advertising dollars provide television stations with a key source of revenue. Unpopular programs will not attract advertisers and, therefore, they will not attract television stations to air them. Such programs are usually cancelled.

What does this mean to how television programming is shaped? It means that makers of television programs will produce programs that reflect popular taste. For example, the popularity of reality shows has resulted in more of the same type of shows in each new television season.

Testing Movies

Before the release of a movie, some moviemakers are now using a test group to measure how a larger audience reacts to the movie. Should a negative reaction result, the release date of the movie might be delayed or parts of the movie changed or edited to suit the audience. In recent years, a few movies are known to have changed their endings using audience reactions.

CREATING VISUALS AND MEDIA WORKS: POSTERS, STORYBOARDS, COLLAGES*

Just as writers gather information, organize it, and create drafts before producing their final version, visual artists plan each and every thing they produce, whether it is drawn by hand or created on a computer. If you are creating a visual product that requires drawing or putting together pictures and type, here are a few helpful hints.

Research

- If you need some background images, look through books and magazines to get ideas for these images.
- Photocopy the pages you like. (Never cut up a book that isn't your own!)
- Take photographs yourself.
- If you want to draw animals, go to the zoo or a pet store or rent a video with animals in it.

Create Thumbnail Sketches

- Thumbnail sketches are just for composition purposes. Do them quickly inside a frame that is the same proportion as the final work. They shouldn't contain any detail.
- Produce as many thumbnail sketches as possible so you will be sure to include your best and most creative ideas (which sometimes come later rather than sooner).
- Experiment with colour and value.
- Avoid tracing your research pictures. Try to change the angle or view of your subject. (Remember, most pictures and drawings, including cartoons, are the property of the artist.)

Choose a Focus

What do you want to put in the foreground, middle ground, and background of your visual presentation?

Create Rough Sketches

- Once you have your subject matter and your thumbnail sketches, you need to put them all together in a final rough layout, larger than the thumbnails but still in proportion to the final.

---

* Information based on Mark Thurman, *How to Plan Your Drawings* (Markham: Pembroke Publishers, 1992).

- Decide on your emphasis. Will it be the characters, the setting, an object, or the action?
- If you need more room, draw outside the border and then draw a new border, ensuring proportions are maintained.
- Ensure you create a definite centre of interest and subordinate the less important information to the special emphasis you've created.

Final Copy

- When you're pleased with your design, create a final, full-sized version of your masterpiece.

Creating a Storyboard

A storyboard is a series of drawings, often composed of thumbnail sketches, that show the camera shots in a video or film, along with the audio for each shot.

When you create a storyboard, you should provide all the necessary instructions for sound/audio and video. Make sure you have considered all six types of information listed below. However, keep in mind that certain types of information may not apply to every shot.

Draw the frames or shots as if you are looking through the lens of a camera. The artwork for the frames can range from stick figures to full-colour pictures. Each frame should represent a separate shot in your video or film.

Sample Storyboard

1. description of shot contents: person approaching mall entrance
2. camera distance: long shot
3. camera angle: eye level
4. camera movement: pan left as subject enters doorway
5. audio: traffic and footsteps
6. shot duration in seconds: five seconds

1. person carrying shopping bag
2. medium shot
3. eye level
4. pan right as subject walks to bus stop
5. footsteps
6. two seconds

(continued)

(continued)

1. shopping bag
2. close up
3. eye level
4. (no movement)
5. (no audio)
6. three seconds

Creating a Collage

A **collage** is a collection of visual materials—photographs, pictures, words, and advertisements from magazines and newspapers, along with other visuals—that create a mood or show a theme.

Here are some suggestions you might want to think about as you plan your collage to help make it interesting and thought-provoking.

Create a Background With Depth

Try using a colour background that suits the mood of the collage. You might collect material from magazines for visual backgrounds such as city skylines, farmlands and countrysides, or typical urban scenes. Placing your other visuals against such backgrounds will help you to create some depth.

Create a Variety of Emotions

Try to create a variety of emotions by
- using visual parallels—things that are similar
- using contrasts—things that are different
- putting together things that might seem to be unrelated

Use Repeated Images

Some of the best collages work well because they focus on repeated images. For example, a collage on the theme of guilt can create a strong impact by including 100 pairs of eyes along with a few simple visuals and text.

Use Words in Different Ways

Because many collages include some words, you should try a variety of approaches, such as contrast or irony or the use of clichés. You might look for quotations in collections of quotations, poetry books, and advertisements. If you have access to a computer, you might input the text and print it out using different fonts and point sizes.

Work with a Partner

Often it helps to work with someone else so that both of you can look for interesting contrasts and ideas as you plan and create your collage.

LAYOUT OF A PAGE

Different kinds of writing have different requirements for presentation on a page. The setup of writing on a page for production is called the layout of the page.

A number of elements are available to you as you prepare an appropriate layout for your work, especially if you are using a computer. Consider the best and most appropriate use of the following when preparing the layout of a page.

- **White Space:** How much space do you want to leave blank? How much space do you want to leave between lines and paragraphs, and for margins?
- **Point Size:** How big do you want the print to be? Do you want to use print of different sizes for titles, headings, and captions?
- **Fonts:** What font will be easiest to read? Do you want to use a variety of fonts for emphasis? Do you want to **bold**, *italicize,* or underline any of the words in your document?
- **Boxes and Sidebars:** Will these special features help your reader to find information more easily?
- **Icons and Illustrations:** Will visual features assist your reader to understand the information better?

TIP

To get ideas for the layout of your work, look at professionally prepared and published documents similar to the one you are producing. Very different layouts are used for advertisements, résumés, reports, and poetry. Select one that will work best for your audience and the information you are presenting.

THE PITCH: HOW ADVERTISERS DRAW ATTENTION TO THEIR PRODUCTS*

Advertisers know we will pay attention to the unusual, interesting, and unexpected. There are several ways in which they grab our attention.

Appealing to Our Senses

Advertisers use some or all of the following elements to appeal to our senses.

- motion
- colour
- lighting
- sound
- music
- visuals
- special effects
- action

Appealing to Our Emotions

When appealing to our emotions, advertisers use associations with an emotional state, such as happiness or sadness.

Appealing to Our Intellect

Advertisers appeal to our "thinking side" through

- news
- claims
- advice
- questions
- demonstrations
- scientific evidence
- real-life stories or testimonials

Building Our Confidence

Advertisers gain our confidence by
- using brand names we know and trust
- using people we think we know and trust (e.g., movie stars, people dressed like doctors, dentists, researchers)
- using cartoon figures, animals, and other friendly figures
- using words associated with trust

Stimulating Our Desire

The products advertised generally make at least one of the following claims:
- They keep a good thing going.
- They help users to obtain something good.

---

* Adapted from Hugh Rank, *The Pitch* (Park Forest, Illinois: Counter-Propaganda Press, 1982).

- They help users to avoid a bad thing.
- They get rid of a bad thing.

Advertisers claim that their products will provide us with something. The following twelve product claims are the most common:

- the best
- the most
- the most effective
- the most beautiful
- the rarest
- the newest
- the most classic
- the most reliable
- the easiest or simplest
- the most practical
- the fastest
- the safest

In addition, advertisers often suggest "added value" as a result of purchasing their products. The following four categories are the most common added values:

- basic needs (food, health, security, money, sex, comfort, activity)
- fitting in (religious acceptance, scientific research, being popular, being elite, being normal)
- love and belonging
- growth (success, respect, creativity, curiosity)

ACTIVITY

In a small group, find an example of one print advertisement, one radio commercial, one television commercial, and one Internet advertisement. For each of them, determine which audience the advertisement is targeting. Using the information above, create a chart demonstrating how each advertisement makes its audience pay attention to it. Be prepared to present your advertisements and commercials and your analysis of each one to the class.

> Glossary

act: A main division of a drama. *Dracula* has three acts.

adaptation: In literary terms, it refers to a work that has been modified or altered. For example, *Dracula* is an adaptation of Bram Stoker's novel.

allusion: An indirect reference to a familiar figure, place, or event that is known from literature, history, myth, religion, or some other field of knowledge. For example, "Shoes" alludes to Imelda Marcos, former first lady of the Philippines, notorious for the hundreds of pairs of shoes that she owned.

analogy: A comparison that focuses on something similar between two things that are otherwise not the same. An analogy is often used to explain a complex idea in terms of a simpler one.

annotated bibliography: A list of citations to books, articles, and documents. Each citation is followed by a brief descriptive paragraph—the annotation. The annotation should reflect the relevance, accuracy, and quality of the sources cited.

anthology: A published collection of literary material including poems, short stories, novels, non-fiction selections, or other material. This textbook is an example of an anthology.

antithesis: A figure of speech in which words or ideas are set up in parallel structure or balance against each other to emphasize the contrast in their meaning. For example, "To err is human, to forgive divine" (Alexander Pope).

argumentative essay: See **essay/magazine article/supported opinion piece/personal essay**.

article: See **essay/magazine article/supported opinion piece/personal essay** and **newspaper article/report/story**.

atmosphere (or **mood**): The prevailing feeling in a literary work created through word choice, descriptive details, and evocative imagery. The atmosphere of "I'm Walking Out of Your Jail Tonight" is one of defiance.

autobiography: The story of a person's life, written by that person.

bias: An underlying preference or prejudice for or against a particular idea, value, or group of people.

biography: The story of a person's life, written by someone other than that person.

brochure: A printed booklet, or pages that are folded into panels, used to advertise or give information about a business, product, place, and so on. It often contains colourful graphics or pictures.

caption: A heading or subtitle that accompanies a photograph, drawing, or cartoon.

caricature: An exaggeration or distortion of a character's most prominent features in order to ridicule him or her.

character: Refers to (1) an individual in a story, narrative poem, or play, and (2) the qualities of the individual. The latter are usually revealed through dialogue, description, and action. In "Apples From the Desert," for example, the mother's prejudice is revealed through dialogue and her own actions.

character sketch: A description of a character's qualities that uses nouns and adjectives to name the character's qualities, and examples and quotations from the story, play, poem, and so on, as evidence of those qualities. A character sketch does not normally describe the character's physical appearance unless it reveals some aspect of his or her qualities or personality.

cliché: An overused expression. For example, "*Tired but happy*, we came home."

conflict: A struggle between opposing characters, forces, or emotions, usually between the protagonist and someone or something else. The central conflict in "Stuck in the Throat" is between the narrator and the ambitious Peter Chen.

connotation: The implications or unstated associations conveyed by a word beyond its basic meaning. Connotations may be widely understood by many people, or may be personal and private, based on an individual's life experiences. See also **denotation**.

consensus: An agreement by members of a group that, although it takes into account individual points of view, focuses on what all members of the group can agree to in order to proceed with a task. For example, there has to be a consensus about the interpretation of a drama by all members of the cast and crew in order for a coherent production of the drama to occur.

context: The situation or background information that helps to explain a word, idea, character, or incident in a text. It could refer to the surrounding event(s) or information in a text, the background of the writer, or the social situation in which the text was written. As well, the context the reader brings to a text affects how a piece of writing is received and experienced.

covering letter: A letter used to introduce a package of materials. For instance, when someone submits a résumé as part of a job application, the covering letter identifies the sender, the position applied for, and the contents of the application (e.g., application form, résumé). It also highlights the applicant's most relevant skills or experience. Covering letters are short and written in a formal business style.

debate: A discussion or argument that presents both sides of a topic. A debate can be formal, such as a televised debate between politicians. Formal debates take place in public, are guided by rules, and are overseen by a moderator. (See also The Reference Shelf, page 401.)

definition: A statement or explanation used to clarify the meaning of words or concepts.

denotation: The basic or specific meaning of a word without associated ideas or emotions. See also **connotation**.

dialogue: A conversation between two or more characters. Dialogue is often used by writers and dramatists to reveal character and conflict. The dialogue between the characters in "Apples From the Desert" shows the conflicts among them.

diction: The deliberate choice of words to create a specific style, atmosphere, or tone. In "Midsummer, Tobago," the poet uses words that evoke the heat of a hot summer's day.

direct speech: The exact words spoken by a character. Direct speech is almost always enclosed in quotation marks. (See also The Reference Shelf, page 356.)

drama: A story written in the form of dialogue intended to be acted out in front of an audience. It consists of plot complication and resolution, character revelation, conflict, setting, and theme. *Life Line* and *Trifles* are examples of drama.

dramatic monologue: see **monologue**.

editorial: A newspaper or magazine article giving the opinion of the editor or publisher regarding a subject.

essay/magazine article/supported opinion piece/personal essay: Non-fiction prose that examines a single topic from a point of view. It requires an introductory paragraph stating the main or controlling ideas, several paragraphs developing the topic, and a concluding paragraph. The title often identifies the topic. Formal essays are usually serious and impersonal in tone. Personal or informal essays reveal the personality and feelings of the author and are conversational in tone. "In and of Ourselves We Trust" is an example of this type of non-fiction writing.

An **informational essay** provides information to the reader. It has supporting details and frequently involves some analysis of the information presented. An example is "25 Things Your Boss Wants You to Know."

A **persuasive essay** uses supporting details and argumentation to persuade the reader to accept the writer's point of view.

An **argumentative essay** argues for or against a question or a position on a topic, issue, and so on.

etymology: The etymology of a word traces its historical origin and development. Most dictionaries provide the etymologies of words.

eulogy: A speech or piece of writing in praise of a person, action, and so on.

explicit meaning: An idea or a message that is stated directly by the writer. For example, Andy Rooney explicitly states in his essay that "the whole structure of our society depends on mutual trust." See also **implicit meaning**.

exposition: A piece of writing that presents information, explains ideas, or presents an argument. It is a generic term for writing that is not drama, narration, or description. An example is "Credit: What Do You Really Know?"

extended metaphor: See **metaphor**.

fiction: Prose writing that is based on imagination rather than on fact.

flashback: A device that shifts the narrative from the present to the past, usually to reveal a change in character or to illustrate an important point. Some parts of "Apples From the Desert" are presented as a flashback to help reveal the conflict and show the change of the mother's character.

flyer: A printed notice used to advertise a product or service.

foreshadowing: Refers to clues that hint at what is going to happen later in the plot. Foreshadowing is used to arouse the reader's curiosity, build suspense, and help prepare the reader to accept events that occur later in the story. For example, in "Hedge-hopping," the description of Mr. John when he is first introduced as an "elegant

stranger" arouses the reader's curiosity and foreshadows events that result from Mr. John's secrecy.

glossary: A list of special, technical, or difficult words with definitions or comments.

graphic organizer: A chart, graph, Venn diagram, or other visual means used to record, organize, classify, analyze, and assess information.

hypothesis: A theory or a proposition assumed to be a likely and true explanation. Usually a hypothesis is created in order to test it out against all known information or through experimentation. In writing, a writer may develop or prove a hypothesis through written discussion and information.

image/imagery: A picture created by a writer using concrete details, adjectives, and figures of speech that gives readers a vivid impression of what or who is being described. Similes, metaphors, personification, and symbols are all specific kinds of imagery.

implicit meaning: An idea or message that must be inferred by the reader. The theme of a short story or the qualities of the characters, for instance, are rarely stated directly, but can be inferred from details provided in the story. For example, we can infer from "Remembrances of Calcutta" the narrator's guilt that while she lived in luxury, others lived in poverty. See also **explicit meaning**.

inclusive language: Language that uses words that are not discriminatory against or exclusive to a gender, culture, age, etc. Inclusive language is used to avoid negative stereotypes. For example, it is preferable to use "humankind" rather than "mankind."

informational essay: See **essay/magazine article/supported opinion piece/personal essay** and **exposition.**

interior monologue: See **monologue**.

interview: A recorded discussion, usually structured in a question–answer format. Examples of interviews are those between an employer and a job applicant (see The Reference Shelf, pages 405–406), a reporter and a politician, or an immigration officer and a new immigrant.

invective: Writing or speech that denounces or is insulting to something or someone.

irony: A literary device that creates a contrast or discrepancy between what is said and what is meant, or between expectations and reality. For example, the reader is aware that Thisbe has not died in the story of "Pyramus and Thisbe." Pyramus, on the other hand, is unaware of this fact. (See The Reference Shelf, page 361, for common types of irony.)

journal: A notebook that contains personal reflections and responses to writing, events, incidents, and people.

layout: A plan or design of a page of a book, advertisement, newspaper, or other printed material that shows the placement of the words and illustrations or photos.

Layouts can be done by hand or by using computer design software.

live-action television program: A program that involves live acting (as opposed to animation) and may be televised as the event or action is taking place. News, sports, and sitcoms are examples.

memoir: A form of autobiographical writing dealing with personal recollections of people or events. An example is "Memoirs of a Really Good Brown Girl."

memorandum (memo): A brief, informal form of business communication used to convey factual information accurately and clearly. All memos identify the date, the person the memo is being sent to, the sender, and the topic. A typical memo template begins in the following way.

Date:

To:

From:

Re:

metaphor: A figure of speech that makes a comparison between two seemingly unlike things without using connective words such as *like* or *as*. In "The Sun," the sun is compared to a bird having "spread its wings." See **simile**.

Sometimes writers use an **extended metaphor**—a metaphor that develops its comparison over several lines or paragraphs or even throughout the entire composition.

monologue: A speech by one person telling a story, revealing character, or describing a humorous or dramatic situation.

A **dramatic monologue** is a form of poetry in which a character speaks to a definite but silent listener and thereby reveals his or her own character.

An **interior monologue** is a form of writing that reveals the inner thoughts of a character.

mood: See **atmosphere**.

narration: Telling a story or recounting an event or series of events.

narrative: Another word for story. Narratives have the following elements: plot, conflict, characters, setting, point of view, and theme. Narratives may be fictional or non-fictional, and include novels and (auto)biographies (or personal stories/narratives) as well as short stories and anecdotes.

narrator: The person or character who tells the story.

newspaper article/report/story: Non-fiction prose that informs readers about an event or issue. It has titles in the form of brief sentences (also known as headlines). The most important information appears at the beginning of a newspaper article so that the reader can stop reading once he or she has sufficient information on the topic.

opinion piece: See **essay/magazine article/supported opinion piece/personal essay.**

panel discussion: A discussion of a particular issue by a selected group of people, usually experts, before an audience.

paraphrase: Restate the meaning of a text in other words.

parody: A humorous imitation of a piece of writing, film, or drama that mocks the original by exaggerating or distorting some of its salient features.

pathetic fallacy: A literary device in which nature or inanimate things are represented as sympathetic to or prophetic about events or the emotions of the characters. For example, the description of stormy weather might be used to reflect the internal conflict of a character.

personal essay: See **essay/magazine article/supported opinion piece/personal essay.**

personal narrative: See **narrative**.

personification: A metaphor in which human attributes are given to inanimate objects. For example, "The kettle whistled loudly, impatient to be lifted off from the heat."

persuasive essay: See **essay/magazine article/supported opinion piece/personal essay.**

play: See **drama**.

plot: A series of events and the thoughtful interrelations of these events, their causes and effects, and so on; the main story in a narrative or drama. The plot of the story usually contains the following elements: narration (introductory background information); rising action or complications (the point at which the plot thickens and conflicts develop); crisis, climax, or turning point (the point at which the plot begins to become less complicated); falling action, resolution, or denouement (the resolution of the major conflicts and problems).

plot graph: A visual representation of a plot.

poem/poetry: A unique form of writing about experiences, thoughts, and feelings, frequently divided into lines and stanzas, which uses compressed language, figures of speech, and imagery to appeal to readers' emotions and imagination. There are a variety of poetic structures with different requirements of length, rhyme, rhythm, stanza formation, and so on. (See also The Reference Shelf, pages 366–367, for types of poetry.)

point of view: The perspective from which a story is told. (See also The Reference Shelf, pages 364–365, for types of point of view.)

proposal: A plan, offer, or suggestion put forward for consideration. The information in a proposal is organized to support the proposed conclusion.

prose: Ordinary language or literary expression not marked by rhythm or rhyme is called prose. As Molière put it in *The Bourgeois Gentleman*, "All that is not prose is verse. All that is not verse is prose." The protagonist of Molière's play is proud and pleased to find out that he has been speaking prose all his life and he didn't even realize it! This type of language is used in short stories, essays, and modern plays.

prospectus: A formal document that describes or advertises the key features of something.

pun: A play on words. For example, in *Romeo and Juliet* (Act III, scene i), as Mercutio lies dying, he says, "Ask for me tomorrow, and you shall find me a *grave* man." The word "grave" could mean both "serious" and "dead in the grave."

report: An oral or written account or opinion formally expressed, based on findings from investigation or inquiry. (See also The Reference Shelf, page 385.)

research report: A form of non-fiction writing intended to inform an audience about a particular topic. It contains factual information that is carefully researched from authoritative sources. (See also The Reference Shelf, pages 374–379.)

résumé: A summary of information about a job applicant's personal, educational, and work experience. There are many formats to choose from, but all require a neat, easy-to-read presentation of factual information. (See The Reference Shelf, pages 411–412 for a sample résumé.)

review: A form of writing that discusses the good and bad points of a book, film, work of art, and so on. It usually provides a synopsis or description of the work and focuses on a few key aspects, using evidence to support arguments.

rhyme scheme: The pattern of end rhymes. A rhyme scheme is indicated by assigning each new end rhyme a different letter of the alphabet. (See also The Reference Shelf, page 366.)

role playing: Assuming and acting the role of a character, fictitious or real, and using dialogue and/or gestures appropriate to the individual to present the character to an audience in an improvisation.

sarcasm: A cutting expression or remark.

satire: A literary work that ridicules human vices and follies, often with the purpose of teaching a lesson or encouraging change. Stephen Leacock is well known for his satires.

scene: The time, place, circumstance, and so on of a play or story, usually involving a particular incident. In a play, a scene is a division of an act, taking place in a single location. See also **act**. (See also The Reference Shelf, page 368.)

script: The written text for a play, video, film, or radio or television broadcast. It includes dialogue, sound effects, stage directions, and so on.

setting: The place and time of a story, play, or poem. The setting of "The Fun They Had" is the year 2155 in Margie's bedroom. (See also The Reference Shelf, page 362.)

short story: A short fictional prose narrative having only one major character, plot, setting, and theme. The short story usually focuses on a single conflict, character, or emotional effect.

simile: A figure of speech that makes a comparison between two seemingly unlike things using a connective word such as *like* or *as*. An example occurs in "Midsummer, Tobago," where the days gone by are "like daughters" who have outgrown and left the arms of the narrator. See **metaphor**.

speech: A public address, usually given in formal language, often to persuade an audience.

stanza: A set number of lines grouped together to form units in poetry.

story: See **short story**.

storyboard: A series of panels with sketches and dialogue, representing the shots in an advertisement, film, or television program, and used to plan a script for a film or video. (See also The Reference Shelf, pages 425–426.)

style: The particular way in which a writer expresses himself or herself in writing. It is the sum effect of the author's choice of voice, vocabulary, and sentence structure, and use of devices such as imagery, onomatopoeia, and rhythm.

summary: A brief account giving the main points of a story or article.

suspense: The condition of being uncertain about an outcome, used by writers to create tension, excitement, or anxiety. In "Hedge-hopping," readers are kept in suspense as to the protagonist's true identity.

symbol: A person, place, thing, or event that stands both for itself and for something beyond itself. For example, the carvings and paintings in "A Family Likeness" symbolize Olivia's identity — the past, the present, and the future — which she inherited from her father.

syntax: The order or systematic arrangement of words in a sentence. Syntax will determine whether ideas expressed orally or in writing are clear and easy to understand.

theme: A statement of the central idea of a work, usually implied rather than directly stated. One theme of "A Family Likeness" is the importance of cultural inheritance.

thesis: A main or controlling idea or statement about a topic that a writer proposes and supports in an essay. The thesis of "In and of Ourselves We Trust" is that we have a mutual trust, a social contract that controls our behaviour. Without it there would be chaos. See **topic**.

tone: The attitude a writer expresses toward his or her subject. The tone of writing may be formal or informal, personal or impersonal, angry or cheerful, bitter or hopeful, and so on. The tone of "Remembrances of Calcutta" is a mixture of guilt and sadness.

topic: The subject that is being written or talked about. The subject of "Turn of the Scrooge" is Ebenezer Scrooge from Charles Dickens' classic novel, *A Christmas Carol*. (Note: Topic and thesis are often confused: **topic** is the subject matter; **thesis** is the statement about the topic.)

topic sentence: A sentence that states the subject of a paragraph. The sentence "Anticipate problems." in "25 Things Your Boss Wants You to Know" is a topic sentence.

typography: The arrangement, appearance, or style of printed words.

voice: This word has three different meanings within this textbook.

Verb voice refers to whether a verb is active or passive. An active voice is usually recommended since it tends to be more direct, hard-hitting, or forceful. The passive voice makes writing more formal and a little bit distant, and is most appropriate in formal, objective reports. (See also The Reference Shelf, page 339.)

Voice is used in the context of oral presentations to discuss volume, clarity, and so on, when speaking.

Voice is also used to describe the distinctive style or tone of an individual writer or speaker. "Memoirs of a Really Good Brown Girl" has the distinctive voice of a young child relating events as they unfold.

> Index

> Acknowledgements

Text

At Seventeen by Janis Ian. Words and Music by Janis Ian © 1975 MINE MUSIC LTD. All Rights for the USA and Canada Controlled and Administered by EMI APRIL MUSIC INC. All Rights Reserved. International Copyright Secured. Used by Permission. **The Fun They Had** by Isaac Asimov from EARTH IS ROOM ENOUGH by Isaac Asimov, copyright © 1957 by Isaac Asimov. Used by permission of Doubleday, a division of Random House, Inc. **Kikaku** translated by Lucien Stryk and Takaski Ikemoto. Reprinted by permission of Northern Illinois University Foundation. **The Sun** by Judah Al-Harizi, translated by T. Carmi (p 389, 31 words) in THE PENGUIN BOOK OF HEBREW VERSE, edited by T. Carmi (Allen Lane, 1981) copyright © T. Carmi, 1981. **The Red Wheelbarrow** by William Carlos Williams, from COLLECTED POEMS: 1909-1939, VOLUME I, copyright © 1938 by New Directions Publishing Corp. Reprinted by permission of New Directions Publishing Corp. **Midsummer, Tobago** by Derek Walcott from COLLECTED POEMS: 1948-1984 by Derek Walcott. Copyright © 1986 by Derek Walcott. Reprinted by permission of Farrar, Straus & Giroux, LLC. **All About Food**. From the Cambridge Reporter. Graphics from Toronto Star. **What Goes Around** by Sarah Sheard. Reprinted by permission of Sarah Sheard. **Remembrances of Calcutta** by Shikha Bhattacharjee. Reprinted by permission of SAMAR (South Asian Magazine for Action and Reflection). **Dracula** by Hamilton Deane & John L. Balderston from Bram Stoker's novel *Dracula*. **Ladies and Gentlemen, start your search engines** by Lisa Sloniowski. Reprinted by permission of the author. **Credit: What Do You Really Know?** by Joanne Thomas Yaccato. Reprinted by permission of American Express Canada. **How to Buy or Sell a Used Car** from Consumer Reports. "How to Buy and Sell a Car" by Consumers Union of U.S., Inc., Yonkers, NY 10703-1057, a nonprofit organization. Reprinted with permission for educational purposes only. No commercial use or photocopying permitted. To subscibe, call 1-800-234-1645 or visit us at www.ConsumerReports.org. **Helping Out** by Scott Edmonds. The Canadian Press. **How Do You Procrastinate?** by Linda Sapadin with Jack Maguire. From IT'S ABOUT TIME by Linda Sapadin and Jack Maguire, copyright © 1996 by Linda Sapadin & Jack Maguire. Used by permission of Viking Penguin, a division of Penguin Putnam Inc. **Everybody Can't Be a Superstar**. Copyright Girls Incorporated of Greater Santa Barbara. Reprinted with permission of Advocacy Press, P.O. Box 236, Santa Barbara, CA 93102. Not to be duplicated in any other form. **Rookie errors close hiring doors** by Kennedy Pires. Reprinted by permission of the author. **Opening Doors** by Joanne Weidner. Reprinted by permission of the Kitchener-Waterloo Record. **Beware of Illegal Questions in Employment Interviews** by Barbara Simmons. Reprinted by permission of the author. **25 Things Your Boss Wants You to Know** by Shirley Sloan Fader. Reprinted by permission of the author. Copyright Shirley Sloan Fader, Paramus NJ 07652, USA. Used of this article without author's written permission if prohibited. **Stuck in the Throat** by Xin Qi Shi, translated by Don J. Cohn. Reprinted by permission of the Research Centre for Translation of the Chinese University of Hong Kong. **Johnny B** by Phil "The Mallet" Voyd. Reprinted by permission of the author. **The Need to Win** by Chaung Tzu , translated from the Chinese by Thomas Merton, from THE COLLECTED POEMS OF THOMAS MERTON, copyright © 1963 by The Abbey of Gethsemani, Inc. 1977 by The Trustees of the Merton Legacy Trust. Reprinted by permission of New Directions Publishing Corp. **The Will to Win** by Laurie Nealin. Reprinted by permission of the author. **1938 400 m Relay: Bell, Cook, Rosenfeld & Smith – Women's Olympic Lib** by Frank Cosentino and Glynn Leyshon. From *Olympic Gold: Canadian Winners of the Summer Games* © 1975 by Holt, Rinehart & Winston Canada. **How writing evolved**. Reprinted with permission – The Toronto Star Syndicate. Copyright Knight Ridder. **It's Etymology, Dude** by Rachel Sauer. Copyright © 2001 The New York Times News Service. Distributed by The New York Times Special Features/Syndication Sales. **Now hear this** by Don Oldenberg. © 2001 The Washington Post. Reprinted with permission. **For Conversation, Press #1** by Michael Alvear. Reprinted by permission of the author. **Blondie cartoon**. Reprinted by permission of King Features Syndicate. **Life Line** by Douglas Craven. Reprinted by permission of the author. **For Reading Out Loud** by Margaret Mary Kimmel and Elizabeth Segel. Reprinted by permission of the authors. **Murmel, Murmel, Murmel** by Robert Munsch © 1982, text Robert Munsch, art Michael Martchenko. Reprinted by permission of Annick Press. **The Letter** by Sally Morgan. Reprinted by permission of the author. **The Story of Pyramus & Thisbe** from *Metamorphoses*, Ovid, translated by Rolfe Humphries, © 1955 Indiana University Press © renewed 1983 by Winifred Davies. Reprinted by permission of Indiana University Press. **Apples from the Desert** by Savyon Liebrecht, translated from the Hebrew by Barbara Harshav. Reprinted by permission of the translator, Barbara Harshav. **Normal is Defined by Life Experiences** by Martin Patriquin. Reprinted with permission – The Toronto Star Syndicate. **All Parents Need a Helping Hand** by Helen Henderson. Reprinted with permission – The Toronto Star Syndicate. **I'm Walking Out of Your Jail Tonight** by Cherry Natural from Utterances & Incantations © 1999, published by Sister Vision Press. **Shoes** by Sylvia Hamilton. Reprinted by permission of the author. **Memoirs of a Really Good Brown Girl** by Marilyn Dumont. Reprinted by permission of Brick Books. **A Family Likeness** by Jacqueline Roy. Reprinted by permission of the author. **The Debate on Ethnicity** by Alison Blackduck. Reprinted by permission of the author. **The Whole Idea of Race is Meaningless** by Mari Rutka. Reprinted by permission of the author. **Love in the Classroom** by Al Zolynas. Reprinted by permission of the author. Originally published in Under Ideal Conditions, Laterthanever Press, San Diego, CA, 1994. **Hand Painting** by Paddy Fahrni. Reprinted by permission of the author. First appeared in Other Voices, Edmonton, AB. **In and of Ourselves We Trust** by Andy Rooney. Reprinted by permission of Tribune Media Services. **A Traffic Light is a Brainless Machine** by David Schoenbrun. Reprinted by permission of Scott Meredith Literary Agency. **Hedge-hopping** by Raul Teixido. Reprinted by permission of the author. Represented by literary agent Rosario Santos. **united colours of benneton** by amuna baraka-clarke. Reprinted by permission of the author. **Turn of the Scrooge** by Philip Preville. Reprinted by permission of the author. **Could Scrolling Ads in the Hallways Be Next?** The Canadian Press. **Ads talkin' about your generation** by Bob Dart. Copyright © 2001 The New York Times News Service. Distributed by The New York Times Special Features/Syndication Sales. **Why is "YKK" stamped on my zipper?** by Philip Preville. Reprinted by permission of the author. **How to Make a Demo CD** by Jim Carruthers. Reprinted by permission of Broken Pencil. Article by

Jim Carruthers and Sarah Welstead. **Maytag Repairman Enters 21st Century** by Peter Goddard. Reprinted by permission of the Toronto Star Syndicate. **The Maytag Man Gets Busy. Text by CXO Media. Graphics courtesy Maytag. Excerpts from The Straight Story** by Mary Sweeney and John Roach. From THE STRAIGHT STORY by John Roach and Mary Sweeney. Copyright © 1999 John Roach and Mary Sweeney. Reprinted by permission of Hyperion. **A Man, a Lawnmower, an Open Road** by Liz Braun. Reprinted by permission of the Toronto Sun.

Photographs

2 Superstock; **11** Two Panel Screen, 18th Century, Kano Roei, Japanese, Watercolor, wood, Gift of Mrs. Joe Price The Philbrook Museum of Art, Tulsa, Oklahoma, 1966.27.4 and 1966.27.5; **26** Eye Wire; **30** Michael S. Lewis/Corbis; **37** Bettmann/Corbis; **61** Peter M. Wilson/Corbis; **70** FPG; **95** Youth Challenge International; **146** John Graham; **159** Canada Sports Hall of Fame; **187** Reprinted by permission of Annick Press; **223** Terrence Jon Dyck; **229** Courtesy Marilyn Dumont. Photo by Barry Peterson and Blaise Enright-Peterson; **235** Comstock; **240** Vancouver Sun; **253** Comstock; 257 *Workers* by Lenka Solan/Archive Inc.; **276** left to right: EyeWire; Image Bank; EyeWire; 282 Courtesy Canadian Tire; **288** CP Archive; **304** Buena Vista/MPTV; **336** First Light;

Illustrations

Kathryn Adams: 106, 119, 172; Drew-Brook-Cormack Assoc.: 197; Cindy Jeftovic: 347; Susan Leopold: 266; Stephen Taylor: 143, 193; Carl Wiens: 99; Tara Winterhalt: 248, 293.